MW01182215

The Vision of Eden

Animal Welfare and Vegetarianism in Jewish Law and Mysticism

DAVID SEARS

אורות
OROT

OROT, Inc
Spring Valley, NY
5763 / 2003

First edition
Copyright © 2003 David Sears
ISBN 0-9674512-7-2

Printed in Israel

Typography: Akiva Atwood

Library of Congress Control Number: 2003103100

Orot, Inc.
Spring Valley, NY
5763/2003

Rabbi Amorai asked: Where is the Garden of Eden?
He replied: It is on Earth.

Sefer HaBahir (The Book of Illumination), 31
Attributed to Rabbi Nechuniah ben HaKanah

Table of Contents

Haskama (Letter of Approbation)

HaRav Shear-Yashuv Cohen, *shlita*
Chief Rabbi of Haifa
President of the Ariel Institutes of Higher Torah Studies

Rabbi David Sears has made a name for himself[1] in the Torah and Chassidus community with his excellent books on Chassidus, such as *The Path of the Baal Shem Tov,* and especially concerning the way of Rabbeinu Nachman of Breslov, may the merit of the *tzaddikim* protect us. His outreach activities in the Breslov spirit have succeeded in deepening the roots and changing the lives of many who now walk in the ways of Torah.

His present book, *The Vision of Eden,* is a comprehensive Jewish sourcebook on vegetarianism and animal welfare, based upon our Rabbis' writings throughout the generations, with a special emphasis on the writings of our Master and Saintly Light of Israel, Chief Rabbi Avraham Yitzchak HaKohen Kook, of blessed memory, and his leading disciples, especially my father and teacher, the saintly Nazir of Jerusalem, HaRav David Cohen, of blessed memory.

The basic definition of Chassidus is that it is a way of life that does not limit itself only to the observance of legal Halachic instructions, based upon the negative and positive commandments; rather, one must go beyond the letter of the Law to "sanctify oneself in the realm of the permissible."[2] Chassidus entails taking on restrictions that will purify

1. Paraphrase of II Samuel 8:13.

and enrich the individual in the service of God, enabling him to reach higher levels that make him fit for divine inspiration.

Being a vegetarian and refraining from eating anything that had to be killed in order to become food fit for human consumption certainly is not required by Halacha. What Rabbi Sears is trying to do in his excellent work is to demonstrate that this reflects a higher degree of piety. The very fact that great and pious Rabbis, well known the world over for their great Torah knowledge, as well as for their holiness as masters of Kabbalah, adopted this very special way of life is indeed irrefutable proof for the positive attitude of Judaism towards vegetarianism.

While one can argue that some biblical personalities, such as Daniel the Prophet, or Chanania, Mishael, and Azaria, or Queen Esther, ate vegetarian foods because, in their special circumstances, this was the only way they could observe the Kashruth laws, nobody can deny the fact that saintly people like my father, the Nazir of Jerusalem, as well as the Kamenitzer Maggid, and last but not least, the Mekubal described by Rabbeinu Chaim Vital, of blessed memory, in the name of his master and teacher, the Ari HaKadosh, may his merits protect us, as "a saintly man of God," were strict vegetarians, and regarded it as a proper, acceptable, and fit way of God's worship.

I found it very important to read in this book an overall view of how HaRav Kook, as interpreted by his leading disciple, my father HaRav HaNazir, explains the entire system of Kosher Dietary Laws as an education towards the ideal of vegetarianism and as a "Divine Compromise" to enable the weak human to prepare for this higher level that at present only exceptional people can take upon themselves as their way of life.

Every reader of this unique and holy book will benefit extensively from it. Indeed, this book, *The Vision of Eden*, makes one feel that he has been handed a key to open the closed gates of the Garden of Eden that were shut to us ever since Adam was expelled, and the angels with swords in hand surrounded it, preventing us even from knocking on its gates, let alone entering it.

---

2. *Yevamos* 20a.

May the inspiration of this book bring many of its readers to reflect deeply upon the right way to feel closer to the Almighty: by leading a pious and Jewish way of life, in order to do His Will with a pure and perfect heart, Amen.

With blessings of the Torah from Zion,

Shear-Yashuv Cohen

Haskama (Letter of Approbation)

HaRav Yaacov Haber, *shlita*
President, TorahLab
Mara d'Asra, Congregation Bais Torah
Monsey, New York

In *The Vision of Eden*, Rabbi David Sears has stepped onto the stage to teach the world how to be more Godly. The world is full of suffering and affliction, some perpetrated even in the name of God. Imagine a world of emulating God, a world full of compassion and sensitivity toward every living creature. The world would be safe, spiritual, and holy, devoid of terror and grief.

In the recently published infamous al-Qaeda guide, there was a description of how little children can be trained to be terrorists by having them pull the heads off live cats. They assured the reader that as their trainees grew up they would have no problem blowing up buildings or crashing planes.

The Torah teaches compassion for every living creature. To study its detail is to study the essence of God. Rabbi Sears has done extensive and valuable research into a topic the world depends on for its existence. Thank you, Rabbi Sears, for bringing more compassion to a spiritually starved world.

Yaacov Haber

Introduction

While researching this book, I often was asked: "Why write about issues considered marginal by most religious Jews?" In keeping with our ancestral tradition, I answered one question with another: What is a "marginal issue" in Judaism? Indeed, our sages have taught, "Treat a minor commandment as carefully as a major one; for no one knows the true value of the commandments" (*Avos* 2:1).

Animal welfare is a more central concern of Judaism than most people realize. The Torah espouses an ethic of compassion for all creatures, and affirms the sacredness of life. These values are reflected by the laws prohibiting *tza'ar baalei chaim* (cruelty to animals); also, they are consonant with the biblical description of the Garden of Eden and the Messianic vision of the ancient prophets. The Midrash asserts, "Just as the Holy One, blessed be He, has compassion for human beings, so does He have compassion for animals" (*Devarim Rabbah* 6:1). Yet the same Torah permits the killing of animals, albeit in a humane manner, to serve various human uses: food, clothing, medicine, etc. Indeed, in ancient times, the Torah mandated animal sacrifice in the Holy Temple. If God has compassion for animals, how could He permit, much less require, their slaughter? This disturbing question demands an explanation. In addition, the practical ramifications of the Torah's attitude toward animals must be clearly defined in legal and extralegal terms, if humanity is to fulfill its divinely-appointed purpose in creation.

The classical texts of Judaism reflect a marked ambivalence toward meat eating. Several authorities argue persuasively that when the Torah permitted Noah and his descendants to eat meat, this was a concession to human weakness, rather than an expression of God's original plan for His creatures. The Kabbalah, too, takes seemingly conflicting positions on the consumption of meat. Because it can accomplish the *tikkun* (spiritual rectification) of the "holy sparks" trapped within the animal kingdom, meat eating is potentially beneficial; yet because of its association with gluttony, as well as its spiritual risks, meat eating should be kept to a minimum, if not avoided entirely. It is true that historically, Judaism has not been a vegetarian religious tradition. However, this does not mean that a religious Jew may not be a vegetarian, but that Judaism does not impose vegetarianism upon its adherents. Moreover, there may be a number of Jewish reasons for practicing vegetarianism today. We shall address these issues in the pages to come.

As a collection of translations from the full spectrum of Torah literature, the present anthology attempts to be comprehensive. To accommodate those who wish to use this work as a source book for their own research, it was necessary to preserve the integrity of the translations, even when certain ideas appear elsewhere in the book. The advantage of presenting a large corpus of original teachings is that the reader may consider what the many voices within the rabbinic tradition actually say. However, in order to make the book more readable, we have divided the source material into two groups: the sources that appear after the chapter essays, and those presented as "Additional Source Texts" in Part IV. Inasmuch as these divisions are somewhat arbitrary, the reader is encouraged to examine all the source material before drawing his or her own conclusions on any issue. Although our research was done without recourse to computer databases, the extent of our findings should be sufficient to accurately represent the range of basic views on these topics.

One of the book's inevitable shortcomings is that while dealing with animal sacrifice and the rites of the Holy Temple, it does not give this subject the full attention it deserves. We did not address this at greater length because animal sacrifice is not immediately relevant to us, and because this issue is too complex to discuss in depth in a book that is already quite long. We refer the reader to *The Temple: Its Symbolism and Meaning, Then and Now* (Jason Aronson 1995) by Joshua Berman, and *Jerusalem: The Eye of the Universe* (Artscroll / Mesorah Publications, 1996) by Aryeh Kaplan. An insightful consideration of the Holy Temple as a spiritual paradigm may be found in Yehoshua Starrett's *The Inner Temple* (Breslov Research Institute 2000).

If the teachings presented here inspire us to become more compassionate toward other creatures, as well as more mindful of what and how we eat, this volume will have served its purpose. If it contributes to actual improvements in the food industry, it will have amply served its purpose. However, my intent goes beyond these immediate concerns. What prompted me to write this book, as well as its companion volume, *Compassion for Humanity in the Jewish Tradition* (Jason Aronson 1998), is a need I have felt since childhood — to find in the faith of my ancestors something beyond what, at first glance, Judaism may seem to be: a highly legalistic and ritualistic religion for a small and insular community. In truth, Judaism is an encompassing doctrine and path that addresses everything in creation, in its every detail as well as in its totality. This vision and its ethical and spiritual implications are most lucidly contained in the mystical dimension of Torah: in the Kabbalah, and especially in the writings of the Chassidic masters. This is why I have included chapters on "Creation and the Holy Sparks" and "Reincarnation," and supplemented other sections of the book with related mystical teachings.

Until recently, this sort of material was reserved for a spiritual elite, and not made available to the public. These teachings are called "secrets of Torah" because they never were intended for the uninitiated. However, today far more esoteric Kabbalistic and Chassidic texts have been translated and published by members of both the religious and academic communities. So those who wish to gain access to similar if not identical teachings already can do so without traveling any farther than their local Judaica shop or college bookstore. (In fact, translations of some of the most abstruse writings of the great Safed mystic, Rabbi Yitzchak Luria, appear on the Internet, available to all.)

There is another reason to approach these issues from a Kabbalistic perspective. While in recent times Torah education in the Orthodox world has reached unprecedented levels, the proportion of the Jewish people as a whole estranged from normative Jewish practice is greater than ever. Among the latter are a sizeable number of Jewish men and women who have been attracted to vegetarianism in connection with various forms of mysticism. The fact that the Kabbalistic and Chassidic masters address their concerns may awaken within them a desire to strengthen their ties to Jewish tradition.

May this book contribute not only to improving the physical plight of animals in our society, but also to the spiritual healing of the Jewish people; and may our eyes behold the restoration of the "House of Prayer for all nations" (Isaiah 56:7) speedily in our days.

David Sears
20 Elul 5762/2002
Yarhrzeit of Rabbi Avraham Sternhartz zt"l

Common Terms and Usages

Hebrew words have been transliterated according to the Ashkenazic pronunciation used by Chassidim and other Jews of European descent. Spelling anomalies occur in a few instances, such as names of institutions or books that are more commonly spelled according to the Sefardic pronunciation.

We have retained certain common Hebrew terms in order to preserve something of the character of the original material. These include:

Torah — the Five Books of Moses, or in certain contexts, the entire corpus of Jewish religious literature.

Tzaddik (pl. *tzaddikim*) — a righteous person.

Kosher — religiously fit or acceptable.

Yeshiva — a school devoted to Jewish religious studies.

Mitzvah — a commandment or religious precept.

Tza'ar Baalei Chaim — the prohibition of causing suffering to animals.

Several titles are often confused with one another:

Rebbe (Yiddish) — rabbi or master. A schoolchild in a yeshiva might call his teacher *rebbe,* and a Chassid invariably will refer to his mentor by the same title.

Reb (Yiddish) — semi-formal term of address, similar to "mister." A familiar rabbinic personage also might be known as "Reb Moshe" or "Reb Nosson," etc., rather than by his formal title, especially in Chassidic circles.

Rav — a synonym for rabbi, but especially indicating an authority in Jewish practical law; e.g., the Rav of Jerusalem is visiting America.

Two formal titles are:

Admor — an acronym for: a*doneinu, moreinu, v'rabbeinu,* our master, teacher, and rabbi. This title is customarily used for Chassidic Rebbes.

Gaon (pronounced "gah-ohn," with the accent on the second syllable) — "eminent one." This title is reserved for outstanding Torah scholars, whether or not they occupy a public position, e.g. the Gaon of Vilna, or the Gaon of Rogatchov.

Dates follow the secular calendar more familiar to English-speaking readers, rather than the traditional Jewish calendar; however, the terms b.c.e. (before the common era) and c.e. (common era) have been substituted for B.C. and A.D., which reflect Christian belief.

Spellings of Eastern European place names reflect the common pronunciation of Ashkenazic Jewry; e.g. Piaceczno (a city in Poland) is Piacetzna, Szydlowiec is Shidlovitz, etc.

Disclaimer

This volume was written as a survey of Jewish teachings on animal welfare, vegetarianism, and related subjects. It should not be used as a source of final decisions in matters of *halacha* (practical Torah law). For such purposes, the reader is strongly urged to consult a qualified halachic authority.

Acknowledgments

First, I must thank my revered teacher, Admor HaRav R' Elazar Mordechai Kenig, *shlita*, leader of the Breslov Community in Tzefat, Israel, for his encouragement and blessings. I also am grateful to my Rosh Yeshiva, Admor HaRav R' Pinchos Dovid Horowitz, Bostoner Rebbe of Flatbush, *shlita*, and *yibadel bein chaim l'chaim*, HaRav HaGaon Shlomo Eisenblatt, *zt"l*, late Mashgiach Ruchani of Yeshiva Darkei Noam. Rav Eisenblatt read the entire manuscript (with the exception of the essay for Chapter 3, which was then incomplete) and expressed his warm approval during the weeks prior to his passing on the first day of Chol HaMoed Pesach, 5761 (2001). Rabbi Bezalel Naor, author-translator and director of Orot, greatly enhanced this work by contributing his editorial acumen, as well as an insightful essay on vegetarianism from a volume of his original writings in Hebrew, *Ben Shanah Shaul*.

I am grateful to the staffs of the libraries that I used while researching this volume: in Brooklyn, those of Mosdos Bobov, under the directorship of Admor HaRav R' Naftule Halberstam, Bobover Rebbe, *shlita;* Haichal HaFla'ah Beis Medrash L'Horaah, under the directorship of Admor HaRav R' Chaim Avraham HaLevi Horowitz, Bostoner Rebbe of New York, *shlita;* Machaneh Levi Kollel L'Hora'ah, under the directorship of HaRav HaGaon R' Moshe Chaim HaLevi Gold, Kruleh Rov of Borough Park, *shlita;* and the Heichal Menachem Library of Borough Park; in Manhattan, the New York University Library; Jewish Theological Seminary Library; and Mendel Gottesman Library of Yeshiva University.

This project also increased my appreciation of the efforts of all those who have contributed to the growing body of English Judaica. Thus, in preparing this book I did not expend my energies "reinventing the wheel," but was able to turn to the research of others. In particular, I am grateful to the staff of Artscroll / Mesorah Publications, Ltd., especially to R. Nosson Scherman, editor of the *Stone Tanach,* and the late R. Hersh Goldwurm, author of *The Rishonim* and *The Early Acharonim* (both volumes incorporating the research of Admor HaRav R' Shmuel Teich, the Pshemishler Rebbe, *shlita*). Similarly, I would like to acknowledge my debt to the late R. Aryeh Kaplan, whose pioneering works have served as a model for a new generation of translators who approach the classic texts of Jewish spirituality as part of a living tradition, and not, to paraphrase Toynbee, as mere "fossils of history."

R. Ozer Bergman, editor of my previous book, *The Tree That Stands Beyond Space: Rebbe Nachman on the Mystical Experience* (Breslov Research Institute 2002), performed an equally skillful and more difficult task in editing the present volume. In addition, I cannot adequately thank R. Zvi Davis, director of Machon Ateres Moshe Aharon, and R. Yaakov Weiss, a senior fellow at Beis Medrash Gavohah of Lakewood, N.J., for taking the time to review the entire text in its first draft. R. Aharon Yonah Hayum of Heichal HaFla'ah Beis Medrash L'Hora'ah checked a number of translations and source references for accuracy, although responsibility for any mistakes remains with me. R. Refael Rosenbaum assisted by tracking down several sources. R. Yisrael Moskowitz shared his great erudition and insight in all areas of Torah. A close friend who has helped me at virtually every turn in life since our first meeting in 1986 is R. Chaim Kramer, director of the Breslov Research Institute. R. Kramer kindly read the "Kabbalistic Issues" section of the book. It also is fitting to mention R. Nosson Zvi Kenig of Bnei Brak, *zt"l*, whose extensive indexes of Kabbalistic works, and Breslov works in particular, have been most helpful over the years. It is hard to believe that this giant of Torah and Chassidus "at whose feet we sat in the dust" is no longer with us.

Having little previous knowledge in the field of *shechitah*, I must thank R. Yisrael Belsky and R. Menachem Genack of the Orthodox

Union's Kashruth Division; R. Chaim Kohen, Executive Mashgiach for Kahal Adas Jeshurun; R. Shimon Lawrence, former Mashgiach at the Empire Poultry plant in Mifflintown, Pa.; and R. Aharon Teitelbaum, the Nirbater Rov, who took the time to explain current procedures in kosher slaughter facilities to me. Dr. Joe Regenstein of Cornell University, a prominent food scientist, kindly reviewed the manuscript and shared his extensive knowledge concerning animal welfare, the food industry, and contemporary slaughter procedures. The masterful essays of R. J. David Bleich on "Animal Experiments" and "Vegetarianism and Judaism" from his *Contemporary Halakhic Problems,* Vol. III, were extremely helpful to me in compiling the source texts and footnotes for Chapters 3 and 6. As this book goes to press another relevant halachic work in Hebrew has been published, *Tza'ar Baalei Chaim* by R. Yitzchak Nachman Eshkoli of Ofakim, Israel. This volume, too, promises to help raise the consciousness of the Jewish public about these issues.

In the Jewish vegetarian community, Richard Schwartz, Ph.D., Professor Emeritus of Mathematics at the College of Staten Island, shared his extensive archives with me, and made himself available for consultation throughout the laborious process of researching, writing, and editing this book. Roberta Kalechovsky, Ph.D., editor of Micah Publications, generously provided me with several of her publications and facilitated other scholarly contacts. During the book's final stages, R. David Rosen of Jerusalem, and Dr. Jay Lavine read the Chapter 3 and 6 essays and offered their helpful comments. At Dr. Schwartz's prompting, I spoke with representatives of The Farm Sanctuary and the Farm Animal Reform Movement (FARM), who were helpful in clarifying several practical issues in animal agriculture and in explaining the legislation that exists, and does not exist, concerning humane treatment and slaughter of animals.

Fishel Bresler and Leibel Estrin edited the essays at various stages. Andy Statman, with whom I have worked in the field of Jewish music for more than a decade, read the manuscript and offered his valuable criticism, as did Yehuda and Chaya Levinson of Toronto, Elana Chaya Risbarg of Fort Lee, N.J., Sholom and Janet Shafner of New London,

Conn., and R. Shraga Fisher of Jerusalem. My *chavrusas* R. David Zeitlin and R. Symcha Bergman provided a number of useful sources, and R. Yitzchak Wolpin co-translated the selections from *Akeidas Yitzchak*. R. Ephraim Berlinsky, an old friend and *chavrusa* during my years in Providence, R.I., often has spoken with me about the primacy of compassion in Jewish ethics, toward both human beings and animals. Translator, poet, songwriter, and editor of *Wings of the Morning*, Yaacov David Shulman looked over the translations from Rav Kook's *A Vision of Vegetarianism and Peace* and *Ein Ayah,* and his sister Chava Nechama Shulman helped me to bid farewell to my old word-processor in favor of a PC. R. Menachem Raymon shared his knowledge as a *shochet,* and read the manuscript. Yosef ben Shlomo HaKohen, author of *The Universal Jew* (Feldheim Books) and director of Chazon, kindly reviewed the manuscript and provided a number of helpful insights and additional sources. R. Nochum Elek of the New York Breslov Center proofread sections of the book, located several hard to find texts with the help of his son, Yisrael Yoel, and provided excellent company as well as scholarly guidance on my trips to the research libraries in Manhattan.

My wife, Shira Sara, was always at my right hand, in this as in all things; and my mother, Mrs. Grace (Gittel) Sears, has been a constant source of encouragement and support. My father, Dr. Lewis (Leibel) Sears, of blessed memory, was a skillful and dedicated healer who loved people, animals, and nature. His example of compassion for all creatures made a profound impression upon me as a child, and has continued to inspire me throughout my life. I am grateful to my son R. Yonah Eliyahu, my daughter-in-law, Simcha, our grandchildren Yehudah Leib, Rochel Esther, Moshe Shneur Zalman, Menachem Mendel, and Rivkah, as well as all our family members and friends, for being such truly wonderful family members and friends. Most of all, I am grateful to God for enabling me to complete this project.

Publishers' Permissions

The following authors and publishers kindly granted us permission to cite their works: **Artscroll / Mesorah Publications, Ltd.:** R. Elie Munk, *The Call of the Torah;* R. Raphael Pelcovitz, trans. / ed., *Sforno: Commentary on the Torah;* Yonoson Rosenblum, *Reb Shraga Feivel: The Life and Times of Rabbi Shraga Feivel Mendlowitz, the Architect of Torah in America;* R. Nosson Scherman, ed., *The Stone Tanach;* R. Shlomo Zalman Sonnenfeld, *The Life and Times of Rabbi Chaim Sonnenfeld;* R. Shlomo Yosef Zevin, *Treasury of Chassidic Tales.* **Feldheim Brothers:** Naftali Herman ("Judaeus"), *The Baal Shem of Michelstadt;* R. Samson Raphael Hirsch, *The Nineteen Letters* (Karin Paritzky, trans.); Simcha Raz, *A Tzaddik In Our Time.* **Soncino / Judaica Press:** R. Samson Raphael Hirsch, *Commentary on the Pentateuch* (Gertrude Hirschler, trans.); *Horeb: A Philosophy of Jewish Laws and Observances* (Dayan I. Grunfeld, trans.). **Kehot Publication Society (Chabad-Lubavitch):** R. Yosef Yitzchak Schneersohn, *Likkutei Dibburim,* Vol. 1, (Uri Kaploun, trans.). **Orot, Inc.:** R. Bezalel Naor, *Kabbalah and the Holocaust.* **Schocken Books Division of Random House:** S.Y. Agnon, *Days of Awe.* We thank **HaModia** (English Edition) for the stories of the Z'vihller and Belzer Rebbes and the late R. Avraham Pam; and R. Akiva Tatz of Jerusalem's Ohr Sameach Yeshiva for permitting us to include a transcription of an excerpt from one of his taped lectures.

Part I:

Human Responsibilities Toward Animals

1

Respect For All Creatures

"God is good to all, and His mercy is upon all His works" (Psalms 145:9). This verse is the touchstone of the rabbinic attitude toward animal welfare, appearing in a number of contexts in Torah literature. At first glance, its relevance may be somewhat obscure. It speaks of God, not man. However, a basic rule of Jewish ethics is the emulation of God's ways. In the words of the Talmudic sages: "Just as He clothes the naked, so shall you clothe the naked. Just as He is merciful, so shall you be merciful..."[1] Therefore, compassion for all creatures, including animals, is not only God's business; it is a virtue that we, too, must emulate. Moreover, rabbinic tradition asserts that God's mercy supersedes all other divine attributes. Thus, compassion must not be reckoned as one good trait among others; rather, it is central to our entire approach to life.

The Unity of All Things

A fundamental premise of Judaism is belief in the absolute and encompassing Oneness of the Creator, Who brings all things into being.[2] In addition to defining our view of the Creator, this premise informs our view of creation. Since creation in all its diversity flows from the Divine Oneness, it follows that in its Essence, all creation is one — a mystical concept that has profound spiritual and ethical implications.

---

1. *Sotah* 14a; cf. *Sifré* on Deuteronomy 11:22. Also see R. Menachem Nachum of Chernobyl, *Me'or Einayim, Tetzaveh*, n. 8.
2. *Mishneh Torah, Yesodei HaTorah* 1:1.

If all creation constitutes a unitary whole, then all things, from the highest to lowest entity in the hierarchy of creation, share a spiritual affinity with one another. Not that the universe as such is divine; the identification of nature and God is pantheism, a belief inconsistent with the doctrine of God's incorporeality. Pantheism also disputes the concept of free choice through its implicit moral determinism. Rather, the spiritual affinity of which we speak exists by virtue of the Infinite One Who produces and imparts existence to all things, while at the same time transcending them. As the verse attests, "How worthy are Your works, O God; You have created them all with wisdom" (Psalms 104:24). For this paramount reason, it is natural and proper for human beings to feel kinship with animals and all forms of life, despite the physical and spiritual differences between them.

Rabbi Moshe Cordovero (1522-1570) states: "Although God transcends creation, He sustains all living beings, from the highest to the lowest, and does not disparage any creature; for if He were to reject any creature due to its inferiority, none could exist even for a moment. Instead, He watches over and shows mercy to all. Similarly, a person should be benevolent to everyone, and no creature should seem despicable to him. Even the smallest living thing should be exceedingly worthy in his eyes."[3]

Kindness Toward Animals

Benevolence entails action. Thus, Judaism goes beyond the subjective factor of moral sentiment and mandates kindness toward animals in *halacha* (religious law), prohibits their abuse, praises their good traits, and obligates their owners concerning their well-being. As we shall see, even man's self-serving use of animals can bring about their spiritual benefit. Certainly, this should be part of our conscious intent in using animals, as well as in using any of the world's resources.

By example of the Patriarchs and Matriarchs, the Torah describes the ways of right action. Abraham personifies the divine trait of *chesed*

---

3. *Tomer Devorah*, chap. 2.

(kindness). Thus, the Midrash cites a dialogue in which Abraham tells Noah and his sons that they survived the flood because of the faithfulness with which they cared for the animals on the Ark.[4] In the Book of Genesis, Abraham's servant Eliezer determines that Rebecca is a worthy bride for Isaac when, after serving him water, she voluntarily gives water to his camels. This act of kindness, both to strangers and animals, proves her worthiness to enter the family of Abraham, and thus to become one of the mothers of the Jewish people. Jacob, too, is distinguished by an act of kindness toward animals. Rabbi Chaim ibn Attar (1696-1743) speculates that Jacob may have been the first person to build animal shelters out of compassion for his flocks.[5]

Not only are animals deserving of our compassion, but we may learn a number of good traits from them. The Talmud attests that had the Torah not been given, "we might have learned modesty from the cat, honest labor from the ant, marital fidelity from the dove, and consideration of one's mate from the rooster."[6]

To be sure, Judaism asserts that the world with all it contains is not an end unto itself, but serves as a backdrop for man — in particular for man's exercise of free will.[7] In the phrase of Chassidic master Rabbi

---

4. *Midrash Tehillim* on Psalms 37:6.
5. *Ohr HaChaim, Bereishis* 33:17.
6. *Eruvin* 100b.
7. *Likkutei Moharan* II, 71, citing *Berachos* 6b. Thus, it is said in the name of Kabbalistic master R. Yitzchak Luria, best known as the Ari z"l (an acronym for "our master, Rabbi Yitzchak, of blessed memory"): "Man is a microcosm, and the cosmos are a macroanthropus." The aphorism may be apocryphal, but is entirely consistent with Lurianic thought; cf. R. Chaim Vital, *Sefer Eitz Chaim, Chelek* II, *Heichal A-B-Y-A, Hakdamah L'haDrush, Sha'ar Tziyyur Olamos; Sha'arei Kedushah* 3:2, s.v. *V'od yesh chiluk,* and 3:5 (beginning); R. Avraham Azulai, *Chesed L'Avraham,* 4:1; R. Yaakov Yosef of Polonoye, *Toldos Yaakov Yosef, Kedoshim,* s.v. *V'hu achar she-kol ha-olam heim komah sheleimah;* R. Moshe Chaim Ephraim of Sudylkov, *Degel Machaneh Ephraim, Bereishis,* pp. 5, 7; R. Chaim of Volozhin, *Nefesh HaChaim* 2:5. That is, all the various levels and facets of creation are contained in each human being—and creation as a whole, including the various spiritual "worlds" beyond the physical universe, reflects the human form in its metaphysical structure. This is why the order of the Ten Sefiros, or divine powers operative in creation, is depicted as corresponding to the human form; cf. *"Pasach Eliyahu," Hakdamah, Tikkunei Zohar.* Moreover, all creation is animated by means of the "Cosmic Soul" known as *Adam Kadmon,* which is the highest spiritual root of all individual souls, and indeed all phenomena. The Kabbalists caution that the nature of *Adam Kadmon* is utterly beyond the grasp of mortal intellect, thus nothing can be said about it.

Nachman of Breslov (1772-1810), "Everything you see in the world, everything that exists, is for the sake of free will."[8] This is the central challenge of our lives; for by choosing the path of belief in God and Torah observance (or, in the case of non-Jews, by heeding the Seven Universal Laws of Noah), a person can achieve intimacy with the Creator. This is not true of a master-slave relationship, which is devoid of the element of choice. Nevertheless, if man is the main performer on the stage of creation, this does not mean that the "supporting cast" is of small consequence. Indeed, the divine call to venture beyond the ego and develop a sense of compassion for the rest of creation is a key part of the cosmic test.

"One should respect all creatures," asserts Rabbi Moshe Cordovero, "recognizing in them the greatness of the Creator Who formed man with wisdom. All creatures are imbued with the Creator's wisdom, which itself makes them greatly deserving of honor. The Maker of All, the Wise One Who transcends everything, is associated with His creatures in having made them. If one were to disparage them, God forbid, this would reflect upon the honor of their Maker."[9]

As the central figure in creation, man is responsible for the rest of the world. The Torah describes how God placed Adam and Eve in the center of Eden and commanded them to "tend" and "watch over" the garden. Symbolically, this defines humanity's continuing role as custodian of nature.[10] As a point of theology, it has important halachic and ethical consequences: we must seek to relieve the suffering of animals; we must

---

8. *Sichos HaRan* 300; also cf. *Si'ach Sarfei Kodesh* I, 385.
9. *Tomer Devorah*, chap. 2.
10. Rabbenu Bachaya (Genesis 2:15) explains this verse on the literal, homiletic, and mystical levels. Like other Rishonim, he interprets the verse in the most basic sense as indicating man's stewardship over nature. Then he cites several Midrashic teachings: according to the first, the terms "tend" and "watch over" allude to the study of Torah and observance of the commandments; the second interprets these terms as alluding to our divine service during the week through creative activity, as contrasted with our divine service on the Sabbath through non-action and rest; and the third relates them to the sacrifices in the Holy Temple, which elicited God's blessings. The Kabbalistic explanation relates the two terms to the "upper" letter *hey* and the "lower" letter *hey* in the four-letter Divine Name YHVH. (The former corresponds to the spiritual source of understanding, whereas the latter corresponds to the spiritual source of action.)

properly feed and attend the domestic animals under our care; our animals must rest on the Sabbath; we only may take the life of an animal to serve a legitimate human need; acts of wanton destructiveness are forbidden; and, according to the *Sefer HaChinnuch* (13th century c.e.), the prohibition of slaughtering an animal and its young on the same day teaches us that it is forbidden to bring about the destruction of any species.[11] Through our emulation of God, we become the instrument of God's compassion for the world that He created and pronounced "good."

The Hallmark of Wisdom

Compassion for animals is the measure of spiritual refinement. In his classic work of Jewish ethics, *Mesillas Yesharim* (Path of the Upright), Rabbi Moshe Chaim Luzzatto (1707-1746) asserts that it is one of the basic characteristics of a *chassid*, by which he means a person striving for spiritual perfection.[12] Indeed, the Midrash states that both Moses and King David were chosen by God to be leaders of Israel because of the compassion they had previously demonstrated toward their flocks.[13] There are countless tales of tzaddikim and their concern for the well-being of animals. As several stories in this volume demonstrate, this concern may extend even to wild creatures for which we bear no direct responsibility.

Despite the apparent multifarious character of the universe, there is an underlying spiritual connection between all things. Kabbalistic works speak of four elements: earth, water, air, and fire; in modern scientific terms, these may be related to the four states of matter: solid, liquid, gas, and energy. The four elements, in turn, parallel the four levels of existence: "silent" things such as minerals, earth, and water (*domem*), vegetation (*tzomei'ach*), animals (*chai*), and human beings (*medaber*), as well as the Four Worlds, or levels of reality. The World of Action (*Asiyah*) includes the entire physical universe; the three higher "worlds" are those of Formation (*Yetzirah*), Creation (*Beriah*), and Emanation (*Atzilus*).

11. *Sefer HaChinnuch*, Mitzvah 545.
12. *Mesillas Yesharim*, chap. 19.
13. *Shemos Rabbah* 2:2.

Beyond these categories are transcendent levels of which we cannot even begin to speak. The universe is wondrously diverse; all things differ in form, intellect, and purpose. Nevertheless, a fundamental interconnectedness exists between all creatures in that everything reflects God's wisdom and plays its part in the divine plan.

This is not merely an abstract concept, but a potent subject of contemplation for anyone who seeks a more enlightened way of relating to the world. The Baal Shem Tov (R. Yisrael ben Eliezer, 1698-1760), founder of the Chassidic movement, declares: "Do not consider yourself superior to anyone else... In truth, you are no different than any other creature, since all things were brought into being to serve God. Just as God bestows consciousness upon you, so does He bestow consciousness upon your fellow man. In what way is a human being superior to a worm? A worm serves the Creator with all of his intelligence and ability; and man, too, is compared to a worm or a maggot, as the verse states, 'I am a worm and not a man' (Psalms 22:7). If God had not given you a human intellect, you would only be able to serve Him like a worm. In this sense, you are both equal in the eyes of Heaven. A person should consider himself, and the worm, and all creatures as comrades in the universe, for we are all created beings whose abilities are God-given..."[14]

Compassion and Enlightenment

The Baal Shem Tov's words proceed from a deeply mystical perception: all things are animated by God, and thus constitute a "garment" for Him. As he observes, "All the worlds are garments, each one for the next, down to the lowest aspect..."[15] This concept is suggested by the verse that states, "He covers Himself with light as with a garment" (Psalms 104:2). In Kabbalistic terms, this alludes to the Infinite Light of Creation (*Ohr Ein Sof*). The Infinite Light, in turn, is "garbed" through

14. *Tzava'as HaRivash* 12.
15. *Sefer Baal Shem Tov, Bereishis* 12, citing *Chesed L'Avraham;* ibid. *Bereishis* 15, citing *Likkutim Yekarim* 17c; also cf. R. Pinchas of Koretz, *Midrash Pinchas,* 2:6, R. Moshe Chaim Ephraim of Sudylkov, *Degel Machaneh Ephraim, Kedoshim,* s.v. *Al tifnu l'elilim,* pp. 162-163; R. Nachman of Breslov, *Likkutei Moharan,* I, 64 (end), citing *Bereishis Rabbah* 21:5.

numerous acts of constriction (*tzimtzum*) that produce the various "worlds," culminating in the physical universe.[16] Thus, the universe may be conceived as the "outermost" garment of God, beneath which His Infinite Light is concealed. Although some elements may be primary and others secondary, all parts of the garment exist in symbiotic relationship with one another, and possess meaning by virtue of the One Who fashioned the garment for His own purpose.

Therefore, the Baal Shem Tov teaches us, the enlightened person will sense the kinship of "man and the worm and all small creatures," and relate to all of God's works with love. As the Maharal of Prague (R. Yehudah Loewe ben Bezalel, 1512-1609) observes, "Love of all creatures is also love of God; for whoever loves the One, loves all the works that He has made."[17] The realization of this truth is the central point of Jewish mysticism, and it is the root of the Jewish ethic of compassion for all creatures.

---

16. *Likkutei Moharan* I: 24, I: 33; *Sefer HaTanya* 1:2, *hagahah*, citing *Sefer Eitz Chaim* of the Ari z"l; R. Yosef Chaim of Baghdad, *Od Yosef Chai, Chut HaMeshulosh*; et al.

17. *Nesivos Olam, Ahavas Re'a,* 1.

Sources

Compassion for Animals in the Bible and Its Commentaries

And the servant took ten camels of the camels of his master, and departed; and all the goods of his master were in his possession; and he arose and went to Aram-Nahara'im, to the city of Nahor. And he made his camels kneel down outside the city by a well of water at dusk, when the women go out to draw water. And he said, "O Lord, God of my master Abraham: Please prepare whatever befalls me today and show kindness to my master, Abraham. Behold, when I stand by the spring of water, and the daughters of the townsmen come out to draw water. Let it come to pass that the maiden to whom I shall say: "Let down your pitcher, please, that I may drink," and she shall say, "Drink, and I also will give drink to your camels" — she will be the one You have designated for Your servant, Isaac. By this may I know that You have shown kindness unto my master." And it came to pass that before he had finished speaking, behold, Rebecca appeared (Genesis 24:10-15).

Commentary: "Let down your pitcher, please, that I may drink." He decided to ask her to lower her pitcher because it would require great effort on her part to remove the pitcher from her shoulder and to give him drink. It would be natural for her to be annoyed by this request and say, "Lift the pitcher from my shoulder and pour yourself a drink, so that I do not have to exert myself."

"Drink, and I also will give drink to your camels." This response would indicate her wisdom and good-heartedness. She would think, "Surely, this man has some sort of pain in his arms that prevents him both from drawing water from the spring and from lifting the pitcher himself. Accordingly, if he lacks the strength to draw water for himself, he certainly cannot attend his camels." Thus, her good-heartedness would be aroused, that she might show compassion for living creatures and give water to the camels as well (Rabbi Meir Leibush Malbim, *HaTorah V'HaMitzvah*, ad loc.).

૭૪૭૩

And shall I not take pity on Nineveh, that great city in which there are more than a hundred and twenty thousand persons who do not know their right hand from their left, as well as many cattle? (Jonah 4:11)

Commentary: "As well as many cattle." The cattle of the city are innocent and deserving of compassion; moreover, they are many (Rabbi David Kimchi, ad loc.).

❦

Bring my soul out of prison, that I may give thanks to Your Name... (Psalms 142:8).

Midrash: This refers to Noah, who was imprisoned in the ark. Rabbi Levi said: For twelve months, Noah and his sons did not sleep, for they were compelled to feed the animals, beasts, and birds. Rabbi Akiva said: Even branches for elephants and glass shards for ostriches they carried aboard by hand in order to feed them.[18] Some animals eat at two o'clock at night, while others eat at three. Thus, you may deduce that they never slept. Rabbi Yochanan said in the name of Rabbi Elazar, son of Rabbi Yosé the Galilean: One time, Noah was late in feeding the lion. Therefore, the lion mauled him, and he came away limping (*Midrash Tanchuma, Noach* 9; also cf. ibid. *Noach* 2; *Sanhedrin* 108b; *Yerushalmi Yoma* 4:41).

❦

Abraham once asked Malkhizedek,[19] "How did you manage to leave the ark [i.e., what merit did you possess at that time of divine judgment]?" Malkhizedek replied, "We performed charitable acts." [Abraham] asked, "What charity could you give? Which poor people were present? Since only Noah and his family were there, upon whom could you bestow charity?" He replied, "We gave charity to the animals,

---

18. Indigenous to the Middle East during ancient times, wild ostriches now live mainly in Africa. The largest birds in the world, they are famous for their plumes, speed, and omnivorous eating habits. The Talmud in *Shabbos* 128a also mentions that ostriches are known to eat glass shards, a fact which has bearing on the laws of *muktzah* (objects that may not be moved on the Sabbath).

19. The Talmudic rabbis identify Malkhizedek (a construct of *Malchi*, meaning "My King," and *tzedek*, meaning "just") as Shem, the eldest son of Noah. He was the priest-king of Salem (later Jerusalem), from whom Abraham received blessings in the name of God following his defeat of the Four Kings (Genesis, chap. 14).

beasts, and birds. We did not sleep at night, but served food to each creature. Once we were late, and my father came away injured."

At this, Abraham reasoned, "Had they not performed charity to the animals, beasts, and birds, they would not have come forth from the ark — and because they were once a bit late, they were punished. Thus, if I act charitably toward human beings, who are created in the form of angels, surely I shall be saved immediately from all harm" (*Midrash Tehillim* on Psalms 37:6).

03છાંછ

And Jacob journeyed to Succos, and built a house for himself and shelters (*succos*) for his flocks; therefore, the name of the place was called Succos (Genesis 33:17).

Commentary: Since this name commemorates Jacob's act of building a shelter, he may well have been the first person to build animal shelters, out of compassion for his flocks. For the sake of this innovation, the place was given the name Succos (Rabbi Chaim ibn Attar, *Ohr HaChaim*, ad loc.).

03છાંછ

The Torah calls Noah a tzaddik because this term specifically refers to one who provides food for God's creatures. Two individuals are called righteous for having provided other creatures with food: Noah and Joseph. Of the latter, it states, "They sold a tzaddik for silver" (Amos 2:6, referring to Joseph and his brothers), and "Joseph sustained" [his family and all the people of Egypt] (Genesis 47:12). [Thus, he is called righteous for having provided their needs.] Rav Achavah son of Rav Zeira said, "The sons of Noah, too, who brought the animals, beasts, and birds into the ark, were all righteous [because they showed compassion toward both animals and humans] (*Midrash Tanchuma, Noach* 5).

03છાંછ

And God remembered Noah and all the beasts and all the animals that were with him... (Genesis 8:1).

Midrash: If a person traveling by ship encounters a great storm, he will throw his possessions and livestock overboard in order to save the passengers. He does not have the same degree of compassion for his animals and possessions as he does for other human beings. However, the Holy One, blessed be He, has compassion for animals just as He has compassion for humans. As it states, "His mercy is upon all His works" (Psalms 145:9). [Thus, the verse places God's "remembrance" of the beasts and animals on the same plane as his remembrance of Noah] (*Midrash Tanchuma, Noach* 6).

෴

When Moses was herding the flocks of Jethro in the wilderness, one of the sheep ran away. He pursued it until he found a rocky ledge. After discovering the ledge, he came upon a stream of water beside which the lost sheep stood drinking. At this he said, "I didn't know that you ran away because of thirst. You must be tired." So he carried it back on his shoulders. The Holy One, blessed be He, declared, "You have shown compassion in tending the flock belonging to mortal man. Thus shall you tend My flock [Israel]" (Midrash: *Shemos Rabbah* 2:2).

෴

David was tested through tending sheep, and found to be a good shepherd. He would restrain the larger sheep for the sake of the small ones. First, he would let the small ones graze on the soft grass, and then let the old sheep graze on the grass that was more difficult to chew, leaving the tough grass for the young bucks. He led them only to the wilderness, in order to distance them from theft. Therefore, the Holy One, blessed be He, told him, "You have proven yourself to be faithful with sheep. Now go and shepherd My flock [Israel]" (ibid.).

෴

"And God will give you mercy, and show mercy to you" (Deuteronomy 13:18). God will instill in you the trait of mercy and compassion; then He will "show mercy to you." If one has mercy upon living creatures, Heaven will have mercy upon him (*Shabbos* 151b).

However, if a person lacks mercy, there is no difference between him and a beast, which is not sensitive to the suffering of other creatures (Rabbi Yehudah HeChassid, *Sefer Chassidim*, 87).

⊂ఖ౭⊃

If you chance upon a bird's nest along the way, in a tree or on the ground, whether it contains young birds or eggs, and the mother is sitting upon the young birds or upon the eggs — you shall not take the mother bird together with the children. You shall surely send away the mother, and only then may you take the young for yourself, so that it may go well with you, and you may prolong your days (Deuteronomy 22:6, 7).

Commentary 1: This precept is a moral instruction, as is the related prohibition not to kill a mother animal and its young on the same day (Leviticus 22:28). The reason for both commandments is that we should not be cruel-hearted and lacking compassion.

Alternately, it could be inferred that the Torah does not permit destruction — the extinction of an entire species — even if it permits the killing [of animals for food or other legitimate human needs] within a given species. One who kills the mother and her young on the same day, or takes them when they are free to fly, is considered as if he had eliminated an entire species.

Maimonides writes in his *Guide for the Perplexed* that the reason for the commandment of sending away the mother bird, as well as that of not slaughtering a mother bird and her young on the same day, is to warn us not to slaughter the offspring in the mother's sight; for this causes the animal extreme grief[20] (Nachmanides, *Commentary on the Torah*, ad loc.).

Commentary 2: This precept aims to instill in our hearts the knowledge that the watchful care of God is over the human species individually, as it is written, "For His eyes are upon the ways of man..." (Job 34:21) and, for other kinds of living creatures, over the entire species in a general way. In other words, His desire is for the endurance of the species. Therefore, no species among all His various creatures will ever

---

20. *Moreh Nevuchim* 3:48.

become extinct, for under the watchful care of the One Who lives and endures forever, [every species] finds enduring existence.[21]

When a person sets his mind on this, he will understand the ways of God, and he will see that the continued existence of the various species — not one of which has become extinct and perished, "from the eggs of lice, to the horns of the wild ox," since the day they were created — is all by His pronouncement, and this is His desire. So, too, will a person realize that when he keeps the precepts of his Creator, and his ways are honest and straight, "with clean hands and a pure heart" (Psalms 24:4), God's providence will be upon him. His body will live long in this world, and his soul will live forever in the World to Come (*Sefer HaChinnuch*, Mitzvah 545).

ೞ

And the superiority (*yisron*) of land is above all... (Ecclesiastes 5:8).

Midrash: The rabbis [rendered the word *yisron* interpretively]: Even creatures you see on the Earth that seem superfluous (*meyusarin*), such as flies, gnats, and mosquitoes — they, too, are part of God's creation (*Vayikra Rabbah* 22:2).

ೞ

People of holiness you shall be unto Me; you shall not eat the flesh of an animal that was torn (*treifah*) in the field... (Exodus 22:30).

Commentary: Distinctive [among the traits of Israel] is the compassion that waits to blossom into manifestation from amidst the feelings of the pure-hearted, and spread from humanity to all living creatures. This compassion is nascent within the prohibition of eating *neveilah* (an animal that has died either due to natural causes, or improper slaughter) or a *treifah* (an animal that has been injured by a predator, or which has a fatal condition).

---

21. During the early medieval period during which the author of *Sefer HaChinnuch* lived it was not known that innumerable species had become extinct. However, his interpretation that the Torah wishes human beings to refrain from contributing to the extinction of any species still stands.

Just as we naturally feel greater pity for sick or injured human beings than we feel for the healthy, the unfortunate injured animal deserves our additional sympathy. Having internalized the ethical implications of the Torah's prohibition of eating the flesh of a torn animal, our hearts can fully experience the spirit of enlightenment that relates the precept of visiting the sick, prompting us to relieve their distress.

The commonality that exists between our feelings of compassion [for both animals and human beings] also expresses itself in connection with the need to guard our health, both spiritually and physically, and in not putting ourselves on the same plane as the predatory beasts. Rather, [the Torah] imposes upon us the further obligation to bring about their good, to benefit and to enlighten them. How could we consume the *treifah* lying in the field, which would appear like "dividing the spoil" with [the wild beasts], and constitute a tacit approval of their predatory habits?

It is true that, among the various categories of *treifah* discussed by the Talmudic sages, we must distinguish between a mortally injured animal in the field and a terminally ill human being. However, the suffering of both creatures calls for our compassion, which initially should be awakened on behalf of the wretched and the outcast. The law of the animal that died as a result of sickness prepares the heart to feel even greater repugnance toward exploiting the misfortune of other creatures in the event of their deaths. This sensitivity signals a sense of comradeship, sharing another's pain, and our having entered the borders of their inner world. With this, the "motivation by virtue of enlightenment" will supersede the "motivation by virtue of the law," causing us to distance ourselves from committing any evil upon these, our comrades in the universe, since we all come forth from the hand of One Creator, the Master of all His works (Rabbi Avraham Yitzchak Kook, *Chazon HaTzimchonut V'HaShalom*, 26, abridged).

Kinship of All Creatures

There is a fundamental principle I would like to share with you, my brother: Just as God is infinite, so all divine attributes are infinite. Thus,

His humility and His providence are infinite. God watches over each of His works, even the least of them. God does not merely watch over the various species in a general manner, as Maimonides, of blessed memory, and others maintain.[22] Do not be perplexed that the Holy King, for Whom "the heavens are His throne," gazes upon and discerns the tiniest creatures in dunghills and unclean places; for also among large animals we see that certain species are not kosher, but the All Seeing One nevertheless watches over them in every detail of their lives.

Indeed, God takes pride in them, as he tells Job: "Do you know the time when the wild goats of the rock give birth — or observe when the hinds calve? ... The wing of the peacock rejoices — are they wings or feathers of a stork? For she leaves her eggs in the ground, and she warms them with the earth ... The young vultures gulp down blood, and where the carrion lies, there is [the parent bird.]"[23]

Before the Blessed One there is no difference whatever between a large creature and a small creature; and the unseemliness of a place is no obstacle to Him, as the author of the Song of Unity wrote in the section corresponding to the third day: "The mighty wind does not repel You; even all foulness does not befoul You." The meaning is that of all lower creatures, none is repulsive before Him but a transgressor, a proud man, and evildoer — he alone is despicable to God and foul smelling.

Rather, know, my brother, remember and do not forget that just as God's providence applies to all the worlds and all creatures, so does His Essence utterly transcend all worlds and all creatures, being hidden and removed from them. This is the meaning of the verse: "Holy, holy, holy, is the Lord of Hosts..."[24] The term "holy" (*kadosh*) indicates the separation and removal of His Essence from everything, due to the loftiness of His sublime and wondrous station, reaching unto infinity. Nevertheless, the verse concludes: "The entire world is full of His glory"

---

22. *Moreh Nevuchim* 3:17; among subsequent Jewish philosophers, R. Albo takes a similar position to Maimonides in *Sefer HaIkkarim* 4:11; for numerous additional sources see R. Aryeh Kaplan's *Handbook of Jewish Thought*, Vol. 2, chap. 19, nn. 34-36. However, R. Moshe (Cheifetz) Gentili (1663-1711) agrees with the author of *Sefer HaBris* in *M'leches Machsheves, Noach* (19a).
23. Job 39:1, 13, 14, 30.
24. Isaiah 6:3.

— as if to say: while God utterly transcends all the worlds, His providence is constantly bound to all the worlds and all His works, down to the smallest detail, even unto this lowly world, which in its entirety is full of His glory (Rabbi Pinchas Eliyahu Horowitz of Vilna, *Sefer HaBris* I, *Ma'amar* 14, *Eichus HaChai,* sec. 8, s.v. *V'klal gadol,* p. 224).

❀

The Baal Shem Tov taught: Do not consider yourself superior because you experience *deveikus* (attachment to God) to a greater extent than someone else. In truth, you are no different than any other creature, since all things were brought into being to serve God. Just as God bestows consciousness upon you, so does He bestow consciousness upon your fellow man.

In what way is a human being superior to a worm? A worm serves the Creator with all of his intelligence and ability; and man, too, is compared to a worm or maggot, as the verse states, "I am a worm and not a man" (Psalms 22:7). If God had not given you a human intellect, you would only be able to serve Him like a worm. In this sense, you are both equal in the eyes of Heaven.

A person should consider himself and the worm and all creatures as comrades in the universe, for we are all created beings whose abilities are God-given. This should always remain in your thoughts (*Tzava'as HaRivash* 12).

❀

The Baal Shem Tov taught that when a piece of straw falls from a wagon loaded with straw, this has been decreed by Heaven. Similarly, when a leaf falls from a tree, it is because Heaven has decreed that this particular leaf at this particular moment would fall at this particular spot. Once the Baal Shem Tov showed his disciples a certain leaf as it fell to the ground and told them to pick it up. They did so and saw that a worm was underneath it. The Baal Shem Tov explained that the worm had been suffering due to the heat, so this leaf had fallen to give it shade (*Sha'ar HaOsios, Hashgachah Pratis*).

ભ્ઠ

The entire universe is included within the mystical paradigm of the human form. Israel and the nations of the world represent the upper part of the body: those who contemplate divine wisdom and engage in holy speech correspond to the head, while those who do the skilled work of the world correspond to the hands. The animals correspond to the legs, for they perform all their activities on their feet. This correspondence extends to the level of creatures that cannot walk, but crawl; and similarly to the rest of creation (Rabbi Pinchas of Koretz, *Midrash Pinchas* I, 22).

ભ્ઠ

Adam was created last of all creatures because the Holy One, blessed be He, asked all creatures to contribute their portion to Adam's body: the lion his might, the deer his speed, the eagle his agility, the fox his cleverness, etc. All these traits were given to Adam Thus, the verse states: "Let us make man in our image... " (Genesis 1:26), indicating that the essential traits of all species are included in humankind (Rabbi Eliyahu ben Shlomo, the Vilna Gaon, *Aderes Eliyahu, Bereishis* 1:26).

ભ્ઠ

Not only for the physical harm that I have caused my fellow men do I beg forgiveness, but also for their spiritual afflictions that I have brought about through my many misdeeds. For our sages taught that one should consider the world to be balanced between good and evil, and one's deeds tip the scales. Similarly, I ask forgiveness from all creatures — whether in the mineral, vegetative, animal or human realms — for my having transgressed against them and caused them suffering, whether physical or spiritual. Also, from the depths of my heart I beg all souls, both the living and the dead, and all celestial beings, from the lowest to the highest, to have mercy and forgive me completely for all my transgressions and sins against them, and for having caused them any form of grief or spiritual defect. Instead, may they intercede for me and tip the scales of judgment to the side of merit. May they beseech God to forgive me for everything, and may I be protected by the shadow of His compassion (Ethical Will of Rabbi Nachman Goldstein, Rav of Tcherin, included in *Kochvei Ohr*, Breslov writings and oral traditions).

ⳡ

The lights of life that animate the entire hierarchy of living creatures according to their species are but shards of one lofty collective soul possessed of all wisdom and talent, divided into many separate parts (Rabbi Avraham Yitzchak Kook, *Orot HaKodesh*, II, p. 358).

ⳡ

The human soul in its greatest breadth contains the individual souls of all creatures. Each living thing is a spark of the vast all-encompassing fire that is the collective soul of humankind (ibid. p. 359).

ⳡ

Man stands and wonders: what need is there for the diversity of creation? He is unable to understand how everything comprises one great unity...

If you are amazed at how it is possible to speak, hear, smell, touch, see, understand and feel — tell your soul that all living things collectively confer upon you the fullness of your experience.

Not the least speck of existence is superfluous, everything is needed, and everything serves its purpose. "You" are present within everything that is beneath you, and your being is bound up with all that transcends you (ibid. p. 361).

ⳡ

We do not know how to measure the invigoration and spiritual well-being that animals incapable of speech confer upon us, simply by virtue of the fact that we coexist.

The vital symbiosis of members of the same nation already has been revealed to us, and those who possess a clearer vision glimpse that of all humanity, as well. However, the spiritual symbiosis of all living beings still remains hidden. As of yet, no researcher dares voice his conviction regarding this perception.

Nevertheless, these far-out propositions arrive before the precise sciences almost as dreams to augur their revelation. Already we can be elevated to that lofty height at which humankind becomes one with the totality of life, even with vegetation and inanimate existence (ibid. p. 363).[25]

King Katzia's Judgment

Alexander [the Great] of Macedonia once came to the land beyond the Dark Mountains[26] and sent for King Katzia. When the latter arrived, Alexander was engaged in a legal discussion. King Katzia presented him a gift of a golden platter containing a golden loaf of bread. [Thus, he alluded to his anxiety that Alexander wished to plunder his kingdom.]

"Do I need your money?" Alexander asked him.

"Perhaps you do not have enough food to eat in your own country, that you must come here?" King Katzia asked.

"I have only come here to learn how you judge disputes," Alexander replied. He sat down beside King Katzia.

One day a man came before the King with a complaint against his fellow. He said, "This man sold me a dung-heap in which I found [hidden] treasure. I bought the dung-heap, not the treasure." [Because he did not wish to steal, he was reluctant to keep the treasure.]

The other man said, "I sold him the dung-heap and all its contents." [He, too, did not wish to keep the treasure, due to his scrupulous honesty.]

King Katzia asked one of the disputants, "Do you have a son?" The man replied affirmatively.

---

25. R. Bezalel Naor shared the following personal anecdote. Meeting Rav Avraham Yitzchak Kook's son, Rav Zvi Yehudah Kook (1891-1982) for the first time, he commented on how much *ahavas Yisrael* (love of Israel) the latter's father had possessed. The octogenarian R. Zvi Yehudah burst out laughing. "*Mai revusa ika?* (What's the big deal?) My father loved the whole world, even *tzomeach* (vegetation), even *domem* (earth and stones)!"

26. This probably refers to a kingdom in Africa; cf. *Tamid* 32a.

"And do you have a daughter?" he asked the other, who also replied affirmatively. The King then declared, "Let them marry one another, and divide the treasure between them."

King Katzia noticed that Alexander seemed disturbed. "Did I rule unfairly?" he asked. "If this case came before the court in your country, how would it be adjudicated?"

"The judge would condemn them both to death, and the king would keep the treasure," Alexander replied.

"Does the rain fall in your country?" King Katzia asked.

"Yes."

"Does the sun shine upon it?"

"Yes."

"Do you have small cattle?"

"Yes."

"Cursed be that man [who would render such evil judgments]!" [King Katzia] declared. "It is only due to the merit of the small cattle that the sun shines and the rain falls upon your country. For the sake of the small cattle you are saved!"

Hence, it is written, "[Your righteousness is like the mighty mountains, Your judgments like the great deep;] man and animal You save, O God" (Psalms 36:7). That is, You save man for the sake of the animal (Midrash: *Bereishis Rabbah* 33:1, with the commentary *Eitz Yosef*).

2

Eden and the Messianic Age

In the second chapter of Genesis, the Torah describes the Garden of Eden, an idyllic environment in which the first man and woman, and with them all living beings, could enter into communion with God. Formed of the dust of the Earth but imbued with a divine soul, Adam and Eve lived in this wondrous place of luxuriant trees and plants together with all the species of animals.

The animals of Eden were neither predatory beasts of the wilderness nor the domesticated animals with which we are familiar; they were awesome beings possessed of beauty and wisdom, which, like Adam and Eve and the first ten generations of humankind, peacefully subsisted on vegetation alone. Their mode of existence was not something to be shunned or pitied, as it is today. Indeed, aquatic creatures and fowl were deemed worthy of receiving the first explicit divine blessing, given on the fifth day of creation (Genesis 1:22). The other animals were created on the sixth day, together with Adam and Eve, and they received a separate affirmation of divine favor (ibid. 1:25).

The dignity of animals is borne out by a number of sources. The Talmud states that God conferred with the souls of all animals prior to creation, and they readily agreed to be created as such, even choosing their own physical forms.[1] This teaches us that they were deserving of

---

1. *Chullin* 60a, with Rashi, s.v. *li'tzivyonam*. Chassidic master R. Kalonymus Kalmish of Piacetzna (1889-1943) infers from this that the specific intelligence that animates each level of life transcends the forms of the creatures on that level. However, by means of each discrete form the transcendent intellect that corresponds to it may attain self-realization; see *Derech HaMelech, Rosh Hashanah* 5686/1925, p. 193 (bottom).

48 The Vision of Eden

God's consideration, and that they were given to understand their destiny in positive terms. Another testimony to the worthiness of animals is their connection to angels. Although angels are incorporeal spiritual beings,[2] their forms as envisioned by the prophets were often those of animals. This suggests that in their spiritual source, animals occupy an exalted rung — an inference supported by the fact that the Torah uses animals to symbolize the Twelve Tribes of Israel.[3]

Animals, too, serve their Creator. The Talmud tells how Rabbi Elazar ben Arach caused his master Rabbi Yochanan ben Zakkai to share with him a mystical vision in which they heard the wondrous song of all creatures, bringing to life the words of the Psalmist: "Praise God from the Earth: sea giants and all the depths, fire and hail, snow and vapor, storm wind that fulfills His word; mountains and all heights, trees and all cedars; animals and all beasts, creeping things and winged fowl..."[4] This is the theme of the Sabbath and Festival prayer *"Nishmas kol chai"* ("The souls of all living things shall praise Your Name..."), as well as the *Perek Shirah* ("Chapter of Song"), an ancient rabbinic work mentioned in the Talmud[5] and much favored by the Kabbalists.[6] Thus, the Torah confers dignity upon the animal kingdom, and does not define it merely in utilitarian terms. Animals belong in the Garden of Eden because they, too, are an integral part of God's world that, in the words of the Mishnah, "He created solely for His glory."[7]

---

2. Cf. *Mishneh Torah, Yesodei HaTorah* 2:3. The *Zohar* I, 101a, 144a, and III, 68b, states that the "bodies" of angels are formed of air or fire, whereas *Pardes Rimonim* 24:11 (51a) describes the angel as a composite of the four elements, even asserting that "an angel is like a physical body in comparison to the sublime level of the *tzaddik.*" However, this does not mean to ascribe actual physicality to the angels. In general, the angelic realm is a spiritual analogue of physical nature, whereas human souls are destined to occupy an altogether higher rung; cf. *Yerushalmi Shabbos* 2:6; *Tikkunei Zohar, Tikkun* 70 (137a); *Likkutei Moharan* II, 1:1.
3. Genesis, chap. 49.
4. *Chagigah* 14b, citing *Tehillim* 148, according to Maharsha.
5. *Chullin* 64b.
6. R. Nosson Slifkin's *Nature's Song* (Jerusalem: Targum / Feldheim 2000) is an excellent English translation of *Perek Shirah* that elucidates the text by combining traditional commentary with contemporary science.
7. *Avos* 6:12; also cf. *Yalkut Reuvaini, Bereishis* 25b (top), citing *Koheles Rabbah.* The term "glory" (Hebrew: *kavod*) specifically refers to divine revelation, as the Ramban states (ad loc.) on the verse, "Please allow me to behold Your Glory" (Exodus 33:18).

Back to Eden

Eden is the biblical paradigm of the original state of accord between God, man, and nature. It represents a state of harmony and peace that since the hour its gates were closed, the world has never known. Eden is our spiritual home, and the longing to return to it is deeply buried within the human psyche. Perhaps the animal rights and vegetarian movements, while seeking to redress what they perceive to be ethical or ecological wrongs, derive their emotional fuel from a deeper source. Aside from the reasons given in the previous chapter, human beings feel a special kinship with animals and nature because they remind us of this "Paradise Lost."

Throughout history, the attitude of Western civilization toward nature has been one of struggle and dominance. Its animating myth has been that of the hero, whose very reason for being is conquest. In biblical terms, this attitude is symbolized by the Tower of Babel; in contemporary cultural iconography, by the spaceship. At the same time, there always have been countervailing attitudes that expressed distrust of human artifice, idealizing the "noble savage" and advocating a return to nature. What is the root of this basic ambivalence that human beings feel toward human productions? Despite all our achievements — or indeed, because of them — we are haunted by the sense that there is something lacking in our approach to life, something amiss in human nature itself.

The Tree of Knowledge

The Torah understands this spiritual lack or confusion as a consequence of the first sin.[8] Human nature is not inherently evil: Adam and Eve were endowed with every manner of physical and spiritual perfection, possessing only the slightest deficiency in order to have free will.[9] Even in contravening the divine will, they only wished to serve God. According to the "Alter" (Elder) of Novhardok (1848-1919), one of the outstanding proponents of the Lithuanian Mussar movement, the rationale by which Adam and Eve were

---

8. *Zohar* III, 107b, et al.

persuaded to eat the Forbidden Fruit was that by internalizing evil and then overcoming it, they might sanctify God's Name to an even greater degree — a task that proved to be far more difficult than they had imagined.[10] Their transgression was not a willful act of rebellion, but the result of confusion and misjudgment.[11] In psychological terms, the Serpent[12] that tempted Eve represents ego: the illusion of self as an entity independent of God, seeking sensory gratification and power.[13] The ego and its associated traits were not always innate tendencies of human nature, but existed only *in potentia;* they were acquired when Adam and Eve heeded the advice of the Serpent and ate the forbidden fruit.[14] We have been spiritually divided ever since.

The Tree of Knowledge represents the conflict between good and evil, produced by our estrangement from God. In a broader sense, it also represents dualistic thinking: seeing things in "positive versus negative" terms, without any sense of their underlying unity. This dualistic consciousness is actually an extremely warped mode of being. When Adam and Eve ate the fruit of the Tree of Knowledge, this produced an existential split between the imaginary "self" built of our egoistic hopes and fears, and the essence of mind that is the divine soul.[15] Thus, Adam

---

9. *Tikkunei Zohar, Tikkun* 67 (98a); Ramchal, *Derech Hashem* I, 3:8; *Nefesh HaChaim* 1:6. Concerning the lofty status of Adam before the first sin, see *Avodah Zarah* 5a; *Eiruvin* 18b; *Yerushalmi Shabbos* 2:6; *Avos D'Rabbi Nosson* 2:5; *Bereishis Rabbah* 8:10, 12:5, 21:1; *Bamidbar Rabbah* 4:8; *Zohar* I, 37b; *Tikkunei Zohar, Tikkun* 57 (91b), *Tikkun* 64 (95b), *Tikkun* 66 (96b).

10. R. Yosef Yoizel Horowitz of Novhardok, *Madreigas HaAdam, Maamar* 1: *B'tekufas HaOlam, Adam HaRishon.*

11. R. Chaim Vital, *Sha'ar HaPesukim, Bereishis* 3.

12. According to one Midrash, even the Serpent was not created with an evil nature, but was influenced by Samael, the Accusing Angel; see *Yalkut Shimoni* 2:25. The trait that made the Serpent susceptible to evil was its cleverness (Genesis 3:1). If not for the sin, the Serpent would have benefited humankind materially and spiritually, as stated in *Sanhedrin* 59b; also cf. R. Gershon Henich Leiner of Radzin, *Sod Yesharim, Bereishis.*

13. *Likkutei Halachos, Orach Chaim, Hilchos Tefillin* 6:4.

14. *Yalkut Reuvaini, Bereishis, 35b,* citing the Ari; *Nefesh HaChaim* 1:6, *hagahah* 2.

15. Concerning the soul as essence of mind, see *Sefer Baal Shem Tov, Vayeilech,* note 6, citing *Nesiv Mitzvosecha; Ohr HaGanuz L'Tzaddikim, Mattos,* citing the Baal Shem Tov; *Teshu'os Chein, Tzav; Likkutim Yekarim* 161; *Likkutei Moharan* I, 35:1, 234; ibid. II, 114. Concerning the existential division of self and soul, see *Derech Hashem* III:1; *Likkutei Halachos, Yoreh De'ah, Orlah* 4:2; ibid. *Choshen Mishpat, Sh'luchin* 5:1. Basing his ideas on a teaching of the Ari z"l, R. Shneur Zalman of Liadi discusses this conflict

and Eve immediately became self-conscious, and sought to hide from God. For most of us, this existential split characterizes the way we commonly think and feel. Although we suffer greatly from it, we may hardly know that we have a problem. However, there is a rabbinic principle that "before God creates a sickness, He creates the cure."[16] In our context, this is reflected by the fact that before the Torah mentions the Tree of Knowledge, it mentions the Tree of Life (Genesis 2:9) — for the Tree of Life bears the power of spiritual healing. It can rectify the dualistic state of mind associated with the Tree of Knowledge by awakening the perception of the Divine Oneness within the very plurality of creation. (Thus, the Tree of Life is associated with the Torah, and its mystical dimension in particular;[17] as stated in Proverbs 3:18, "She is a Tree of Life to those who grasp her.") It is significant that both trees are described as standing in the "center of the Garden."[18] This suggests that they are interdependent and share a common purpose.

---

in terms of an animal soul vs. the divine soul in *Likkutei Amarim-Tanya*, esp. chaps. 1, 6, 9, et passim.

16. *Megillah* 13b.

17. The Torah describes both trees as standing in the center of the Garden. How was this possible? Nachmanides (R. Moshe ben Nachman, 1194-1270) citing the interpretation of Targum Onkelos (ad loc.) describes the two trees as standing side by side in a common area designated generally as the "center" of the garden. Accordingly, the two trees symbolize two separate modes of being which spring forth from the Divine Oneness the center point, concerning which Nachmanides adds that its exact location is known "only to God."

Another answer is that from a common trunk and root system, the two trees separated from each other: the Tree of Knowledge below, and the Tree of Life above (Rabbenu Bachaya on *Bereishis* 2:9). This symbolizes that the dualistic reality of "knowledge of good and evil" devolves from the Divine Oneness and is inseparable from it.

According to other Kabbalistic sources, the Tree of Life was surrounded on all sides by the branches of the Tree of Knowledge (*Yalkut Reuvaini*, *Bereishis,* p. 68, citing *Asarah Ma'amaros*). This indicates that within every appearance of dualism, the Divine Oneness is present (cf. *Likkutei Moharan* I: 33). From either point of view, however, the dualistic aspect of the Tree of Knowledge is subsumed within the transcendent unity expressed by the Tree of Life. Their central position in the Garden indicates their primacy in creation, due to the higher consciousness they confer.

Alternatively, Chassidic master R. Kalonymus Kalman HaLevi Epstein of Cracow (1751-1823) opines that the term "Tree of Knowledge" does not indicate any particular tree, but that state of mind in which one takes the pursuit of physical desire to be an end in itself; see *Ma'or VaShemesh, Bo, s.v. V'kachah tochlu oso.*

If the original divine intent in creation was to confer the ultimate good to His creatures,[19] why did God create the Tree of Knowledge? In truth, it was not created merely as a temptation for Adam and Eve to overcome, but its fruit was meant to be their Sabbath food. If they had waited the remaining two hours until the onset of the holy day, they would have received permission to partake of this tree, as well.[20] First, they would have eaten from the Tree of Life, and then partaken of the fruit of the Tree of Knowledge, thereby attaining an even higher spiritual state.[21] Their perception of the essential unity of all creation would have extended into the realm of multiplicity and dualism; thus, they would have gained a more vivid knowledge of the Divine Oneness.

Unfortunately, the first man and woman had no way of anticipating the nature and extent of the damage their transgression would cause. The *Zohar* states that as a result of eating the Forbidden Fruit, thirty-nine curses were brought upon creation,[22] including the mortality of all living beings, the difficulty of earning a livelihood, inequality of the sexes, and the pain of childbirth and child-rearing. The greatest punishment of all was estrangement from God, resulting in our distorted perception of the world and ourselves. This condition of estrangement is enforced by the Cherubim, the angels that guard the gates of Eden, wielding "revolving swords of flame" (Genesis 3:24). Rabbi Nosson Sternhartz (1780-1844) states that these swords are the mental confusions that eclipse the soul's knowledge of its own essential nature.[23]

18. *Midrash HaGadol, Bereishis* 3:24. For the Tree of Life as symbolic of the mystical dimension of Torah, see *Zohar* III, *Naso*, 124b-125a (*Raya Mehemna*); *Tikkunei Zohar*, *Tikkun* 55 (89a); *Sha'arei Orah*, Gate 5, 61b; *Sefer HaTanya, Iggeres HaKodesh*, Epistle 26; *Likkutei Halachos, Yoreh De'ah, Sefer Torah* 3:10.
19. R. Chaim Vital, *Eitz Chaim, Sha'ar HaKlalim* 1; *Pardes Rimonim* 2:6; Ramchal, *Derech Hashem* I, 2:1, *K'lach Pis'chei Chochmah* 2; *Likkutei Moharan* I, 64:1. Note ms. version in appendix of some editions of *Likkutei Moharan* that R. Nachman initially used the term *chesed* (kindness) to describe the divine intention in creation, and subsequently changed it to *rachmanus* (mercy).
20. R. Chaim Vital, *Eitz Chaim* 49:3; *Shaar HaKavanos, Inyan Rosh Hashanah, Drush* 1; *Sefer HaLikkutim*, 3 (pp. 25-27); R. Chaim of Chernowitz, *Be'er Mayim Chaim, Bereishis* 2:9, 2:16, 2:17; R. Shlomo Elyashiv, *Leshem Shevo V'Achlamah, Drushei Olam HaTohu*, 2:4:2, 4.
21. *Derech Hashem* I: 3:6.
22. Adam, Eve, and the Serpent each received ten curses, while the Earth received nine. These correspond to the 39 forms of constructive activity forbidden on the Sabbath; cf. R. Yaakov Zvi Yolles, *Kehillas Yaakov*, s.v. *Lamed-Tes Melachos*; for additional sources, see n. 25 below.

The Messianic Age

However, the original state of divine favor and bliss that Adam and Eve had known in the Garden of Eden and the mutual harmony that existed among all creatures was not lost forever. The Prophets assured all humankind that a time is coming when God will fulfill all the blessings He gave His works at the very beginning of creation.[24] Then the Thirty-Nine Curses (*lamed-tes klallos*) will be transformed to the Dew of Illumination (*tal oros*).[25] That is, not only will we regain the state of Adam and Eve before the first sin, but also everything we formerly experienced as "negativity" will now serve as a lens through which to perceive God. The meaning of human history, with all its agonies and ecstasies, will be revealed. We will understand how the political, interpersonal, and existential conflicts we have suffered were, in truth, "birth pangs of the Messiah"[26]— birth pangs of enlightenment. The Jewish people, chosen to bear witness to God's existence and oneness, will no longer suffer exile, misunderstanding, and persecution, but will return in peace to the land of Israel. And with their political redemption, a religious renaissance will begin to flower: prophecy will return to the world, heralding the spiritual redemption of all creatures.[27]

Isaiah describes a future world in which the peace and joy of Eden will be restored. Indeed, the prophet speaks as if the divine promise had already been fulfilled:

---

23. *Likkutei Halachos, Netilas Yadayim Shacharis* 4:12; ibid. *Birkhas HaShachar* 3:2. This concept also is implied by the Baal Shem Tov's words in *Tzava'as HaRivash* 58.
24. Rabbenu Bachaya, *Bereishis* 2:15.
25. In Hebrew, the number 39 is spelled with the letters *lamed-tes*. When transposed, these letters spell the word *tal*, meaning "dew." Thus, the affliction we suffered will be transformed to the medium of our enlightenment; cf. *Zohar* III, 243b; *Tikkunei Zohar, Tikkun* 48 (85a); *Likkutei Moharan* I, 11:4, 38:7 (end). The word *arur* ("cursed") that the Torah uses in connection with the Serpent is phonetically similar to *ohr*, meaning "light."
26. *Sanhedrin* 97af; *Sotah* 49b; *Derech Eretz Zuta* 10; *Zohar* III, 67b, 124b, 125b (*Raya Mehemna*), 153a; Maharal, *Netzach Yisrael*, chap. 36; *Sichos HaRan*, 35, 220; also note *Likkutei Moharan* II, 2, with *Parparaos L'Chochmah*, sec. 8.
27. Zechariah 8:22, 23; Isaiah 2:2-4; Jeremiah 3:17; *Shemos Rabbah* 23:11; *Avos D'Rabbi Nosson* 35:19; *Mishneh Torah, Hilchos Melachim* 11:4 (end), 12:5; Ramchal, *Maamar HaIkkarim*, "*BaGe'ulah*." Concerning the return of prophecy, see Joel 3:1, 5; Maimonides, *Igeres Teiman* (p. 30); *Likkutei Moharan* II, 8:5; Rav Kook, *Arpelei Tohar*, 40; *Orot*, 34-35.

Truly God has consoled Zion,
Consoled all her ruins;
He has made her wilderness like Eden,
Her desert like the Garden of the Lord;
Gladness and joy shall abide there,
Thanksgiving and the sound of music

                                            (Isaiah 51:3).

Each level of creation will be elevated in a continuous process of spiritual ascent. According to one Midrashic opinion,[28] all animals will become kosher (ritually pure); in any case, they all will become spiritually perfected, regaining their status prior to the sin of Adam. Moreover, all animals will share what we presently consider human intellect and wisdom.

To a limited extent, this has already happened. The Talmud cites several cases in which the animals of tzaddikim refused to violate Torah laws, although these laws apply only to humans. Indeed, the cow that demurred from working on the Sabbath inspired a Roman farmer to embrace Judaism. This convert later achieved renown as the Torah sage, Rabbi Yochanan ben Torsa.[29]

As in Eden, animals during the Messianic age no longer will be carnivorous. Not only will war between nations cease, but even animals will desist from preying upon one another. "And a wolf shall dwell with a lamb, and a leopard will lie down with a kid, and a calf and a lion cub and a fattened ox will flock together, and a small child shall lead them. And a heifer and a bear will graze together, their young will lie down together, and a lion, like the ox, will eat straw. A suckling babe will play at a viper's hole, and over an adder's den an infant will stretch forth his hand. They will do no harm or damage in all My holy mountain, for the knowledge of God shall fill the Earth as the water covers the sea" (Isaiah 11:6-9). Although Maimonides understands this prophecy as strictly allegory, Ravad (Rabbi Avraham

---

28. *Midrash Shocher Tov, Tehillim* 146.
29. Literally, "son of a cow"; see *Pesikta Rabbasi* 14.

ben David of Posquières, 1120-1197) and other authorities interpret it literally, as well.[30]

Spiritual Repair

The key that opens the Gates of Eden is *teshuvah*: return to God. In a hidden way, each one of us, every day, goes through the moral scenario implicit in the biblical account of the Garden of Eden.[31] We are constantly faced with the challenge to trust God, and not rely upon our own guile; to heed the Torah and the tzaddikim, and not follow our own desires; to be patient, and not impulsive; to refrain from taking what belongs to others; not to listen to gossip or evil speech; and if we fail in some way, not to blame our associates or circumstances, but accept responsibility for our own actions.

Having engaged in *teshuvah*, we also must engage in *tikkun*: spiritual repair of the damage we have done. However great its extent, this damage may be fixed through Torah study and observance of the commandments; through meditation and prayer; through acts of kindness and charity; and through using the things of this world in order to serve God thereby. Rabbi Nachman of Breslov taught: "Ultimately, everything can be transformed to the good,"[32] even the worst moral failings. We have the power to make this world a Garden of Eden, to

---

30. Maimonides, *Mishneh Torah, Melachim* 12:1, and gloss of Ravad, ad loc.; also Abarbanel on Hoshea 2:18 and Isaiah 11:3; Radak, Mahari Kara, Metzudas David, and Malbim on Isaiah 11:3-9; R. Nosson Sternhartz, *Likkutei Halachos, Choshen Mishpat, Nezikin* 2:6; R. Kook, *Chazon HaTzimchonut V'HaShalom*, 32.

31. Kabbalistically, each person shares a measure of responsibility for the sin of Adam and Eve, since all future souls were included in the soul of the first human being; *Sha'ar HaGilgulim, Hakdamah* 3, et passim. Thus, these same moral tests repeat themselves in every incarnation. According to the Ari, this is why the Talmudic formula for the confession of sins states: "We and our fathers transgressed..." Why must the children atone for the mistakes of their forebears? The term "fathers" refers not to the confessor's physical ancestors, but to his previous incarnations. We must engage in *teshuvah* for our sins in previous incarnations, as well as our more recent strayings; see *Chakal Yitzchak (Spinka)*, citing the Ari, p. 155d, s.v. *U'lifi hama'amar*. Similarly, Moses reproved the congregation for their fathers' sins prior to their entry into the Holy Land, although the younger generation was apparently innocent of blame. The Ari explains that they were reincarnations of their fathers, and therefore deserved such reproof (cited in *Chakal Yitzchak-Spinka, Devarim* 158c, d).

spiritually benefit all creatures, and to fulfill the Torah's directive to "know God in all our ways,"[33] if we but will it.

---

32. *Likkutei Eitzos, Hischazkus* 36, citing the principle in *Yoma* 86b that through the power of *teshuvah*, one may retroactively transform former wrongs to spiritual merits by using them as a means to bring about the good.

33. *Shulchan Aruch, Orach Chaim* 231, citing Proverbs 3:6. The concept that the Garden of Eden is the spiritual "essence" hidden within the confusions of this world is suggested by *Sefer HaBahir* 31; *Zohar* II, 150a; *Likkutei Moharan* II, 119, with *Parpara'os L'Chochmah*; et al. The *Zohar Chadash (Midrash HaNe'elam)* 17b, states, "Rabbi Shimon Bar Yochai taught in the name of Rabbi Yochanan ben Zakkai: The Holy One, blessed be He, called the Garden of Eden the 'nut garden' [in the Song of Songs], because just as a nut is enclosed by a series of shells and the fruit is within, so, too, the Garden of Eden is concealed in world beyond world, and it is within..."

Sources

The Messianic Age

And a wolf shall dwell with a lamb, and a leopard shall lie with a kid, and a calf and a lion cub and a fattened ox will flock together, and a small child shall lead them. And a heifer and a bear shall graze together; their young shall lie down together, and a lion, like the ox, shall eat straw. And a suckling babe shall play over a viper's hole, and over an adder's den a weaned child shall stretch forth his hand. They shall neither harm nor destroy in all My holy mountain; for the knowledge of God shall fill the Earth as the water covers the sea (Isaiah 11:6-9).

Commentary 1: Some authorities explain that in the Messianic era, the nature of animals and beasts will revert to its original state, as it was at the beginning of creation and in Noah's ark.[34] For in the beginning of creation, if the lion had eaten the lamb, the [divine order of] creation would have been destroyed. What did the lion or the other carnivorous animals eat? If they had consumed the flesh of other animals and beasts, the world would have lacked that species; for they were created male and female, not more, and they did not wait to eat until their prey had offspring. Surely, they consumed the grasses of the field until their prey mated and increased. From then on, their nature was carnivorous. Similarly in Noah's ark, if they had eaten their prey, that species would have been lacking in the world; for they entered the ark in pairs, not more, except for the "clean" species, which entered in pairs of seven. However, other authorities interpret this entire passage as an allegory for the peace that will exist between all people and all nations during the Messianic era (Rabbi David Kimchi, ad loc.).

Commentary 2: "And a heifer and a bear shall graze together." If you wonder what predatory animals will eat then, the verse goes on to explain that the bear will graze in the meadow and no longer need to kill its prey. Also, the offspring [of predatory animals and their prey] will grow up together, as if they belonged to the same species. Not only the

---

34. See n. 30 above.

bear, which even today eats other foods [i.e., vegetation], but also the lion, which is strictly a carnivore, shall eat straw, as does the ox (Rabbi Meir Leibush Malbim, *Chazon Yeshayahu,* ad loc.).

Commentary 3: The main cause of harm is a lack of enlightenment (*da'as*). Thus the verse states, "They shall neither harm nor destroy in all My holy mountain; for the knowledge of God shall fill the Earth..." Through the spreading forth of knowledge, the animals and wild beasts will desist from harm, as well. For the knowledge of God will not be complete until all the "holy sparks" hidden in the animal kingdom have been elevated to the realm of holiness. Then animals, too, will partake of the human level and attain such a degree of enlightenment that there will be no harm in all creation, even among them (Rabbi Nosson Sternhartz, *Likkutei Halachos, Choshen Mishpat, Nezikin* 2:6).

೦ঙৎ౦

And it shall be on that day, says God, that you shall call Me "my Husband (*Ishi*)," and you shall no longer call Me "my Master (*Ba'ali*)."[35] And I will remove the names of the idols from her mouth, and no more shall they mention their names. I will make a covenant on that day with the beasts of the field and the birds of the heavens and the creeping things of the ground; and the bow and sword and warfare shall I destroy from the Earth, and I shall cause them to lie down in security. And I will betroth you to Me forever; and I will betroth you to Me in righteousness, and in justice, and in kindness, and in mercy. And I will betroth You to me in faith, and you shall know God (Hoshea 2:18-22).

Commentary: "And I shall cause them to lie down in security." This refers to the animals, which "shall neither harm nor destroy" one another, as Isaiah states, "The wolf shall dwell with the lamb..." (Isaiah 11:6, 9). The condition of peace on Earth will not only be for humanity but also will include the animals (Rabbi Yitzchak Abarbanel, ad loc.).

೦ঙৎ౦

---

35. The term *ba'al* has the double connotation of a master or owner and a pagan deity.

When Adam sinned, all souls and all animals fell into the depths of the *klippos* [literally, "evil husks," or forces of unholiness]. Now the souls must ascend [to their Supernal Source] through the mystery of the Feminine Waters [i.e., through self-sacrifice in divine service]. Only animals deemed pure by the Torah attain spiritual rectification through our partaking of them, as do vegetation and minerals. However, in the future all animals will be rectified, even those deemed impure today (Rabbi Chaim Vital citing his mentor, Rabbi Yitzchak Luria, *Eitz Chaim* II, *Hechal A-B-Y-A, Sha'ar Klippas Nogah*, 3).

ぼ❀

At the end of days an inner thirst will prompt each person to search for someone upon whom to confer benevolence, upon whom to pour forth his overflowing spirit of kindness, but none will be found. For all human beings already will have attained happiness, living lives of delight, gratification, and prosperity in every sense materially, ethically, and intellectually.

Then, with all its store of wisdom, its collective insight and experience, humanity will turn toward its brothers on lower levels of creation, the mute and the downtrodden, including the animal kingdom. And they will seek means to share wisdom with them, to instruct and enlighten them according to their abilities, [thus to elevate them] from level to level. There is no question that humanity will take an active part in this when the time comes to accomplish this mission. Beyond all doubt, humanity will share the enlightenment of the Torah with the animal kingdom, affecting their physical development and, all the more so, their ethical and spiritual development. This state of enlightenment will reach such a lofty level that we cannot imagine it at present, due to our lowliness and lack of wisdom. All beings shall receive a new, exalted form a new world. This is implied by the words of our sages: "If they so desired, the tzaddikim could create a world" (*Sanhedrin* 65b) (Rabbi Avraham Yitzchak Kook, *Chazon HaTzimchonut V'HaShalom*, 31).

ぼ❀

As a consequence of their spiritual elevation in general, the lofty level attained [by animals] in the course of their development will also affect their senses and feelings, to attune and refine them. Indeed, a higher nature comes with this. "And the oxen and the young donkeys who work the soil shall eat enriched food that was winnowed with the shovel and with the fan" (Isaiah 30:24). For according to the loftiness of their souls, the faculty of taste will be developed to a higher degree of sensitivity, as befits their spiritual stature.

With a "still, small voice" does the wisdom of Israel, the Kabbalah, speak: the level of animals in the future will be as the level of humanity today, due to the "ascent of the worlds."[36]

This is the radiant vision the prophets disclosed to us of the civilized state that will be attained by the predatory animals of today: "And a wolf shall dwell with a lamb, and a leopard shall lie with a kid, and a calf and a lion cub and a fatling together, and a small child shall lead them. And a heifer and a bear shall graze together; their young shall lie down together, and a lion, like the ox, shall eat straw. And an infant shall play over a viper's hole, and over the den of an adder shall a weaned child stretch forth his hand. They shall neither harm nor destroy in all My holy mountain; for the knowledge of God shall fill the Earth as the water covers the sea" (Isaiah 11:6-9) (Rabbi Avraham Yitzchak Kook, *Chazon HaTzimchonut V'HaShalom*, 32).

---

36. See R. Chaim Vital, *Sha'ar HaMitzvos, Ekev*, 42a. Kabbalistic literature describes the sequential emanation of four "worlds," or levels of reality: Emanation, Creation, Formation, and Action. When the disharmony on a given level is rectified, that level achieves unification with the level above it. This process is known as *aliyah*, or ascent.

3

Judaism and Animal Welfare

Political movements in the United States typically use the rhetoric of "rights," no doubt because the foundation of our legal system is the Bill of Rights. Defenders of "animal rights" insist that in order to be protected from cruelty and abuse, animals, like humans, deserve effective legislation backed up by vigorous enforcement of the law.

Since the prohibition of cruelty to animals is included within the Seven Laws of Noah that apply to all humanity, in principle most rabbinic authorities probably would endorse this sort of legislation; their only philosophical reservation might be the use of the term "rights." As a rule, the Torah does not speak of rights, whether concerning Jews or non-Jews, men or women, employers or employees, masters or slaves, or animals. In truth, all "rights" belong to the Master of the Universe: "The Earth and all that fills it belongs to the Lord, the world and those who dwell therein" (Psalms 24:1). Rather, the Torah imposes upon the Jewish people, as well as humanity as a whole, duties and responsibilities toward God, and toward one another.[1] As the source-texts in this chapter

---

1. Rabbi J. David Bleich mentions this point in his treatise, *"Judaism and Animal Experimentation," Contemporary Halakhic Problems* (1989), Vol. III, p. 204, ff. Regarding the religious duties of non-Jews, see my *Compassion For Humanity in the Jewish Tradition* (1998). The Seven Universal Laws are: to respect, and therefore refrain from blaspheming God; not to practice idolatry; not to commit murder or suicide; not to steal, whether money, property, or persons; not to engage in sexual immorality; not to tear a limb from a living animal or consume its flesh, but rather to treat all animals humanely; and to establish courts of justice based upon these principles and their ramifications. Aaron Lichtenstein's *The Seven Laws of Noah* (1981) and Nahum Rakover's *Law and the Noahides: Law as a Universal Value* (1998)

demonstrate, the Torah considers compassionate treatment of animals an important area of human responsibility. Thus, it mandates that we consider the physical and emotional well-being of animals, not because they have rights per se, but because the Master of the Universe requires this of us — in His compassion for animals, and, as we shall see, in His compassion for human beings.

An Ancient Legacy

Primarily due to misunderstandings surrounding the Jewish method of slaughter (*shechitah*), many uninformed Jews and non-Jews assume that Judaism is less concerned with animal welfare than other religions. If anything, the opposite is true. From its earliest origins, Judaism has been distinguished by its concern for the humane treatment of animals, often in marked contrast to surrounding religions and cultures. Where the wall paintings and bas-reliefs of ancient Assyria and Egypt extol the drama of the hunt, the Torah associates such pursuits exclusively with villains such as Nimrod and Esau. Not only is hunting for sport forbidden; to the Jewish mind, it is almost unthinkable.[2] Where Roman citizens flocked to attend animal fights in the Colosseum, such gruesome entertainments were unheard of among the Jews. According to the Talmud, animal fights

---

discuss the parameters of these laws, as does the Orthodox Forum volume on *Tikkun Olam: Social Responsibility in Jewish Thought and Law* (1998). For primary and secondary rabbinic sources, see *Mishneh Torah, Hilchos Melachim*, chap. 9; *Teshuvos HaRambam*, no. 364; *Teshuvos HaRashbash*, no. 543; Maharatz Chayes on *Sota* 32b; *Sanhedrin* 56b, 59a, esp. Meiri, ad loc.; *Tosefta Avodah Zarah* 9:4; *Bereishis Rabbah* 16:9; *Vayikra Rabbah* 6:5; *Devarim Rabbah* 2:17; *Shir HaShirim Rabbah* 1:16; *Tanna D'vei Eliyahu* 6:17; *Zohar* I, 35b; *Kuzari* 3:73; *Sefer HaIkkarim* 1:25, et al. Maimonides states that non-Jews who uphold these laws due their own reason are deemed wise; those who uphold them because they were given by God to Noah and his descendants and were renewed through Moses at Mount Sinai are considered religiously devout non-Jews (*chassidei umos ha-olam*) who have a place in the World to Come (*Mishneh Torah, Hilchos Melachim* 8:11).

2. R. Yechezkel Landau, *Teshuvos Noda B'Yehudah (Tinyana), Yoreh De'ah*, no. 10. Other sources that forbid hunting for sport include Rashi, *Avodah Zarah* 18b, s.v. *kenigyon*; *Ohr Zaru'a, Hilchos Shabbos* 83:13; *Teshuvos Maharam MiRothenberg*, no. 27; *Teshuvos Mahari Bruna*, no. 17; *Givat Sha'ul, Vayeishev*, pp. 87-88; *Pachad Yitzchok* (R. Yitzchak Lampronti), s.v. *tzeidah*; Rama, *Shulchan Aruch, Orach Chaim* 316:2; *Teshuvos Shemesh Tzedakah, Yoreh De'ah*, nos. 18 and 57; *Teshuvos Toldos Yaakov, Yoreh De'ah*, no. 33; *Darkei Teshuvah, Yoreh De'ah*, 117, sec. 44.

epitomize the "dwelling place of scorners" so vehemently decried by the Book of Psalms.[3] Indeed, the author of *Chavas Da'as* (a classic work on Jewish law) deems one who attends a bullfight or similar event "an accomplice to murder."[4] To be sure, there were great thinkers of antiquity who disavowed such practices; in the West, Pythagoras (582-507 b.c.e.) and Empedocles (490-430 b.c.e.) advocated compassion for animals, as did Lao Tzu (604-531 b.c.e.) and Buddha (566-480 b.c.e.) in the East. However, centuries before these non-Jewish sages, King Solomon declared: "A tzaddik considers the needs of his animal..." (Proverbs 12:10).

A Talmudic Problem

On what grounds are acts of cruelty to animals (*tza'ar baalei chaim*) prohibited? Nowhere does the Torah state, "Thou shalt not afflict animals." Yet the rabbis of the Talmud all tacitly accept that such acts are forbidden by virtue of an unbroken tradition beginning with Moses at Mount Sinai. They only question the specific grounds and ramifications of the prohibition.[5]

The Talmud (*Bava Metzia* 32b) cites a dispute as to whether *tza'ar baalei chaim* is forbidden by scriptural law or rabbinic decree. The discussion concerns the case given in Exodus 23:5 in which a traveler encounters the animal of his enemy "lying under its burden," and the Torah's mandate that he intervene. The Gemara (the portion of the Talmud that presents the debates and traditions of the sages) considers the nuances of the text: Does the term "lying" indicate a temporary condition, excluding an animal that habitually lies down under its burden? Does "lying" exclude an animal that is standing? The Gemara reasons that such possible distinctions only apply if the prohibition is a rabbinic enactment, which would entail a lesser degree of stringency; if the prohibition is scriptural, no exclusions apply. Although the Talmudic

---

3. *Avodah Zarah* 18b.
4. R. Yaakov of Lisa, *Chavas Da'as* III, 66.
5. *She'arim Metzuyanim B'Halacha, Issur Tza'ar Baalei Chaim*, 191, cites the view of *Teshuvos HaRashba*, nos. 252 and 257, that the prohibition of *tza'ar baalei chaim* applies to humans as well as animals. *Teshuvos Chavas Yair*, 191, rejects this opinion.

discussion is inconclusive, Maimonides (R. Moshe ben Maimon, 1135-1204) and most authorities treat the prohibition as scriptural.[6] Yet there are dissenting opinions.[7]

What practical difference does this make? One difference is that if *tza'ar baalei chaim* is scripturally prohibited, one must not only refrain from causing an animal pain but actively intervene to relieve it. According to some authorities, this is implied by the Torah's injunction in the above-mentioned case, "You shall surely help him with it."[8] If *tza'ar baalei chaim* is prohibited by rabbinic decree, one is exempt from active intervention (although a compassionate person would surely relieve the animal, even in the absence of any obligation to do so). Another practical implication concerns the laws of the Sabbath. If the prohibition is scriptural, certain Sabbath restrictions may be waived to

---

6. Maimonides, *Mishneh Torah, Hilchos Rotze'ach* 13:9, according to *Kesef Mishneh*, ad loc. This is supported by *Mishneh Torah, Hilchos Shabbo*s 25:26 and Maimonides' *Commentary on the Mishnah, Beitzah* 3:4. Most authorities agree that *tza'ar baalei chaim* is scripturally prohibited, including the Rif on *Shabbos* 128b; *Sefer HaChinnuch*, 450, 451; *Rosh* on *Bava Metzia* 2:29 and *Shabbos* 3:18; *Nimmukei Yosef, Bava Metzia* 32b; Me'iri, *Bava Metzia* 32b; *Shitah Mekubetzes, Bava Metzia* 33a; *Sefer Yere'im*, 267; *Sefer Chassidim*, 666; Rama, *Choshen Mishpat* 272:9; *Levush, Orach Chaim* 305:18; and *Magen Avraham, Orach Chaim* 305:11. These sources are all listed in R. Bleich's essay (op. cit.). Although most are of a technical nature, I have translated several for the present volume.

7. Some authorities understand Maimonides' position in *Hilchos Rotze'ach* 13:9 as following the view that the prohibition is rabbinic. They include: *P'nei Yehoshua, Bava Metzia* 32b; *Hagahos HaGra al HaRosh, Bava Metzia*, chap. 2, sec. 29; *Biur HaGra, Choshen Mishpat* 272:11; also see *Minchas Chinnuch*, 80.

  The Chasam Sofer advances the opinion that, although causing pain to an animal is scripturally forbidden, the obligation to rescue an animal in distress applies only to one's own animals; see *Teshuvos Chasam Sofer, Yoreh De'ah*, nos. 314, 318, and *Choshen Mishpat*, no. 185. This appears to be consistent with the view of Maharam Schick on the *Taryag Mitzvos, Mitzvah* 80. Authorities who do not make such a distinction include: *Noda B'Yehudah, Mahadurah Kama, Yoreh De'ah*, nos. 81-83; *Shulchan Aruch HaRav*, Vol. 6, *Tza'ar Baalei Chaim*, 4; *Kitzur Shulchan Aruch*, 191:1; *Orach Maysharim*, 15:1; et al. The Netziv in *Ha'amek Davar*, Deuteronomy 22, maintains that one is not obligated by Torah law but is required to intervene by rabbinic decree. In *Eishel Avraham: Tinyana, Yoreh De'ah* 305:20, R. Avraham of Butchatch argues that the relief of *tza'ar baalei chaim* directly or indirectly caused by a human being is incumbent upon any Jew capable of intervening by scriptural law. For further discussion see R. Yitzchak Nachman Eshkoli, *Tza'ar Baalei Chaim* (2002), chap. 11.

8. See Rashi on *Shabbos* 128b, according to the view that *halachos* may be derived from reasons explicitly stated in the Torah. Also note Rabad as quoted in *Shitah Mekubetzes, Bava Metzia*, 32b; *Levush* on *Orach Chaim* 305:18.

relieve the pain of an animal.[9] However, if the prohibition is rabbinic, due to the gravity of the Sabbath laws, these restrictions remain in force; thus, in certain situations, the compassionate person wishing to conduct himself in a manner "beyond the letter of the law" would be constrained from directly intervening. Still another variable is the severity of punishment for transgressing scriptural, as opposed to rabbinic laws. But, again, all this is theoretical. The prevailing halachic view is that *tza'ar baalei chaim* is scripturally forbidden.[10] Therefore, we are obligated to assist an animal; and, on the Sabbath, this obligation takes precedence over all rabbinic restrictions.

Given that most authorities consider the prohibition of cruelty to animals to be of scriptural origin, which verse or verses come to establish these laws? Rashi (R. Shlomo Yitzchaki, 1040-1105) cites the verse that describes an animal collapsing under its burden: "And you shall surely release it with him" (Exodus 23:5).[11] Since the prohibition of *tza'ar baalei chaim* is only implied but not openly stated here, other Rishonim (medieval authorities) seek its basis elsewhere. Both Maimonides and Rabbi Yehudah HeChassid (1150-1217) derive it from the Torah's censure of Balaam the Midianite for angrily striking his donkey.[12] The anonymous author of *Sefer HaChinnuch* (13th century) relates it to the prohibition not to take the limb of a living animal[13] (this being one of the Seven Laws of Noah). The same author also invokes the prohibition of *tza'ar baalei chaim* in discussing the negative commandment of plowing

9. Specifically, a Jew may violate rabbinic prohibitions for the sake of relieving the pain of an animal, and a non-Jew may be requested to intervene where scriptural prohibitions apply; see Ritva, *Bava Metzia* 32b; Rosh, *Bava Metzia* 2:29 and *Shabbos* 18:3; *Magen Avraham, Orach Chaim* 305:11; *Korban Nesanel, Shabbos* 18:3. If indirect intervention fails or is not possible, *Shiltei HaGibborim* on the Rif, *Shabbos* 51a, note 3, permits one to assist the animal directly.
10. However, there are mitigating factors. According to *Nimmukei Yosef* citing Rabbenu Nissim on *Bava Metzia* 32b, a Torah scholar, elderly person, or one who holds a communal position of honor, is exempt from the obligation to intervene. Also, the prohibition of *tza'ar baalei chaim* may be contravened to serve a legitimate human need, as stated by Ramban on *Avodah Zarah* 13b; also cf. Tosefos and *Nimmukei Yosef* on *Avodah Zarah* 11a and *Bava Metzia* 32b. This is the *halacha*; see Rama on *Shulchan Aruch, Yoreh De'ah* 24:8 and *Even HaEzer* 5:14; *Shach* on *Yoreh De'ah* 24:8; et al.
11. Rashi on *Shabbos* 128b.
12. *Moreh Nevuchim* 3:17; *Sefer Chassidim*, 666.
13. *Sefer HaChinnuch*, Mitzvah 452.

with two different species of animals yoked together.[14] Rabbi Menachem Meiri of Perpignan (1249-1306) relates it to the law of not muzzling an ox while it is treading grain.[15]

The latter case presented the sages with an interesting legal quandary. The laws of *terumah* (portions of the harvest of Israelites and Levites given to the Kohanim-priests) forbade the animal working on the threshing floor from eating the grain; yet muzzling is scripturally prohibited. Therefore, the sages advised the owners to muzzle their animals with a feedbag containing grain similar to that being threshed, so the animals would not feel frustrated while at their labors.[16]

The Commandments as Moral Instructions

Additionally, we must consider the philosophical and ethical ramifications of these laws. The Kabbalists teach that the Torah has four dimensions: *p'shat* (literal meaning), *remez* (allusion), *d'rush* (homiletic meaning), and *sod* (mystical meaning).[17] Thus, in addition to their primary concerns, the laws of *tza'ar baalei chaim* have ethical and philosophical implications. Aside from demonstrating God's compassion for animals, which we must emulate, they bear the greater purpose of increasing our compassion for other human beings.[18]

---

14. *Sefer HaChinnuch*, Mitzvah 550.
15. R. Menachem Meiri, *Beis HaBechirah, Bava Metzia* 32b. Some authorities ascribe the prohibition of *tza'ar baalei chaim* to the principle of emulating God's ways. Thus, R. Moshe ibn Chaviv (*Yom Teru'ah, Rosh Hashanah* 27a) relates it to the verse, "And you shall bring forth water out of the rock for them; thus you shall give the congregation and their cattle to drink" (Numbers 20:8). The Chasam Sofer (*Hagahos Chasam Sofer* on *Bava Metzia* 32b) relates the prohibition to the verse, "And His tender mercies are upon all His works" (Psalms 145:9). In *Sefer Chareidim*, chap. 4, Safed Kabbalist R. Eliezer Azkari similarly views this prohibition as an offshoot of the precept, "And you shall walk in His ways" (Deut. 28:9).
16. *Terumos* 9:3; also cf. *Bava Metzia* 90a. Another solution would be to employ the animal of a Kohen, which may be fed *terumah*.
17. Together, the initial letters of these four categories form the word *pardes*, or "orchard," which is suggestive of the Garden of Eden. See R. Chaim Vital, *Hakdamah* to *Sefer Eitz Chaim; Sha'ar HaMitzvos, Va'eschanan* (Ashlag ed., p. 79); *Sha'ar HaGilgulim, Hakdamah* 11; R. Meir Poppers, *Ohr Tzaddikim* 22:18; et al. It is likely that the Hebrew *pardes*, which appears in Song of Songs 4:13, Ecclesiastes 2:5, and Nehemiah 2:8, is the origin of the Greek *paradeisos*, the Iranian *pairidaeza*, and the English "paradise."

The sages of the Talmud debate the ascription of such meanings to the commandments. How can the mortal mind understand the commandments, which reflect the divine will and wisdom?[19] As a wise man once said of God, "If I could know Him, I would be Him."[20] Nevertheless, the notion that the commandments possess an edificatory dimension is strongly supported by rabbinic tradition.[21] Thus, we may say that, among their many meanings, the laws of *tza'ar baalei chaim* call upon the Jewish people to strive for higher levels of spiritual refinement.

---

18. R. Yosef Rabi, a brother-in-law of Rav Kook, probes the question of whether the prohibition of *tza'ar ba'alei chaim* primarily reflects concern for animals as such, or is meant to instill finer ethical sensitivities in humans; see Tziburi (pseudonym), *"LeHilkhos tza'ar ba'alei chaim," HaTarbus HaYisraelis* (Jaffa, 1913), pp. 76-81, cited in R. Moshe Zvi Neriyah, *Tal HaRayah* (Bnei Brak, 1993), p. 149.

19. This issue is debated by two Amoraim (Talmudic masters) cited in *Megillah* 25a and *Berachos* 33b. The case concerns the communal prayer leader who declares, "You have shown mercy to the bird's nest; show mercy and compassion to us!" The Mishnah states that he should be silenced. According to one authority, this is because such words would create jealousy among God's creatures; according to the other, it is because God's laws are decrees beyond mortal understanding.

20. R. Yosef Albo, *Sefer HaIkkarim* II, 30 (p. 194). R. Nachman of Breslov in *Likkutei Moharan* I, 21:11, explains this teaching in a mystical sense. Concerning God's unknowability in general, see *Kuzari* 5:21; *Emunos V'Deos* 2:10; *Zohar* I, 103a; *Shomer Emunim HaKadmon* 2:11, Principle 6; *Mishneh Torah, Yesodei HaTorah* 2:10; *Sefer Chareidim*, chap. 5; et al.

21. The Midrash and Targum Yonasan both frequently ascribe such meanings to the commandments. However, Maimonides carried this approach into the realm of philosophy with his *Moreh Nevuchim* (Guide for the Perplexed), which reflects the influence of Aristotle. This work incurred the fierce opposition of many Rishonim, including R. Shlomo of Montpellier and Rabbenu Yonah, who placed a ban on the controversial work. The pre-eminent Spanish authority of the late 13th century, R. Shlomo ibn Adret (Rashba), similarly took objection to the *Moreh Nevuchim*, although Nachmanides, the Rashba's teacher, was more equivocal. (For other authorities opposed to philosophy, see Chapter 5, n. 8). Nevertheless, the *Moreh* had a profound effect upon later Rishonim, including the anonymous author of *Sefer HaChinnuch*. Its influence is also evident in the late medieval homiletic writings of the Yemenite scholars; cf. Y. Tzvi Langermann, *Yemenite Midrash* (HarperCollins, 1996).

    Several modern thinkers have carried on the search for philosophical and ethical meanings within the commandments. One such figure was 19th century humanist R. Samson Raphael Hirsch, who paved a path for the observant Jew seeking to participate in modern society without religious compromise. R. Hirsch's works are replete with such interpretations. In the early 20th century, R. Avraham Yitzchak Kook propounded a Messianic Zionism, drawing freely upon Maimonidean and Kabbalistic concepts. Several of R. Kook's ethical readings of the commandments have been included in the present volume.

The sages define the Jewish people as inherently compassionate, modest, and kind.[22] The recognition of animals as sentient creatures deserving of human consideration also has heightened our sensitivity to the needs of our fellow human beings. Thus, the trait of compassion ascribed to the Jewish people is bound up with that of kindness, not merely in religious sentiment, but in actual deed.

Permitted Uses of Animals

One issue about which Judaism and the animal rights movement (or at least one trend within the animal rights movement) must disagree is the philosophical view that puts animals and humans on the same plane.[23] The Torah states, "God blessed [Adam and Eve], and God said to them: Be fruitful and multiply, fill the Earth and subdue it; and rule over the fish of the sea, the bird of the sky, and every living thing that moves on the Earth" (Genesis 1:28). This verse contains both an implicit hierarchical distinction between humans and animals, and a divine mandate for man to benefit from the natural world.

As a consequence, the prohibition of *tza'ar baalei chaim* does not apply to situations in which human beings are permitted to make use of animals, namely to serve legitimate human needs. As a concession to the desire for meat, the Torah permitted the slaughter of animals to Noah and his descendants. (This issue will be discussed at greater length in the

---

22. *Yevamos* 79a; *Midrash Shmuel*, 28.
23. The best-known proponent of this idea is Peter Singer, author of *Animal Liberation* (New York, 1975) and with Jim Mason, *Animal Factories* (New York, 1990). Although in Western philosophy it is difficult to find a precedent for such a thorough-going moral equivalence of the species, it may exist among certain Eastern religious sects; cf. Schochet, *Animal Life in Jewish Tradition*, chap. 14. However, the "theology" of animal rights is not an import from the Far East; it is a consequence of materialist philosophy, and Darwinian theory in particular. If the existence of God and the divine intention in creation are denied, good and evil must be seen as human constructs that vary according to each individual or group. (Indeed, from this standpoint, the moral impulse itself may be understood as a form of self-aggrandizement.) If contrary to Torah thought, man is not the central figure in creation, there can be no fundamental difference between humans and animals. Therefore, the quasi-religious fervor of some animal rights advocates may be an expression of this materialist "article of faith"; see Joshua Berman, *The Temple: Its Symbolism and Meaning, Then and Now* (Jason Aronson, 1995), pp. 148-154.

chapter on "Judaism and Vegetarianism.") Since, within certain limitations, animal slaughter is permitted, any resultant pain the animal might suffer would not fall under the halachic prohibition of *tza'ar baalei chaim*.[24] According to most authorities, this exemption extends to all other religiously sanctioned reasons for animal slaughter, such as to provide human beings with clothing or products for medical purposes, or to benefit us in any significant way.

However, as Rabbi Avraham Yitzchak Kook (1865-1935) states in *"A Vision of Vegetarianism and Peace,"* the Torah's mandate that humankind subdue the Earth "does not mean the domination of a harsh ruler, who afflicts his people and servants merely to fulfill his personal whim and desire, according to the crookedness of his heart."[25] Rather, it comprises a form of stewardship for which humanity is answerable to God. Both Talmudic and Kabbalistic sources state that it is forbidden to kill any creature unnecessarily,[26] or to engage in wanton destruction of the Earth's resources.[27] All forms of life are precious by virtue of the divine wisdom that brings them into existence, whatever rung they may occupy

---

24. R. Bleich (op. cit.) includes among those who exempt the act of slaughter from the *issur* of *tza'ar baalei chaim*: *Teshuvos Avodas HaGershuni*, no. 13; *Noda B'Yehudah*, Vol. I, *Yoreh De'ah*, no. 83; and *Seridei Eish*, Vol. III, no. 7. Apparently Tosafos on *Sanhedrin* 80a agrees in stating that withholding food and drink from an animal constitutes *tza'ar baalei chaim*, but killing it by a swift, direct act does not. Dissenting opinions include *Shitah Mekubetzes* on *Bava Basra* 20a, citing Ri Migash; *Teshuvos Sho'el U'Meshiv, Mahadurah Tinyana*, III, no. 65, as well as *Sefer HaChinnuch*, 451. Later authorities that include putting an animal to death in the category of *tza'ar baalei chaim* include the *Bach* on *Yoreh De'ah* 116, s.v. *mashkin*; *Sheilas Ya'avetz*, I, no. 110; *Teshuvos Shevus Yaakov*, III, no. 71; *Teshuvos Imrei Shefer*, no. 34; and *Ohel Moshe*, I, no. 32.
25. *Chazon HaTzimchonut V'HaShalom*, 2, included in Additional Source Texts for Chapter 6 on "Judaism and Vegetarianism."
26. This is the view of R. Pinchas ben Ya'ir in *Chullin* 7b; *Shulchan Aruch, Orach Chaim* 316:2; *Zohar* II, *Yisro*, 93b; R. Yehudah HeChassid, *Sefer Chassidim* 667; R. Chaim Vital, *Sha'ar HaMitzvos, Noach*.
27. Concerning wanton destructiveness (*bal tash'chis*) and ecological issues in general, cf. Deut. 20:19-20; Isaiah 5:8; *Berachos* 52b; *Kiddushin* 32a; *Bava Kamma* 50b, 91b; *Bava Basra*, chap. II; *Shabbos* 67b; *Sefer Chassidim*, 667; Maimonides, *Sefer HaMitzvos*, Neg. Commandment 57; *Mishneh Torah, Shoftim, Hilchos Melachim* 6:10; Ramban on Deut. 22:6; *Sefer HaChinnuch*, 545, 529; *Shulchan Aruch HaRav, Choshen Mishpat, Hilchos Shemiras Guf VaNefesh U'Bal Tashchis*, pp. 1772-1774 (Kehot ed.); *Ben Ish Chai, Halachos* I, *Ki Seitzei* 14, 15; Hirsch, *Horeb*, Vol. II, chap. 56, sec. 402, p. 282 (Dayan I. Grunfeld, trans.). Much of this and similar material is discussed in Richard Schwartz's *Judaism and Global Survival* (Lantern, 2002).

in the hierarchy of creation. Thus, in the words of Rabbi Moshe
Cordovero, "One should neither uproot plants unless they are needed,
nor kill animals unless they are needed. One should choose a humane
manner of death for them, using a carefully inspected knife, in order to
be as compassionate as possible."[28]

The divine mandate for man to dominate the natural world is a
sacred trust, not a carte blanche for destructiveness. And the permission
to slaughter animals for food was given within a complex set of
limitations, an important part of which is concern for the suffering of
those creatures who forfeit their lives for our benefit.[29]

Animal Slaughter

The commandment of kosher slaughter is given in the verse: "You
may slaughter from your cattle and your flocks that God has given you, as
I have commanded you..." (Deuteronomy 12:21). The instructions to
which the verse alludes were taught to the entire nation of Israel by
Moses at Mount Sinai, and have been preserved through an unbroken
chain of transmission down to the present day. These procedures are
defined technically in the Talmudic tractate *Chullin* and in the *Shulchan
Aruch* (Code of Jewish Law), *Yoreh De'ah*, chapters 1-28. In keeping with
the holiness of this commandment, the *shochet* (slaughterer) must recite
a blessing before carrying out his task: "Blessed are You, O Lord our God,

---

28. *Tomer Devorah*, chap. 3. This is supported by a discussion of capital punishment in
    Kesubos 37b, which states that execution by the sword must be at the "neck." Rav
    Nachman adds in the name of Rabbah bar Avuhah that this is called an "easy death"
    because it is quick (Rashi, ad loc.). The same principle may be applied to animal
    slaughter. For this reason, some authorities insist upon *shechitah* of animals needed
    for non-food purposes whenever possible; see *Sefer HaChinnuch*, Mitzvah 451;
    Rabbenu Nissim on *Chullin* 18b; *Teshuvas HaGeonim*, Vol. I, no. 375. However, Rashi
    disagrees in his glosses on *Shabbos* 75a, s.v. *shochet*, and *Chullin* 27b, s.v. *chayav
    le'chasos*. This is the *halacha*, as stated in *Shulchan Aruch*, *Yoreh De'ah* 28:18; cf. also
    Drishah on *Yoreh De'ah* 28:6; *Turei Zahav* on *Yoreh De'ah* 116:6 and 117:4.
29. *Galya Raza*, pp. 209-210, cites a Kabbalistic tradition that the souls of animals
    protest before the Divine Throne against Jews and non-Jews alike for having
    slaughtered them improperly, unnecessarily, or in a cruel manner; also cf. the
    pre-Lurianic *Sefer HaKanah*, *Mussar L'Morei Hora'os V'Shochtim*, p. 307.

King of the Universe, Who has sanctified us with His commandments and has commanded us concerning *shechitah.*"

Aside from any ritual or other significance it possesses, *shechitah* seeks to minimize the animal's pain.[30] Indeed, after more than three thousand years since the Torah was given at Mount Sinai, no other form of slaughter has proven itself superior in this regard. Contemporary halachist Rabbi J. David Bleich states: "*Shechitah* is the most humane method of slaughter known to man. The procedure involves a traverse cut in the throat of the animal with an extremely sharp and smooth knife. Due to the sharpness of the knife and the paucity of sensory cutaneous nerve endings in the skin covering the throat, the incision itself causes no pain... The resultant massive loss of blood causes the animal to become unconscious in a matter of seconds."[31] This assertion is supported by a substantial body of scientific evidence.[32]

In order for meat to be kosher, the animal must come from a kosher species as specified in the Torah.[33] It must be physically sound and free of

---

30. *Tomer Devorah,* chap. 3. Maimonides offer this rationale in *Moreh Nevuchim* 3:26, 48. A mystical reason for *shechitah* is given in *Sefer HaTemunah* III, *Os Hey,* p. 100.
31. R. Bleich, op. cit., p. 205, ff.
32. The objection to *shechitah* is by no means new, having been a common anti-Semitic subterfuge in various times and places. Hundreds of scientific studies have been published on *shechitah,* beginning with Dr. Isaac Dembow's *Hachanah L'Shechita (Preparation For Animal Slaughter)* (1892) and *The Jewish Manner of Slaughter* (1894). Perhaps the most thorough volume on the subject addressed to laymen is *Shechitah in the Light of the Year 2000* by Dr. I.M. Levinger (1995).

    In Chapter 11, Levinger addresses the question of the animal suffering during *shechitah,* and concludes (p. 75): "Within 8-10 seconds [after *shechitah*] the centers for maintaining equilibrium lose their regulatory capacity. Corneal reflex disappears in small animals, though in larger animals it takes longer to disappear. Since it is known that the neo-encephalon is more oxygen sensitive than [other sections] of the brain, it may be assumed that the functional ability of the cortex ceases within less than 10 seconds after *shechitah.* Since the animal does not move within 10 seconds, it may be concluded that the animal does not feel pain..."

    Another study cited by Levinger is *An Electroencephelographic Study of the Effect of Shechitah Slaughter on Cortical Function in Ruminants* (1979) by L.I. Nangeroni and P.D. Kennett, Dept. of Physiology, New York State Veterinary College, Cornell University, Ithaca, NY. The latter report states that among the sheep, calves, and goats tested, consciousness was lost 3.3 to 6.9 seconds after the incision. The researchers conclude that under normal circumstances, the act of *shechitah* is painless, or nearly so.
33. The Torah enumerates the species permitted for Jewish consumption. However, the Talmud stipulates that in practice, only those species may be consumed for which there is a reliable tradition that they have been eaten by Jews (*Chullin* 62b).

The Vision of Eden

life-threatening diseases (the latter ascertained in large animals after slaughter by examining the lungs for lesions). Also, *shechitah* must be performed with a perfectly sharp knife called a *chalaf*, and the act of slaughter must be free from five disqualifying movements:[34]

1. *Shehiyah*: hesitation or interruption
2. *Derasah*: excessive pressure
3. *Chaladah*: digging or burrowing
4. *Hagramah*: cutting beyond the designated area
5. *Ikkur*: tearing of the tissues.

The cut is accomplished in a precise, swift, uninterrupted back and forth gesture, severing the esophagus and trachea, as well as the jugular vein and carotid arteries. The esophagus and trachea are known as *simanim*, or "signs." Although it is proper to sever both *simanim*, in fowl it is sufficient *ex post facto* to have severed one *siman*.

The humane handling of livestock immediately prior to slaughter is also required by *halacha*. For example, an animal should not be slaughtered in the sight of another living animal,[35] and restraining the animal should be done as carefully as possible.[36] For centuries it has

---

Permitted mammals include both wild and domestic animals. Their distinguishing signs are that they have split hooves and chew their cud (Leviticus 11:3). The Torah specifies those birds that may not be eaten, although it does not exactly define those that are permitted (ibid. 11:13-19). The Talmud states that they are not predators, and that they possess an extra claw, a crop, and/or a gizzard that can be peeled away (*Chullin* 59a). Some commentators define the "extra claw" as one claw that is longer than the others, while others take it to be one claw that is turned backward, whereas the others are directed forward. The crop is a storage area in the middle of the esophagus, found mainly in birds that eat seeds. The gizzard is made of two distinct layers that can be separated from one another. All fish with fins and scales that are visible to the naked eye are kosher, as stated in Leviticus 11:9-10. Shellfish are prohibited. Of the non-vertebrates, only a few species of grasshoppers are permitted. However, since the tradition concerning these species has been lost, they are no longer consumed. (An exception to this is the ancient Yemenite community that still possesses such traditions.) The kosher species of fish and grasshoppers do not require *shechitah*. For a more detailed explanation, see Levinger, *Shechitah in the Light of the Year 2000* (1995), Appendix I, pp. 137-147.

34. *Chullin* 27a, b. Primary sources for the laws of *shechitah* are the first two chapters of tractate *Chullin; Mishneh Torah, Hilchos Shechitah; Shulchan Aruch, Yoreh De'ah*, 1-28.
35. *Shulchan Aruch, Yoreh De'ah* 36:14, with *Yad Ephraim* and *Pischei Teshuvah*, both of whom explicitly relate this to the prohibition of *tza'ar baalei chaim*; similarly, cf. *Aruch HaShulchan, Hilchos Treifos* 36:70 (end).
36. *Shulchan Aruch, Yoreh De'ah*, 58.

become an additional requirement that the slaughterer (*shochet*) be a Torah scholar, fully conversant with the complex laws of *shechitah*, as well as those of *neveilah* and *treifah*. Indeed, in order to work in the kosher food industry today, a *shochet* must have received rabbinic certification. In addition to having demonstrated mastery of the relevant laws and procedures, he must be a God-fearing person of good moral character who regularly attends the communal prayer services.[37]

To say the least, these standards of animal slaughter compare favorably with those of every non-vegetarian society in which the Jewish people have lived. Indeed, it is one of the many bitter ironies of Jewish history that *shechitah* has been repeatedly criticized and even banned as an inhumane practice. By contrast, once upon a time, slaughter of cattle in this country was accomplished by crushing the animal's skull with a sledgehammer. (Today animals for non-kosher use are "stunned" by being shot in the head with a metal bolt, or by electrical means prior to killing. Sheep, calves, and swine also may be stunned by the inhalation of CO_2 gas.) For centuries, it was not uncommon practice in Europe to torture animals before slaughter, beating them with knotted ropes and even skinning them alive, in the belief that this would improve the flavor of the meat.[38] In most times and places, cruel methods of slaughter were performed by savage individuals unqualified for any other trade or profession.

---

37. R. Alexander Sender Shor, *Tevu'os Shor* on *Hilchos Shechitah*; also *Beis Yosef* on *Tur Yoreh De'ah*, 18, s.v. *Kasav HaRav Rabbenu Yonah*; R. Yeshaya Horowitz, *Shnei Luchos HaBris*, Vol. I, *Sha'ar HaOsios, Os Kuf: Kedushas HaAchilah*, 6; R. Zvi Hirsch Spira of Munkatch, *Darkei Teshuvah, Shechitah* 1:1, no. 50, citing R. Chaim Palagi's *Ruach Chaim* and R. Moshe Rivkahs' *Hadras Zekenim*; R. Zvi Pesach Frank, *Teshuvos Har Zvi, Yoreh De'ah*, no. 5.

38. Diane Ackerman, *A Natural History of the Senses* (Random House, 1990), p. 147. This is also the origin of the "bulldog," which was bred specifically to attack bulls prior to slaughter in the belief that this would enhance the tenderness of the meat. Dogs, too, may be victims of a similar evil fate. According to a Reuters news report, St. Bernard dogs are raised as food animals in China. The popular Sino-Korean Gourou Wang ("Dog Meat King") restaurant in Beijing offers more than 50 dog dishes ("Love for St. Bernard Meat Angers Swiss," by Paul Eckert, 3.18.01, www.dailynews.yahoo.com). Animal activist Grace Gabriel asserts, "Many beat the dog to death, others burn the skin of an animal that is still alive," in order to produce more tender meat ("SOS St. Bernard Dogs," www.interportail.net). Sarah Hartwell's "Cats Friends or Food?" includes documentation of cats and dogs killed and sometimes tortured for human food in Korea and elsewhere (http://messybeast.com/eat-cats.htm).

In America, the standard practice of shackling and hoisting animals by one or both hind legs after stunning and prior to bleeding (during which most animals expire) was instituted as a consumer health measure by the Federal Meat Inspection Act of 1906.[39] This system also was imposed upon the American Jewish community, and initially it was a source of controversy among rabbinic authorities.[40] *Shechitah* of cattle and sheep traditionally is performed on an animal lying on the ground. This method of restraint is known as *hagbahah v'harbatzah*, literally, "picking up and putting down," or simply "casting." Aside from humane considerations, the act of casting must not be violent, or the animal might be injured and thus rendered unfit. However, because Jewish law prohibits stunning prior to *shechitah*, the Federal Government's requirement of shackling and hoisting introduced an additional element of causing animals pain and distress.[41]

After almost a century, shackling and hoisting has become nearly obsolete for kosher slaughter of both cattle and sheep in the U.S., although it is still used in certain slaughterhouses for veal calves.[42] The

---

39. However, this law did not address animal welfare concerns. The first such legislation in the U.S. was the Humane Methods of Slaughter Act of 1958, which applied only to meat packers selling to federal agencies. Not until 1978 were these regulations imposed on all slaughter facilities. Two amendments to the Humane Methods of Slaughter Act were passed by the U.S. House of Representatives in 2001, one of which established some basic ground-rules for dealing with "downed animals," i.e., farm animals that due to illness or injury are too lame to walk, requiring that they be humanely euthanized.

40. *Darchei Teshuvah, Shechitah,* 6:4, sec. 47, citing *Nofes Tzufim, Lev Aryeh,* and others; *Teshuvos Har Zvi* on *Yoreh De'ah,* no. 17, which invalidates slaughter of an animal suspended by a block placed around the neck, but permits suspension by the legs; and R. Chananiah Yom Tov Lipa Teitelbaum (previous Nirbater Rov of New York), *Levushei Yom Tov,* no. 20, citing the Ran and *Nekudas HaKessef,* et al., to support his leniency. R. Teitelbaum mentions that the Satmar Rov and other American Gedolim investigated these procedures and gave their assent to performing *shechitah* on a suspended animal. Within the limitations of *halacha,* industry standards in general have determined contemporary Jewish practices.

41. Because shackle and hoist restraint systems are standard in most slaughter facilities, including those in South America, certain kosher slaughter operations outside of the U.S. have used this equipment to position the animal, after which the workers lower the animal onto a casting table, where the *shochet* may slaughter it in the traditional manner. Despite the halachic preferability of *shechitah* after *harbatzah* as compared to slaughtering an animal while suspended, this unusual procedure causes the animal great pain and distress, and therefore has been subject to criticism from both Jewish and secular quarters.

new procedures employ a holding pen approved by the American Society for the Prevention of Cruelty to Animals (ASPCA), or the high-speed V-Conveyor restraint system developed by an Iowa-based company, Spencer Foods. (Another system, the Double Rail conveyor, has become standard equipment in many large, non-kosher facilities.) These systems require that *shechitah* be performed on the standing animal from below. Although this method of restraint, too, departs from tradition, it has been endorsed by Rabbi Moshe Feinstein (1895-1986) and other rabbinic authorities,[43] and is widely used in kosher slaughterhouses today.

In order to allow *shechitah* to be performed from above, an earlier design, the Weinberg casting pen, allows the constrained animal to be rotated. However, the operation of this system is more time-consuming, hence more costly than the others, and it is far more stressful to the animal than the modern ASPCA design.[44] As a result, the Weinberg pen is no longer used in the United States. The Facomia pen (presently used by the Rubashkin facility in Postville, Iowa) also permits rotation of the animal to facilitate *shechitah* from above, in the traditional manner.[45] Ideally, these restraint systems are so efficient that the act of slaughter

---

42. This information was kindly provided by R. Chaim Kohen of Kahal Adas Yeshurun (KAJ), who also informs me that the Rubashkin facility does not perform shackling and hoisting on cattle. The Meal Mart Company under the supervision of the Nirbater Rov uses veal facilities in Montreal and Pennsylvania that are equipped with ASPCA pens or the V-Conveyor system designed by Temple Grandin.

43. One of the halachic concerns was *derasah*, making the cut with undue pressure, and thereby rendering the animal *treife*; see R. Moshe Feinstein, *Igros Moshe* (1973), Vol. 5, no. 13; R. Yitzchak Yaakov Weiss, *Minchas Yitzchak* (1969), Vol. 10, no. 59; R. Zalman Sorotzkin, "Be'inyan Shechitah B'tzavor LaMa'alah V'Sakin LeMatah," published in *Ma'asaf Sha'arei Torah* (1961); R. Zvi Pesach Frank, *Har Zvi* on *Yoreh De'ah*, no. 11 (incomplete). R. Menachem Genack, Administrator of the Kashruth Division of the Union of Orthodox Jewish Congregations of America states: "We have found that the [ASPCA] pen not only mitigates pain to the animal, but also has advantages in terms of securing the safety of the *shochet* and carefully insures proper *shechitah*, in that it immobilizes the head of the animal" (letter cited in Temple Grandin's "Humanitarian Aspects of Shechitah in the United States," *Judaism*, No. 156, Vol. 39, No. 4, Fall 1990). While a majority of American and British rabbis have accepted the upright restraint pens, the Israeli rabbinate has been reluctant to abandon the traditional casting methods.

44. Temple Grandin, ibid.

45. Temple Grandin and other animal scientists have deemed the Facomia system inferior to the ASPCA pen. An improved casting pen recently was designed that soon may render the Facomia system obsolete, as well. See "Slaughter and Animal Welfare" by Dr. Joe and Carrie Regenstein, *Kashrus Magazine*, 12.01, pp. 59-62.

may be completed with minimal pain or trauma on the part of the animal.

Recent Improvements

It would be nice to say that the use of holding pens and other recent improvements in the handling of livestock prior to slaughter were innovated by the Jewish religious community. However, the nature of the halachic process, coupled with the historical Jewish experience, militates against such a possibility. Orthodox Judaism is perforce extremely conservative when it comes to modifying established practices, particularly when they are part of a complex halachic framework.[46] In fact, these changes came about through the efforts of animal welfare activists, particularly those of animal scientist Dr. Temple Grandin of Colorado State University. Diagnosed in early childhood as autistic, Grandin considers her medical disorder a "blessing in disguise" in that it enables her to empathize deeply with animals. This empathy has prompted her to pinpoint a number of problems, and thus innovate major improvements in standard systems of animal slaughter.[47]

Grandin designed circular pens and chuted ramps to avoid frightening the animals being led to slaughter, as well as the Double-Rail conveyor system mentioned above, to make them feel more secure. Additionally, she proposed that slaughterhouses train employees to herd the animals without excessive electrical prodding and to refrain from making disturbing sounds, install non-slip grates on slippery floors, and ensure proper maintenance of stunning equipment so that animals suffer no pain. These improvements gradually were accepted by the industry, and today are required by the new Federal Humane Slaughter regulations.[48] She also served as an advisor to Spencer Foods during the

---

46. Thus, most rabbis have viewed with suspicion those who sought to modify the traditional method of casting prior to *shechitah*; e.g., R. Dovid Feldman of Manchester, England, *Shimushah Shel Torah*, p. 103. The often undisguised anti-Semitism of critics of *shechitah* in various times and places has greatly contributed to this suspicion.
47. Anne Raver, *The New York Times*, 8/5/97.
48. Code of Federal Regulations, Title 9, Vol. 2, sec. 313.

1970s in developing the V-Conveyor restraint system,[49] and has served as a consultant to several kosher plants. Her posture toward ritual slaughter in general demonstrates understanding and respect.

Despite the abuses she has seen, Dr. Grandin does not reject animal slaughter altogether. "I believe that we can use animals ethically for food," she asserts, "but we've got to treat them right. None of these cattle would have existed if we hadn't bred them. We owe them a decent life — and a painless death. They're living, feeling things. They're not posts, or machines."[50]

What Happens Prior to Slaughter

Having discussed some of the religious and ethical aspects of *shechitah*, we also must address the treatment of animals prior to slaughter. Here it must be acknowledged that the raising of animals for food remains problematic.

Until recent times, animals belonging to Jews were raised on private farms, under relatively humane conditions. The *shochet* was a familiar figure to his community; he worked for each customer on an individual basis, and probably slaughtered large animals relatively infrequently. In modern society, however, all this has changed. Almost a century ago, mass production began to take over the food industry, beginning with the great stockyards of Chicago and the first supermarkets. Since the 1940s, in addition to the traditional methods of agronomy, we have witnessed the steady rise of corporate-owned "factory farms" that produce beef cattle by the millions and fowl by the billions every year for

---

49. Temple Grandin, ibid.
50. A rather amazing experience of this empathy is described in the New York Times feature article on Temple Grandin cited above: "When a kosher system was installed in Alabama a few years ago, Dr. Grandin operated the hydraulic gears of the restraining box herself, concentrating on easing the animal into the box as gently as possible. 'When I held his head in the yoke, I imagined placing my hands on his forehead and under his chin and gently easing him into position... Body boundaries seemed to disappear, and I had no awareness of pushing the levers.'

"She compared it to a state of Zen meditation: 'The more gently I was able to hold the animal with the apparatus, the more peaceful I felt. As the life force left the animal, I had deep religious feelings. For the first time in my life, logic had been completely overcome by feelings I did not know I had' " (ibid.).

human consumption.[51] Given the economic realities of today's food industry, the Jewish community ineluctably has been enlisted into this system. It is not commercially feasible for kosher meat suppliers to raise their own livestock, and none do so. In fact, the only American kosher meat packing company that has its own exclusive slaughter facility is Aaron Rubashkin and Sons, Inc., in Postville, Iowa.[52] Other producers of kosher beef must resort to time-sharing arrangements at non-kosher facilities.

According to the methods of factory farming, animals are raised in intensely crowded, artificial environments in which their emotional needs are largely ignored. The Federal Animal Welfare Act specifically excludes food animals. Thus, the industry has developed new systems of raising animals that have exponentially increased production and profits, with limited concern for the well-being of the animals they have bred. The ethical ramifications of these methods are the subject of ongoing debate among advocates of animal rights (who condemn them roundly), animal welfare (who are more equivocal), and the farmers, cattlemen, and food corporations who typically defend them. From a Jewish point of view, they are highly questionable. Rabbi Aryeh Carmell, a founder of the Association of Orthodox Scientists of Great Britain who for many years has served on the faculty of Israel's D'var Yerushalayim Yeshiva, has written: "It seems doubtful... that the Torah would sanction factory farming, which treats animals as machines, with apparent insensitivity to their natural needs and instincts. This is a matter for decision by halachic authorities."[53]

---

51. According to the USDA's National Agricultural Statistics Service (NASS), 9,853.5 million animals (i.e. nearly 10 billion) were killed for food in the US in 2001. This includes 41.6 million cattle and calves, 118 million pigs, 4.2 million sheep and lambs, 8,902 million "broiler" chickens, 450 million laying hens, 309 million turkeys, and 27.7 million ducks. The total number is expected to rise by 2.4% to 10,090 million in 2002. The worldwide number of animals killed for food in 2001 was 47.9 billion according to the U.N. Food and Agriculture Organization.
52. The Berig Brothers kosher veal facility in Vineland, NJ, is owned by Orthodox Jews, however, they also rent their premises to non-kosher companies on a part-time basis.
53. Aryeh Carmell, *Masterplan: Judaism It's Programs, Meanings, Goals* (1991), p. 69.

A related issue is that factory farming engages in the chemical and hormonal regulation of the animals' life cycles, both for reasons of production and health. As a result of overcrowding, the threat of disease and infection must be battled with an arsenal of animal drugs, which a U.S. Congressional committee acknowledged several decades ago, "may have potentially adverse effects on animals or humans."[54] This, too, is a subject that warrants serious halachic consideration.

Other Food Animals

If the treatment of large animals raised for human consumption raises some difficult ethical questions, the treatment of calves raised for the production of "white veal" is far less defensible. After nursing for only one or two days, the calf is separated from her mother and confined to a narrow slatted stall too small for the animal to lie down. To obtain the veal's desired paleness, the calf is given a high-calorie, iron-deficient diet. As a result, the calf craves iron to the extent that her head must be tethered, lest she lick the stall's iron fittings, or even her own urine. The pen is kept warm and the calf deprived of water, so that she will drink more of her high-calorie liquid food.[55] After enduring this treatment for 14 to 18 weeks, the animal is taken to slaughter. Aside from causing *tza'ar baalei chaim*, these conditions may render as many as 85% of the calves raised for white veal unfit for kosher consumption due to sickness. Thus, Rabbi Moshe Feinstein, widely regarded as America's foremost rabbinic

---

54. Union Calendar no. 24: Human Food Safety and the Regulation of Animal Drugs, 27th Report of the Committee on Government Operations, U.S. Printing Office, 1985. More recently, the journal *Science* (1998) 279: 996-997 declared the meat industry to be "the driving force behind the development of antibiotic resistance in certain species of bacteria that cause human disease." The Centers for Disease Control similarly blamed the meat industry for the emergence of new, antibiotic resistant bacteria; see K. Glynn, "Emergence of multidrug-resistant *salmonella enterica* serotype... infections in the U.S.," *New England Journal of Medicine* (1998) 338: 1333-1338. The first significant response to this problem at the federal level would be HR3804, which proposes to phase out the use of eight specific antibiotics in the immediate future, including penicillin and tetracycline that are used in human medicine or which are so closely related to human-use drugs that they trigger cross-resistance.
55. C. David Coates, *Old MacDonald's Factory Farm* (1989), pp. 65-66.

authority, ruled in 1982 that a Jew is forbidden to raise veal calves in this cruel and unhealthy manner, or even to sell such meat.[56]

Nevertheless, this ruling has not eliminated veal as a kosher commodity. Since kosher meat suppliers obtain veal calves, like all other livestock, from non-Jewish sources, they do not directly violate the laws of *tza'ar baalei chaim* (notwithstanding that, according to some authorities, *tza'ar baalei chaim* is prohibited equally to non-Jews).[57] It also must be said that kosher suppliers buy whatever livestock is available, and the number of veal calves raised by these cruel methods is said to have declined (although to what actual extent remains uncertain.) The Nirbater Rov has informed me that although the calves still are taken away from their mothers and their natural environment, today many veal producers allow the calves to roam within their shelters, ventilation is better than it used to be, and the animals' liquid feed (primarily milk powder and warm water) includes vegetable-derived fats, as well as vitamin supplements and a small amount of iron to prevent illness.[58] The animals are thoroughly examined for disqualifying signs by the *mashgiach* (rabbinic supervisor), and if none are found, the meat is deemed kosher. Thus, despite Rabbi Feinstein's prohibition of selling veal, today's vendors do so, relying upon the kosher supervisory agencies presently involved.[59]

---

56. *Igros Moshe, Even HaEzer,* Vol. IV, no. 92. R. Feinstein prohibits selling veal on grounds of fraud: the customer likely will assume from its appearance that it is meat of a better quality, when in fact it is inferior, being far less healthful.

57. This position is held by *Sefer Chassidim,* 666 (also note *Mekor Chesed* 666:7, ad loc.), and *Teshuvos Imrei Shefer,* no. 34. sec, 2, 8. The latter relates this to the Noahide prohibition of eating the limb of a living creature. However, *Pri Megadim (Mishbetzos Zahav)* on *Orach Chaim* 467:2, and *Teshuvos Maharsham,* Vol. III, no. 364, disagree; see R. Bleich, op cit., n. 43.

58. Also see American Veal Association, *Facts About Care and Feeding of Calves* (2000). In recent years animal fats have been used in some milk-based feeds, creating the possibility of a forbidden mixture of meat and milk from which it would be forbidden even to derive benefit. However, R. Yisrael Belsky of the Orthodox Union's Kashruth Division and other contemporary authorities have investigated this problem and determined that, for technical reasons, no prohibition is created for the Jewish consumer by the veal industry's use of such mixtures.

59. The Farm Sanctuary has spearheaded a campaign by which livestock growers may certify that their calves were not raised by inhumane methods. This certification, which restaurants and butcher shops subsequently can display to their customers, has proven to be an effective strategy in combating this problem (www.farmsanctuary.org).

Animal advocates also have voiced objection to the treatment of fowl, both those used for egg production and human consumption. At present, the poultry industry is largely self-regulated, and fowl are excluded from Federal Humane Slaughter Laws. As a result, their conditions of living and dying are considerably worse than those of larger animals.[60] Laying hens in factory farms are typically housed in artificially illuminated, windowless buildings containing 140,00 birds, each hen producing 250 eggs per year. By contrast, in 1940 an average laying hen produced only 134 eggs per year. Overcrowding and unnatural conditions also have led to widespread foot and feather damage resulting from contact with wired cages. Lack of exercise coupled with intensive egg production causes osteoporosis, predisposing the hens to broken bones.[61] Since eggs of a kosher species are themselves kosher (with the single requirement that they be checked for blood spots), religious Jews buy the same eggs as everyone else, obtained by the same methods.

The differences between non-kosher and kosher slaughter systems for poultry are significant. In the non-kosher industry, the procedure for killing both "broiler chickens" and "spent hens" no longer capable of producing their quota of eggs consists of three phases: motor paralysis by means of an electric current (commonly called "stunning"), throat-cutting, and bleeding. In fact, stunning does not mean that the birds are rendered unconscious or anesthetized. Rather, they are shackled

---

60. Since they have no value to the egg or poultry industries, most male chicks are destroyed shortly after birth. In the U.S., approximately one half-million newborn male chicks per day are stuffed into plastic bags, where they are manually crushed, or left to suffocate. Alternately, poultry workers grind them up while still alive to use them as fertilizer or feed; see Mark O. North and Donald Bell, *Commercial Chicken Production Manual,* 4th ed. (1990), p. 105. I am told by the RSPCA of West Sussex, England, that in the UK the figure approaches 45 million male chicks annually. Such blatant disrespect for life and wastefulness grossly contradicts the ethical and Kabbalistic teachings cited in Part IV: Additional Source Texts, Chapter 1; e.g. *Zohar* II, *Yisro,* 93b, *Sha'ar HaMitzvos, Noach,* etc. R. Yitzchak Halevy Herzog, former Chief Rabbi of Israel, ruled that if Jews owned these businesses, such chicks would require individual *shechitah* and *kisui hadam* (covering the blood) once they had opened their eyes. R. Herzog's responsum, citing the *Noda B'Yehudah,* is included in R. Shimon Efrati's *Sh'vi Zion, Kuntres Tza'ar Baalei Chaim,* no. 1, printed with *Gaon Zvi* on *Chullin* (1971). (According to *Simlah Chadasha* 16:1, if the chick was born covered with feathers it need not have opened its eyes prior to *shechitah.*)
61. These statistics were provided by the Humane Society of the U.S. (www.hsus.org).

upside-down to an overhead conveyor belt and rinsed with electrically charged water in order to render them docile as a preparation to slaughter — a highly traumatic procedure. If the amperage of the stunner is too high, it may cause red wing tips, broken bones, muscle hemorrhages, and impede subsequent blood drainage; if the amperage is too low, it may result in increased agitation resulting in poor or missed neck cuts, broken wings, and survival of the mechanized slaughter process.[62] Following slaughter, usually at the rate of 90 birds per minute, the carcasses are put into a scald tank, after which the feathers may be removed more easily. However, for many birds the agony is not quite over. Due to the sheer quantity of poultry slaughtered in the U.S., inevitably millions of birds enter the scald tank alive every year.[63]

Whatever its shortcomings, at least kosher slaughter of poultry is free of these evils. The largest producer of kosher chickens in the world today is the Empire Poultry Corporation. It, too, relies upon mass production methods, slaughtering a total of 100,000-110,000 birds per day, four days per week, at its plant in Mifflintown, Pa. A rival firm based in Postville, Iowa, Aaron Rubashkin and Sons, slaughters approximately 40,000 chickens per day; while Vineland Poultry of Vineland, New Jersey, slaughters approximately 20,000 chickens per day. The systems at all three plants have several important differences from their non-kosher counterparts. Jewish law disallows the stunning of kosher chickens prior to slaughter. In addition, since *shechitah* must be performed manually and not by a mechanical process, there is less chance for mutilating live birds and prolonging death.

---

62. University of Georgia Cooperative Extension Service Poultry Tips, 5.00, by poultry scientist Douglas P. Smith, cited in University of Nebraska Poultry News, Fall 2000.
63. USDA *Guidelines for Establishing and Operating Broiler Processing Plants* (1993) states that missed birds (known as "cadavers" in the industry) should not exceed more than 1 or 2 per thousand slaughtered. Total poultry slaughtered in the U.S. in 2002 exceeded nine billion. Thus, it is likely that more than nine million birds will enter the scald tank alive. In her animal rights polemic *Prisoned Chickens, Poisoned Hens* (1996), industry nemesis Dr. Karen Davis contends that the total number of missed birds annually may exceed 20 million. By the author's admission, her figures are highly imprecise, being based upon worker affidavits and factors such as production line speeds and slaughter methods. Since the USDA has not investigated this problem, more accurate statistics are unavailable.

In the larger kosher operations, slaughter of each bird is quite labor intensive. At least two attendants assist the *shochet:* the first removes each hen from the crate and passes it to a second attendant, who holds the bird during *shechitah.* After the *shochet* plucks away the neck feathers and slaughters the bird, he inspects its throat; then the attendant transfers the carcass to a cone in a conveyor. All this takes a matter of several seconds. A *mashgiach* (rabbinic supervisor) periodically checks the slaughterers' knives for knicks, a task which the *shochtim,* too, perform regularly. (Due to the high quality of modern steel knives, knicks are found relatively infrequently.) Kosher slaughter disallows the use of scald tanks, requiring that birds be defeathered by a cold-water process. Several *mashgichim* (supervisors) inspect the slaughtered birds for *treifos* (disqualifying signs), and still other *mashgichim* oversee the washing and salting process. From the standpoint of *tza'ar baalei chaim,* the main problem is that the greater percentage of kosher chickens, like other food animals, must be purchased from the same factory farms that rule the industry.[64]

Inhumane practices have a long, dark past in the American food industry, and the Jewish community cannot be blamed for them. However, we must not implicitly condone such practices by taking advantage of them without protest, rationalizing that we have not directly violated the laws of *tza'ar baalei chaim.* The establishment of higher humane standards in our society as a whole is a moral undertaking for which we, as willing participants in the system, must take responsibility. Animal welfare as a political concern may be a novel "Jewish issue," but it is fully consistent with traditional Jewish values.

---

64. It must be acknowledged that not all factory farms are equally problematic. All broiler hens are "free-roaming," i.e., floor raised; however, spaciousness and sanitariness of the coops vary widely. Most "broilers" are fed a mixture of corn and soy treated with growth hormones and steroids, although certain growers do allow the chickens to develop naturally. Empire Poultry states that their chickens are not treated with growth hormones. However, given the size of such operations and the high probability of disease, the use of antibiotics is virtually ubiquitous.

Beyond the Letter of the Law

The Torah advocates sensitivity to the feelings of animals above and beyond the permissibility of acts that may cause them pain. A well-known example of this involves Rabbi Yehudah HaNasi, the 2nd century sage who redacted the Mishnah. The Talmud tells how Rabbi Yehudah was punished at the hand of Heaven for speaking callously to a frightened calf that sought refuge at his feet while being taken to slaughter.[65] The various commentaries question the nature of Rabbi Yehudah's wrong-doing; after all, he neither afflicted the calf, nor did he speak falsely. One explanation is that a person of Rabbi Yehudah's spiritual stature should have displayed greater compassion, beyond the letter of the law.[66]

In keeping with this principle, many of our greatest sages showed diligence in saving animals from distress, even when not compelled to do so by *halacha*. As we learned in the first chapter, Rabbi Yisrael Salanter (1810-1883), founder of the modern Mussar movement, once spent the evening of Yom Kippur, the holiest day of the year, rescuing a lost calf belonging to a Christian neighbor, while his congregation unknowingly waited for him. The revered Rabbi Eliyahu Lopian (1876-1970) personally attended a stray cat that sought refuge in his yeshiva. During his youth, the Chazon Ish (R. Avraham Yeshaya Karelitz, 1878-1953) lowered himself into a deep pit to save an animal of a non-kosher species.

This call to a higher moral sensitivity is not only addressed to great tzaddikim (righteous individuals) like Rabbi Yehudah HaNasi; it is relevant to all. Another example of such behavior is cited by the Rama (R. Moshe Isserles, 1530-1572) in his authoritative glosses on the *Shulchan Aruch* (Code of Jewish Law). "The law permits one to pluck feathers from a live

---

65. *Bava Metzia* 85a.
66. R. Yehudah Leib Zirelson, *Ma'archei Lev*, no. 110. In his essay on "Animal Experimentation" (sec. IV), R. Bleich notes that the Maharsha on *Bava Metzia* 85a and *Teshuvos Imrei Shefer*, no. 34, sec. 10, 12, each propose different explanations for R. Yehudah's censure, but their conclusions agree with that of *Ma'archei Lev*. This is related to the principle of sanctifying oneself within the realm of the permissible, which varies according to the spiritual level of the individual. As the verse states, "You shall be holy, for I, the Eternal, Your God, am holy" (Leviticus 19:2). Nachmanides explains that without this call to holiness, "one could become a sordid person within the realm of the permissible" (ad loc.).

goose, but people refrain from doing so because this is an act of cruelty."[67] Thus, we see that even the extralegal conduct of ordinary folk constitutes a halachic factor, and that the suffering of animals in the service of human needs may not be discounted as morally inconsequential.

Surely this higher sensitivity should be applied to areas of questionable human necessity. Several examples include:

Animal Experiments: Scientific experimentation using animals is countenanced by Jewish law in order to obtain concrete benefits for mankind. It is undeniable that such experimentation in the past has led to a number of important medical breakthroughs.[68] Yet many ethically concerned scientists and physicians feel that the extent of animal research could be reduced, if not eliminated, without adversely affecting progress in finding new treatments for disease.[69] Arguments for and against animal research are beyond the purview of this book, but are the affair of the scientific community. However, according to one current in halachic thought, if alternate means of gaining the same knowledge were to become available, such animal experiments would cease to be halachically justifiable.[70] The parameters of what constitutes "human

---

67. Rama on *Shulchan Aruch, Even HaEzer* 5:14. This ruling, cited in *Issur v'Heter* 59:36, is supported by Tosefos on *Bava Metzia* 32b. Also cf. *Kitzur Shulchan Aruch* 191:1; *Shulchan Aruch HaRav, Ovrei Derachim V'Tza'ar Baalei Chaim*, 4.
68. In support of this widely held assertion, see Kevin O'Donnell, M.D., representing the Research Defense Society of the U.K. (www.cix.co.uk). A brief history of medical treatments developed through animal experimentation may be found on the website of Americans for Medical Progress (www.amprogress.org/history.htm). These presentations were created to defend existing practices in the scientific and medical communities.
69. Founded in 1985, The Physicians Committee For Responsible Medicine, headed by Neal Barnard, M.D., opposes animal experimentation for any reason (www.pcrm.org). The PCRM's advisory board lists a number of prominent health professionals, among them Drs. Dean Ornish, T. Colin Campbell, Henry Heimlich, and Andrew Weill. However, the proportion of advisors and members who take an unequivocal position like that of the organization's founder is unclear.
70. R. Bleich's *Judaism and Animal Experimentation*, sec. IV, cites *Teshuvos Imrei Shefer*, no. 34, sec. 16, as questioning the permissibility of causing *tza'ar baalei chaim* "for the purposes of tests and experiments," the human benefits of which are uncertain. This is supported by *Teshuvos Noda B'Yehudah, Mahadura Kamma, Yoreh De'ah*, no. 83. *Teshuvos Chelkas Yaakov*, Vol. I, No. 30, sec. 6, maintains that even permissible experiments involving animals should be curtailed as much as possible if they cause *tza'ar baalei chaim*. Similarly, see *Shevus Yaakov*, Vol. III, no. 71. However, *Da'as Kedoshim, Yoreh De'ah* 24:12, *Seridei Eish*, Vol. III, no. 7, and *Tzitz Eliezer*, Vol. XIV, no. 68, citing the Chasam Sofer, take a lenient view of experiments that have any

need" are an important factor in determining the halachic legitimacy of such research, as well. Several rabbinic authorities have forbidden or questioned the conducting of animal experiments in order to manufacture cosmetics and luxury items.[71] Of course, at the practical level, most of this sort of research is conducted under the auspices of corporations that have no connection to Judaism or Jewish law.[72] Nevertheless, the Torah viewpoint is significant as a moral posture: animals may not be exploited to serve every human whim, or simply to satisfy intellectual curiosity, but only to contribute to the betterment of human life. Thus, vivisection as part of an educational curriculum is forbidden.[73] Whenever possible, anesthesia and analgesia must be used in the course of permissible animal experiments to minimize suffering.[74]

Pate De Foie Gras: The forced feeding of geese and other species of fowl for the production of *pate de foie gras* was the subject of debate among rabbinic decisors during the 18th and 19th centuries, when many Jewish families in Eastern Europe subsisted from the breeding and sale of livestock. Stuffing geese was deemed halachically unacceptable by most prominent authorities, although several, including the Chasam Sofer (R. Moshe Sofer, 1762-1839), permitted it.[75] Thus, Jewish farmers in

---

reasonable possibility of human benefit.

71. R. Bleich, ibid. sec. 5, citing *Pri Megadim (Mishbetzos Zahav)* on *Orach Chaim* 468:2, which differentiates between "great need" and "minor need"; *Teshuvos Sho'el U'Meishiv, Mahadura Tinyana*, III, no. 65. Also note R. Chaim HaLevi, cited at the end of the responsum below regarding killing animals for their furs, and his invocation of the principle of *tzorech chiyuni*, legitimate human need. More recently former Sefardic Chief Rabbi of Israel, R. Ovadiah Yosef, forbade animal experiments for cosmetics in a responsum dated 23 Adar 5762 (2002). In a letter dated 21 Cheshvan 5763/27.14.02, R. Shear-Yashuv Cohen, Ashkenazic Rav of Haifa, has informed me that he forbids such experiments and is preparing a formal responsum on this issue.

72. Israel's support of medical experimentation involving large animals has declined to the lowest per capita rate in the Western world: 0.56 of all animals used for medical research, according to statistics for 2001 released by Israel's Health Ministry. Of those large animals used for research, most did not undergo invasive procedures, and were rehabilitated from any injury rather than euthanized (*Jerusalem Post* 6.21.02).

73. *Teshuvos Issur V'Heter*, 59:36; Rama on *Shulchan Aruch, Even HaEzer* 5:14; *Shevus Yaakov*, III, no. 71; *Teshuvos Imrei Shefer*, 34:1; *Chelkas Yaakov*, 1:30-31; also note R. Yoel Schwartz, *V'Rachamav Al Kol Maasav*, p. 56, s.v. *limud*.

74. *Tzitz Eliezer*, Vol. XIV, no. 68, sec. 7. Anesthesia of animals during medical experiments is required by government regulations in the U.S., Canada, Great Britain, the European Union, and elsewhere.

Hungary force-fed their geese, while those living in Rumania, Poland, Ukraine, and Russia did not.

Both the unnatural method of feeding and the suffering the birds inevitably endure as their sclerotic livers become enlarged to as much as eight times their natural size raise the issue of transgressing the laws of *tza'ar baalei chaim*. Of pressing halachic concern is whether or not forced feeding renders the birds *treifos* (internally damaged). The smallest puncture in the animal's esophagus as a result of foreign matter or a coarse particle of grain in the feed would render it non-kosher. Therefore, religious Jews today almost universally abstain from *pate de foie gras*. Most European countries forbid raising geese for *pate de foie gras* for humane reasons, but some allow it to be imported.[76] Ironically, among the world's main producers of *foie gras* are the secular Kibbutzim (farming collectives) in Israel.[77]

Furs: European Jews, like their non-Jewish neighbors, traditionally made use of animal furs to survive the bitterly cold winters, a practice that is supported by *halacha*. As the *Noda B'Yehudah* (R. Yechezkel Landau, 1720-1793) remarks, "The animal world is subordinated to

---

75. Authorities opposed to this practice include the *Bach* on *Yoreh De'ah* 33:9; *Chochmas Adam* 16:10; *Sha'arei Tzedek* on *Yoreh De'ah* 33; *Divrei Menachem (Divrei Shalom)*, p. 143, col. 2; *Darkei Teshuvah, Yoreh De'ah* 33:131, 142, 143, citing *Teshuvos HaTzemach Tzedek*, no. 17, *Nekudas HaKessef*, et al.; *She'ilas Shalom Tinyana*, no. 154 (end); *Tzitz Eliezer*, Vol. XI, nos. 49, 55 (end), citing the Chida in *Machzik Beracha*, *Yoreh De'ah* 33:19, and R. Zvi Elimelech Spira of Dinov, et al.; ibid. Vol. XII, no. 52; *Teshuvos Har Tzvi*, no. 26; *Shema Shlomo, Yoreh De'ah*, no. 1. The *Taz* is inclined to permit it if the birds are fed gently. On this basis the Chasam Sofer takes a lenient view in *Teshuvos Chasam Sofer*, Vol. I, no. 25. Nevertheless, I am told that most Chassidim in Hungary before the Holocaust would not eat force-fed geese due to uncertainty as to their *kashrus*. For a comprehensive halachic perspective, see R. Binyamin Adler, *Kashrus U'Treifos B'Ohf*, chap. 33, sec. 98-129.
76. Austria, Czech Republic, Denmark, England, Finland, Germany, Norway, Poland, Sweden, Switzerland, as well as Australia have banned this practice. Italy has recently implemented such legislation, to be complied with by 2004.
77. The Knesset, Israel's parliament, recently initiated a process of reassessing its standards for raising fowl in order to produce *pate de foie gras*. As of July 2001, the forced feeding of ducks, which represent 12% of the birds slaughtered for *foie gras* in Israel, has been banned. However, Israel's rabbinate has opposed the forced feeding of fowl all along; see above n. 75, *Teshuvos Har Tzvi, Tzitz Eliezer*, op cit. R. Ovadiah Yosef, the most influential contemporary halachic authority in the Sefardic world and former Sefardic Chief Rabbi of Israel, forbids the forced feeding of fowl in Israel in *Yabia Omer*, Vol. 9, *Yoreh De'ah*, no. 3 (originally issued in 1976), both for reasons of *kashrus* and *tza'ar baalei chaim*.

humanity to provide for human needs. It makes no difference if we slaughter kosher animals for food, or take the lives of non-kosher animals for their hides or furs..."[78] The wearing of mink and other furs long ago became an esthetic preference and a status symbol. Just as medieval Polish nobility wore fur-trimmed hats (possibly due to the influence of the Mongol hordes that invaded Eastern Europe during the 13th century), so did prominent rabbis and Jewish communal leaders. Most Chassidim still wear the traditional *shtreimel* made from tails of the sable or marten, an object widely perceived as the movement's cultural logo.

Nevertheless, at least one major rabbinic authority seems to have been influenced by the animal rights movement's critique of the contemporary fur industry. Given the brutality of obtaining seal-furs for women's coats by beating the animals to death with clubs, the cruelties of trapping, and the sometimes inhumane procedures of fur farms, the late Rav Chaim David HaLevy, Sefardic Chief Rabbi of Tel Aviv, ruled that furs obtained by such means should be boycotted. In a 1992 responsum, Rav HaLevy states: "If the killing of animals for the obtainment of their furs were accomplished by a quick, easy death, that would be one thing; but in actuality, this is not the case... The animals are caught in a kind of ring trap that causes them great anguish until they are released and killed and stripped of their furs. This constitutes actual *tza'ar baalei chaim*; there can be no disagreement about it."

The same authority adds: "I have been informed that nowadays there are farms where animals are raised for the purpose of killing them and using their furs... However, as explained above, according to many authorities, even killing without *tza'ar baalei chaim* is forbidden if there is no compelling human need (*tzorech chiyuni*). According to all views, it is clear that such acts are tainted by cruelty, which is foreign to the character traits of the children of Abraham, Isaac, and Jacob... Therefore, one should refrain from wearing furs."[79]

---

78. "However," R. Landau concludes, "when the act [of killing an animal] is not prompted by such motives, it is wanton cruelty"; *Noda B'Yehudah Tinyana, Yoreh De'ah*, no. 10.

79. Also note R. Chaim ibn Attar, *Ohr HaChaim* on Leviticus 17:13, citing *Mishneh Torah, Ma'achalos Asuros* 8:17, as well as his *Sefer Pri To'ar*, sec. 117, which prohibit the trapping of non-kosher animals by Jews on the grounds of *tza'ar baalei chaim*. However, R. HaLevy apparently objects to complicity in such acts even when performed by others.

While this remains an unusual halachic position, at the very least it lends weight to public demand for a greater degree of government involvement in imposing humane methods of raising and slaughtering fur-producing animals.[80] (At present there are no animal welfare or

---

80. It is difficult to ascertain how many animals are killed for furs annually in the U.S. The Humane Society places the total number at approximately 30 million animals (www.hsus.org). However, if this figure once was accurate, it is probably considerably lower today. Based on information from the National Agricultural Statistics Service and the U.S. Dept. of Agriculture, the Humane Society states that the number of cage-raised minks killed for fur in the U.S. declined from 4.12 million in 1987 to 2.84 million in 1997. The number of cage-raised foxes killed in the U.S. fell from 100,000 to 20,000 over the same ten years. According to the International Association of Fish and Wildlife Agencies, an estimated 4 million fur-bearing animals are trapped annually, as compared to more than 17 million in the mid-1980s. This dramatic change is the combined result of public objection to animal abuse and the availability of less expensive alternative products.

According to the Fur Commission of the USA, approximately half the animals killed for their pelts are raised in confinement on "fur farms," where eventually they are euthanised by carbon dioxide, pure carbon monoxide gas, or lethal injection. The American Veterinary Medical Association and the Geulph University Research Facility in Canada deem these methods to be humane (www.furcommission.com). However, because the industry is for the most part self-regulated, a sizeable percentage of cage-raised animals are not killed by these methods, but by carbon monoxide generated by engine exhaust, anal electrocution, genital or ear-to-foot electrocution, or by having their necks broken.

Pressure from animal activists has led to the banning of the steel-jawed leghold trap in 89 European countries. In 1999, the U.S. House of Representatives banned the use of leghold traps and strangling snares on all National Wildlife Refuges. In 2001 H.R.1187 was introduced in the House of Representatives, which proposes to ban all uses of such traps in the U.S., as well as importing or exporting any article of fur obtained by such means. An alternative to these devices, the body grip or "Conibear" trap, was developed decades ago as an instant-kill trap; however, some studies indicate that as many as 85% of its victims may languish in agony for substantial periods of time with broken backs and other mortal injuries; see H.C. Lunn, "The Conibear Trap: Recommendations for its Improvement," Canadian Federation of Humane Societies, 1973.

The Humane Society states that for each trapped animal used in a fur coat, at least twice as many animals, including dogs, cats, and birds, are mistakenly caught and subsequently "trashed." Thus, to produce one 40" long mink coat, more than 150 animals of various species will spend a combined total of approximately 3000 hours in traps. One out of four trapped animals succeeds in chewing off its own leg to escape, and soon dies of sickness, exposure, or the inability to defend itself from predators (www3.sympatico.ca/taniah/animal/fur.html). An average fur coat, depending on its type, variously requires 125 ermines, 100 chinchillas, 55 wild minks, 40 sables, 35 ranch minks, 30 muskrats, 30 rex rabbits, 27 raccoons, 25 skunks, 18 red foxes, 15 bobcats, 14 otters, 11 silver foxes, 9 beavers, or 8 seals (www.idausa.org).

humane laws regulating the housing, handling, or killing of cage-raised fur-bearing animals in the U.S., although certain USDA regulations do apply. Strict regulations have been imposed on the fur industry by the European Union.) Rav HaLevy's ruling also may influence religious Jewish consumers to see this as another area in which it is proper to "sanctify oneself within the realm of the permissible." Animal activists argue that the killing of animals for their furs has become ethically unjustifiable since high quality synthetic furs, as well as synthetic fabrics that are warmer and lighter in weight, are readily available.

Kapparos: Although some early authorities questioned the propriety of this custom, the Ari and virtually all later Kabbalists, including the Chassidic masters, accepted it.[81] As a consequence, it has become widespread in most devoutly Orthodox circles today. However, the handling of live chickens used for the pre-Yom Kippur Kapparos rite

---

The fur industry disputes the claim that its procedures are inhumane, arguing, "The practices used in fur farming are no more cruel than those used in rearing pigs and chickens." Spokesmen for the industry also deny that business has declined, but assert: "The worldwide demand for mink... has averaged nearly 30 million pelts per year since 1980" (National Center for Policy Analysis, www.ncpa.org). These statements are taken from Richard North's "Fur and Freedom: In Defense of the Fur Trade," published by the Environmental Unit of the U.K.'s Institute of Economic Affairs (www.iea.org.uk/wpapers/fur.htm). The Fur Commission of the USA through its website at www.furcommission.org explains and defends current fur industry practices.

81. R. Chaim David HaLevy in a 1992 ruling traces the origins of this rite, pointing out that its observance in Sefardic communities is due to the influence of the Ari, whose customs Sefardim generally follow. The Ari would perform the rite of *Kapparos* at the break of dawn on the morning before Yom Kippur (*Sha'ar HaKavanos, Drushei Yom HaKippurim*, 100a). However, R. HaLevy argues, this was done primarily for Kabbalistic purposes that are beyond the ken of the uninitiated. The *Beis Yosef* (the foremost later decisor among Sefardim) rejects this custom, following the view of the Rashba and the Ramban, while the Rama (the foremost later decisor among Ashkenazim) strongly endorses it as a time-honored practice (*Orach Chaim* 605:1). A compromise solution is to substitute money, which should be given to charity (*Mishnah Berurah*, ad loc., sec. 2; *Chayei Adam* 144:4). This is recommended by R. HaLevy, who concludes: "Thus, one will be saved from any risk of *neveilos* and *treifos* on the eve of the Day of Atonement, as well as from the cruelty inherent in excessive and unnecessary animal slaughter prior to the day presided over by "The One Who is Merciful in Judgment" (Ramban on Leviticus 23:24). For the essence of Yom Kippur is the divine mercy that tempers divine judgment (*Zohar* I, 114b); and it is especially unbefitting to show cruelty on the eve of the Day of Mercy, when all creatures arise to beseech mercy and to supplicate the King Who sits on the Throne of Mercy."

prior to their slaughter can be problematic. Every year, various entrepreneurs, some of whom are insufficiently experienced in caring for livestock, offer this service to the public in the larger Orthodox Jewish communities. After setting up their trailers on the streets, certain vendors leave the birds in crates in which they can barely move, sometimes for as long as two days. During this time they may neglect to feed or water them altogether. Thus, a non-obligatory rite meant to inspire repentance and to elicit God's mercy may become tainted by cruelty. Another halachic concern, given the pressures of the hour, is the likelihood of producing quantities of *treifah* chickens that subsequently will be given to the Jewish poor.[82] It is encouraging that in recent years, during the weeks before Yom Kippur, the rabbinic court of Jerusalem's *Eidah HaChareidis* under HaRav Yisrael Moshe Dushinsky has issued strongly worded proclamations warning vendors of chickens to keep their animals in the shade, and to feed and water them regularly. It is hoped that this rabbinic response will be widely emulated.[83]

The Talmud states that the Jewish people are praiseworthy for their desire to serve God beyond the letter of the law.[84] Since we diligently apply this expression of religious devotion to many ritual precepts, such as *tefillin, tzitzis,* and *mikveh,* should we not apply it with equal diligence to precepts that affect other living creatures? Moreover, this directly benefits God's works and improves the world. By engaging in acts of compassion, we become worthy of receiving the blessing of our sages that God will show mercy to those who are merciful.[85]

82. R. Chaim David HaLevy (ibid.) citing *Sdei Chemed, Ma'areches Yom HaKippurim* 1:2; also cf. *Mishnah Berurah*, 605:1, sec. 1.
83. R. Yosef Wikler, Rosh Yeshiva of Brooklyn's Birkhas Reuvain Rabbinic Seminary and Editor of *Kashrus Magazine,* in the Dec. 2001 issue of *Kashrus* advances a similar assessment of the problem. The solution he proposes is rabbinic certification for Kapparos vendors and *shochtim,* comparable to that used elsewhere in the contemporary kosher food industry.
84. *Berachos* 20b.
85. *Shabbos* 151b; *Bava Metzia* 85a; *Megillah* 12b; *Yerushalmi Bava Kamma* 8:7; *Zohar* III, 92b; also note *Likkutei Moharan* I, 119.

Sources

Rabbi Yehudah HaNasi and the Calf

Once a calf being led to slaughter thrust its head into the skirts of Rabbi [Yehudah HaNasi]'s robe and began to bleat plaintively. "Go," he said, "for this is why you were created." Because he spoke without compassion, he was afflicted [at the hand of Heaven].[86] Then one day, his maidservant was cleaning his house and came upon some young weasels. She was about to chase them away with a broom, when Rabbi Yehudah said to her, "Let them be — for it is written: 'His tender mercies are upon all His works'" (Psalms 145:9). They said [in Heaven], "Since he is merciful, let him be treated with mercy." [Thereafter, his pain ceased.] (Talmud: *Bava Metzia* 85a[87]).

Commentary 1: "His tender mercies are upon all His works." This should be understood in its literal sense. God has mercy upon all creatures, including insects and reptiles (*Eitz Yosef* on *Bereishis Rabbah* 33:3).

Commentary 2: Since the calf had fled the slaughterer's knife and buried its head in the skirts of Rabbi Yehudah HaNasi's robe seeking refuge, his giving it over immediately to the slaughterer seemed like an act of cruelty. If Rabbi Yehudah had shown mercy by at least allowing the calf a temporary reprieve, the observer might have taken this as a proper example and learned to be merciful himself. Seeing Rabbi Yehudah deliver the animal that had fled the slaughterer's knife immediately, without a trace of pity, the observer might have become more hard-hearted toward other people, as well as toward animals.

---

86. According to the Midrash, R. Yehudah was afflicted with a toothache for 13 years. Kabbalistically, the 32 teeth correspond to the "32 Paths of Wisdom (*chochmah*)"; see Pseudo-Ravad on *Sefer Yetzirah* 1:1; R. Avraham ben Nachman's *Chochmah U'Tevunah* on *Sippurei Maasiyos*, Story 7. The 13 years of affliction correspond to the *gematria* of *echad* ("one"), which is 13. This suggests that R. Yehudah's punishment reflected a failure on the part of a sage of his lofty stature to fully appreciate the unity of all creatures. However, for a person of lesser spiritual attainments, the same act might have gone unpunished.
87. Also cf. *Yerushalmi Kila'im* 9; *Bereishis Rabbah* 33:3; *Yalkut Shimoni, Tehillim* 145, with minor differences

It is also possible that sufferings befell Rabbi Yehudah because of his statement, "This is why you were created." It is true that animals were created for this fate, in that human beings have been permitted to slaughter them. Nevertheless, God does not allow any good deed to go unrewarded, and we believe that all animals slaughtered on behalf of humanity will be rewarded for their pains. For, without a doubt, the Holy One, blessed be He, does not withhold recompense from any of His creatures (*Pesachim* 118a). Thus, the animal was not created for an evil fate, but in order that good be done to it; nor was it created for the sole purpose of being slaughtered, although this has been permitted to man[88] (Rav Sherira Gaon, *Teshuvos HaGeonim*, Harkavy ed., Vol. I, No. 375, pp. 190-191).

The Pain of Animal Slaughter Must Be Minimal

The act of slaughter must be sanctified in a unique manner — "as I have commanded you" — with a minimum of pain to the animal. Thus, the person will take to heart the fact that he is not involved with a random object that moves about like an automaton, but with a living, feeling creature. He must become attuned to its senses, even to its emotions, to the feeling it has for the life of its family members, and to its compassion for its own offspring. Thus, it is biblically forbidden to kill the mother bird with her children on the same day, or to slaughter a calf before it is eight days old; and it is a positive precept to send away the mother bird before taking her young (Rabbi Avraham Yitzchak Kook, *Chazon HaTzimchonut V'HaShalom*, sec. 14).

---

88. The above responsum was addressed to the Jewish community of Kairouan, Tunisia, circa 992 c.e. Apparently following Rav Sherira's approach, R. Yehudah Leib Ginsburg, early 20th century Rav of Jaroslavl, Russia, and later Denver, Colorado, wrote in his *Yalkut Yehudah* (I, p. 24): "It appears that [Rabbi Yehudah HaNasi was punished] because he sinned in saying, 'This is why you were created.' In truth, at the beginning, animals were not created for the purpose of slaughter, inasmuch as Adam was not permitted to consume meat. It was not the original intent of the Holy One, blessed be He, to create animals in order that they die. Rather, death came to the world as a consequence of Adam's sin when he ate from the Tree of Knowledge." Cited in R. Bezalel Naor's essay *HaTzimchonut B'Ri'i HaYahadut*, published in B. Naor, *Ben Shanah Shaul*, p. 296.

ಛೀಶಾ

When the Lord your God shall expand your border, as He has told you, and you will say, "I will eat meat," for your soul desires to eat meat, according to your desire you may eat meat. If the place that God has chosen to put His Name thereupon be too far from you, you may slaughter from your herds and from your flocks that God has given you, as I have commanded you, and you may eat within your gates according to your desire (Deuteronomy 12:20-21).

Midrash: What difference does it make to the Holy One, blessed be He, whether an Israelite eats the flesh of an animal that has been ritually slaughtered, or whether an Israelite slaughters at the neck or at the leg? [That is, since the Torah permits the slaughter of animals, why should the specific means be a matter of importance?] Israel was only given the laws of ritual slaughter to refine their moral sensitivities (*Midrash Tanchuma, Shemini*, 7).

Commentary: *Shechitah* is done at the throat and with a carefully inspected knife so that the animal will not experience any more pain than necessary. The Torah permitted man in his superiority [above animals] to use them for food and for all his requirements, but not to afflict them needlessly (*Sefer HaChinnuch*, Mitzvah 451).

Helping a Beast of Burden

If you see the donkey of your enemy lying under its burden, would you refrain from unloading it? — you shall surely unload it with him (Exodus 23:5).

Talmud: One is obligated to assist an animal, whether it belongs to a non-Jew or an Israelite. Now, if you say that relieving the suffering of animals is a scriptural commandment, this law is consistent with your point of view... In either case, the Torah mandates relieving the suffering of animals (*Bava Metzia* 32b).

Codes: When one chances upon two animals, and one is collapsing under its burden, while the other's master needs to reload his animal, and there is no one whose assistance he may hire, it is a religious duty to help in unloading immediately, and then to load the other. The first concern is to relieve the animal's suffering. This applies when both parties are either one's enemies or one's friends. However, if one of them is an enemy and the other is a friend, a person must help his enemy load first, in order to overcome his evil inclination (Maimonides, *Mishneh Torah, Nezikin: Rotzei'ach* 13:13; also cf. *Shulchan Aruch HaRav, Choshen Mishpat, Ovrei Derachim V'Tza'ar Baalei Chaim* 1).

Commentary: When the Torah says "a donkey," it means any animal. The verse speaks of what is commonplace, as donkeys are beasts of burden... At the root of this precept lies the purpose of teaching us the praiseworthy trait of compassion. [If we must consider the plight of animals,] it goes without saying that we must show compassion to another human being experiencing physical difficulty. Even if that person merely suffers the loss of money or possessions, it is a religious duty to have compassion for him, and come to his aid (*Sefer HaChinnuch,* Mitzvah 80).

Sefer Chassidim on Tza'ar Baalei Chaim

For every act by which a person needlessly causes pain to another creature, he shall be punished. This applies even if he needlessly causes distress to an animal — for example, if he overloads an animal, and then, when it does not move, beats it. That person will be called to judgment before the Heavenly Court, because inflicting cruelty upon animals is a biblical prohibition.

Thus, concerning Balaam it is written: "For what reason did you strike your donkey?" in response to his having declared, "If I had a sword in my hand, I would kill you right now" (Numbers 22:29-32). That is why he was killed by the sword. [As the verse states: "And Balaam son of Beor they slew by the sword" (ibid. 31:8).] (Rabbi Yehudah HeChassid, *Sefer Chassidim*, 666).

೦ළන

One who hurts an animal for no reason — by placing an excessive burden upon it, by beating it when it is unable to proceed, etc. — violates the prohibition of causing pain to animals. One who pulls the ears of cats in order to make them wail, additionally violates a decree of our sages. It is written, "In that day, declares God, I will strike every horse with alarm and its rider with madness" (Zechariah 12:4). The Talmudic rabbis homiletically infer from this verse that in the future the Holy One, blessed be He, will punish the horsemen who goad their horses with their spurs (*Sefer Chassidim*, 44).

⋘⋙

The angel said to Balaam, "For what reason did you strike your donkey these three times?" One might think that it is forbidden to beat an animal unless it bears a burden and refuses to go. [This would render it impossible even to train an animal.] Thus, the verse specifies "three times." Since the animal already had been trained, [Balaam] should have assumed that it balked because it was sick. In that case, it would have been sinful to make it work.

Similarly, when an animal snorts loudly at night, it is surely because it sees an evil spirit or demon and does not wish to proceed. One should not strike it, for the animal is afraid of both [the evil spirit] and its rider. [Under such circumstances,] one should not show one's animal ingratitude, nor should one beat it (ibid. 668, citing Numbers 22:32).

⋘⋙

I heard the following from the Kohen of Vedona. The verse states: "A tzaddik considers the needs of his animal, but the mercy of the wicked is cruelty" (Proverbs 12:10). A cruel person will show his animal compassion by feeding it to excess one day, and the next day racing it over mountains and hills. For he says, "Did I not give it plenty of food?" Then, if the animal is unable to run according to his fancy, he beats it savagely. This is the meaning of "the mercy of the wicked is cruelty" (ibid. 669).

⋘⋙

If a dog that does not bite enters one's house, one may chase it away with a small stick. However, it is forbidden to scald it with boiling water, strike it with a large stick, or squeeze it between the door and the jam; certainly, one may not blind it (ibid. 670).

ભૂજ

He who behaves like an animal in this life [by pursuing physical desires] will be forced to labor as an animal in the next world. A person who willfully intimidates his fellow men or needlessly hurts his animals will receive the same punishment [at the hand of Heaven] (ibid. 169).

Hunting for Sport

Rabbi Shimon ben Pazi expounded: "Fortunate is the man who has not walked in the counsel of the wicked..." (Psalms 1:1). That is, he has not attended the theaters and animal circuses of the other nations. "And in the way of sinners they do not stand" (ibid.). This refers to one who does not participate in a *kenigyon*" (Talmud: *Avodah Zarah* 18b).

Commentary: A *kenigyon* is a hunt with dogs in pursuit of wild animals, which is forbidden (Rashi, ad loc.).

ભૂજ

Whoever hunts wild animals with dogs, as do the non-Jews in these regions, will not witness the celebration of the Leviathan [in the World to Come] (Rabbi Yitzchak ben Moshe of Vienna, *Ohr Zaru'a*, 83:17).

The Noda B'Yehudah on Hunting for Sport

Throughout the Torah, we find the sport of hunting imputed only to [such villains as] Nimrod and Esau. This is not the way of the descendants of Abraham, Isaac, and Jacob. Indeed, according to Mahari Weill, the customary blessing given to a person who wears a new garment for the first time, "May you wear it out and acquire a new one," is omitted in the case of a fur coat. Such a blessing might make it appear that the killing of animals is not merely condoned, but is actually desirable. This would contradict the verse, "And His tender mercies are over all His works" (Psalms 145:9).

It is true that the Rama (Rabbi Moshe Isserles) in his glosses on the *Shulchan Aruch* remarks that this reason is weak. However, the weakness lies only in the fact that putting on a fur coat does not necessarily imply that the animal was killed specifically for this purpose. The fur may have been taken from an animal that died a natural death, in which case [although the meat would not be deemed kosher] it is permissible to use the hide. Nevertheless, the Rama concludes that many people are particular [to refrain from offering the customary blessing to one who wears a new fur coat, in agreement with Mahari Weill]. Therefore, how could a Jew waste his precious time in the wanton pursuit of hunting and killing animals, without any legitimate need to do so?

Some have tried to justify the hunting of bears, wolves, and other wild animals because they are liable to injure human beings. These individuals base their view on the Talmudic statement [of Rabbi Eliezer]: "Whoever is first to destroy them is meritorious" (*Sanhedrin* 2a). This assumption, however, is mistaken for two reasons. First, the *halacha* does not follow Rabbi Eliezer's opinion. Even regarding a snake, Maimonides and the Ravad differ in their views (*Mishneh Torah, Hilchos Sanhedrin* 5:2). Second, even according to Rabbi Eliezer, we follow the view of Resh Lakish that this [mandate to kill a predatory animal] only applies to one that already has proven itself to be of murderous disposition (op cit.).

Another view has been advanced that [the prohibition of *tza'ar baalei chaim*] only pertains to animals that have been raised among people and therefore have become somewhat tamed, not to wild beasts. The latter are presumed to be dangerous at all times; therefore, it is permitted to kill them even on the Sabbath, at least in an indirect manner (*Shulchan Aruch, Orach Chaim* 316:14). This reasoning, too, is mistaken, and has nothing to do with our case. The above [mandate to kill wild animals] only applies when such animals are found in inhabited places, so that they constitute a menace to society, whereas we are discussing animals in the forests, etc. It is certainly no meritorious act to pursue them in their own habitat. Rather, it is an act of blood-lust (Rabbi Yechezkel Landau, *Noda B'Yehudah (Tinyana), Yoreh Deah,* no. 10, s.v. *V'amnam me'od ani tame'ah,* abridged).

Part II:
Kabbalistic Issues

4

Creation and the Holy Sparks

Light is one of the primary symbols in Judaism. The biblical account of creation begins: "And God said, 'Let there be light,' and there was light" (Genesis 1:3). The mystical *Sefer HaBahir* observes that the verse might have stated, "And God said, 'Let there be light, and it was so'" or something similar; instead, the Torah repeats the phrase, "And there was light." From this, the *Sefer HaBahir* infers that the light had already existed, hidden within the mystery of the Infinite One.[1] Thus, light is a symbol for the primordial essence of reality.[2]

The Book of Psalms also speaks of God "covering Himself with light like a garment"[3] (Psalms 104:2). This is a metaphor for God's will to bring about the spiritual illumination of His creatures — that supreme act of divine grace, to which another verse from Psalms attests: "In Your light, we see light" (36:8). As such, light is the interface between the Creator

---

1. *Sefer HaBahir* 25; also cf. ibid. 13, 16, 190. There are conflicting views among the Kabbalists as to whether the Infinite Light (*Ohr Ein Sof*) may be considered a creation, inasmuch as it partakes of the nature of *Ein Sof*. See *Sefer Eitz Chaim* (*Heichal A-B-Y-A, Sha'ar D'rushei A-B-Y-A*) 42:1; R. Shalom Sharabi, *Nahar Shalom* on *Sefer Eitz Chaim*, ad loc., chaps. 1 and 2; R. Shneur Zalman of Liadi, *Torah Ohr, Mikeitz* 39a; et al.

2. The sages of the Midrash ask what became of this divine light, and conclude that it was "hidden away for the righteous in the Torah"; note *Bereishis Rabbah* 12:5, 42:4; *Esther Rabbah, P'sicha* 11; *Rus Rabbah, P'sicha* 7; *Midrash Tanchuma, Shemini*, 9; *Sefer HaBahir* 147; 148, 160, particularly in the mystical dimension of the Torah; cf. *Zohar* II, 148b; *Zohar Chadash, Bereishis* (8a). Also cf. R. Menachem Nachum of Chernobyl, *Me'or Einayim*, p. 268, n. 4. Thus, several Kabbalistic works bear the title "*Ohr HaGanuz L'Tzaddikim*," "The Light Hidden Away For The Righteous."

and creation. Jewish men customarily recite these verses while donning the *tallis* (fringed garment) before the Morning Prayer service. In so doing, they recall the divine origin of creation and reenact the macrocosmic event at the beginning of every day. This, too, is an emulation of God's ways. The Jew garbs himself with the *tallis*, just as the Creator garbs Himself with light. [4]

Seeking the Light

A Chassidic master once discussed the difference between philosophy and Kabbalah. The philosopher, he explained, presumes the universe to be real, and asks, "Does God exist?" whereas the Kabbalist presumes God to be real, and asks, "Does the universe exist?" (In the style of the Talmud, the latter goes on to prove that there must be a universe by citing a verse from Genesis, etc.)

One of the basic theological problems Jewish mysticism seeks to resolve is: if in its essence everything is part of the undifferentiated divine light, how can the apparent diversity of the phenomenal world exist? At the practical level, this question has an important corollary: if in its outer manifestation, everything exists in a state of division and conflict, how

---

3. *Sha'ar HaKavanos, Inyan Tzitzis, D'rush* 2 (pp. 27-28), citing *Bereishis Rabba, Parsha* 3; *Baal HaTurim* on *Bereishis* 1:2, s.v. *V'ruach Elokim*; *Midrash Shocher Tov* 104:4; *Tikkunei Zohar, Tikkun* 21 (55b). Also cf. *Rosh Hashanah* 17b in the name of R. Yochanan, that the Holy One, blessed be He, revealed Himself to Moses "covered with a *tallis* like a prayer leader." The Baal HaTurim observes that the *gematria* of the phrase, "And He said: I shall make all My goodness pass before you, and I shall call out with the Divine Name before you..." (Exodus 33:19) is equivalent to that of the Gemara's words, "For the Holy One, blessed be He, wrapped Himself [in a *tallis*] as does a prayer leader" (*Rosh Hashanah* 17b). By additionally counting each letter in both the scriptural verse and the phrase from the Gemara, their respective totals are 2256 and 2257. Following the principle that one may be added for the *kollel* (representing the word or group of words as a discrete unit), these numbers may be considered equal (*Ittur Bikkurim*, ad loc.).

4. R. Chaim Vital states that the *tallis* represents the "encompassing light" (*ohr makif*); see *Pri Eitz Chaim, Sha'ar HaTzitzis*, chap. 1. Therefore, it should be put on before the *tefillin*, which represent the "inner light" (*ohr pnimi*); see *Sha'ar HaKavanos, Inyan HaTzitzis, D'rush* 5 (p. 45); also cf. *Eitz Chaim* (*Heichal Nukva, Sha'ar HaChashmal*) 41:3. *Likkutei Moharan* I, 49:3 (*LaShemesh Sam Ohel Bahem*), states that the *tzitzis*-strings on the four corners of the *tallis* correspond to the various *tzimtzumim* (constrictions), and the *tefillin* to the light of creation.

may the primal unity of creation be restored? These are not merely abstract, intellectual questions, for they go to the root of the problem of suffering. As long as disharmony persists, there can be no true security or joy or peace.

In Kabbalistic thought, the restoration of the essential unity of creation is called *tikkun*. This is bound up with a process figuratively known as *aliyas hanitzotzos* (elevating the "holy sparks"). In order to understand these terms, it is necessary to present a brief overview of some of the most basic concepts in Jewish mysticism. Once we have a map of the "cosmological landscape," we may begin to understand why the Torah permits us to use animals for our own needs, and to appreciate the spiritual benefits obtained by those uses. In a broader sense, these mystical teachings will enable us to understand how studying and contemplating the Torah and fulfilling the commandments are the main ways the Jewish people accomplish the ultimate *tikkun* of all creation.

The Paradox of Tzimtzum

The *Sefer HaBahir* speaks of the primordial light of creation, but we commonly experience a dualistic world of light and darkness, revelation and hiddenness, unity and division, good and evil. How did this state of affairs come about? Basing himself on the *Zohar* and other earlier Kabbalistic sources, the Ari (R. Yitzchak Luria, 1534-1572) explains the paradox of dualism and unity with the notion of *tzimtzum*: the "constriction" of the Infinite Light that produces the "elemental darkness" — the absence of divine revelation that is the spiritual source of every manifestation of darkness and negativity in creation.[5] This is suggested by the verse, "And there was darkness upon the face of the deep..." (Genesis 1:2). Conceptually, *tzimtzum* is the device through which the Divine Oneness gives rise to the plurality of creation —

---

5. According to *Shefa Tal* 3:5, *Sha'arei Gan Eden* 2:3, and others, the opening passage of the *Zohar, Bereishis* (15a), alludes to this concept when it states: "In the beginning of the revelation of the King's will, He carved out of the supernal radiance a Lamp of Darkness, and from the Hidden of the Hidden, from the mystery of the Infinite, there emerged an unformed line imbedded in a ring..."; also note *Tikkunei Zohar, Tikkun* 5 (19a); *Zohar Chadash, Va'eschanan* (57a).

without compromising God's absolutely simple unity and omnipresence.[6] In the first chapter of his *Sefer Eitz Chaim*, the Ari formulates his classic allegory for the mystery of creation:

> Before all things were emanated and created, the Supernal Light was perfectly simple, suffusing all of existence. There was no empty space. Everything was filled with the Infinite Light in its perfect simplicity. There was no aspect of beginning or end; rather, everything was one simple, undifferentiated light. This is what is meant by the term "Infinite Light." When it arose within His simple will to create all the worlds, to emanate the various emanations, and to bring forth the entirety of His works, holy names, and attributes (the latter being the causative factor in the creation of all the worlds), God constricted the light to the sides (i.e., in all directions) from a central point, leaving a void or Vacated Space. This space was perfectly round, its perimeter being equidistant from the central point...[7]

After the *tzimtzum*, there was a "place" in which all things could be brought into existence. The Creator then drew a "straight thread" (*kav*) from the Infinite Light and beamed it into the Vacated Space. Through that *kav*, the Infinite Light was drawn below.

Inasmuch as the realities they describe precede the creation of the physical universe, these mystical concepts inevitably must remain recondite. However, one insight we may glean from the Lurianic allegory is that the first act of creation, the emanation of the *kav*, prefigures the

---

6. *Eitz Chaim* (*Heichal Adam Kadmon, D'rush Igulim V'Yosher*), 1:1:2; *Sha'ar* 1, 1:1; *Sha'ar HaHakdamos*, p. 14; also cf. Ramchal, *K'lach Pischei Chochmah*, 24; R. Shneur Zalman of Liadi, *Sefer HaTanya, Sha'ar HaYichud V'haEmunah*; idem, *Torah Ohr, Vayeira*, 13c, ff; idem, *Likkutei Torah, Nitzavim*, s.v. *Ki k'eretz totzi tzim'chah*, sec. 3 (51b); R. Nachman of Breslov, *Likkutei Moharan* 1:49 (*LaShemesh Sam Ohel Bahem*) and 1:64 (*Bo El Par'oh*).

7. *Eitz Chaim* (*Heichal Adam Kadmon, D'rush Igulim V'Yosher*), 1:1:2.

linear character of time and development. Past, present, and future are among the most basic components of what we take to be reality. Thus, the *kav* is a symbol of time issuing forth from eternity, albeit at the subtlest level.[8] Another fundamental dichotomy presented here is that of the light of creation and the Vacant Space. This dichotomy is responsible for the positive and negative polarities of the dualistic mode of perception.

The Ten Sefiros

The Ari goes on to describe the primordial ten "vessels" of creation, also known as the Ten Sefiros, or "Divine Powers."[9] These vessels were first created as one homogeneous whole, "ten lights in one vessel."[10] In other words, the quantum essence of creation was brought into being in a collective, inchoate state. Then the individual Sefiros were emanated into the Vacated Space as a series of concentric orbs. That is, they existed in causal relation to one another, but, nevertheless, remained separate entities, incapable of interaction. These vessels are called the Ten Sefiros of *Tohu* (Chaos or Formlessness), and the context in which they exist is the "World of *Tohu*."[11] The Ari finds an allusion to this concept in the verse which states that "the Earth was chaos (*tohu*) and emptiness, and darkness was upon the face of the deep..." (Genesis 1:2).

During the next stage, the Creator caused the intensity of light to increase until seven of these vessels of *Tohu* "exploded" (the eighth and

---

8. Perhaps it was this concept to which R. Nachman of Breslov alluded when he said: "Everything that takes place is merely like working a thin strand of metal in relation to the Infinite" (*Chayei Moharan* 280).

9. On the basis of *Sefer Yetzirah* 1:1 and 2, the term *sefirah* is related to the Hebrew words *safar*, meaning "number"; *sefer*, meaning "text"; or *saper*, meaning "to tell" or "to express." The latter is also the view of *Sefer HaBahir*, 125; *Zohar, Terumah*, 136b; *Tikkunei Zohar, Hakdamah*, 12b. Other sources see it as related to *sapir*, meaning "sapphire" or a precious stone, because the *sefiros* "refract" the undifferentiated divine light like a prism; note *Pardes Rimonim* (*Sha'ar Mahus V'Hanhagah*) 8:2.

10. *Eitz Chaim* (*Heichal Adam Kadmon, Sha'ar Akudim*) 1:6:1.

11. *Eitz Chaim* (*Heichal HaNekudim, Sha'ar D'rushei HaNekudos*) 2:1:1; ibid. (*Heichal Ze'er Anpin, Sha'ar Reish-Pey-Ches Nitzutzin*) 5:18:1 (end); *Likkutei Torah* (*Ari z"l*), *Bereishis*, 7b, *Yirmiyahu*, 122b. A profound explanation of the precedence of darkness before light in the order of creation may be found in R. Nosson Sternhartz, *Likkutei Halachos, Orlah* 4:13; also cf. ibid. *Minchah* 4:1.

last vessel being only partially damaged). This cosmic cataclysm is known as the *Sheviras HaKeilim* (Shattering of the Vessels).[12] However, this seeming disaster was also part of the divine plan, resulting in a new cosmic order in which the Ten Sefiros became compounds of one another. This new array follows a structure that parallels what will come to be the human form. These are called the Ten Sefiros of *Tikkun* (Repair), because of their ability to interact with one another, and the context in which they exist is the "World of *Tikkun*."[13] This transformation of *Tohu* to *Tikkun* through the Shattering of the Vessels reflects the Midrashic teaching that "the Holy One, blessed be He, created and destroyed worlds" prior to the creation of the world in which we exist.[14]

---

12. Based on *Zohar* III, 128a (*Idra Rabba*) et passim, the Ari associates this event with the verse that enumerates the seven kings who reigned in the land of Edom and died (Genesis 36:31-39). However, I Chronicles 1:51 enumerates eight kings who died. Kabbalistically, this is because the shattering of the vessels of *Da'as* through *Yesod* was complete, whereas the shattering of *Malchus*, the last vessel, was only partial. Therefore, the account in Genesis lists only seven kings. Regarding *Sheviras HaKeilim* in general: In the writings of R. Chaim Vital, see *Eitz Chaim* (*Heichal Nekudim, Sha'ar Sheviras HaKeilim*) 8:1:4; ibid. (*Heichal Ze'er Anpin, Sha'ar Reish-Pey-Ches Nitzutzin*) 18:2:1; *Mevo She'arim* 2:1-11; *Sha'ar HaHakdamos, D'rush* 1 *B'Olam HaNekudim*. In Chassidic works, see R. Shneur Zalman of Liadi, *Torah Ohr, Vayeishev*, s.v. *V'hinei anachnu m'almim alumim*, and *Yisro*, s.v. *L'havin shorshei hadevarim*, sec. 3; also, R. Shmuel Teich's *Lahavas Eish, Inyan Sheviras HaKeilim V'Olam HaTikkun*, cites a broad spectrum of Chassidic sources, including *Ateres Tvi (Ziditchov), Teshu'os Chein, Zohar Chai (Komarno), Noam Elimelech*, et al. The comparison to kings denotes the independence of each Sefirah.
13. *Eitz Chaim (Heichal Nekudim, Sha'ar Sheviras HaKeilim)* 2:8:6; *Likkutei Torah (Chabad), Shelach*, s.v. *Vayom'ru el kol adas b'nei Yisrael*, sec. 2 (37c).
14. *Bereishis Rabbah* 3:17, 9:2. The Kabbalists perceive a hidden allusion to these three basic stages of creation in the biblical narrative that describes Jacob's breeding of Laban's sheep and goats (Genesis 30:31-43). An angel appears to Jacob in a vision and reveals the method by which he should go about breeding his own flocks from the predominantly white flocks of the deceitful Laban (whose Hebrew name actually means "white"). Jacob personifies the Torah, into which God "gazed and created the universe." Thus, his act of breeding the sheep recapitulates the divine act of creation. In Jacob's vision, the white sheep and goats with bands (*akudim*) on their ankles correspond to the level of "ten lights in one vessel." The white sheep and goats with black spots (*nekudim*) on their bodies correspond to the Ten Sefiros of *Tohu* (Chaos). The black sheep and goats with white streaks (*berudim*) on their bodies correspond to the Ten Sefiros of *Tikkun* (Repair). These stages in creation, differentiated by the relation of light and darkness, are sometimes called the Worlds of *Akudim, Nekudim*, and *Berudim*. The division and subdivision of lights into vessels, and the evolution of the levels of creation known as the Four Worlds, accounts for the coming into being of what we experience as reality.

The Fallen Sparks

The source of disharmony and evil may be ascribed to the two main ways in which the primordial light became concealed: the original constriction (*tzimtzum*), and the Shattering of the Vessels. This constriction is the necessary precondition for creation; but, at the same time, it inevitably causes the concealment of the Divine Essence. At the level of consciousness, this gives rise to the sense of self as an autonomous entity. The Vacant Space — and the problem of ego — will not be rectified completely until the Messianic Age. Then, to paraphrase the words of King David, "night will shine like the day" (Psalms 139:12). This alludes to the *tikkun* of all the spiritual darkness that proceeds from Vacant Space.[15] The Divine Oneness will be apparent even in those realms of the human experience in which Godliness had seemed to be absent.

However, the world of dissonance and strife we experience is also a consequence of the Shattering of the Vessels. As a result of this metaphysical cataclysm, a more integrated network of relationships was forged among the Ten Sefiros of *Tikkun*, creating the potential for improvement (as well as the potential for damage). After the Shattering of the Vessels, "sparks" or refractions of the original light were displaced from their proper locus in the cosmic hierarchy, falling to lower and lower levels, and ultimately giving power to the realm farthest from the Source, the realm of impurity and death.[16] As the sparks fell from one level to the next, they divided and subdivided, until on this lowest plane of creation, the World of *Asiyah* (Action), their number is beyond calculation. In a sense, they are like snowflakes continually falling in a vast, mysterious space: just as each crystal forms around a speck of dust, so each speck of creation forms around a fallen holy spark.

---

15. R. Nachman of Breslov explains that the nature of the Vacant Space is a paradox, for concerning it two contradictory statements necessarily apply: God must be absent from the Vacant Space, otherwise there would be no "place" for creation to exist; and God must be present there, for it is axiomatic that God is infinite and omnipresent. The ultimate resolution of this paradox is the essence of the *da'as* (enlightenment) associated with the Messianic Age; see *Likkutei Moharan* 1:64 (*Bo El Par'oh*). Concerning the allegorical meaning of "the night will shine like the day," see R. Nosson Sternhartz, *Likkutei Halachos, Netilas Yadayim Shacharis* 2:1, 8; *Nefilas Apayim* 4:21.

The Shattering of the Vessels created the possibility of free will. This was manifested on the first day of the creation of Adam and Eve in the Garden of Eden. They could have accomplished the *tikkun* of the Shattering of the Vessels had they not transgressed the divine word and prematurely eaten of the fruit of the Tree of Knowledge. As a result of their failure and exile, even more holy sparks descended into the widening darkness, and the dissonance in creation increased. With every generation a degree of healing has been effected by the deeds of the righteous — and further damage has been done through human wrongdoing.

Thus, we now face an almost unimaginably difficult spiritual task: nothing less than the elevation of the holy sparks and the spiritual repair of all creation. However, at the same time we must remember God's affirmation of all His works as "good," and recognize the Shattering of the Vessels to be "very good" — in that it made possible our very ability to serve God. Because the fallen sparks give life to the realm of evil and the profane, it is possible to serve God amidst all the confusions of this world, through the exercise of free will. As it is written in *Tanna D'vei Eliyahu Zuta* (12:1): "Why did the Holy One, blessed be He, create the Evil Inclination? Does He not possess nine hundred, ninety-nine myriads of angels who sanctify His great Name every day? Only for the sake of

---

16. *Eitz Chaim (Sha'ar HaKlallim)* 1:1; R. Shneur Zalman of Liadi, *Torah Ohr, Va'erah,* s.v. *Vayomer Hashem... kach es mat'chah;* R. Menachem Nachum of Chernobyl, *Me'or Einayim, Chayei Sarah,* s.v. *V'zeh she'kasuv.* An allusion to this descent of the holy sparks is found in the verse, "And the spirit of God (*Elokim*) fluttered (*m'rachefes*) upon the face of the water" (Genesis 1:3). The Divine Name *Elokim* is associated with the Sefirah of *Binah,* the level from which the holy sparks fell. The sparks themselves are associated with the next word in the verse, *m'rachefes* ("fluttered"). The middle letters of *m'rachefes* are *reish-ches-pey,* which have the numerical value of 288; the first letter *mem* and the final letter *tav* spell "*mes,*" or "dead." This indicates that 288 sparks fell, or "died," after the Shattering of the Vessels (a spiritual descent being a form of death). As mentioned above, the descent of the holy sparks also corresponds to the death of the seven kings of Edom; see *Eitz Chaim (Heichal Ze'er Anpin, Sha'ar Reish-Pey-Ches Nitzutzin)* 18:2:1; *Mevo She'arim* 2:2:9; *Sefer HaLikkutim, Bereishis,* pp. 8-9. *Likkutei Halachos, Tolaim* 4:3. Just as the first and last letters of *m'rachefes* spell *mes,* indicating death, the middle three letters bear the numerical value of *chai,* meaning "life," according to the method of *gematria* known as *mispar katan.* That is, the number 288 is spelled *reish-pey-ches.* The letter *reish* equals 2, *pey* equals 8, and *ches* equals 8; together they add up to 18, which spells *chai,* or "life."

mortal man, who eats and drinks like an animal, excretes like an animal, and nevertheless brings himself to serve God." That is, by negating evil and choosing the good, we can come closer to God from the very ground upon which we stand, with a closeness exceeding even that of the angels.[17]

Tikkun Olam: Spiritual Repair

All commandments, if properly performed, bring about an elevation of holy sparks. The sages of the Talmud state that the 365 negative commandments parallel the 365 blood vessels and tendons, and the 248 positive commandments parallel the 248 limbs.[18] What similarity exists between the corpus of the commandments and the human form? The Kabbalists explain that through the collective performance of the Torah's laws by the Jewish people, the human form below becomes spiritually aligned with its source in the "human form" above, i.e., the Ten Sefiros of *Tikkun*. The meaning of this alignment is that the Sefiros now become conduits for the revelation of God's Oneness. Thus, the "miniature world" of the individual becomes suffused with Godliness; and since everything depends upon man, all creation is transmuted from substance to Essence — to Godliness.[19] That is, all aspects of reality are facets of the

---

17. Thus, the Talmud states: "The *tzaddikim* are destined to occupy a rank higher than the ministering Angels" (*Yerushalmi Shabbos*, chap. 2); also cf. *Tikkunei Zohar, Tikkun* 70 (137a); R. Nachman of Breslov, *Likkutei Moharan* II:1 (*Tik'u/Memshalah*); R. Shneur Zalman of Liadi, *Sefer HaTanya*, chap. 39.

18. The Mishnah in *Ohalos* 1:8 specifically lists the 248 limbs; *Targum Yonasan* on Genesis 1:27 cites the tradition that there are 248 limbs and 365 veins and tendons. Regarding the comparison of the mitzvos to the human form, see *Midrash Tanchuma, Ki Seitzei*, 2; *Zohar* I:170b, II:25a, 228b; *Tikkunei Zohar, Tikkun* 30 (74b); R. Moshe Cordovero, *Pardes Rimonim* 31:8; R. Shneur Zalman of Liadi, *Sefer HaTanya*, chap. 23 and 24.

19. R. Chaim Vital, *Sha'ar HaMitzvos, Hakdamah* (esp. s.v. *Od matzasi bazeh*); various implications of this concept are discussed in *Ben Poras Yosef* 74b, as quoted in *Sefer Baal Shem Tov, Mikeitz*, 1; *Kesser Shem Tov* 53, 127; *Tzava'as HaRivash* 109, 126, 127; *Avodas Yisrael (Koznitz), Bo,* s.v. *Ha'chodesh hazeh; Degel Machaneh Ephraim, Korach,* s.v. *V'yesh lifaresh,* citing the Baal Shem Tov, pp. 182-183; *Sefer HaTanya, Igeres HaKodesh,* Letter 7, Letter 29. The intrinsic harmony of creation also is restored by elevating the holy sparks through words of Torah and prayer; see *Likkutei Moharan* 1:75 (*Y'vorcheinu Elokim*) and its explanation in *Likkutei Halachos, Beis HaKnesses* 4; also ibid. *Minchah* 7:38.

"cosmic diamond" through which the Infinite Light now can shine forth.[20]

This spiritual transformation not only depends upon our words and deeds, but our thoughts;[21] thus, Kabbalistic works are replete with mystical meditations related to the performance of religious precepts. The Baal Shem Tov taught that even mundane acts could be invested with holiness if performed "for the sake of heaven." (Chassidic legend therefore depicts the movement's founder meditating upon Divine Names as he sat in silence, smoking his long-stemmed pipe.) However, the situation that presents the greatest single opportunity for the elevation of holy sparks is the act of eating.

Perhaps this is why so much of Jewish law is directly or indirectly concerned with food. The Sabbath and Festivals, highlights of the Jewish calendar, are celebrated through festive meals. Indeed, most of the rites of the Holy Temple centered on eating. Even today, nearly two thousand years since the *Korban Pesach* (Paschal Lamb) was offered in Jerusalem, the Passover Haggadah that recounts the ancient exodus from Egypt is still recited over a ritual meal. This is because eating is uniquely an act of transformation. If approached as a spiritual task, this mundane necessity may be elevated from a simple means of physical survival to one of the most sublime ways of serving God.

This form of divine service also has an experiential component. Rabbi Nachman of Breslov taught that while eating, a spiritually refined person experiences what he calls *he'aras ha-ratzon*: an illumination of the deepest desire of the soul for God.[22] When one eats in such a state, this

---

20. A diamond is luminous, enduring, and beautiful. Hence it symbolizes the spiritual perfection of both the individual and all creation in R. Nachman of Breslov's *Sippurei Maasiyos* (Collected Tales), Story 5 (The Prince of Gems); also cf. *Chayei Moharan* 281.
21. R. Chaim Vital, *Sha'ar HaMitzvos, Eikev*, esp. s.v. *V'nachzor l'kavanas ha-achilah*, et al., and throughout the writings of the *Ari z"l*; also cf. *Me'or Einayim, Shemos*, s.v. *V'noda she'ha-machashavah*, citing *Zohar, Pekudei*, 254b (end); *Sefer Baal Shem Tov, Pekudei* 1, citing *Ben Poras Yosef, Hakdamah*. The Tzemach Tzedek of Lubavitch discusses how higher knowledge (*da'as*) is actually a consequence of elevating the holy sparks, and is attained through withstanding evil temptations and spiritual challenges; see *Derech Mitzvosecha, Ma'amar "Acharei Hashem Elokecha Teileichu."*
22. *Likkutei Moharan* II, 7:10 (*Ki M'rachamam Y'nahagem*).

effects a spiritual unification of an extremely high order — even if one does not know the right Kabbalistic meditations.

Eating As A Spiritual Practice

Therefore, we should approach eating neither as a meaningless, sensual indulgence, nor even as a necessary means of maintaining our physical well-being (although this is surely a legitimate concern), but as a responsibility to God and to all creation.[23] This is why Jews are commanded to eat kosher food — and not, as some mistakenly think, merely for health reasons or to reinforce communal bonds, etc. This, too, is the Kabbalistic reason for the Torah's concession to slaughter animals and use them for food or other legitimate needs. By so doing, we human beings may elevate the holy sparks that have fallen to the lower levels of creation.[24] (Non-Jews, too, may elevate the holy sparks in their food; but the price of being exempt from the complex and demanding laws of *kashrus* is that they cannot accomplish this *tikkun* to the same degree.)[25]

---

23. A number of teachings on eating as a means of divine service have been translated into English by Yitzhak Buxbaum, *Jewish Spiritual Practices* (Jason Aronson, 1990), esp. chaps. 10, 20; also see Susan Schneider's *Eating As Tikkun* (A Still Small Voice, 1996). In Hebrew, see *Lechem HaPanim (Breslov)* (rev. ed. Jerusalem, 1985) and R. Shmuel Stern's *Kedushas HaAchilah* (London, 1994); also cf. R. Aharon Roth, *Shulchan HaTahor*, R. Tzadok HaKohen, *Pri Tzaddik*, Vol. I, *Kuntres al HaAchilah*; R. Yeshaya HaLevi Horowitz, *Shnei Luchos HaBris*, Vol. I, *Inyan Kedushas HaAchilah*; R. Chaim of Volozhin, *Nefesh HaChaim, Likkutei Ma'amarim*, no. 33.
24. The centrality of humankind in the divine scheme is reflected by the symbolism of Ezekiel's vision of the *Merkavah* (Divine Chariot). Kabbalistically, the lowest level of the *Merkava* corresponds to the mineral realm and to vegetation; the angels (*Chayos*) in the vision correspond to the animal kingdom; and the Human Form (*Adam*) seated on the Supernal Throne corresponds to the perfection of all human souls. This indicates that humankind is the crown of creation, through which everything is spiritually elevated. This symbolism has profound esoteric meanings, as well; cf. *Shivchei HaBaal Shem Tov*, 201 (Rubenstein ed.); *Degel Machaneh Ephraim, Lech Lecha,* s.v. *Vayashav es kol harechush,* p. 14; R. Nosson Sternhartz, *Likkutei Halachos, Rosh Chodesh* 6:20, *Birkhas HaPeiros* 5:18; et al.
25. *Pardes Rimonim, Sha'ar* 24:10; *Sefer Baal Shem Tov, Chayei Sarah* 4, citing *Me'or Einayim, Matos; Sh'nos Bikkurim: Tiferes Mordechai, Middos,* Vol. II, s.v. *Yashuv Yerachameinu,* p. 817, citing *Kisvei Chassidim Rishonim;* also cf. R. Yitzchak Isaac Yehudah Yechiel Safrin of Komarno, *Heichal HaBerachah,* Vol. IV, *Shelach (Otzar HaChaim),* 100a (end). However, one who lacks virtue cannot bring this about; therefore, the holy spark remains in a state of exile within him, or must transmigrate elsewhere.

Of central importance to the act of eating is the recitation of the blessings before and after; if performed with proper intention, the blessings bring about the elevation of the holy sparks contained in the food.[26]

The opposite is also true. If we are negligent in these matters, we do a gross disservice to the rest of creation. Thus, Rabbi Nachman Goldstein (1823-1898), Rav of Tcherin and a leading figure in the Breslov Chassidic community during the latter part of the 19th century, included in his *tzava'ah*, or "spiritual will," an eloquent apology to all souls and all beings on all levels of creation for his having possibly failed to elevate them during his sojourn in this world.[27] Chassidic master Rabbi Yaakov Yosef ben Yehudah of Ostrog, better known as "Rav Yaivi" (1738-1791), would apologize after every meal to the holy sparks in the leftover food for his inability to redeem them.[28] This posture toward the rest of the universe befits us all. If we acknowledge our spiritual responsibilities, we may truly fulfill the lofty purpose for which we are destined: to become, in the golden expression of the Talmudic sages, "partners with the Holy One, blessed be He, in the work of creation."[29]

26. *Sha'ar HaMitzvos, Eikev;* R. Nosson Sternhartz, *Likkutei Halachos, Terumos U'Ma'aseros,* 1; also see *Berachos* 35a-b; *Yerushalmi Berachos* 1:6; *Zohar, Vayakhel,* 218a; R. Bachaya on Deut. 8:10; R. Menachem Nachum of Chernobyl, *Me'or Einayim, Matos,* s.v. *Al kein tzarich;* R. Zvi Hirsch of Ziditchov, *Sur Me'Ra V'asei Tov, Kesav Yosher Divrei Emes,* s.v. *V'gam b'uvdos tzorchei haguf,* pp. 112-113, et al.
27. *Kochvei Ohr, Tzava'as HaRav MiTcherin,* sec. 16, p. 58.
28. *Imrei Kodesh,* cited in *Sefer Kedushas HaAchilah,* 139.
29. *Shabbos* 119b.

Sources

Revealing the Divine Life Force

In truth, God is everywhere; as the verse states, "And You give life to them all" (Nehemiah 9:6). It is only that the lower the level of a thing, the greater the extent to which Godliness is hidden and concealed within it. The purpose of all our divine service in this world is to elevate and bring forth Godliness from concealment to revelation, [as we pray during the Days of Awe], "And every created thing shall know that You created it..." (*Rosh Hashanah Machzor*).

However, it takes great effort and many forms of divine service to transform the state of concealment to revelation, for this is the ultimate spiritual task of a person in this world. Due to the extent of this concealment, not everyone has sufficient spiritual merit to succeed in this task. This capability only belongs to the great tzaddikim, the true sages who can draw forth wondrous perceptions from the depths of divine wisdom. Through them, concealment can be transformed to revelation, and Godliness can be made known to the world. They can reveal the truth, that what the world takes to be important is "vanity of vanities," a passing shadow, a gust of wind; moreover, they can offer spiritual advice and a reliable path to every person, according to his or her level. Thus, one can be saved from the false sense of reality produced by the concealment of Godliness in the world, and all one's efforts will be directed toward the true goal: knowledge of God.

Everyone really knows that the world is transitory and without substance. Nevertheless, the concealment is so great that people still pursue the illusory pleasures of the world, losing sight of the ultimate purpose. Even if they sometimes remember and say, "What will come of this in the end?" they have no practical guidance as to how to save themselves. Therefore, the main thing is to have faith in the true sages. Only they, in their great wisdom, can reveal that which is hidden in the proper manner and give wondrous advice to each person, according to his unique nature and spiritual level (Rabbi Nosson Sternhartz, *Likkutei Halachos, Shechitah* 5:5, abridged).

Freeing the Captives

"He appoints an end to darkness" (Job 28:3). On this, the Midrash comments: "As long as the Evil Inclination exists, darkness and death exist... " (*Bereishis Rabbah*, 89:1).

The Kabbalistic meditations of the Ari discuss the elevation of the holy sparks that fell through the Shattering of the Vessels, and how man must bring about their ascent from the mineral to the animal, vegetative, and human levels. Thus, the holy sparks will be disencumbered from the "evil husks." This is the spiritual task of every Jew, both in Torah study and performance of the commandments, as well as [for the Kabbalistic initiate] by engaging in the meditations for eating.

It is known that every spark on each plane of creation possesses a complete structure that consists of 248 spiritual "limbs" and 365 spiritual "tendons." As long as it remains imprisoned on an inferior level, it cannot stretch out its hands and feet, but sits with its head on its knees. However, one who is able to elevate the spark to the human level through his meditative intent brings it forth to freedom. There is no "redeeming of captives" greater than this. Moreover, if it is the King's son who is in prison, and one strives mightily until he frees him, surely his reward will be very great. However, all this is in accordance with Heaven's decree that "appoints an end to darkness" — how long [the holy spark or reincarnated soul] must remain in prison, and when, and through whom, it will merit to be released (Rabbi Yisrael Baal Shem Tov, cited by Rabbi Yaakov Yosef of Polonoye, *Ben Poras Yosef* 74b; also *Sefer Baal Shem Tov, Mikeitz* 1).

ভস্তু

My grandfather [Rabbi Yisrael, the Baal Shem Tov] taught: Each tzaddik possesses certain holy sparks that are related to the root of his soul. Even his servants, animals, and vessels contain these holy sparks, which he must perfect and elevate to their spiritual source (Rabbi Moshe Chaim Ephraim of Sudylkov, *Degel Machaneh Ephraim, Lech Lecha,* s.v. *Vayeshev es kol ha-rechush,* p. 14).

The Maggid of Chernobyl on Elevating the Holy Sparks

Our sages state: "A day of rain is as great as the Resurrection of the Dead" (*Ta'anis* 6b). The matter is as follows: Sometimes a soul cannot ascend after death, but must remain in the "silent" or mineral realm, buried in the dust of the Earth. When the rain falls and the Earth gives forth vegetation, this soul ascends to the vegetative level. An animal eats the vegetation, and the soul ascends to the animal level. Should a religious Jew consume the animal and recite a blessing over it, he sanctifies it [with the holiness of the commandments], causing the soul to regain the human level. When that person prays and speaks words before God, the soul comes forth, garbed in the breath of his mouth and his words, and returns to the One Above; this is its *tikkun*. What causes all this? The rain. This [process of *tikkun*] actually is a resurrection of the dead: for that which had been in the category of the "silent," a state comparable to death, now ascends [through prayer and holy speech]. Thus, *Great is a day of rain...* In truth, it is the divine life-force that descends to the Earth; however, when it enters this physical world, it becomes manifest as rain (Rabbi Menachem Nachum of Chernobyl, *Me'or Einayim, Likkutim*, s.v. *Ach ha-inyan*, p. 410).

⊂ঈ৲⊃

Doing business is called *masah u'matan* [literally: "picking up and giving"], because one "picks up" the holy spark from the place to which it fell, and "gives" it back to its original place in the realm of holiness (ibid. *Vayeitzei*, s.v. *V'al kein*, 116).

⊂ঈ৲⊃

The Torah states, "And Jacob lifted up his feet... " (Genesis 29:1). That is, he lifted up the paradigm of the "footstool" [as in the verse, "The heavens are My Throne, and the Earth is my footstool"] (Isaiah 66:1). This alludes to the lower levels [in the hierarchy of creation] that Jacob spiritually elevated to the transcendental plane. [Therefore, the verse continues,] "And he walked to the land (*eretz*) of children of Kedem" (ibid.). He transferred whatever earthliness (*artzius*) he encountered to

the "children (*b'nei*) of Kedem" — that is, to build (*boneh*) the kingdom of
the Primordial One (*Kadmono Shel Olam*).

The term "building" denotes our efforts to extricate the sparks from
the *klippos*. Through this spiritual work, we build and expand the borders
of the realm of holiness, and the "cosmic form" of the Primordial
Creator.[30] This is why Torah scholars are called "builders" (*Berachos* 64a)
(ibid. *Kedoshim*, s.v. *V'Yaakov Avinu*, p. 240).

ભજ

"God will wage war with Amalek from generation to generation"
(Exodus 17:16). This alludes to the war against the Evil Inclination that
will continue until the advent of the Moshiach, may it be speedily in our
days. Then, "the Divine Throne will be complete" (Rashi citing *Midrash
Tehillim*, ibid.). That is, the Godliness that had animated the lower levels
of creation will ascend, each holy spark being gathered to the next, until
they become a collective vehicle (*merkavah*) for Godliness. However, at
present, the ongoing war against the Evil Inclination precludes all this.
The Divine Throne is not complete, for the Jewish people have not
succeeded in spiritually rectifying the [lower levels].

When the verse [from Isaiah cited in the previous section] juxtaposes
the Supernal Throne and the "footstool," this teaches us that the
perfection of the sublime depends upon the perfection of the lowly. This
task has been entrusted to the Jewish people. Thus, [regarding the war
with Amalek, Rashi comments:] "The Divine Name is not complete, and
the Divine Throne is not complete" (op cit.). As is known, the divine life
force garbed within the lower levels is called "God's Name" (*Sha'ar
HaKavanos, Kavanas HaAmidah, Drush* 32). Due to the war with the Evil
Inclination, the task of the Jewish people remains unfinished.
Ultimately, however, the prophecy will be fulfilled: "And I will remove
the spirit of impurity from the Earth" (Zechariah 13:2) (ibid. *Kedoshim*,
s.v. *V'Yaakov Avinu*, p. 240).

ભજ

---

30. By this, the Maggid of Chernobyl alludes to the order of the various "worlds,"
    culminating in the physical universe.

Why is the sciatic nerve called the *gid hanasheh* (literally: "displaced tendon")? Because when Jacob wrestled all night long with the angel of Esau, it was moved from its proper place (Genesis 32:33). This symbolizes the dislocation of the lower levels of creation from their true "place": the Creator, Who is the "Place of the Universe."[31] For all the vitality and all the holy sparks in the world have their "place" within God. It is only that at present, they have fallen from that Place (ibid. *Kedoshim*, s.v. *V'noda*, p. 241).

CBEO

One devoted to the service of God must seek to bind himself to all created things. This is the meaning of the Talmudic dictum: "A prayer leader should not stand in a high place, but in a low place" (*Berachos* 10b). One must stand in the "low place" where the holy sparks have fallen, and pray, binding oneself to them and elevating them to their source (ibid. *Va'eschanan*, s.v. *V'al kein*, p. 339).

CBEO

The thoughts of every Jew are taken from the "World of Thought" [i.e., the animating divine wisdom that is the essence of creation]. However, due to the Shattering of the Vessels, these thoughts have fallen from their source. One who has a knowing heart can extricate them from the state of being "shattered," and restore them to the Supernal Thought. The Supernal Thought is also called wisdom (*chochmah*), as the *Zohar* states: "Everything is spiritually refined in wisdom (*chochmah*)" (*Pekudei* 254b). Through this wisdom, through this ascent to the Supernal Thought, they are extricated from the state of being "shattered" and are transmuted to the complete good. Our main spiritual task is to refine the holy sparks, which are the thoughts trapped in the *klippos* — to extricate and elevate them, and bring about their reunification with their Source (ibid. *Shemos*, s.v. *V'noda*, p. 153).

CBEO

---

31. *Bereishis Rabbah* 68:9.

In truth, there is no soul that will not receive its *tikkun*, for it will ascend from level to level until it attains perfection. As the verse states, "God devises strategies so that no one should remain banished from Him" (II Samuel 14:14). When there is no one to intervene in the process of *tikkun*, the soul must advance from level to level, a process that takes a long time. However, another person can expedite this *tikkun* through words of Torah and prayer. The soul is bound up with the holy letters that fell [after the Shattering of the Vessels]; therefore, its ascent also depends upon the letters of speech. [Through encountering a person who engages in Torah study and prayer, the estranged soul] can skip over many levels, and attain its *tikkun* at once (ibid. *Bamidbar*, s.v. *Vi'hinei kol ha-neshamos*, p. 254).

⊂ℑ৪৩

The taste of all food and drink is derived from the sparks of souls contained therein. The food and drink is a vessel for these souls. If one eats and drinks with proper intent, "for the sake of Heaven," one may declare: "This is the table that stands before God [in the Holy Temple]" (Ezekiel 41:22). This is truly like bringing a sacrifice, for one is bringing those souls back to their Source (ibid. *Noach*, s.v. *V'tishaches ha'aretz*, p. 30).

⊂ℑ৪৩

All souls are connected to the letters of the Torah. Therefore, when one engages in Torah study, properly upholds its commandments, and devotes himself to serving God, he elevates the souls that are related to the Torah he studies (ibid. *Lech Lecha*, s.v. *V'es*, p. 38).

⊂ℑ৪৩

According to divine providence, a person must travel from place to place in order to elevate the holy sparks. As the verse states: "A man's footsteps are established by God, and He shall favor his way" (Psalms 37:23). The terms "footsteps" and "his way" appear to be redundant. However, the Baal Shem Tov explained: "A man's footsteps are established by God" — for God causes a person to travel to a certain place, although he thinks he is going there for his own reasons. Nevertheless, "He shall favor his way." That is, God desires his benefit. God wishes to rectify the person's soul by enabling him to elevate the holy sparks found in that place. Therefore, God accomplishes His own plan and purpose, despite the person's mundane reasons for going there (ibid. *Vayak'hel,* s.v, *"Nach'zor l'inyaneinu..."* p. 212).

∽◦∾

There is a type of *deveikus* (attachment to God) that is brought about by taking the holy sparks that have fallen to lower levels and binding them to the Creator. This is the mystical meaning of the teaching that eating in holiness is like bringing a sacrifice in the Holy Temple. As our sages state: "A man's table is like the Altar" (*Chagigah* 27a), and, "Since the destruction of the Holy Temple, a man's table effects atonement for him" (*Berachos* 55a). One must elevate the holy sparks and the divine life force garbed within food and drink. This life force is experienced as the taste of one's food, for the taste is spiritual, not physical. When a person eats, the divine life force remains within him, increasing and adding to his own vital soul, which is a "portion of Godliness Above" (Job 31:2); with that power and strength he serves God, speaking words with *deveikus* and performing commandments with *deveikus*. And all this is by virtue of the increased vitality he has gained from the food. This brings about the ascent of the holy spark that was contained therein. The external aspect of the food is expelled after the life force has been removed. Its beauty and attractiveness were due to the life force; lacking this, it becomes repulsive, like a corpse (ibid. *Emor,* s.v. *V'hinei noda,* p. 246, abridged).

∽◦∾

While eating, one should meditate upon the inner aspect (*p'nimius*); that is, one's entire intention should be for the sake of Heaven, in order to fulfill the verse, "Know Him in all your ways" (Proverbs 3:6). This is the secret of *da'as* (enlightenment): to realize that nothing exists apart from God and His service. Indeed, through [the very object or situation that seems estranged from the spiritual] one becomes bound to God.

When [approached in this manner,] one's eating is comparable to a sacrifice in the Holy Temple. In so doing, one offers up the portions of holiness from the lower levels of creation to their Supernal Source. One also causes the divine soul within him to attain a more profound experience of *deveikus*. The Creator derives great delight when the lower levels draw closer to Him. This is why the Moshiach has been delayed so long: all the holy sparks must be elevated[32] (ibid. *Emor*, s.v. *V'hinei b'eis*, p. 246).

∞

The entire universe and all that fills it was formed by the divine speech, "and all the celestial hosts by the breath of His mouth" (Psalms 33:6). Through the divine speech all things came into being, from the smallest to the greatest. It sustains and gives life to them, as the verse states, "And You give life to them all" (Nechemiah 9:6). If not for the divine life force within an object, it immediately would cease to exist.

However, as a result of the Shattering of the Vessels, as well as the sin of Adam and the sins of subsequent generations, many fallen sparks of souls became clothed in the things of this world, [particularly] in the various types of food and drink derived from the various species. Nothing in this world exists that does not contain a holy spark, which was emanated from the divine speech, and this spark within each element of creation is its animating force (ibid. *Matos*, s.v. *L'havin ha-inyan*, pp. 280-281).

∞

One who strives to serve God must gaze upon the inner aspect of the words he speaks. All his deeds should be for the sake of Heaven, including his eating and drinking, in order to elevate the holy sparks from the state of being "shattered," from exile and captivity, to their source in the realm of holiness. [This is accomplished particularly] through the blessings one recites, for in this manner one "crowns" the Creator [by recognizing His benevolence]. Afterwards, one serves God with the energy derived from

---

32. Cf. *Tzafnas Pane'ach*, *Shemos*, citing the Baal Shem Tov.

the food, speaking words of holiness, and causing the energy to enter his words. Thus, one binds his mind to the Supernal Speech, and through this, the fallen letters, which are the holy sparks, ascend (ibid. *Matos*, s.v. *Al kein tzarich,* p. 10).

5

Animals and Reincarnation

To many Jews, reincarnation is a foreign concept, more commonly associated with Eastern religions. The immortality of the soul and resurrection of the dead are fundamental Jewish beliefs,[1] but not once does the Talmud or Midrash openly mention reincarnation.[2] Thus, many early authorities did not accept this doctrine. Rav Saadia Gaon (882-942), head of the Babylonian Academy at Sura and the first post-Talmudic arbiter of rabbinic creed, devotes less than four pages to a critique of reincarnation in his *Emunos V'De'os* ("Beliefs and Opinions"). One of this doctrine's most compelling features is that it offers a cogent explanation for the suffering and premature death of

---

1. *Mishneh Torah, Hilchos Teshuvah* 3:6; Rambam, *Perush al HaMishnah, Sanhedrin* 10:1; *Emunos V'De'os, Ma'amar* 6:4, *Ma'amar* 7 (also cf. variant version); *Kuzari* 1:109-111; *Zohar* I: 114a, II: 108b, III: 216a; *Derech Hashem* 1:3:9-13, 1:4:2, 2:2:4. Talmudic sources include *Sanhedrin* 90a-91b, citing various scriptural verses; *Berachos* 18b; *Kesubos* 111b; *Eiruvin* 19a; *Yerushalmi Kilayim* 9:3; et al. Observant Jews profess their faith in these two interrelated doctrines three times a day in the second blessing of the *Shemoneh Esrei* prayer. For further study, see R. Aryeh Kaplan's *Immortality, Resurrection, and the Age of the Universe* (Ktav, 1993), which includes R. Yaakov Elman's translation of the *Tiferes Yisrael's* profound sermon on death and the afterlife, *D'rush Or ha-Hayyim* (originally delivered in Danzig, 1842).
2. However, the *Maharsha* (R. Shmuel Eliezer Edeles, 1555-1631) does understand the Talmud to allude cryptically to reincarnation; see his *Chiddushei Aggados* on *Niddah* 69b, s.v. *she'sha'alu gimmel divrei aggada.* I am grateful to R. Chaim Kramer for this reference. R. Moshe Alshech on Job 16:25 understands the Talmudic story of R. Elazar ben Pedas in *Taanis* 25a as alluding to reincarnation. In *Galya Raza* (p. 306), R. Avraham of Safed sees a reference to reincarnation in the Talmud's remark, "Pinchas is Elijah" (*Bava Metzia* 14b, and Rashi, s.v. *lav kohen mar*). This interpretation is shared by R. Velvel of Brisk and many other authorities.

young children.[3] However, Rav Saadia summarily dismisses this rationale, arguing that it is more reasonable to believe that the Merciful One compensates these unfortunates for their sufferings in the afterlife. He also examines several scriptural verses commonly cited in support of reincarnation, which he refutes through exegetical analysis.[4] Rav Saadia's critique is shared by medieval philosophers Rabbi Chisdai Crescas (1340-1415), author of *Ohr Hashem*,[5] and his famous disciple, Rabbi Yosef Albo (1380-1444), author of *Sefer HaIkkarim*,[6] while the preeminent codifier Rabbi Moses Maimonides (1135-1204) fails to mention the subject.

Yet today the doctrine of reincarnation is accepted by virtually all authorities, representing Sefardim (Jews of Middle Eastern descent) and Ashkenazim (Jews of European descent), Chassidim and Misnagdim (their one-time opponents). The Baal Shem Tov (1698-1760), founder of the Chassidic movement, reinforced this already widespread belief among the masses of his time and place. And the Vilna Gaon (1720-1798), one of the most revered sages in the non-Chassidic world, wrote an entire commentary on the Book of Jonah as an allegory for reincarnation.[7] The concept also figures prominently in the writings of

---

3. This rationale is cited by R. Yechiel Michel Epstein in his *Kitzur Shelah* (Ashdod, 1998), *Inyan S'char Va'Onesh*, p. 62, based upon earlier sources, e.g. R. Yitzchak of Acco, *Me'iras Einayim* (Jerusalem, 1993), *Bereishis*, s.v. *Da ki yon'kei shadayim hameisim*, p. 47; R. Chaim Vital, *Sefer Likkutim, Mishpatim* 3, *Koheles* 4. It is also a common motif in Kabbalistic stories, particularly those of the Baal Shem Tov and his followers. R. Chaim Vital in *Sha'ar HaGilgulim, Hakdamah* 38, extends this idea to explain the phenomenon of child prodigies. However, the rabbis also give other reasons for the suffering and premature death of children, including atonement for the sins of the generation; see *Shabbos* 33b; *Zohar* III: 17b; *Likkutei Moharan* 1:282 (end); also cf. Ramban, *Toras HaAdam* 26a, 73b, 76a; *Nishmas Chaim* 4:11, no. 2, 3.

4. *Emunos V'De'os, Maamar* 6:8, which actually heaps scorn upon those who maintain this belief. Although Rav Saadia Gaon's writings do not mention Kabbalistic works or concepts, the Chida (citing *Matzref L'Chochmah*) states that Rav Saadia was conversant with them; cf. *Shem HaGedolim, "Saadia,"* 2. The illustrious Rav Sherira Gaon (906-1006) and his son, Rav Hai Gaon (938-1038), both possessed deep knowledge of Kabbalah; however, their views on reincarnation are not known to us.

5. *Ohr Hashem, Ma'amar* 4, *D'rush* 7; for biography, see Goldwurm, *The Rishonim* (1991), pp. 108-109.

6. *Sefer HaIkkarim, Ma'amar* 4, *Perek* 29; for biography, see *The Rishonim*, p. 112.

7. In English translation, see R. Aaron Werner, *Three Beacons on Jonah* (Jerusalem 1979); also cf. R. Moshe Schapiro, *The Book of Yonah: Journey of the Soul* (Artscroll / Mesorah 2000), based upon *Aderes Eliyahu*.

the legendary Sefardic sage known as the Ben Ish Chai (Rabbi Yosef Chaim of Baghdad, 1834-1909). What caused this seemingly radical "amendment" of normative rabbinic theology? The answer is: the dissemination of Kabbalah.

The "Reincarnation" of Reincarnation

Although the "secrets of the Torah" were preserved by various elites throughout the Mishnaic-Talmudic and Geonic periods (roughly 200 b.c.e.-1000 c.e.), the major texts that explicitly endorse the belief in reincarnation were not widely known until the era of the Rishonim (medieval authorities). Prior to what today is considered the classical period of the Kabbalah, the predominant orientation of many Spanish-Jewish scholars was, albeit qualifiedly, philosophical. The affluent and relatively tolerant society of 9th century Spain under the Cordovan caliphs was fertile soil for the cross-pollination of ideas; thus, Greek concepts also found their way into the world of Jewish thought.[8] This intellectual climate persisted for several centuries until the advent of the conquering Almohades (Arabic: al-Muwahidin, an Islamic fundamentalist sect) during the mid-1100s.[9] In the wake of harsh persecutions of the Jews, the quasi–Aristotelian rationalism of Rabbi Avraham ibn Ezra (1089-1164) and Maimonides began to be displaced by the mystical worldview of the Kabbalah.

Evidence of this shift may be seen in the writings of 13th century Spain's foremost rabbinic leader, Nachmanides (R. Moshe ben Nachman,

---

8. Goldwurm, *The Rishonim,* Historical Introduction, pp. 20-21. The influence of Greek philosophy upon many Torah scholars during this period also elicited pointed opposition, e.g. Rav Hai Gaon on *Chagigah* 14b (in *Ein Yaakov*). The critique of philosophy is echoed by *Teshuvos HaRivash,* no. 45; *Teshuvos Chavas Yair,* no. 210; *Teshuvos HaRashba,* no. 419; *Teshuvos HaRosh,* no. 25; *Sefer HaYashar* 6:13; R. Ovadiah of Bartinuro on *Mishnah Sanhedrin* 10:1; Maharal of Prague, *Hakdamah Sheniyah* to *Gevuros Hashem,* et passim; R. Shlomo Luria, *Yam Shel Shlomo, Hakdamah* to tractate *Bava Kamma;* R. Yeshaya Horowitz, *Shnei Luchos HaBris, Maseches Shavuos* II, 92b, ff. R. Pinchas Eliyahu Horowitz of Vilna, *Sefer HaBris* I, *Ma'amar* 2: *Chug HaShamayim,* sec. 6, 9, et passim; *Be'ur HaGra* on *Yoreh De'ah* 179:13; R. Nachman of Breslov, *Chayei Moharan,* 407-423, with *hashmatos,* et passim; *Sichos HaRan,* 5, 40, 102; R. Zvi Hirsch of Ziditchov, *Sur MeRah V'Aseh Tov,* p. 65 (with *hagahah* of R. Zvi Elimelech Spira of Dinov), and pp. 95-111.
9. *The Rishonim,* pp. 20-23.

1194-1270). The latter's biblical commentary often cites the *Sefer HaBahir*, which he calls the "Midrash of Rabbi Nechuniah ben HaKanah."[10] Attributed to this first century Talmudic saint and his school, the *Bahir* is one of the oldest works extant that advances the belief in reincarnation. The commentaries of Rabbi Menachem Recanati (1223-1290)[11] and Rabbeinu Bachaya ben Asher (1263-1340) reflect an orientation similar to that of Nachmanides;[12] and the number of scholars who share their viewpoint increases exponentially in subsequent generations. Thus, the doctrine of reincarnation, although of esoteric origin, came to be recognized as an authentic part of the unbroken chain of transmission that begins with the biblical prophets and continues through the Talmudic sages, until the present day.[13]

Although questioned by scholars due to the relative absence of early manuscripts, this assertion of the antiquity of reincarnation as a normative belief is not unfounded. Among the ancients, reincarnation played an important role in the thought of Pythagoras (582-507 b.c.e.),

10. Nachmanides cites the *Bahir* in his commentary on Genesis 1:1, 38:29, 46:1; Exodus 2:25, 15:27, 20:8; Leviticus 23:40, 26:16; Numbers 15:31; Deuteronomy 16:20, 22:6 (end), 33:12, 33:23; as well as in other works. He mentions reincarnation in his *Sha'ar HaGemul*, p. 275 and 279 (chap. 5, end); *Perush HaRamban* on Genesis 38:8; *Perush HaRamban* on Job 33:29-30; also cf. *Hakdamah*. Concerning the line of transmission for the Spanish school of Kabbalah, R. Menachem Recanati states: "Elijah [the Prophet] revealed himself to R. David, head of the Rabbinical Court, and taught him the wisdom of the Kabbalah. He taught this to his son, the Ravad (R. Avraham ben David of Posquières, 1120-1198), and he also experienced a revelation of Elijah. The tradition was passed on to his son, R. Isaac the Blind, who was blind from birth, and to whom Elijah also revealed himself. He gave the tradition to two disciples, the first being R. Ezra, who wrote a commentary on the Song of Songs, and the second was R. Azriel [of Gerona]. From them, it was given over to the Ramban (Nachmanides)" (*Perush HaRecanati, Naso*, 36d, as translated in R. Aryeh Kaplan's *Meditation and the Kabbalah*, chap. 6, p. 207).
11. *Perush HaRecanati* mentions both reincarnation and *ibbur* ("impregnation" of the soul of a living person by that of a deceased person) in *Vayeishev* 64b and *Pinchas* 189a (see commentary *Even Yekarah*, beg.), et passim. The Recanati quotes the *Zohar* and *Bahir* extensively.
12. Rabbenu Bachaya mentions reincarnation in his commentary on *Vayishlach* 38:1; also see ibid. *Toldos HaMechaber* (preface), "*Rimazei HaKabbalah B'Divrei Chazal*," Vol. 1, p. 8 (Jerusalem 1995 ed.).
13. R. Meir ibn Gabbai, *Avodas HaKodesh* II: 32 states that the doctrine of reincarnation was given at Mount Sinai; also cf. Ramak, *Pardes Rimonim, Sha'ar* 31:7; idem, *Shiur Komah, Perek* 4, p. 166. Regarding the chain of transmission in general, see R. Meir Zvi Bergman, *Gateway to the Talmud*, chaps. 1-7.

the revolutionary Greek mathematician and philosopher-mystic. According to the historian Josephus Flavius (37-93 c.e.) and other Jewish sources, Pythagoras received certain traditions of the prophets of Israel.[14] Rabbi Yaakov Emden (1698-1776) specifically states that the doctrine of reincarnation was part of that esoteric Jewish wisdom.[15] One may object that such inferences cannot take the place of hard facts. However, it must be remembered that this body of knowledge was highly restricted, even among the greatest scholars. The Talmud itself attests to this, stating that it is forbidden to teach *Ma'aseh Merkavah* (i.e., the "hidden teachings") even to one student, unless he is sufficiently learned in the "revealed teachings," and wise enough to have intuited these truths on his own.[16] Therefore, it should not be surprising that only a few of the ancient

---

14. *The Complete Works of Josephus* (Kergel, 1981), "Wars of the Jews," Book 2, chap. 8, pp. 478, 637; ibid. "Against Apion," Book 1, chap. 22, p. 614; also cf. R. Eliyahu de Vidas, *Reishis Chochmah, Sha'ar HaYirah* 13:80, *Sha'ar HaAhavah* 6:42; R. Eliezer Azkari, *Sefer Chareidim*, chap. 33 (end); R. Menachem Azariah of Fano, *Asarah Ma'amaros, Ma'amar Olam Katan*, 4. This also would explain certain similarities between Pythagorean mysticism and that of the *Sefer Yetzirah*, a Kabbalistic text of major importance attributed to the Patriarch Abraham (although R. Saadia Gaon in his commentary asserts that it was arranged in its present form at a later period); cf. R. Aryeh Kaplan, *Sefer Yetzirah: The Book of Creation*, Introduction, p. xvii.
15. *Migdal Oz, Aliyos HaGilgulim.*
16. Concerning the restrictions imposed by the Talmudic sages in teaching the *Ma'aseh Merkavah*, see *Chagigah* 11b, 13a, 14b; *Kiddushin* 71a; *Gittin* 60b. This reticence surely extended to the discussion of reincarnation. Even later Kabbalists who share this belief disagree about the propriety of its dissemination; e.g., *Emek HaMelech* (*Hakdamah* 2, *Perek* 2) by R. Naftali Herz Bacharach (17th century), strongly advocates publicizing the doctrine, as does R. Yom Tov Lipman Heller of Prague (1579-1654), the celebrated author of *Tosefos Yom Tov* on the Mishnah, in his approbation for *Emek HaMelech*. By contrast, R. Levi ben Yaakov ibn Chaviv (1485-1545), son of the compiler of *Ein Yaakov* on the Aggadata and the commentary *HaKoseiv*, cautions against openly discussing such matters in *Teshuvos Ralbach*, chap. 8.
   As modern people living in an open society, we are unaccustomed to intellectual restrictions. We may wonder: what were the Talmudic sages afraid of? One basic concern was the inevitable confusion of intellectual and religious boundaries. The Rabbis, too, lived among a host of diverse Jewish and non-Jewish religious sects, and were well acquainted with the thought of many Greek and Roman philosophers. The Rabbis fully realized that in the hands of those who lacked faith in God and Torah, Jewish mystical ideas would be taken from their proper context and grafted onto foreign systems of thought. Thus, the wisdom of the prophets and the *tzaddikim* would be misunderstood, and their esoteric practices misused.

mystical texts mentioned in the Talmud and in the *Zohar* have come down to us.[17]

Reincarnation in Early Kabbalah

Despite the Talmud's reticence about the subject, the *Bahir* discusses reincarnation quite openly. Written in the terse style of the Midrash, it contains many of the key concepts discussed in more technical language and at greater length in medieval Kabbalistic works. Concerning the transmigration of souls, the *Bahir* offers the following scriptural interpretation:

> Rabbi Pinchas cited the verse, "A generation goes, and a generation comes" (Ecclesiastes 1:4). Rabbi Akiva said, "A generation comes (Hebrew: *bah*) — it already came (*bah*)."[18]

The Hebrew verb *bah* can denote either present or past tense; hence, Rabbi Akiva infers that the Book of Ecclesiastes alludes to reincarnation. The *Bahir* goes on to discuss the main reason for reincarnation: the purification of the soul for past spiritual failings, a process that it compares to laundering unclean garments. (The essence of the soul cannot be sullied, being utterly bound to God.) This process may be quite

---

17. The Talmud mentions the *Sefer Yetzirah* (still extant, according to some opinions) and a lengthy tract on idolatry which has been lost, both written by the Patriarch Abraham; see *Shabbos* 156a, *Chagigah* 13a, *Avodah Zarah* 14b, *Sanhedrin* 65b; *Yerushalmi Pe'ah* 1:1, *Yerushalmi Sanhedrin* 7:13 (ms. version). Regarding the occult knowledge Abraham gave to the sons of his concubines, see *Sanhedrin* 91b and *Zohar* I, 99b; the latter states that this is the source of certain Eastern mystical traditions. *The Greater and Lesser Hechalos* from the first century c.e are still extant; cf. R. Aryeh Kaplan's *Sefer Yetzirah: The Book of Creation*, Introduction. Several lost mystical texts mentioned in the *Zohar* include *Sifra D'Chanoch, Sifra D'Adam Kadma'ah, Sifra D'Rav Yaivi Sabba, Sifra D'Rav Yaisi Sabba, Sifra D'Rabbi Kruspedai Chamid Liba, Sifra D'Rav Hamnuna Sabba;* see R. Meir Zvi Bergman, *Gateway to the Talmud*, chap. 11, p. 115.
18. *Bahir* 121; also cf. 122, 155, 184, 185. This teaching also appears in the *Zohar, Eikev (Raya Mehemna)*, 273a; R. Yitzchak of Acco, *Me'iras Einayim, Bereishis*, s.v. *V'sod ha-mekubal*, p. 43; R. Chaim Vital, *Sha'ar HaGilgulim, Hakdamah* 9; et al. R. Moshe Alshech finds numerous scriptural allusions to reincarnation, e.g. "If a man dies, will he live [again]? All the days of my life I will wait, until the coming of my replacement" (ibid. 14:14), et passim.

time-consuming. In fact, the *Bahir* intimates that a soul may be reincarnated as many as a thousand times.[19]

The *Zohar* frequently discusses reincarnation. Rabbi Moshe de Léon (1250-1305) of Guadalajara, Spain, brought to light this collection of mystical teachings from the school of Talmudic sage Rabbi Shimon Bar Yochai during the 1290s, and its influence on subsequent generations has been immeasurable.[20] Like the *Bahir*, the *Zohar* was composed for a select group of disciples during the Roman persecutions, when the chain of transmission (*mesorah*) was in danger of being lost. Under such circumstances, it was deemed permissible to commit the mystical teachings to writing, albeit in cryptic form, in order to preserve them.[21] (Also, there seems to have been a Messianic agenda behind the dissemination of these writings at that moment in history.)[22]

The *Zohar* explains many facets of reincarnation hitherto unknown beyond a small circle of initiates. For example, it discusses several reasons for reincarnation: the moral obligation to repay a debt;[23] the unwillingness or inability of a couple to bear children;[24] and, again, the need to cleanse the soul of impurity.[25] The *Zohar* also reveals the

---

19. *Bahir* 195; also cf. R. Moshe Cordovero, *Shiur Komah, Inyan Gilgul*, sec. 84 (p. 167); *Sha'ar HaGilgulim, Hakdamah* 4; R. Avraham Azulai, *Chesed L'Avraham* 5:19.

20. See R. Avraham Zacuto (1448-1515) citing R. Yitzchak of Acco (1240-1295), *Sefer HaYuchsin*, Vol. I, p. 29 (Constantinople, 1510 ed.). The relevant passages and anecdotal material may be found in English translation in R. Aryeh Kaplan's *Meditation and Kabbalah* (Northvale, NJ: Jason Aronson 1995), pp. 147-154.

21. In general, the permissibility of writing down the Oral Torah (*Torah She'b'al Peh*) is based upon the verse, "It is time to act for God; they have breached His Torah" (Psalms 119:126). See Rashi on *Gittin* 60b, s.v. *U'devarim she'b'al peh*; Ritva on *Gittin* 60b; Ran on *Megillah* 14a, s.v. *Amar lei* (end); *Perishah* on *Orach Chaim* 49:1; *Shevilei Emunah* 8 (80a); Rambam, *Hakdamah* to *Mishneh Torah*. This same principle is invoked by the *Zohar, Naso*, 128a; also cf. *Chayei Moharan*, 419.

22. The *Zohar* states that its teachings should be revealed in preparation for the Messianic Redemption 1,200 years after the destruction of the Holy Temple, which took place in 70 c.e.; see *Zohar* II, *Shemos*, 9b. It further states: "Because Israel is destined to taste of the Tree of Life, which is this *Sefer HaZohar*, she will go out from her exile with mercy" (*Naso, Raya Mehemna*, 124b); also cf. *Likkutei Moharan* I, *Hashmatah* ("*L'chu chazu*"); *Likkutei Halachos, Minchah*, 7:56; *Chayei Moharan*, 189.

23. *Zohar* II: 98a.

24. *Zohar* I: 91b, 186b; II: 105b, 106a, 186b.

25. *Zohar Chadash, Ki Setzei* (96b); for further discussions of reincarnation in the *Zohar*, see I: 187b, 194a; II: 91b, 99b, 100a, 111a; Vol. III: 88b, 116b, 182b, 213a, 216a, et passim.

underlying purpose of the legal procedure known as levirate marriage (*yibbum*) to be the spiritual benefit of the deceased husband, who consequently will be reborn as the son of his brother and former wife. This interpretation often recurs in later mystical works.[26] The *Tikkunei Zohar* from the same school (although not widely circulated until the 16th century by the Safed Kabbalists) describes a number of physical irregularities indicating that a person bears a reincarnated soul.[27] However, rather than presenting these teachings in a coherent manner, the *Bahir* and the Zoharic writings mention them as scattered topics of discussion in various contexts. The task of articulating this doctrine as a systematic and sustained thesis was left to the Ari (Rabbi Yitzchak Luria, 1534-1572) and his closest disciple, Rabbi Chaim Vital (1543-1620). The latter's *Sha'ar HaGilgulim* ("Gate of Reincarnation") remains the most theologically developed and detailed work on the subject in Kabbalistic literature.[28]

26. *Zohar* I: 92a, 96b, 187b; *Zohar* II: 99b-101b; *Zohar* III: 167a, 177a, 181a, 215bff, 281a; *Tikkunei Zohar, Tikkun* 47 (83b). This concept also is discussed at length in subsequent Kabbalistic works, e.g. Ramban on *Bereishis* 38:8 (Chavel Hebrew ed. pp. 214-215); R. Yitzchak of Acco, *Me'iras Einayim, Bereishis*, p. 43, 47; *Sefer HaKanah, Sod HaChalitzah*, pp. 250-256; Ramak, *Ohr Yakar al HaZohar, Vayeishev, Sha'ar* 8:6:6, 81a; ibid. *Ki Seitzei*, sec. 32, 163a; ibid. *Saba*, sec. 7, pp. 30-31; ibid. *Raya Mehemna, Sha'ar* 3:16:16, pp. 140-141; R. Chaim Vital, *Eitz Chaim, Sha'ar HaMelachim*, 6:54a; idem, *Sha'ar HaPesukim, Devarim* 39b-40a, *Tehillim* 48a; idem, *Sha'ar HaGilgulim, Hakdamah* 2, 3, 29; *Zohar HaRaki'a* 97a, 107b-108a; also see anonymous, *Galya Raza*, p. 306; R. Moshe Alshech on Job 14:1; R. Nachman of Breslov, *Likkutei Moharan* 1, 21:6; R. Nosson Sternhartz, *Likkutei Halachos, S'chiras Po'alim* 2:4.

27. *Tikkunei Zohar, Tikkun* 70 (137b-138a); for further discussion of reincarnation in the *Tikkunei Zohar*, see *Tikkun* 6 (22b, 23a-b), *Tikkun* 10 (132b), *Tikkun* 32 (76b), *Tikkun* 69 (99b, 110b, 115a); *Tikkun* 70 (131a, 132b, 133a, 136b), et passim. The pioneering scientific researcher into reincarnation, Dr. Ian Stevenson of the University of Virginia, discovered a correspondence between birthmarks and mortal injuries a number of his subjects claimed to remember from previous lifetimes; see *Twenty Cases Suggestive of Reincarnation*, pp. 91-105, 149-171, 231-269, 381-385, et passim. Stevenson addresses this subject in his later works, as well.

28. Another version of this material with a similar title, *Sefer HaGilgulim*, which the Chida assumes to have been edited by R. Meir Poppers (1624-1662), was available in Europe during the early Chassidic period. However, the *Sha'ar HaGilgulim* edited by R. Chaim Vital's son, R. Shmuel Vital, was not. Preserved for almost three centuries by the leading Sefardic Kabbalists, the latter was first published in Jerusalem, 1863. Similarly, the Chassidic masters possessed R. Meir's *Pri Eitz Chaim*, widely circulated in manuscript and first published in Koretz, 1782, but not the *Sha'ar HaKavanos*, edited by R. Shmuel Vital and first published in Salonika, 1852. Related works include *Gilgulei Neshamos* by R. Menachem Azariah of Fano (Jerusalem, reprinted 1978) and the more recent compendium *Toras Nosson: Shorashei Neshamos* (Bnei

The Blessing of Mortality

To understand the purpose of reincarnation according to Jewish mysticism, we must consider the ultimate purpose of death — and of life. The Torah is a life-affirming doctrine. Indeed, it teaches us that in the original divine scheme, death had no place. Adam and Eve were created as immortal beings; death came into existence only as the result of sin — and for the sake of its *tikkun*. (Thus, when the Children of Israel stood together at Mount Sinai to receive the Torah, the curse of death was removed from them. This condition lasted until the sin of the Golden Calf.)[29]

Yet there is a seemingly positive allusion to death at the end of the biblical account of the sixth day of creation. The verse states, "And God saw all that He had made, and behold it was very good" (Genesis 1:31), upon which the Midrash remarks that the term "very" (Hebrew: *me'od*) alludes to death.[30] The mortal condition is "very good," because, death is the gate through which the spiritual damage brought about by our misdeeds is repaired. Through death, we gain the eternal life of the World to Come.[31] This is the spiritual dimension in which we may attain the purpose for which we were created: the direct experience of Godliness. Concerning this, the Prophet Isaiah declares, "All Israel has a place in the World to Come."[32] Indeed, rabbinic tradition states that righteous non-Jews also merit a place in the World to Come.[33] Even animals receive divine recompense for their sufferings.[34]

In his classic treatise on the afterlife, *Sha'ar HaGemul* ("The Gate of Reward"), Nachmanides explains that what generally is called the "World to Come" (*Olam HaBah*) consists of two stages: the World of Souls (*Olam HaNeshamos*) and the World of the Resurrection (*Olam HaTechiyah*).[35] After experiencing the bliss of the former, the dead will be

---

Brak, no date) by R. Nosson Zvi Kenig. Aside from *Sefer HaGilgulim* and *Sha'ar HaGilgulim*, the writings of the Ari are replete with discussions of reincarnation in various contexts.

29. *Shabbos* 146a.
30. *Bereishis Rabbah* 9:5, 6.
31. *Bereishis Rabbah* 9:10, 12; also cf. *Emunos V'De'os, Ma'amar* 6:4.
32. Isaiah 60:21; *Mishneh Torah, Teshuvah* 3:5; *Derech Hashem* I, 3:3, 4; et al.

restored to life in their previous bodies, which during the interim have been cleansed of spiritual impurity. Thus all worthy beings will live in a perfected world, according to the Creator's original intention.[36] However, in order to attain this goal we must use our time in this world to proper advantage. Only in this world can we create the spiritual "vessels" capable of receiving the divine light. These vessels are formed by repudiating evil and choosing the good, and by fulfilling the Torah's commandments.[37] This may seem a nearly impossible task. If, however, we fail, all is not lost. We may be given another chance through reincarnation.

---

33. *Sanhedrin* 105a; *Yalkut, Melachim* II, 296; *Tanna D'vei Eliyahu* 20:6; *Pirkei D'Rabbi Eliezer* 34; *Mishneh Torah, Hilchos Teshuvah* 3:5, *Hilchos Eidus* 11:10; Meiri on *Sanhedrin* 57a; *Zohar* II, *Pekudei*, 268a. This material has been translated to English in my *Compassion for Humanity in the Jewish Tradition* (1998).

34. R. Saadia Gaon, *Emunos V'De'os, Ma'amar* 3:10; R. Sherira Gaon, *Teshuvos HaGeonim*, Vol. 1, 375. Also cf. Abarbanel on Hoshea 2:18; R. Nosson Sternhartz, *Likkutei Halachos, Nezikin* 2:6 (translated in the sources for Chapter 2, "Eden and the Messianic Era"); R. Moshe (Cheifetz) Gentili, *M'leches Machsheves, Noach*, s.v. *vayizkor Elokim es Noach ve-es kol ha-chayah ve-es kol ha-behemah*. I am grateful to R. Bezalel Naor for showing me this source.

35. *Sha'ar HaGemul* 9-12, citing various scriptural and rabbinic sources; cf. Ramchal, *Ma'amar HaIkkarim, "BaGemul"* ("Reward and Punishment"); idem, *Derech Hashem* 1:3:11.

36. *Sanhedrin* 91a. There is a dispute among the post-Talmudic authorities concerning the Resurrection and the World to Come. Some consider the Resurrection to be the ultimate reward, since both body and soul will experience it; see Ramban in *Sha'ar HaGemul* 11, 12, citing *Emunos V'De'os* 7:8; similarly cf. *Zohar* I, *Vayeira* (*Midrash HaNe'elam*), 114a, 116b; *Zohar* III, *Pinchas*, 216a; Ritva on *Rosh Hashanah* 16b; Ravad on *Mishneh Torah, Teshuvah* 8:2; R. Yeshaya Horowitz, *Shnei Luchos HaBris, Beis David* I: 31b; Ramchal, *Derech Hashem* 1:3:9, 11; Chida, *Avodas HaKodesh* 2:42-43; R. Menachem M. Schneersohn of Lubavitch (Tzemach Tzedek) , *Derech Mitzvosecha, Tzitzis*, 14b. Others maintain that the ultimate reward will be the entirely spiritual life of the World to Come; esp. Rambam, *Mishneh Torah, Teshuvah* 8:2 and *Igeres Techiyas HaMeisim*; also cf. *Tanchuma, Vayikra* 8; *Kuzari* 1:115, 3:20, 21; *Chovos HaLevavos* 4:4:6; *Ohr Hashem* (Crescas) 3:4:2; *Sefer HaIkkarim* 4:30, 33. The Kabbalists subscribe to the first opinion.

37. *Chesed L'Avraham*, 4:4, citing *Zohar* II, *Pekudei*, 229b, states that the Torah and its commandments create a spiritual lens (*aspaklaria*) through which to perceive the divine light.

The Commandments and Reincarnation

In the *Sha'ar HaGilgulim*, R. Chaim Vital states in the name of the Ari that every Jew must perform all 613 commandments to attain *tikkun ha-neshamah*, perfection of the soul.[38] (Exceptions to this rule include those precepts related to the Holy Temple that we cannot fulfill at present, and those performed only under special circumstances, such as the commandment of *shilu'ach ha'ken* sending away the mother bird. Also, as a rule, women are exempt from time-bound commandments.)[39] If one succeeds, he or she returns to the spiritual level of Adam and Eve in the Garden of Eden, prior to the first sin — and even higher. For our sages tell us, "The place where penitents (*baalei teshuvah*) stand is superior to that of perfect tzaddikim."[40]

Why is such cosmic import ascribed to the performance of the commandments? In the previous chapter, we discussed the primordial light of creation that was hidden away for the righteous in the World to Come. Where was it hidden? "In the Torah," the Baal Shem Tov declares.[41] The Torah can "hold" the light of creation, because it is the very divine will and wisdom that animates all things; as the Midrash figuratively says, "God looked into the Torah and created the world."[42] According to its wisdom, all that transpires is determined, and all beings receive life. Thus, the Torah may be described as the "genetic code" of creation.

---

38. *Sha'ar HaGilgulim, Hakdamah* 3, et passim; also cf. *Sha'ar HaMitzvos, Hakdamah; Sha'arei Kedushah* 1:1, 2:3 (end); *Tikkunei Zohar, Tikkun* 70 (132a); *Sefer HaTanya, Igeres HaKodesh,* Letter 7 (112a) and Letter 29 (148b); R. Yitzchak Isaac Weiss of Spinka, *Chakal Yitzchak,* 131d.
39. *Sha'ar HaGilgulim, Hakdamah* 15, et passim; also cf. *Chakal Yitzchak, Bamidbar,* 118a, *Devarim,* 158c. For non-Jews, heeding the Seven Noahide Laws accomplishes this to a significant degree, therefore, their souls, too, must undergo reincarnation; see *Galya Raza,* pp. 307-309. However, the ultimate *tikkun* of all humanity and all creation depends primarily upon the divine service of the Jewish people by virtue of their devotion to performing the Torah's commandments; see *Derech Hashem* 2:4:6, 9. This *tikkun* will be completed during the Messianic age.
40. *Berachos* 34b; also cf. R. Nosson Sternhartz, *Likkutei Halachos, Geneivah,* 3:3; *Toras Nosson: Pardes* (based on *Likkutei Halachos*), *Zera'im, Berachos* 265.
41. *Sefer Baal Shem Tov, Bereishis,* 27, citing *Degel Machaneh Ephraim.* Although the Baal Shem Tov is best known for this saying, the concept derives from the Midrash and *Zohar;* see Chapter 4, "Creation and the Holy Sparks," n. 2.
42. *Bereishis Rabbah* 1:2, 8:2; *Zohar* I, *Toldos,* 134a; ibid. *Terumah,* 161a-b.

We also have described the primordial light of creation as "God's *tallis*" or outer garment. To carry this metaphor one step further, we must say that God's *tallis* has *tzitzis*, the specially tied fringes mandated by the Book of Numbers, on each of its four corners. Kabbalistically, the four corners of a *tallis* allude to the four letters of the Essential Divine Name, *Yud-Hey-Vav-Hey.*[43] These four letters in turn give rise to the four "worlds" of *Atzilus* (Emanation), *Beriah* (Creation), *Yetzirah* (Formation), and *Asiyah* (Action).[44] The *tzitzis*-fringes tied to each corner of a *tallis* allude to the dimension of Torah that animates each of these four worlds. This concept is underscored by the fact that the *gematria* (numerical value) of the word *tzitzis* is 600; together with its eight strings and five knots, this adds up to 613, the number of biblically prescribed commandments. Also, the Torah states of the *tzitzis*, "And you shall look at them and remember all the commandments..." (Numbers 15:37-41). This teaches us that by performing the 613 commandments symbolized by the *tzitzis*, the Jewish people cause the Infinite Light to be revealed in a measured way.

By fulfilling the 613 commandments of the Torah, we may cleave to God through the very limitations of the temporal world. This cleaving (*deveikus*) accomplishes the purpose of creation — and in so doing, purifies and perfects creation. Thus, it follows that the number 613 corresponds to the structure of the body, the structure of the soul and her separate powers, as well as the structure of all the worlds.[45] By studying the Torah and performing its commandments, we bring all creation into accord with its supernal source. This is what the Kabbalists call the *aliyas*

---

43. Regarding the Essential Divine Name (*Shem HaEtzem*), see *Shnei Luchos HaBris* I, *Ma'amar Beis Hashem*, esp. sec. 4.

44. This is inferred from the verse: "All that was called [into existence] for the sake of My Name (YHVH): for My Glory (*Atzilus*) I have created it (*Beriah*), formed it (*Yetzirah*), and also made (i.e., completed) it (*Asiyah*)" (Isaiah 43:7). See *Tikkunei Zohar, Hakdamah*, 6b; *Pardes Rimonim* 19:2, 3; *Eitz Chaim* (*Heichal A-B-Y-A*) 42:1, 2; *Sha'arei Kedushah* 3:1; *Tanya, Igeres HaKodesh*, Letter 5, 108b; *Likkutei Halachos, Tola'im*, 4:3, 5; et al.

45. *Sha'arei Kedushah* 1:1,3, 2:3, 3:5; *Sha'ar HaGilgulim, Hakdamah* 4, 11, 16; *Sha'ar HaMitzvos, Hakdamah*. However, the attainment of divine wisdom also requires meditative practice; see *Sha'arei Kedushah* 3:5, 3:8; *K'savim Chadashim L'Rabbenu Chaim Vital* (Jerusalem, 1988), *Sha'arei Kedushah*, Part 4; *Sefer HaBris* II, 8:6, 11:7; *Ohr Ganuz L'Tzaddikim, B'ha'alosecha*, s.v, *Vay'hi binso'ah ha-aron; Likkutei Moharan* 1, 52 (which mentions both paths of action and contemplation), II: 100; et al.

ha'olamos, the spiritual elevation of all the "worlds": the transformation of separateness to Oneness, substance to Essence, and the incorporation of the finite into the Infinite Light (*Ohr Ein Sof*). Through the Torah, the primal unity of the cosmos is restored.

This is why every Jewish man and woman must fulfill all the commandments that apply to them in order to attain *tikkun ha-neshamah*; and, according to their differing abilities and circumstances, Jewish men are required to study all four levels of Torah: *p'shat* (simple meaning), *remez* (implied meaning), *drush* (homiletical meaning), and *sod* ("secret" or mystical meaning).[46] Otherwise, the vessels we have formed to perceive the "light hidden away for the tzaddikim" will be incomplete. To be sure, this is an extremely difficult task to accomplish in one lifetime; therefore, we must endure reincarnation until our duties have been fulfilled.[47] Even a completely evil person, the *Zohar* states, is given three incarnations to return to God; if he remains unrepentant, he forfeits his place in the World to Come.[48] Nevertheless, few souls come to such an unhappy fate; for the

---

46. *Sha'arei Kedushah* 1:2, s.v. *U'zchor v'al tishkach*; *Sha'ar HaMitzvos, Hakdamah*, s.v. *Gam b'inyan eisek haTorah*; R. Yehudah Ftayah, *Minchas Yehudah, Yirmiyahu*, 86 (p. 131), and *Tehillim*, 93 (p. 202). Kabbalistically, the formal obligation of Torah study is not incumbent upon women because their souls are considered more complete; see R. Aryeh Kaplan's essay "Male and Female," in *Immortality, Resurrection, and the Age of the Universe* (Ktav 1993), pp. 58-59; Maharal, *Drush al HaTorah* (included in *Be'er HaGolah*, 27a); R. Avraham Azulai, *Chesed L'Avraham, Mayan* 5, *Nahar* 20; also note R. Menachem M. Schneerson of Lubavitch, *Likkutei Sichos*, Vol. 31, *Yisro*.

47. *Sha'ar HaGilgulim, Hakdamah* 22, s.v. *Ki ki'm'at ein adam ba'aretz*; also cf. *Me'iras Einayim, Bereishis*, s.v. *V'im tirtzeh lir'os*, p. 48; *Chesed L'Avraham, Mayan* 2, *Nahar* 7; *Minchas Yehudah, Yechezkel*, 88 (pp. 190-191); *Likkutei Halachos, Basar B'chalav* 5:7, *Givi'as Chov MehaYesomim* 4:7. However, *Sha'ar HaGilgulim, Hakdamah* 14, explains that this only refers to the portion of the soul that did not attain its *tikkun* in a former life. Although reincarnation is an expression of divine mercy, it entails great risks. Instead of rectifying one's past misdeeds, one may get into even more trouble. For this reason the Ramak considers reincarnation "worse than Gehenna (Purgatory)"; see *Ohr Yakar al HaZohar, Mishpatim, Sha'ar* 6:1, *K'rach* 8 (pp. 249-250). R. Nachman of Breslov instructed his disciples to insist before the Heavenly Court that they "finish things over there," rather than decree further incarnations upon them (*Chayei Moharan* 446); also cf. R. Menachem Nachum of Chernobyl, *Me'or Einayim, Bamidbar*, s.v. *V'hinei Yisrael*.

48. *Zohar* II, *Yisro*, 91b; *Zohar* III, *Pinchas*, 216a; *Zohar Chadash, Ki Seitzei*, p. 107; *Tikkunei Zohar, Tikkun* 32 (76b); also cf. R. Yitzchak of Acco, *Me'iras Einayim, Bereishis* 4:1, p. 43; Ramak, *Pardes Rimonim* 6:2; *Ohr Yakar al HaZohar, Tikkunim, Sha'ar* 1:1, *K'rach* 1 (p. 5); *Ohr Yakar al Tikkunei Zohar, Bereishis, K'rach* 3, *Sha'ar* 1:14 (p. 32) and 1:19 (pp. 42-43); ibid. *K'rach* 3, *Sha'ar* 3:16 (p. 145); R. Eliezer Azkari, *Sefer*

Merciful One "devises ways that the banished will not remain estranged from Him" (II Samuel 14:14).[49]

The *Zohar* explains that when a person possesses a reincarnated soul, inevitably certain things happen to him as a result of his deeds in a former life. He may encounter other reincarnated souls with whom he must settle a debt or rectify an injustice. Or he may be led into a particular set of circumstances in order to correct an error in judgment, or to perform a religious precept previously neglected. The Chassidic masters maintain that in these generations, virtually everyone has lived before. Rabbi Aharon Roth of Jerusalem (known as "Reb Ahreleh," 1894-1944) observes: "Everything that happens to a person is the result of divine providence and is necessary to rectify [one's misdeeds and failings] in previous incarnations."[50] At the end of these successive incarnations, the soul is judged. However, the Kabbalists assure us that this judgment will be tempered with mercy, taking into account all mitigating factors. As the verse states, "God's work is perfect, for all His ways are just" (Deuteronomy 32:4).[51]

Chareidim, chap. 33; R. Chaim Vital, *Sha'ar HaGilgulim, Hakdamah* 4; R. Naftali Herz Bacharach, *Emek HaMelech* 2:3; R. Avraham Azulai, *Chesed L'Avraham*, 5:19; R. Moshe Alshech on Job 9:21; R. Moshe Chaim Luzzatto, *Pischei Chochmah vaDaas*, pp. 44f; et al.

49. *Me'or Einayim, Bamidbar*, s.v. *Vay'daber Hashem El Moshe*. Kabbalistic sources state that the morally corrupt generation of the Flood reincarnated a second time as the generation of the Dispersion that built the Tower of Babel, and a third time as the people of Sodom; see R. Chaim Vital, *Sha'ar HaPesukim, Shemos; Sha'ar HaKavannos, Chag HaMatzos*, et al. R. Avraham of Safed mentions in *Galya Raza* (p. 138) that these souls also were reincarnated as Laban's sheep, and then as those of Yaakov. The *Imrei Yosef* of Spinka (R. Yosef Meir Weiss, 1838-1909) explains: "The Patriarch Abraham raised them up from *domem* (the mineral realm) to *tzomei'ach* (vegetation). The Patriarch Isaac raised them up from *tzomei'ach* to the lower forms of animal life, e.g. vermin and insects. And the Patriarch Jacob elevated them to become Laban's sheep, over which he was shepherd"; *Chakal Yitzchak*, 67b. Chassidic tradition has it that the Maggid of Koznitz (R. Yisrael Hapstein, 1737-1814), once remarked: "I remember when our *zeideh* (grandfather) Jacob struck me with the lash" (ibid. *Vayeitzei*, 37b). A similar statement is ascribed to the author of *Yismach Moshe* (R. Moshe Teitelbaum of Ujhely, 1759-1841). Subsequently, these souls were reincarnated as the Children of Israel in Egypt, whom Moses redeemed from bondage and elevated to the lofty spiritual plane at which they were deemed worthy to receive the Torah at Mount Sinai.

50. *Shomer Emunim*, p. 143.

The exceptions to this rule are the great tzaddikim who return to this world for the benefit of humanity, in order to teach the ways of righteousness and divine wisdom.[52] They have no need to return to this imperfect world.[53] Their presence among us is one of the most visible manifestations of God's mercy on His creatures.

---

51. *Derech Hashem* 2:3:10. A commonly asked question is: which body will arise with the resurrection of the dead? This issue is discussed in the *Zohar* I, *Chayei Sarah*, 131a. According to R. Yossi, only the last body will arise, because it has attained the greatest degree of spiritual refinement. However, R. Yitzchak contends that each body will arise in order to have a last chance to acquire greater merit, by virtue of its previous good deeds; see *Yedid Nefesh al HaZohar*, Vol. 3, *Biur HaMa'amar*, ad loc., citing *Mishneh L'Melech* and *Ohr HaChamah* ("*Iyunim*"). Elsewhere, the *Zohar* states that each body will be resurrected, even if it merely performed one religious precept (*Zohar* II, *Mishpatim*, 100a, 105b; also cf. *Zohar* III, *Tosafos*, 308b, no. 17). In *Reishis Chochmah, Sha'ar Kedushah,* 15:12, R. Eliyahu de Vidas states that the body in which the soul exerted itself to the greatest degree in divine service will arise, whereas the Ari states that since the soul is reincarnated in components (i.e., "sparks" of *nefesh, ruach, neshamah*), each component will be resurrected with the body that it formerly occupied (*Sha'ar HaGilgulim, Hakdamah* 4, 11). The 13th century Kabbalist, R. Yitzchak of Acco, cites a similar view in *Me'iras Einayim, Bereishis,* s.v. *V'nishal mimenu b'sod ha'ibbur,* p. 46. However, Chassidic master R. Levi Yitzchak of Berditchev contends that the body restored at the Resurrection of the Dead will be a composite form, each of its limbs corresponding to the precepts and good deeds performed during the soul's various incarnations; *Kedushas Levi, Va'eschanan, Ma'amar "V'shamartah es HaChukim."*
52. *Tikkunei Zohar, Tikkun* 32 (76b), s.v. *V'im hu tzaddik itmar;* also Ramak, *Ohr Yakar al HaZohar, Saba,* sec. 1 (p. 5). However, sometimes *tzaddikim* must reincarnate in order to rectify a slight mistake. Because Gehenna has no power over them (*Chagigah* 27a), they only can rid their souls of this trace of impurity through reincarnation. In *Sha'ar HaGilgulim, Hakdamah* 4, the Ari states that *tzaddikim* often reincarnate as fish. Just as a fish is "nullified" to the water in which it exists, so, too, the *tzaddik* is "nullified" to the encompassing Divine Oneness; cf. R. Menachem Azariah of Fano, *Kanfei Yonah* II, 104. R. Zvi Elimelech of Dinov (1785-1841) points out that fish do not require *shechitah;* therefore, he presumes their death to be less painful than that of other kosher animals; see *B'nei Yissaschar, Chodesh Sivan, Ma'amar* 5 (" *Ma'alas HaTorah*"), sec. 18 (Toldos Aharon ed., p. 141b); similarly, cf. *Ohr HaChaim* on Genesis 1:26; R. Yehudah Ftayah, *Minchas Yehudah, Tehillim,* 91 (p. 201); *Likkutei Halachos, Tola'im* 4:10; et al.
53. *Zohar* III, *Pinchas,* 213a; *Galya Raza,* p. 182; *Sha'ar HaGilgulim, Hakdamah* 8; concerning the selfless devotion of *tzaddikim,* see *Chayei Moharan* 307; *Avodas Yisrael, Likkutim, Ta'anis; Divrei Emes, Noach;* et al.

Reincarnation Into Non-Human Forms

The texts we have cited discuss reincarnation from one human body to another. This issue of reincarnation to animals and other non-human forms receives greater attention with the emergence of the Safed (Hebrew: Tzefat, or Tzefas) school of Kabbalah during the 1500s.

In the wake of the Spanish Inquisition and its cruel persecutions, the fate of the Jewish people seemed highly precarious. Then a new dawn of wisdom began to shine forth from the ancient city of Safed in the mountains of northern Israel. At that time, Safed was the center of Torah scholarship in the Holy Land, so it was natural that the great Kabbalists should gravitate to her. However, Rabbi Avraham Azulai (1570-1643), author of *Chesed L'Avraham*, also offers a mystical reason for the renaissance of Kabbalah in this city. Dividing the land of Israel according to influences of the Ten Sefiros, he identifies Safed with the Sefirah of *Netzach* (Eternity), this being the root of prophecy. He also declares, "The air of Safed is the purest in the entire land of Israel."[54]

Prior to the arrival of the holy Ari in 1570, the leading Kabbalist in Safed was Rabbi Moshe Cordovero (1522-1570), also known as the Ramak. His encyclopedic *Pardes Rimonim* (Orchard of Pomegranates) is a systematic distillation of virtually all Jewish mystical teachings extant prior to the Ari. The Ramak discusses reincarnation in a number of works, particularly *Ohr Yakar*, his voluminous commentary on the *Zohar*. In another tract, *Shiur Komah* (definitions of mystical concepts), he affirms that reincarnation of human souls into the bodies of animals is an ancient Jewish doctrine "about which we possess many stories from the Kabbalists."[55] This is supported by textual evidence, as well.[56]

---

54. *Chesed L'Avraham*, 3:13, s.v. *V'hinei Tzefat*. Nevertheless, the Moroccan-born R. Avraham Azulai spent most of the latter three decades of his life in Chevron, where the Patriarchs and Matriarchs (with the exception of Rachel) are buried; see Goldwurm, *The Early Acharonim*, pp. 145-146.

55. *Shiur Komah, Inyan Gilgul*, sec. 84.

56. Mention of reincarnation into non-human forms that predates the Safed Kabbalists may be found in the late 13th century Torah commentary of R. Menachem Recanati, cited in *Yalkut Reuvaini, Noach*, pp. 139-140, and *Sefer HaKanah, Sod V'Onesh Gilgul al HaArayos*, et passim. The latter, although attributed to the father of first century sage R. Nechuniah ben HaKanah, more likely derives from a later period. The Chida in *Shem HaGedolim, Ma'areches Sefarim* 71, speculates that *Sefer*

The Safed Kabbalists teach that there are many reasons why a human may be reincarnated as an animal.[57] A number of them are related to sexual transgressions. In general, however, this fate reflects Rabbi Yehudah HeChassid's teaching that "if one behaves like an animal in this life, he will be forced to labor as an animal in the next world."[58] This follows the principle that God rewards each person "measure for measure" (*midah k'neged midah*), a concept that *Tanna D'vei Eliyahu* applies equally to "Jews and non-Jews, all families of the Earth."[59] The Kabbalists also state that as part of its punishment (and *tikkun*), the soul reincarnated in non-human form knows its own condition.[60] In certain cases, the soul may be reborn as a plant or a stone, and remain in that state for as long as Heaven decrees.[61]

HaKanah was written by one of the Geonim. R. Hersh Goldwurm, *The Rishonim*, p. 151, adds that some scholars identify the author as R. Avigdor Kara of Prague (mid-1300s-1439).

57. *Sha'ar HaGilgulim, Hakdamah* 22, s.v. *V'hinei niva'er atah k'tzas minei gilgulim*, until end; *Sha'ar HaMitzvos, Eikev; Shiur Komah, Inyan Gilgul*, sec. 84. Transgressions rectified through reincarnation in non-human forms include murder; engaging in damaging speech (*lashon harah*); abusing political power for personal gain; causing other Jews to eat non-kosher food; neglecting the precept of washing the hands upon awakening or before eating bread; omitting the blessings before and after eating; and stealing from one's parents. R. Shmuel Vital, editor of the teachings of the Ari preserved by his father, R. Chaim Vital, adds at the end of *Sha'ar HaGilgulim, Hakdamah* 22, a section from the notebook of another Safed Kabbalist that lists a number of sexual sins and their specific corresponding forms of reincarnation. However, R. Shmuel questions if this teaching comes from the Ari. *Tikkunei Zohar* mentions reincarnation as a dog in *Tikkun* 70 (133a); also cf. *Sha'ar Ruach HaKodesh, Tikkun* 20; and *Minchas Yehudah, Yechezkel*, 88 (pp. 154, 172), which point out a seeming inconsistency regarding this punishment in *Zohar* III, *Behar* (*Raya Mehemna*), 111a. *Galya Raza* (p. 96) relates reincarnation in non-human forms to cheating the poor in business or through usury, and to the pursuit of gluttony, in addition to being a punishment for sexual immorality. *Chakal Yitzchak (Spinka), Shemini*, 104b, cites a tradition that those who eat vermin or crawling insects will reincarnate as such creatures.

58. *Sefer Chassidim*, sec. 169 (translated in the source texts for Chapter 3, "Judaism and Animal Welfare"), may be understood as a cryptic reference to reincarnation in animal form; see commentary of Chida there.

59. *Tanna D'vei Eliyahu Rabbah* 16:1, 17:19; regarding the principle of *midah k'neged midah*, see *Sanhedrin* 90a; *Bereishis Rabbah* 9:13; also cf. *Mishnah Sota* 1:7, *Avos* 2:6; *Zohar* III, *Emor*, 92b.

60. *Shiur Komah, Inyan Gilgul*, sec. 84; *Sha'ar HaGilgulim, Hakdamah* 22 (p. 59, top); *Sefer Chareidim*, chap. 33.

61. *Sha'ar HaGilgulim, Hakdamah* 22 (end); *Sefer HaLikkutim, Bereishis*, s.v. *Bereishis barah; Sha'ar HaMitzvos, Eikev; Galya Raza*, p. 100; *Sefer Chareidim*, chap. 33; *Chesed*

Reincarnation and Jewish Ethics

One practical implication of all this is, of course, that we should seek to avoid such a fate. The Kabbalists clearly state that through *teshuvah* — return to God — one may be spared these afflictions. A moment of true remorse, accompanied by sincere resolve to change one's actions, can benefit the soul more than centuries of reincarnation.[62] Recognizing the divine gift of having been created as human beings, we must strive to live up to our spiritual potential. As the *Zohar* declares, "Worthy are the tzaddikim who know what is of true value. Their heart's desire is directed to the One Above, and not toward this world and its empty passions."[63]

At the same time, the doctrine of reincarnation imposes upon us even greater responsibilities toward other creatures. If, indeed, animals possess human souls, the demands of animal activists take on a new dimension. When we consider the inhumane aspects of raising and slaughtering animals, the mystical perspective outlined here discloses even greater vistas of horror. According to the Kabbalists, most animals today possess reincarnated human souls.[64] Therefore, from this standpoint we must view these ill-fated creatures as we would our fellow human beings — even while rejecting the doctrine of the moral equivalence of all species.

It might be argued that since these animals deserve their suffering, we are blameless of any responsibility for causing it. Why must we concern ourselves with God's hidden ways of purifying the wicked?

Although the rabbis of the Talmud are silent on the subject of reincarnation, they are lucidly clear on that of moral subterfuge. In his commentary on the Torah, Rashi (R. Shlomo Yitzchaki, 1040-1105) discusses the law of a balcony without a railing or parapet. If someone

---

L'Avraham 2:47, 5:17; *Kitzur Shelah, S'char V'Onesh*, s.v. *Yesh resha'im she'misgal'gilim*; R. Pinchas Eliyahu Horowitz of Vilna, *Sefer HaBris* II, *Ma'amar* 8:2; R. Yosef Chaim of Baghdad, *Otzros Chaim* I, *Tikkun HaM'gulgolim*; R. Yehudah Ftayah, *Minchas Yehudah, Eikev*, 70, p. 99.

62. *Chesed L'Avraham*, 1:13; Ramak, *Shiur Komah, Inyan Gilgul*, p. 168 (bottom); *Kitzur Shelah, Sha'ar HaOsios, S'char Va'Onesh*, s.v. *V'chol hanal b'd'lo asah teshuvah*; also cf. *Chayei Moharan*, 37, 91; *Likkutei Moharan* I:8.

63. *Zohar* II, 134b; also cf. *Tzava'as HaRivash* 84, sec. 3.

64. *Likkutei Halachos, Shechitah* 2:10-11, 3:2, 4:2.

should fall off and injure himself, the owner might contend that the victim deserved this fate; otherwise God would not have allowed it to happen. This may be true, say the sages. "But let not his death be brought about through you; for good things are brought about through the worthy, and evil things through the unworthy."[65] This principle may be applied to the issue at hand. If such harsh punishments are deserved by our fellow beings, we do not have to serve as the agents of their affliction. Moreover, there are consequences for such heartless acts. As the well-known Mishnah states, Hillel once saw a skull floating down a stream, at which he remarked, "Because you drowned others, you were drowned; and in the end, those who drowned you will be drowned in turn" (*Avos* 2:6). If animal slaughter is permitted to serve human needs, gratuitous cruelty surely is not. Those who engage in such abuses may bring a similar fate upon themselves.

Aside from this moral concern, reincarnation into animals presents us with still another dilemma: who is spiritually equipped to elevate such lost souls? And, if one cannot elevate them, at least how can one avoid being harmed by them? According to the Ari, the spiritual responsibilities — and risks engendered by eating animal foods — are great. These are among the questions we shall consider in the concluding chapter on "Judaism and Vegetarianism."

---

65. Rashi on Deuteronomy 22:8, citing *Sifré*; also cf. *Emunos V'De'os, Ma'amar* 4:4.

Sources

Reincarnated Souls in Food

The verse states: "For your soul desires to eat flesh..." — "your soul" alludes to a kindred [reincarnated] soul, which thus "belongs" to you [and desires that you redeem it] — "after all the desire of your soul you may eat flesh" (Deuteronomy 12:20). That is, your intention must be to spiritually elevate the soul for which you are responsible that dwells within the food. However, the one who eats must be spiritually elevated in order to accomplish this task. Then the Holy One, blessed be He, will prepare for him appropriate food. If the one who eats does not have this intention, but eats merely to satisfy his craving, the [captive soul within the] food will ascend above to its proper place, whereas the one who eats will descend to the spiritual level formerly occupied by the [soul that had been captive within the] food he consumed. Thus, the status of a human may become exchanged with that of an animal, and vice versa. [66]

Consider this well, my child, and you will see that the Tannaim (Mishnaic masters) and Amoraim (Talmudic masters) permitted meat to themselves alone, for all their deeds were for the sake of Heaven. Thus, our sages ask, "And as for others, when is it eaten?" and they reply, "From one Sabbath eve to the next,"[67] for then divine mercy prevails, and one's intent is perfect. Moreover, one who saves a soul of Israel is considered to have kept the entire Torah.[68] However, in these subsequent generations, when the commandments have come to be performed as if by rote, even Talmudic scholars should not risk losing their souls as a consequence of eating meat. Nevertheless, one who understands the meaning of eating, and the mystery of the verse stated above, is permitted to eat meat [and in

---

66. R. Chaim Vital citing the Ari in *Sha'ar HaMitzvos* (below) apparently disagrees with the contention of the author of *Sefer HaPeliah* that the transmigrated soul may be redeemed even in the absence of proper intent by the one who consumes the food.
67. *Pesachim* 49b.
68. This appears to be a variant of the Mishnaic teaching: "If one saves one soul of Israel, it is as if he had saved an entire world" (*Sanhedrin* 37a); also cf. Talmud Yerushalmi, *Sanhedrin* 4:9, and *Pirkei Rabbi Eliezer*, 48 (115a), both of which omit the phrase "of Israel."

so doing, engage in the risks of elevating the reincarnated souls contained therein].

Indeed, we find that our sages were so moved by this concern that they declared: "One ignorant of Torah (*am ha'aretz*) is forbidden to eat meat."[69] Since an *am ha'aretz* is comparable to an animal, for what purpose may he consume the soul of one who is superior to him, and himself turn into an animal that will be consumed by another *am ha'aretz*, and still not attain purification? By eating without proper intent, he will bring about his own destruction. It is better for such a person to consume the herb of the Earth, rather than damage his soul (*Sefer HaPeliah*, s.v. *U'r'ei v'havain*, pp. 282-283).

გჳ80

Sometimes, due to certain transgressions, a soul may be reincarnated in an article of food or drink. Even if no reincarnated soul is present, one's food or drink contains spiritual impurities and *klippos*. A tzaddik and a Torah scholar will not come to harm through food and drink; on the contrary, he will extricate the good from the coarse physical component of what he consumes, and rectify any souls contained therein. However, an evil person or one ignorant of Torah not only will fail to rectify any souls reincarnated in his food or drink, but may cause even further harm to those souls, beyond that which they brought upon themselves through their own misdeeds. Additionally, these [transmigrated souls] may attach themselves to him, causing him to sin and leading him along an evil path, until he damages his soul beyond remedy (Rabbi Chaim Vital citing his mentor, Rabbi Yitzchak Luria, *Sha'ar HaMitzvos, Eikev*, pp. 100-101).

გჳ80

Our master, Rabbi Chaim Vital, writes that sometimes a person eats an article of food in which the soul of an evil-doer has been reincarnated, and he cannot redeem it: "The reincarnated soul may attach itself to him, causing him to sin and leading him along an evil path, until he has

---

69. *Pesachim* 49b.

damaged his soul beyond repair. This is why certain people suddenly turn to evil and eventually renounce Judaism altogether, may Heaven protect us. This, too, is what caused Yochanan the High Priest to become a Sadducee,[70] as the Talmud states (*Berachos* 29a). Everything depends upon the nature of the soul that attaches itself to a person."[71]

He also writes: "Similarly, [this danger exists] if one who lacks Torah knowledge eats an article of food in which a transmigrated soul is present — albeit from the animal realm, which is [a descent of] but one level — and he cannot rectify it; or if a Torah scholar who lacks the wisdom of Kabbalah eats vegetables which bear a transmigrated soul that he cannot rectify, this soul may cleave to him and lead him to transgress" (ibid.).

It is known that vegetables that grow directly from the Earth have more spiritual impurities than animals. This helps us understand the statement of Rav Chisda: "This Torah scholar did not eat vegetables because of *g'rir* (whetting the appetite)" (*Shabbos* 140b). [The word *g'rir* also can mean to drag or carry along.] Because a [vegetable] possesses more spiritual impurities, it may "carry" a transmigrated soul; if so, it has become an "evil portion" that could lead the one who eats it to sin. Although the individual [to whom Rav Chisda referred] was a Torah scholar, his knowledge might have been insufficient to protect him.

All this was said concerning vegetables that grow entirely in the ground. The fruits of trees that do not grow directly from the ground, but from the body of the tree, are less problematic. Since something intervenes between the fruit [and the ground], it is less likely that their relatively fewer spiritual impurities would attract a transmigrated soul, thus rendering them an instrument of evil. It seems to me that this is why our sages taught that King Hezekiah ate a *litra* of vegetables every day,

---

70. The Sadducees (Hebrew: *Tzadokim*, after their leader, Tzadok) were members of a deviant Jewish sect that rejected the traditional rabbinic interpretation of the Written Law, attempting to substitute a more fundamentalist, "common sense" understanding. Influenced by the prevailing cultural Hellenism, the sect won many followers among the Kohanim (priestly caste) and the aristocracy during the late Second Temple period. Based upon similar theological premises, the Karaite (from the word *mikra*, meaning "scripture") movement arose during the latter part of the 8th century c.e. Although cut off from the rest of the Jewish people, a small remnant of the Karaites has survived until this day.

71. *Sha'ar HaMitzvos, Eikev.*

and this sufficed for his meal (*Sanhedrin* 94b). He knew that he possessed great spiritual power, sufficient to overcome any possible impurity.

However, any [vegetable] cooked in fire will be free of impurity. As our master, Rabbi Yonasan Eibeshutz (1696-1764) writes in his *Ya'aros Devash*: "Any fresh herb that has not been cooked or otherwise purified is potentially harmful" (Rabbi Yosef Chaim of Baghdad, *Otz'ros Chaim* I, *Tikkun Ha'm'gulgolim B'Domem, Tzomei'ach, Chai, Medaber*).

⋘⋙

"Hungry and thirsty, their souls fainted within them" (Psalms 107:5). A great and awesome mystery is contained here. Why did the Holy One, blessed be He, create the various sorts of food and drink that man craves? The reason is because there are actually sparks of Adam hidden in the mineral realm (*domem*), in vegetative life (*tzomei'ach*), in the animal kingdom (*chai*), and in mankind (*medaber*). They long to attach themselves to holiness, [which in Kabbalistic doctrine is called] "the arousal of the Feminine Waters." Concerning this mystery it has been taught, "No drop descends from above unless two corresponding drops ascend from below."[72] All the food and drink a person consumes contains sparks which actually belong to him, and which he must rectify. Thus, the verse states, "Hungry and thirsty" — when people crave after food and drink, what happens? "Their soul fainted within them" — [the holy sparks remain] in exile, in alien garments. For all the things one uses are actually his children, held in captivity (Rabbi Yisrael Baal Shem Tov, *Rimzei Yisrael*).

⋘⋙

"If three people ate together at one table and did not speak words of Torah, it is as if they partook of slaughter to the dead" (*Avos* 3:4). Citing a teaching of his master, the Baal Shem Tov, the Maggid of Mezeritch (R. Dov Ber ben Avraham, 1704-1772) said: Souls of the deceased are reincarnated in food and drink, waiting for a person to speak words of Torah and give them life. However, if one does not say words of Torah, he

---

72. *Taanis* 25b; also cf. *Zohar* III, 247b.

"slaughters the dead" who had been thus reincarnated and casts them back to the inanimate realm (*Be'er Mayim, Haggadah Shel Pesach*).

The Shochet's Responsibility

When those who perform *shechitah* are worthy individuals, [the meat they provide causes] others to show compassion toward one another. The opposite is also true (Rabbi Nachman of Breslov, *Sefer HaMidos, Shochet*, II, 1).

ଔଞ୍ଚ

Wicked slaughterers who cause people to eat non-kosher meat bring about an increase of theft in the world[73] (ibid. II, 2).

ଔଞ୍ଚ

My soul went out when he spoke. I sought him but could not find him; I called but he did not answer. I met the watchmen who patrol the city. They struck me, they bruised me; they stripped me of my mantle (Song of Songs 5:6-7).

Commentary: When an unworthy person slaughters an animal, this causes anguish to the animal's soul, which cries out bitterly. [The above scriptural passage alludes to this.] "My soul went out when he spoke" — [the soul] went out [of the animal's body] in order to enter into the words of the blessing [recited by the *shochet*]. This is an aspect of [the ascent of] the Feminine Waters [a Kabbalistic term for the Godly life-force concealed within creation, which is spiritually elevated through the divine service of the Jewish people]. However, when I went out, "I sought him but could not find him; I called out but he did not answer" — because he was not mentally present at the time of the blessing and had disqualifying thoughts.[74] Through this, "I met the watchmen who patrol the city. They struck me, they bruised me; they stripped me of my mantle." That is, whatever advantage the soul had gained while it was in

---

73. Cf. R. Moshe Teitelbaum of Ujhely, *Yismach Moshe, Toldos*, 3 (274a), citing Kabbalistic sources that one who consumes even the kosher meat of an immoral *shochet* damages his soul.

the animal aspect was also taken from it. Now it [is like the dove that Noah sent forth from the ark, and] has "no place to rest its feet" (Genesis 8:9). Woe unto that *shochet*, woe unto the soul — for he murdered the soul and gave it over to the hands of its enemies (Rabbi Nachman of Breslov, *Likkutei Moharan* I, 37:6).

〇

Rabbi Nachman of Breslov once said: "I do not want any of my followers to become ritual slaughterers. But if a person is already a ritual slaughterer, at least he should be one of my followers" (Rabbi Levi Yitzchak Bender, *Siach Sarfei Kodesh* II, 1:15).

〇

Rabbi Shimon wished to learn the laws of *shechitah*. He asked his master, Rabbi Nachman of Breslov, who told him that it would be better to study medicine. [It was well known to Rabbi Nachman's disciples that he was deeply critical of doctors, and cautioned against the blind faith people often invest in them.] Rabbi Shimon exclaimed, "Do you want me to become a murderer?" The master replied, "Is it not an act of murder to take a chicken in which the soul of an old man has been reincarnated, hold him by the beard, and cut his throat?" Thereupon, Rabbi Shimon ceased studying to become a *shochet* (*Avaneha Barzel, Kisvei Rabbi Nosson MiTerovitz*, 65).

〇

Once a young man approached Rabbi Avraham Sternhartz (1865-1955), a leading figure in the Breslov Chassidic community, and asked if he should become a *shochet*. "First study the teachings in *Likkutei Halachos* (a fundamental Breslov Chassidic text by Rabbi Avraham's great-grandfather, Rabbi Nosson Sternhartz) on the laws of *shechitah*,"[75] Rabbi Avraham advised. The young man agreed to do so. However, after

---

74. The term used is *pigul*. Although only certain thoughts actually render a slaughtered animal unfit (see *Yoreh De'ah*, chaps. 3-4), R. Nachman's point is that anything less than proper, holy intent will fail to accomplish the spiritual elevation of the animal's soul and any reincarnated soul it may bear.

75. See "R. Nosson Sternhartz on Reincarnation" in Additional Source Texts below.

he saw what Reb Nosson had to say about the profound mysteries involved in ritual slaughter, he decided to pursue a different career (Breslov oral tradition).

CG೪೦

A tradition has been preserved in one branch of the family of Rabbi Yaakov Yitzchak of P'shischa, better known as the *Yid HaKadosh* ("Holy Jew"), that he did not want any of his female descendants to marry *shochtim* (ritual slaughterers). According to another branch of the family, the Yid HaKadosh did not want any of his male descendants to become *shochtim (Sefer Minhagei Nisuin L'Beis Lelov*, p. 26, citing Rabbi Yosef Yerucham Fishel Hagar's *Toras HaYehudi HaKadosh*, p. 226, no. 31).

CG೪೦

When the late Mashgiach Ruchani of Yeshiva Darkei Noam in Brooklyn, NY, Rabbi Shlomo HaKohen Eisenblatt, was a young man, he accepted a rabbinic post in a small community where it was difficult for him to obtain kosher meat that met the highest halachic standard. Therefore, he learned to become a *shochet* in order to slaughter chickens for his own family. However, when he informed his saintly mentor, the Boyaner Rebbe, Rabbi Mordechai Shlomo Friedman (1891-1971), of blessed memory, the latter exclaimed, "You want to be a *shochet*? A *shochet* is an *achzor* (a cruel individual)!" Hearing this, Rabbi Eisenblatt resolved never again to practice *shechitah* (heard directly from Rabbi Eisenblatt).

Reb Tzadok HaKohen on Reincarnation

The Torah is a "spice" for the evil inclination, as our sages state (*Kiddushin* 30b). That is, even if one's heart is not absolutely pure, because he has not slaughtered the evil inclination, nevertheless if he fills himself with Torah, his evil inclination will be "spiced" and become worthy. Thus, a Torah scholar is permitted to eat meat, whereas one ignorant of Torah may not (*Pesachim* 49b).

The Ari explains this Talmudic teaching in terms of the rectification of souls reincarnated as animals.[76] When a person spends his life sunken in bestial deeds, after death his soul may cleave to the soul of an animal and remain there without a trace of human intellect or wisdom. The nature of the particular animal the soul must enter will be determined by the person's former actions.

I heard[77] that the deeds one performs without proper intention have far-reaching consequences. If they are virtuous, a pure animal will be created; if they are evil, an impure animal will be created. For man includes all creation within himself, and everything is affected by him. All animals reflect human traits; therefore, they are many and diverse. An animal that embodies the trait of the person responsible for its creation will attract that person's errant soul after death. [However, divine providence mercifully causes] kosher animals to provide food for a living person [who either shares the same "spiritual root" as the reincarnated soul] or possesses a corresponding good trait. Of its own accord, this good trait can extricate the portion of the soul trapped in the evil trait [of the animal].

All food produces foreign thoughts and fantasies, in the manner of "a full stomach itself is harmful food" (*Berachos* 32a). [This especially is true of animal foods,] since the reincarnated soul is garbed in the trait of the animal. Since the Torah scholar extricates the good, he spiritually rectifies it. One ignorant of Torah, however, is forbidden [to eat meat], for this may bring about his downfall. When he encounters a quality similar to his own, his [evil inclination] will be aroused. Even a Torah scholar who does not possess a completely pure heart is still superior to the beast, due to his wisdom. By thinking Torah thoughts, he can redeem the reincarnated soul garbed within the animal.

Physically, the flesh of an animal is transformed to human flesh when a person derives sustenance from it. Similarly, the spiritual quality of the animal is transformed to a human spiritual quality. This is the

---

76. *Sha'ar HaGilgulim, Hakdamah*, et passim.
77. It is known that whenever Reb Tzadok writes *shamati* (I heard) without further qualification, what follows is a teaching of his master, Rabbi Mordechai Yosef Leiner of Izhbitz (1800-1854).

meaning of the *Zohar*'s teaching that "in wisdom, everything is purified." A Torah scholar is able to purify and rectify souls, although he has not attained perfection himself, as long as he is immersed in Torah. Through the Torah, he can elevate and spiritually rectify all foreign thoughts.

However, one ignorant of Torah is permitted only vegetables and grains. Although animals have an evil inclination, this is not true of plants (cf. *Berachos* 61a). The [souls] garbed in plants cannot cleave to the thoughts and evil inclinations of those [who consume them], but only to the outer garment of evil deeds. For the physical act serves as a garment for this evil spirit, in order to conceal the spark of a holy soul. These are the malevolent spirits of the world. They are also able to conceal themselves in vegetation. Although they lack the power to affect a person's thoughts and fantasies, they may affect his actions. Nevertheless, when it comes to action, "even the empty ones of Israel are as full of commandments as a pomegranate [is full of seeds]" (*Berachos* 57a). Through the commandments performed [by a simple religious Jew], the [sparks of souls contained in the vegetables and grains] he eats are subsequently rectified (Rabbi Tzadok HaKohen of Lublin, *Tzidkas HaTzaddik,* chap. 240, abridged).

A "Litvisheh-Chassidisheh" Tale

In a lighter moment, Rabbi Yehoshua Leib [Diskin, the "Brisker Rav," 1817-1898] once told Rabbi Chaim [Sonnenfeld, 1848-1932], "Come, I'll tell you a 'Chassidic' story[78] that happened while I was Rav (Chief Rabbi) of Kovno. One of Kovno's residents came to me with a problem. The man was extremely poor and barely eked out enough for his family to subsist on. This man had had a terrifying dream. His father, who had died during the previous year, appeared to him and told him that he had been

---

78. Editor's note: R. Diskin referred to this tale of reincarnation as a "Chassidic story" despite the fact that Lithuanian (Yiddish: "Litvisheh") non-Chassidim uphold the same Kabbalistic traditions, based upon the same classic texts. The main difference is that Lithuanian Kabbalists have tended to preserve the traditional reticence about such matters, while their Chassidic counterparts have been inclined to be more open about mystical teachings, miracles (particularly those performed by their *Rebbes,* or teachers), and paranormal occurrences.

reincarnated in a black bull that was owned by a certain non-Jew in a certain town some distance from Kovno. His father ordered him to go and buy the bull, adding that the owner would ask eighty rubles for the animal but that he would settle for forty. After buying the animal, the son was to bring it back to Kovno and have it slaughtered by a God-fearing *shochet* in the presence of the Rav, who would answer "amen" to the *shochet's* blessing. The Rav was to eat some of the meat, and the rest was to be distributed to other Jews. Only then would the father's soul find eternal peace. Although this dream had been repeated on three consecutive nights, the man had paid no attention to it. Some time later, however, the man had been reciting *chazaras hashatz* (repetition of the communal prayer service, often led by a mourner during the first eleven or twelve months after the death of a parent) in the *shul* (synagogue), when he collapsed in a dead faint. After he was revived, he explained that he had seen a vision of his father, who had again commanded him to go purchase the bull and have it slaughtered.

"The people present in the *shul* at the time accompanied the man to my house. I held a private conversation with the man, in which he recounted to me the entire episode, and it was then confirmed by the people accompanying him. I asked them if they would provide the money for the purchase, and they readily agreed. When I noted that the trip would take some time, and that someone would have to temporarily support the man's family, they agreed to provide for that, as well.

"I called the man back and told him that he should go purchase the bull, but only if its description, price, location, and owner all tallied exactly with the dream. Otherwise, he would be squandering Jewish money. The man took the money and went to the specific town and looked up the gentile. When he described the bull to him, the gentile said that yes, he had a bull fitting that description, but it was extremely wild and dangerous, and to approach it was to place one's life in jeopardy. If he still wanted to buy the bull, it would cost him eighty rubles. The Jew offered forty rubles, which the gentile quickly accepted. He advised the man to hire several men to help transport this dangerous animal, but the man declined. To the utter amazement of the gentile and his friends, he slipped a rope over the bull's horns and led the now docile animal away.

"The bull was brought to Kovno, where it was slaughtered by a God-fearing *shochet* and was found to be kosher. The meat was distributed among the city's *talmidei chachamim* (Torah scholars), and a portion was sent to my house," concluded the Brisker Rav (Rabbi Shlomo Zalman Sonnenfeld, *Guardian of Jerusalem: The Life and Times of Rabbi Yosef Chaim Sonnenfeld* [Brooklyn: Artscroll / Mesorah Publications, 1985] pp. 91-92).

Part III:
Animals As Food

6

Judaism and Vegetarianism

It would be hard to imagine Jewish life without chicken soup. Indeed, for many American Jews, chicken soup (or at least little books with "chicken soup" in their titles) may be one of the few overt connections to Judaism they have left. Nevertheless, in both Israel and America, the number of Jewish vegetarians is on the rise. This phenomenon may be attributed to increased public awareness of health risks engendered by a meat-centered diet, as well as ethical concerns raised by animal rights and animal welfare advocates. In any event, it has become commonplace for many "health food" and vegetarian products to bear the symbol of a kosher supervisory organization (*hechsher*). Despite its departure from convention, vegetarianism as a personal preference is condoned by *halacha*. Moreover, vegetarianism does have a significant connection to Jewish tradition in that it constitutes the diet of the Garden of Eden and the Messianic Age. In this final chapter, we will consider some of the arguments for and against vegetarianism from a Jewish point of view. These arguments may be classified as philosophical, mystical, and halachic.

Philosophical Views

Several major rabbinic thinkers have espoused philosophical views that support vegetarianism. They include Rabbi Yosef Albo and Rabbi Yitzchak Arama among the medieval authorities, as well as 20th century visionary Rabbi Avraham Yitzchak Kook. An important biblical commentator of the 17th century, Rabbi Shlomo Ephraim Lunshitz of Prague, also deserves mention for his pointed criticism of meat eating. Their ideas as they pertain to vegetarianism may be summarized as follows:

Rabbi Yosef Albo

In his classic presentation of rabbinic doctrine, *Sefer HaIkkarim* ("Book of Fundamentals"), Rav Yosef Albo (1380-1444) defines animal slaughter and meat eating as an intermediate phase in the spiritual evolution of humankind. The use of animals to serve human needs, he contends, leads man to recognize the superiority of his moral stature and its attendant responsibilities; however, when at last man overcomes his lower nature and actualizes his innate spiritual essence, there will be no further reason to eat meat. Thus, the Messianic Age will be marked by a return to the vegetarianism of Eden.

Rav Albo develops his ideas in relation to the story of Cain and Abel, which he interprets as a theological dispute. Both brothers erroneously believed that humans and animals are on an equal moral plane. This led Cain to assume that animal sacrifice is forbidden; thus, Cain, tiller of the soil, offered God a sacrifice of flax from the harvest. However, God rejected this offering because Cain had failed to appreciate man's true status. Abel, the shepherd, recognized man's right to make use of animals, and, therefore, assumed that it would be proper to sacrifice a sheep from his flock. Although Abel was not much better than Cain, considering man to be no more than a superior animal, God accepted his offering. At this, Cain became jealous. Still under the misconception of the equivalence of the species, he speculated that just as it was permissible for Abel to kill an animal, so it would be permissible for him to kill his brother — with tragic results.[1]

---

1. Taking a view antithetical to that of R. Albo, early 20th century Chassidic master R. Shlomo of Z'vihl proposes that since Adam was not permitted to eat meat, Abel may have offered an animal sacrifice without divine consent. Yet God accepted it above the flax offered by Cain. This seeming injustice provoked Cain's anger, leading him to rationalize that there would be no wrong in killing his brother. According to the Z'vihler Rebbe, Cain's error was not his failure to understand the moral primacy of

The widespread currency of this concept led to such depths of immorality that a divine decree of destruction was visited upon the world. By bringing an animal offering after the Flood, however, Noah demonstrated that he had attained a deeper understanding of the meaning of life, and acknowledged his greater responsibilities. Thus, the Torah permitted his descendants to slaughter animals, in order to underscore this distinction between animals and men. Because Cain had failed to recognize this distinction and misunderstood the meaning of animal slaughter, the very next verse warns against killing other human beings: "for in the image of God He made man" (Genesis 9:6).

A highpoint in the spiritual evolution of humanity was reached at Mount Sinai, when the Children of Israel were given a more complex set of dietary laws, and a more difficult method of slaughter. This implicit limitation on meat eating indicated that now it was less necessary to remind man of his pre-eminence above the animals. Therefore, the "beginning of the end" of animal consumption was set in motion. This process will culminate in the Messianic Age, when meat eating will cease forever.

It is not clear if Rav Albo associates vegetarianism with the eschatological era exclusively. In a bold comparison, he relates the Torah's concession to eat meat to the law regarding the beautiful woman captured in battle.[2] While the woman may be taken captive, clearly the Torah does not approve of this course of action; in fact, the sages of the Talmud warn that such a base deed only will lead to grief for everyone concerned. Rather, the Torah implicitly acknowledges that war, even when mandated by necessity, will inevitably interfere with the normal ability of some human beings to restrain themselves. Similarly, says Rav Albo, due to our lack of enlightenment, we may slaughter animals to satisfy our desire for meat; however, the many laws surrounding this concession instruct the wise person to refrain from taking advantage of it.

---

man over animals, but the primacy of a sincere heart in the sight of God; see *Kuntres Yesod Tzaddik, Acharei*, s.v. *Kisui HaDam*, p. 176. Neither explains how Cain apparently was unaware of the prohibition of murder, one of the laws given to Adam and later to Noah; see *Sanhedrin* 59b; *Bereishis Rabbah* 24:5, 34:13, 18; *Devarim Rabbah* 2:25; also note Maimonides, *Mishneh Torah, Melachim* 9:1.

Rabbi Yitzchak Arama

In his Torah commentary *Akeidas Yitzchak* ("The Binding of Isaac"), Rabbi Yitzchak Arama (1430-1494) declares vegetarianism to be the ideal human diet. This is why in the Garden of Eden, Adam and Eve ate only vegetarian foods, as did Moses and the Generation of the Wilderness, who were sustained each day by Manna from heaven. Manna was the ideal food: it required minimal effort in its acquisition or preparation, possessed all tastes, and was the most spiritually refined food conceivable, having been directly provided by God.

On the one hand, the Torah's concession to eat meat does not apply to immoral people, for such individuals are comparable to wild beasts, and creatures of the same species are forbidden to consume one another. On the other hand, the author of *Akeidas Yitzchak* contends, spiritually evolved individuals are affected adversely by the coarse physicality of animal foods. Therefore, a meat-based diet is appropriate only for those in the middle category, who have begun to improve themselves but have not yet actualized their higher potential. Referring to ancient religious traditions that have affirmed vegetarianism, he adds a striking statement: "From time immemorial, men of spiritual attainment, possessed of divine wisdom and removed from worldly desires... refrained from consuming the flesh of animals." This suggests that vegetarianism once may have played a greater role in Jewish pietism than we know today.

---

2. Deuteronomy 21:10-14. Even while making this concession to an evil desire, the Torah does not allow the Israelite soldier to enslave or abuse the captive woman. On the contrary, he must marry her according to *halacha*, whereupon she gains the full status of a Jewish wife. The Torah further stipulates that the captive woman must shave her head, allow her nails to grow long, and dwell in the house of her prospective husband while mourning the loss of her parents for a full month before she enters into marriage. According to *Yevamos* 48a and the *Sifri*, these restrictions are meant to inhibit such relationships. This is borne out by the fact that the Torah places the law of the disrespectful and gluttonous son immediately after the law of the captive woman. From this juxtaposition, the sages infer that one who takes a captive woman will be cursed with unworthy children (Rashi on Deut. 21:11, citing *Tanchuma*). R. Chaim ibn Attar offers a mystical explanation of this law in *Ohr HaChaim, Ki Seitzei*, 21:10, 11.

Rabbi Shlomo Ephraim Lunshitz

In his homiletical Torah commentary *Kli Yakar* ("A Precious Vessel"), Rabbi Shlomo Ephraim Lunshitz (d. 1619), like Rav Albo, observes that the grudging tone of the Torah's permission to slaughter animals reflects tacit disapproval of a debased craving. Animal slaughter is only justified as a component of the rites of the Holy Temple (which themselves are meant to restore the innocence and peace of the vegetarian Edenic state). The restrictions that disallow an animal to be killed or injured through trapping, as well as the complex laws of *shechitah* and the subsequent preparation of meat, were given in order to deter the Jewish people from this morally inferior manner of conduct. At the very least, concludes the *Kli Yakar*, one should indulge such desires infrequently. However, elsewhere in his commentary he does acknowledge that spiritual benefit accrues to animals slaughtered for the benefit of those who devote themselves to Torah study and the fulfillment of the commandments.

Rabbi Avraham Yitzchak HaKohen Kook

The main work of Rav Kook (1865-1935) cited in the present anthology is *Chazon HaTzimchonut V'HaShalom* ("A Vision of Vegetarianism and Peace") edited by his saintly and erudite disciple, Rabbi Dovid Cohen (also known as the "Nazir" of Jerusalem).[3] This tract has been a favorite of Jewish vegetarians since its first publication in the early 1900s,[4] because it acknowledges the legitimacy of the moral sensitivities underlying ethical vegetarianism.

Why did Rav Kook, Chief Rabbi of pre-State Israel, concern himself with such a long neglected issue? A major thread that runs through Rav Kook's thought is a teleological principle also found in the works of Rabbi

---

3. A Nazir is one who vows to abstain from wine and grapes, from cutting his hair, and from contact with the dead (*tumah*). Purification from the latter cannot be accomplished outside the land of Israel; thus, Naziriteship is confined to the Holy Land. Moreover, this purification requires the ashes of the Red Heifer. Therefore, whether it is permissible to take a Nazirite vow today in the land of Israel is the subject of a dispute between Maimonides and Ravad, *Mishneh Torah, Hilchos Nezirus* 2:21. Despite his sobriquet, the Nazir of Jerusalem never took a formal vow of *nezirus*, but merely adopted the behavior of a Nazir.

Nachman of Breslov (whose thought exerted a major influence on Rav Kook).[5] From this vantage point, the Messianic Age is not only a political goal achieved by the cumulative religious efforts of the Jewish people — it is a spiritual paradigm that illuminates the exile from without, and, in so doing, increases the momentum of the redemption, particularly as the End of Days draws near.[6] In Rav Kook's conception, Zionism (at that time a fledgling movement to bring about the return of the Jewish people to their national homeland) was understood to be a Messianic undertaking. A corollary of this utopian vision was the resurgence of interest in vegetarianism as the "Messianic diet," recalling the mystical kinship between humans and animals that characterized the Garden of Eden, and anticipating the enlightened future world order.

However, despite his strongly pro-vegetarian stance, Rav Kook considers this diet to represent a spiritual rung that presently remains beyond the grasp of most human beings. When people take on austerities for which they are insufficiently prepared, their uncorrected evil traits inevitably will manifest themselves in other, possibly more harmful ways. He also observes that a common psychological strategy for a corrupt person is to whitewash his self-image by finding an extremely idealistic cause to champion. Both dangers apply to ethical vegetarianism. If the premature embrace of this lofty expression of compassion for animals should fail, Rav Kook warns, it could lead to moral regression — even to cannibalism.[7] Echoing Rav Albo's

---

4. The first section, *Afikim BaNegev* (Streams in the Desert), was published in serial form in the Berlin Hebrew journal *HaPeles* (The Balance), 1903-1904; the concluding essay, *Talelei Orot* (Dew of Light) originally appeared in *Tachkemoni* (Wise Counsel), 1910, a publication of the Union of Jewish Students of Switzerland. R. Cohen subsequently combined and edited the two parts as *Chazon HaTzimchonut V'HaShalom*, however this new version was not published until 1961 in Jerusalem; see R. Moshe Zvi Neriyah, *Tal HaRayah* (Bnei Brak, 1963), p. 149.

5. *Likkutei Moharan* 1:49, discusses "remembering the future world" as a way of spiritually magnetizing the present state of creation and nullifying its negative potential. By binding one's thoughts to the transcendent level, one infuses the domain of constriction and disharmony with an illumination of the ultimate goal, which is the revelation of the Divine Oneness.

6. R. Jonathan Sacks, *Tradition in an Untraditional Age*, chap. 3, pp. 26-27, citing *Orot HaKodesh*, *Orot HaTeshuvah*, et al.

7. *Chazon HaTzimchonut V'HaShalom*, sec. 6; 9, 11; *Ein Ayah, Berachos* Vol. II, 7:41. This apprehension is not borne out by studies of vegetarian societies or communities,

sentiments, he equivocates: "If the obligation of righteousness toward animals had been practiced as toward fellow humans, this would have greatly hindered the lofty spirit of human uprightness and those noble ideas that it has inculcated in human beings. For it was quite necessary for humanity to elevate itself from the lowly ways of other living creatures, whose entire universe consists of their stomach and their physical gratification. As a consequence, people would have forgotten their human superiority and come to think of themselves as beasts."[8]

Nevertheless, by extolling the virtues of such compassion and the moral inferiority of the desire for meat, Rav Kook rightfully may be seen as the most forceful rabbinic advocate of ethical vegetarianism in modern times. Indeed, in another of his philosophical works, he expresses the view that during the Messianic Age, the sacrificial offerings in the Holy Temple will consist of vegetation alone.[9]

An Ambiguous Prohibition

A Talmudic teaching often cited in support of vegetarianism is: "An *am ha'aretz* (one ignorant of Torah) is forbidden to eat meat" (*Pesachim* 49b). Since most human beings are not Torah scholars, they should restrict their eating habits to vegetarian foods. Upon closer examination, however, the actual intent of the Gemara is ambiguous. This is reflected by a wide range of interpretation among the authorities. Some take the statement at face value and interpret it in a legalistic sense: an ignoramus does not know the necessary laws and procedures related to the preparation of meat.[10] Other authorities take it as a philosophical statement: such a person has not fully attained the human level, thus his fellow creatures on the animal level are forbidden to him.[11]

---

such as those in the Far East. If anything, it appears that vegetarian societies are less prone to moral regression (much less cannibalism) than others. However, there are numerous precedents for societies with meat-based diets turning to cannibalism when unable to obtain sufficient meat from animals; see Louis Berman, *Vegetarianism and the Jewish Tradition* (1982), pp. 19-20, citing Reay Tannahill, *Flesh and Blood: A History of the Cannibal Complex* (1975) and other sources.

8. Ibid. sec. 8 (end).
9. *Olat Rayah*, I, 292. Also see Additional Source Texts, n. 107.
10. Rabbenu Nissim, Maharsha, ad loc.; *Teshuvos Rama*, no. 65.

However, in practical terms no rabbinic decisor actually forbids an ignorant or spiritually coarse individual to eat meat. The urbane *am ha'aretz* of today's consumer culture need not restrict his culinary habits, since he readily may rely upon those trained in *shechitah* and kosher food preparation. As for the philosophical interpretation, the Gemara's statement should be understood not as the basis for an additional dietary restriction, but as an implicit reproof: let the ignorant person remedy his shortcoming, and apply himself to studying the Torah. Only the Kabbalistic interpretation of this teaching may be understood as endorsing a limited form of vegetarianism. The Ari understands the Gemara as alluding to a mystical issue: one ignorant of Torah lacks the spiritual power to elevate the holy sparks and reincarnated souls trapped within animals. Therefore, he should sustain himself only with vegetarian foods.[12]

In this connection, contemporary scholar Rabbi Bezalel Naor postulates a basic dichotomy in Kabbalistic thought regarding vegetarianism. One trend affirms meat eating as an ideal: it is the responsibility of every tzaddik and Torah sage to elevate the holy sparks within the animal kingdom by doing so. This is the approach of the Chabad school of Chassidism, which Rabbi Naor traces back to the early medieval author of *Ma'areches Elokus*.[13] This would support the view that interprets the Talmud's restriction of the *am ha'aretz* along spiritual, rather than practical lines. By contrast, Rav Kook's perception of vegetarianism as the ideal diet and eating meat as a moral concession, seems to be aligned with the view of Nachmanides and his school, which gives greater emphasis to the underlying kinship between all living beings.[14] Ironically, this lends support to those who interpret the Talmud's restriction in a non-mystical manner.

11. *Sefer HaKanah, Sod Mi Mutar B'Achilas Basar*, pp. 277-279; R. Yitzchak Arama, *Akeidas Yitzchak, Beshalach*; Maharal, *Nesivos Olam*, chap. 15; R. Ephraim Lunshitz, *Kli Yakar*, Genesis 9:2; R. Moshe Feinstein, *Igros Moshe, Choshen Mishpat*, Vol. II, no. 47, sec. 1.
12. *Sha'ar HaMitzvos, Eikev*, p. 100; also cf. the pre-Lurianic *Sefer HaPeliah*, s.v. *U'r'ei v'havain*, pp. 282-283.
13. Translated in Additional Source Texts on Chapter 6, in "Benefits of Eating Meat."

Arguments In Favor of Vegetarianism

Aside from the various implications of the Talmudic teaching in *Pesachim*, a number of compelling reasons may be brought in favor of renouncing the traditional meat diet — whether one is qualifiedly ignorant or not.

1. Kashrus: Several biblical heroes and heroines, including Daniel and his comrades, Queen Esther, and the Maccabees became vegetarians in order to survive under religiously hostile conditions.[15] Jewish immigrants followed their example in various times and places; thus, many refugees from European poverty and persecution who came to America at the turn of the 20th century gave up the consumption of meat. Even under the best circumstances, the kosher status of animal products in particular demands careful scrutiny. This applies especially in this era of mass production. Ideally, one should be personally acquainted with the *shochet* of the meat one purchases, knowing him to be skillful at his profession and God-fearing.[16] Although *hashgachah* (kosher supervision) serves this purpose, the present system is by no means failsafe.[17] Most religious Jews who refrain from eating meat do so because of halachic scrupulousness.

2. Asceticism: It is surprising that for a non-vegetarian religion, Judaism has much to say in criticism of meat eating and comparatively little to say in defense of it. Perhaps this is because the sages wanted the Jewish people to exercise restraint in all matters of physical desire. One of

---

14. R. Bezalel Naor, *Ben Shanah Shaul, Divrei Aggadah: HaTzimchonut B'Ri'i HaYahadut*, pp. 291-298; also cf. *Sefer HaKanah*, s.v. *Sod Mi Mutar B'Achilas Basar*, pp. 277-279, which in certain places reads verbatim like *Ma'areches Elokus*.

15. Daniel 1:8-16; Ibn Ezra on Daniel 1:5; *Avodah Zarah* 36a; *Mayanei HaYeshuah* 5:3; *Me'am Loez* on Esther 2:9, citing R. Eliyahu Cohen Itamari of Izmir, *Dena Pishra*; II Maccabees 5:17. Josephus Flavius mentions that certain Kohanim on trial in Rome ate only figs and nuts to avoid non-kosher meat; see *Josephus* (Harvard University Press, 1926), Vol. I, p. 7. Native Americans used to call Jewish peddlers "egg-eaters" because they would not consume the flesh of animals killed by hunting or trapping.

16. This requirement was instituted at various times by regional rabbinic tribunals in response to the preponderance of unqualified *shochtim*. Regarding *hashgachah* in general, see *Yoreh De'ah, Shechitah*, 1:14, and *Shach*, ad loc. *Shechitah* by followers of the antinomian Karaite sect that accepted the Written Law but rejected the authority of the Talmud posed a frequent problem in both Sefardic and Ashkenazic lands; see *Yoreh De'ah, Shechitah* 2:9, and *Shach*, note 24.

the Torah's most striking examples of reckless immorality is the rebellious son who habitually feasts on meat and wine (Deuteronomy 21:18-21). Given this negative association of meat and wine, religious Jews have always treated their use with moderation. This reflects the Maimonidean virtue of the "golden mean" that avoids both extremes of hedonism or total renunciation. Moreover, ascetic practices have been a part of the Jewish mystical tradition since the times of the prophets. Rav Yosef Karo (1488-1575), author of the *Shulchan Aruch* and one of the greatest luminaries in Jewish history, limited his consumption of meat for such reasons.[18] To this day, many devoutly religious Jews partake of meat only on the Sabbath and Festivals, or at a *se'udas mitzvah* (feast in honor of a religious occasion). Rabbi Chaim Chizkiyahu Medini (1833-1903), author of *Sdei Chemed,* cites the example of a well-known Kabbalist-ascetic who would never partake of meat. "It is forbidden to disparage such a person, God forbid," the *Sdei Chemed* warns. "Fortunate is his lot. He abstained even from wine, except when performing a religious precept."[19]

3. Health: Maimonides interprets the scriptural mandate to "guard your souls well" (Deuteronomy 4:15) to mean that we must preserve our health to the best of our abilities.[20] This principle is an important factor in many areas of practical *halacha*, including the foods we choose to eat — aside from our concern as to whether or not they are kosher.[21] Since

---

17. I am told that it has become commonplace even for highly reputable *hashgachos* to avail themselves of the greatest halachic leniencies in examining *sirchos* (lesions). Even so-called glatt kosher meat may be designated as such if the slaughtered animal had no more than two *sirchos* of a minor degree (such a lesion is known as a *rir*). This criticism does not apply to the standard of "Beis Yosef glatt kosher" observed by many Sefardim. However, Ashkenazim traditionally follow the more stringent views of the Rama in other aspects of *shechitah,* disallowing them from using Beis Yosef glatt kosher meat. Exceptions to this rule are several Chassidic groups that insist on the stringencies of both the Beis Yosef and the Rama, and therefore slaughter their own meat, e.g. the Karlin-Stolin Chassidim.
18. See *Maggid Mesharim, Azharos V'Tikkunim U'Siyagim,* et passim. Some of this material appears in the Additional Source Texts for this chapter.
19. *Sdei Chemed,* Vol. 5, *Inyan Achilah.*
20. *Mishneh Torah, Hilchos Rotze'ach* 11:4; also cf. Hirsch, ad loc.
21. *Mishneh Torah, Hilchos De'os* 4:1, et passim, contains Rambam's views on dietary and other health issues. A good deal of this material is derived from the Talmud, although some reflects the scientific thought of his day. Another halachic ramification of this principle would be the institution of prophylactic measures against animal diseases that are passed on to humans through consumption of

red meat is high in saturated fat and cholesterol, when consumed regularly it may constitute a serious health concern. Cross-cultural studies have revealed that populations with the highest levels of saturated fat consumption also have the highest death rates from breast and colon cancer.[22] According to some studies, this is particularly evident among Ashkenazic Jews.[23] The relation of diet to heart disease has been well known for decades. The pioneering Framingham Study demonstrated a significant correlation between total cholesterol level and coronary risk.[24] Other chronic diseases that have been linked with meat consumption in at least some studies include prostate cancer, lymphoma, and kidney stones.[25]

In addition, the widespread use of growth hormones, antibiotics, and chemical food additives in modern factory farms has created a host of new consumer health hazards.[26] (Aside from *tza'ar baalei chaim*

---

animal products; see Laurence S. Shore, "Efforts by Jewish Communities to Prevent Zoonoses," *The Torah U-Madda Journal,* Vol. 8, 1998-99 (Yeshiva University 1999), pp. 277-283. The author cites *Yam Shel Shlomo* on *Bava Basra, Perek HaGozel,* 37; *Sifsei Zahav* on *Yoreh De'ah* 111:7; *Aruch HaShulchan, Yoreh De'ah* 60:3; and *Sho'el U'Meishiv Tinyana,* Sec. I, *Yoreh De'ah* 267.

22. Lane and Carpenter, "Breast Cancer: Incidence, Nutritional Concerns, and Treatment Approaches," *Journal of the American Dietetic Association,* 1987, 87:765-769; David P. Rose, et al., "International Comparisons of Mortality Rates for Cancer of the Breast, Ovary, Prostate, and Colon, and Per Capita Food Consumption," *Cancer,* 1986, 58:2363-2371. For a more recent study, see P.N. Singh, and G.E. Fraser, "Dietary Risk Factors for Colon Cancer in a Low-risk Population," *American Journal of Epidemiology,* 1998, 148:761-764. The latter study indicated approximately twice the cancer risk for those who consume red meat one or more times per week versus those who consume no red meat; and more than three times the risk for those who consume white meat one or more times per week versus those who consume no white meat.

23. G.E. Feldman, "Do Ashkenazi Jews Have a Higher Than Expected Cancer Burden? Implications for Cancer Control Prioritization Efforts." *Israel Medical Association Journal* 2001; 3:341-346. This proclivity is attributed to diet rather than genetics.

24. See P. W. F. Wilson, W. P. Castelli, and W. B. Kannel, "Coronary Risk Prediction in Adults (The Framingham Heart Study)," *The American Journal of Cardiology* 63 (1987): 91G-94G. Dr. Dean Ornish presented evidence that a combination of exercise, stress reduction, and a vegetarian diet can reverse heart disease in *Lancet* (1990) and *The Journal of the American Medical Association* (1995).

25. See note 28 below.

26. The European Union has accepted the research that links hormones used to treat cattle with several cancers. Therefore, it has banned the importation of such beef. U.S. scientists, however, claim that they have determined the threshold for causing cancer, and can therefore instruct farmers as to the dosages they may safely use. The

concerns, this is another reason why many non-vegetarians prefer "free-range" chickens raised on organic feed. In recent years, free-range chickens have been made available to kosher consumers, as well.[27]) By contrast, the superior health benefits of a balanced diet of whole grains, fresh fruits, and vegetables have been demonstrated persuasively.[28]

EU does not accept this claim. Also, a 1998 EU spot check of 258 "hormone free" beef cows imported from the U.S. showed that 12% contained hormones, some of which were altogether illegal. The effects of hormones on animals are largely unknown. Virtually all commercial poultry feed now contains some type of medication, inasmuch as sickness is rampant in factory farms. Of the estimated $87 million U.S. poultry producers spend annually on drugs, $75 million is spent on antibiotics, and the remainder on drugs to prevent intestinal parasites (www.hsus.org).

27. There are several wholesale and retail distributors of kosher organic free-range chickens in the New York area. Wise Kosher Natural Poultry, Inc., of Brooklyn, NY, offers Cornish game hens, ducks, and turkeys raised on organic feed under humane conditions by Amish and other farmers in Winfield, Penn., and slaughtered on the premises of the David Elliot Poultry Farm, Lake Ariel, Penn. Rabbinic supervision is provided by the Orthodox Union and Beis Din Tzedek of Crown Heights. Gertner Kosher Poultry of Monroe, NY, produces organic free-range chickens that are raised without hormone or antibiotic injections on several small farms in Pennsylvania. Rabbinic supervision is provided by the Vaad HaKashruth of Monsey, NY. Another family business, Pelleh Poultry of Monsey, NY, in conjunction with Bethel Farms, Bethel, NY, and under the supervision of Rabbi Dovid Miller, serves a limited clientele. However, animal activists caution that the term "free-range" can be misleading. Free-range chickens typically are de-beaked at the hatchery the same as battery-caged hens. In many cases such birds are kept indoors constantly, although the area in which they roam may be more spacious. Given the relative lack of government regulation of this industry at present, organic free-range poultry sometimes may be more contaminated than the standard product; see www.consumeralert.org/issues/food/organicfood.htm.

28. *Journal of the American Dietetic Association* 1997; 97:1317-1321. This thesis is supported by the "China Project," an epidemiological study involving more than 6,500 people in 65 provinces of China, undertaken collaboratively by Cornell University, Oxford University, and the Chinese Academy of Preventative Medicine. This study indicated that those who ate more animal products had the highest rates of heart disease, cancer, and chronic degenerative diseases; see T. Colin Campbell and Christine Cox, *The China Project: Keys to Better Health, Discovered in Our Living Laboratory* (Ithaca, NY: New Century Nutrition, 1996). Also see H. A. Kahn, R. L. Phillips, D. A. Snowdon, and W. Choi, "Association between Reported Diet and All-Cause Mortality," *American Journal of Epidemiology* 199 (1984): 775-87; D. A. Snowdon, "Animal Product Consumption and Mortality Because of All Causes Combined, Coronary Heart Disease, Stroke, Diabetes, and Cancer in Seventh-Day Adventists," *The American Journal of Clinical Nutrition* 48 (1988): 739-48; J. Chang-Claude, R. Frentzel-Beyme, and U. Eilber, "Mortality Pattern of German Vegetarians after 11 Years of Follow-up," *Epidemiology* 3 (1992): 395-401; J. Chang-Claude and R. Frentzel-Bayme, "Dietary and Lifestyle Determinants of

4. Esthetic Sensitivity: Some people simply do not like meat. Thus, the halachic view that it is a mitzvah to partake of meat on the Sabbath or Yom Tov in order to increase one's pleasure (*oneg*) or joy (*simcha*) does not apply to those who do not enjoy these foods.[29] Sometimes one may develop such an aversion as a psychological reaction to death. After the Holocaust, Rav Shraga Feivel Mendlowitz (1886-1948), legendary Menahel (principal) of New York's Mesivta Torah Vodaath, renounced eating meat, saying, "There has been enough killing in the world."[30] It is not an uncommon psychological phenomenon to lose one's taste for meat after the loss of a loved one.

5. Tza'ar Baalei Chaim: While *shechitah* as the method of animal slaughter designated by the Torah cannot be attacked on grounds of *tza'ar baalei chaim*, present slaughterhouse and factory farming procedures are not exempt from criticism. Despite ongoing efforts of animal welfare advocates, shackle and hoist restraint systems have not been eliminated completely; cruel methods of raising and slaughtering veal calves have not been banned; and, despite the existence of internal regulations developed by the large corporations, strict health and humane treatment laws still have not been imposed upon the poultry industry. Enforcement of existing USDA regulations also has been inconsistent in a number of areas related to animal transport and slaughter. Given the Judaic ethic of compassion for animals, kosher meat production should be a model to the rest of the industry for animal-slaughter with minimal *tza'ar baalei chaim*; thus, Jewish meat packing companies should welcome improved procedures for handling livestock prior to slaughter. Unfortunately, this has not always been the case.[31]

Mortality among German Vegetarians," *International Journal of Epidemiology* 22 (1993): 228-36; T. J. A. Key, M. Thorogood, P. N. Appleby, and M. I. Burr, "Dietary Habits and Mortality in 11,000 Vegetarians and Health Conscious People: Results of a 17 Year Follow Up," *BMJ* 313 (1996): 775-79. I am grateful to Dr. Jay Lavine for many of these references.

29. See R. Bleich, "Meat on Yom Tov," *Contemporary Halakhic Problems*, Vol. III, p. 248, n. 19, citing R. Moshe HaLevi Steinberg, *Chukkas HaGer, Kuntres HaTeshuvah*, no. 1.

30. R. Aharon Soraski, *Sh'lucha D'Rachmana* (Jerusalem: Feldheim, 1992), p. 249; similarly, note Yonoson Rosenblum's biography of R. Mendlowitz in *The Jewish Observer*, Oct. 1998, p. 19.

6. Ecological Consequences: Surprising as these facts may seem, 70% of the grain grown in the United States is fed to animals, 50% of the nation's acreage is devoted to feed crops for animals, and livestock production consumes 80% of our fresh water — an increasingly precious commodity.[32] Leading ecologists such as Robert Goodland, Environmental Advisor to the World Bank, and David Pimentel of Cornell University point out that vastly disproportionate amounts of the Earth's resources are expended to support meat-based diets, while people in many parts of the world are starving. This already has created serious environmental problems. Goodland and Pimentel observe that the worldwide demand for water has tripled in the last two decades, while pollution and wasteful agricultural practices have further reduced natural resources.[33] Cattle raised for food purposes produce more than 2 billion tons of waste annually, causing extensive water pollution; and the Environmental Protection Agency (EPA) lists pathogens from bird wastes (manure and corpses) as the third most primary pollutant from agricultural runoff.[34] Chemical fertilizers and the vast quantities of

31. Temple Grandin, *"Humanitarian Aspects of Shechitah in the United States,"* incl. in Kalechovsky, *Judaism and Animal Rights: Classical and Contemporary Responses,* (Micah 1992), esp. "Economic Factors," p. 96.
32. U.S. Department of Agriculture, Foreign Agriculture Service, "World Cereals Used For Feed," (unpublished printout), Washington, DC, 4.91; USDA Agricultural Statistics, 1989; p. 389, table 554, "Crops: Area, Yield, Production and Value, United States, 1986-88" (Washington, DC: GPO, 1989). Pimentel, et al., "The Potential for Grass-Fed Livestock: Resource Constraints," Science, 2.22.80. According to Robert H. Brown in *Feedstuffs* 1.31.94, almost a decade ago broiler operations used an estimated 96.3 billion gallons of water annually, and the demand has increased every year. In California, the leading dairy state in the U.S., livestock agriculture consumes nearly one-third of all irrigation water. Similar figures apply across the western states; see Durning and Hough, *Taking Stock: Animal Farming and the Environment* (Worldwatch 1991), pp. 17-18. Worldwatch Institute estimates that more than 3,000 liters of water are required to produce a kilogram of American beef (ibid.).
33. Goodland and Pimentel, included in Pimentel, Westra, and Noss, *Ecological Integrity: Integrating Environment, Conservation, and Health* (Washington, DC: Island Press, 2000), Chapter 5, "Sustainability and Integrity in the Agricultural Sector," pp.128-130.
34. Animal agriculture accounts for one third of surface water pollution in the U.S. Yet chicken manure, no matter how great the quantity, remains unregulated under the Clean Water Act. More than 360 million birds weighing a combined 470,000 tons that die each year prior to slaughter must be safely disposed of (www.hsus.org).

dangerous pesticides necessary for livestock production in particular are responsible for significant air and water pollution.[35]

Another related environmental problem is that enormous tracts of tropical rainforests continue to be bulldozed and burned in order to create additional rangelands for cattle.[36] Aside from the loss of these irreplaceable natural resources and the many species of wildlife they support, destroying the world's rainforests promises to bring in its wake ecological changes of such proportions as to alter global climatic conditions and reduce the world's rainfall. This would have a devastating effect upon world agriculture. By contrast, the increased cultivation of vegetarian sources of food would impact far less negatively upon the environment and help relieve the problem of hunger in underdeveloped countries.

As Orthodox vegetarian Dr. Richard Schwartz has written, "By adopting a diet that shows concern and lovingkindness for the hungry people of the world, by working for righteousness through more equitable sharing of God's abundant harvests, we can play a significant role in moving the world toward that day when 'nations shall not learn war anymore' (Isaiah 2:4)."[37]

---

35. Goodland and Pimentel, op cit., pp. 131-132, and Laura Westra, pp. 282-287; Frances Lappe, *Diet for a Small Planet*, pp. 80, 136.

36. Based on estimates of forest conversion made by the Food and Agriculture Organization of the U.N., ecologist T.C. Whitmore states that tropical deforestation throughout the 1980s exceeded 150,000 sq. km per year. If impacts such as selective logging are included, this rate exceeds 200,000 sq. km per year. Whitmore estimates that 154 million hectares (a hectare is 2.471 acres) were lost from 1981 to 1990. At this rate, an additional third of the world's remaining rainforests will be cleared or modified by 2025. Though occupying only 7% of the Earth's land surface, these forests probably sustain more than half of the planet's life forms. Thus, their depletion threatens biological diversity as well as ecological stability (Lawrence and Bierregaard, *Tropical Forest Remnants: Ecology, Management, and Conservation of Fragmented Communities* [Chicago: University of Chicago Press, 1997]). Conservation efforts are presently underway to regulate rainforest depletion.

37. *Judaism and Vegetarianism* (Lantern 2001), p. 101; also note the same author's discussion of vegetarianism and environmental issues in *Judaism and Global Survival* (Lantern 2002), Chapter 12. However, dietary change is only a partial solution to the problem of world hunger. Even under present conditions, there would be no lack of food if the majority of economic and political leaders resolved to eliminate world hunger. Russia, Ukraine, China, and India, for example, possess vast natural resources, but their populations have insufficient food. Even countries whose lands have been purchased by western corporations for livestock production commonly

7. Ethical Principles: Although not a practicing vegetarian,[38] Rav
Kook affirmed the moral sensitivity that leads to this practice as
emanating from the enlightenment of the Messianic Age, when all
creatures will coexist in harmony and peace. His views are based upon
those of the *Akeidas Yitzchak, Sefer HaIkkarim,* and the Ari. A similar
sentiment is voiced by the Chasam Sofer (although the latter was not a
vegetarian, either). However, Rav Kook's disciple, Rabbi Dovid Cohen
(1887-1973), did become a devout vegetarian after moving to an
apartment near a slaughterhouse. Distressed by the anguished cries of the
animals, the sensitive Torah scholar resolved never again to eat meat. He
even refrained from wearing leather shoes. However, we have no
indication that his philosophy differed from that of his mentor, Rav
Kook. As such, it arguably may be classified as a personal sensitivity,
rather than a full-fledged ethical vegetarian position.

More outspoken in his views was Rabbi Chaim Maccoby
(1858-1916), better known as the Kamenitzer Maggid, who preached the
virtues of ethical vegetarianism and compassion for animals on the
streets of London during the early 1900s. In his refusal to benefit from the
killing of other creatures, he stopped wearing leather shoes, and added a
second hard-boiled egg to his Passover Seder plate to replace the
traditional shank bone (*zero'ah*) or chicken wing that commemorates the
Paschal Lamb. (Like his contemporary Rav Kook, the Kamenitzer Maggid
was an ardent religious Zionist, who took issue with the secularist
ideology of Theodor Herzl and its proponents within England's Chovevei
Zion Society.)[39]

An obscure but erudite vegetarian activist from the same period,
Rabbi Yitzchak Hebenstreit of Reisha, Poland, authored a fiery

---

suffered from food shortages prior to this. Poverty exists not simply because of a lack
of natural resources, but due to unrestrained human greed and ruthless indifference
to the plight of the less fortunate.

38. When as a young student in Europe, R. Zvi Yehudah Kook sought parental approval
to adopt a vegetarian diet, it appears that his father, Rav Kook, demurred *(Zemach
Zvi: Letters of Rav Zvi Yehudah HaKohen Kook* [Jerusalem, 1991], pp. 110, 138-139).
39. R. Maccoby's biography and a small collection of his sermons was published as *Imrei
Chaim* (Tel Aviv: Mansky, 1928); also see entries on the Kamenitzer Maggid in the
Encyclopedia Judaica and *Encyclopedia of Zionism* (Hebrew). The Kamenitzer Maggid's
grandson, Dr. Hyam Maccoby of Surrey, U.K., kindly furnished this information.

denouncement of meat eating and other human uses of animals entitled *Kivros HaTa'avah* ("The Graves of Lust"), published by a Jewish vegetarian society.[40] The title recalls the biblical incident when the Children of Israel, unappreciative of the Manna from heaven, demanded meat, and so brought upon themselves divine retribution.

In addition to these points in support of vegetarianism, two Kabbalistic reasons may be cited:

8. Spiritual Risks: Some time ago, proponents of the macrobiotic diet popularized the slogan, "You are what you eat." Perhaps to the surprise of many readers, a number of rabbinic sources seem to agree — at least to the extent of recognizing that food affects personality. The Ramban (R. Moshe ben Nachman, or Nachmanides, 1194-1270) proposes that predatory creatures are forbidden to Jews in order to distance us from the traits of ruthless aggression and cold-bloodedness, etc.[41] The anonymous author of *Sefer HaChinnuch* takes a similar stance.[42] Rav Yosef Albo implicitly extends this rationale to the kosher species, although presumably to a lesser degree. "In the killing of animals there is cruelty, rage, and habituation to the evil of shedding innocent blood," he states. "Moreover, the eating of certain animals produces emotional coarseness, physical ugliness, and intellectual weakness."[43] (However, one who adheres to the dietary laws and eats in a spirit of sanctity is less susceptible to such negative influences than one who eats without proper restraint or intention.)

---

40. Although an articulate spokesmen for vegetarianism and what today would be called "animal rights," R. Hebenstreit must be faulted for imposing his agenda on his source material, rather than developing the actual case for these ethical concerns from within the parameters of normative rabbinic tradition; e.g., in chap. 3 (end) he summarily dismisses the entire concept of spiritually elevating the lower levels of creation, even interpreting the incident of R. Yehudah HaNasi and the calf as an implicit refutation of this thesis. Yet nowhere is this novel interpretation supported by the Rishonim, nor can it be reconciled with the Kabbalah of the Ramak or the Ari. His treatment of the sacrificial rites is similarly idiosyncratic.

41. *Commentary on the Torah, Vayikra*, chap. 11, et passim. A Kabbalistic precedent for this view is found in *Sefer HaKanah, Simanei Ofos Tehoros V'Treifos*, p. 272, which adds that kosher animals, by contrast, generally display a greater degree of compassion and peacefulness.

42. *Sefer HaChinnuch*, Mitzvah 73, 148, 154, et passim.

43. *Sefer HaIkkarim* 3:15.

9. Reincarnated Souls: The Kabbalists teach that eating is not merely a biological need, but a spiritual responsibility by which one may elevate the holy sparks and reincarnated souls trapped within the food. According to the Chassidic masters, most animals today contain reincarnated human souls. Eating kosher food and reciting the appropriate blessings with mindfulness is of critical importance in accomplishing their *tikkun*. One who neglects to recite these blessings or to eat in a holy manner not only fails to elevate the souls present in the food, but also renders his soul susceptible to harm. Rabbi Moshe Cordovero and the Ari concur in stating that of all foods, meat presents the greatest spiritual danger.[44]

Arguments In Favor of Meat Eating

Having enumerated the basic reasons in favor of vegetarianism, we must consider the opposite point of view: the defense of meat eating as a diet that is supported by common Jewish practice.

1. Need: In various times and places throughout history, humans have depended on animal foods, as well as hides and furs, for their survival. Several biblical commentators (Sforno, Abarbanel, Malbim and Hirsch) offer this as the reason why divine consent was given to Noah and his descendants to slaughter animals after the world's vegetation had been depleted by the biblical flood, and the Earth's climate changed.[45] Indigenous populations of mountainous regions such as Tibet or the Andes, as well as those who dwell in deserts or regions where there is a short growing season, invariably rely upon herding to supplement the limited range of crops they can raise.

2. Permissibility: When asked their opinion of meat eating as opposed to vegetarianism, most observant Jews probably would reply, "If it's permissible, it's permissible." The restrictions imposed by the Torah

---

44. R. Moshe Cordovero, *Shiur Komah*, 84c; R. Chaim Vital citing the Ari, *Sha'ar HaMitzvos, Eikev*, p. 100.
45. R. Ovadiah Sforno on Genesis 8:22, 6:13; R. Yitzchak Abarbanel on Genesis 9:1, sec. 3; R. Meir Leibush Malbim on Genesis 9:3; R. Samson Raphael Hirsch on Genesis 9:3. See "Permission to Eat Meat as a Practical Concession" in Sources for the present chapter.

upon non-Jews (not to consume the limb of a living animal) and Jews (the kosher laws) were given with full knowledge of the needs and limitations of humankind. Just as some people are repelled by meat, others prefer it — and to judge from the fare served at most restaurants, the latter are in the majority.

3. Rabbinic Affirmation: The vast majority of Torah sages did consume meat, at least on the Sabbath and Festivals. It is inconceivable that these saintly individuals were incapable of restraining their desires, while millions of people all over the world subsist without meat, often for religious reasons. Notwithstanding the view of the *Kli Yakar* cited above, it is hard to believe that the rabbis took such great pains to work out the halachic intricacies of *shechitah,* forbidden mixtures of meat and milk, salting, etc., simply in order to coax the masses toward vegetarianism. One would expect there to be greater significance in their affirmation of meat eating. Kabbalistically, this would be the task of elevating the holy sparks.

4. Elevating the Holy Sparks: The *tikkun* of all levels of creation depends upon the divine service of humankind, particularly the fulfillment of the Torah's commandments by the Jewish people. By partaking of meat in a holy manner — by ascertaining that the animal has been properly slaughtered and prepared, reciting the appropriate blessings, and eating with holy intention — one can spiritually elevate the sparks contained in food. At the same time, this enhances the state of mind of the one who engages in eating meat. Among Jewish mystics, the Baal Shem Tov took issue with his ascetic predecessors in emphasizing the advantages of serving God through the very things of this world; thus the early Chassidim were less inclined to renounce meat eating than non-Chassidic pietists. Asceticism, the Baal Shem Tov warned, can lead to gloom, and what is worse: the sin of pride.

5. Enjoying the Sabbath and Festivals: This is an extremely strong point in favor of meat eating, being explicitly supported by the Talmud and legal codes. In fact, the sages considered this to be such an integral part of these sacred occasions that they permitted animal slaughter on the Festivals in order to provide for the needs of the day. (However, it is

scripturally prohibited to slaughter an animal, or even to kill an insect on the Sabbath, unless it presents a threat to human life.)[46] Maimonides rules that in order to enhance one's enjoyment of the Festivals, it is an actual mitzvah to eat meat.[47] Some authorities extend this to Purim, as well.[48] On the Sabbath, the consumption of meat and fish is customary, although not strictly required. As mentioned above, this does not apply to an individual who dislikes meat, abstains for reasons of health or *kashrus*, or has another legitimate objection to eating meat.

6. Increasing One's Physical Strength: Eaten in moderation, meat and other animal foods contain certain health benefits not as readily available to vegetarians if they do not eat a variety of plant-based foods. The Gemara recounts how Rav Nachman was unable to refute a rabbinic colleague because he had not eaten beef on the previous evening.[49] Rabbinic sources also enumerate various maladies for which meat and fish have a medicinal effect.[50] However, these benefits must be weighed against the dangers to health posed by harmful substances in the meat commonly produced today, as well as the proven deleterious effects of meat and other animal products when used as dietary staples.[51]

7. Religious Humanism: According to medieval philosopher Rav Yosef Albo, meat eating is an implicit refutation of the philosophical idea of the equivalence of the species. Of all living things, humankind alone is

46. *Shulchan Aruch, Orach Chaim,* 316:9; also see *Chayei Adam, Hilchos Shabbos, Klal* 31 ("HaShochet"), 2, 7; et al.

47. Rambam, *Sefer HaMitzvos,* Positive Mitzvah 54; *Mishneh Torah, Yom Tov* 6:18; *Tur Shulchan Aruch, Orach Chaim* 529; also note *Sifré, Devarim* 16:11. However, the *Beis Yosef* (ad loc.) and *Magen Avraham* on *Orach Chaim* 696:15 disagree, as does the *Sha'agas Aryeh.* See *Darkei Teshuvah, Yoreh De'ah* 89:19, at length.

48. See Rambam, *Mishneh Torah, Hilchos Megillah* 2:15. Citing the *Taz* on *Orach Chaim* 693 and other Acharonim, R. Menashe Klein of Ungvar, in his *Mishneh Halachos* Vol. 7, no. 93, interprets the Rambam's words to mean that it is appropriate to eat meat in order to rejoice, but not that one has failed to perform the mitzvah of feasting on Purim if one does not eat meat. R. Moshe Sternbuch in *Moadim U'Zmanim,* Vol. II, no. 175, argues that the Torah designates Purim as a day that is intrinsically joyous, therefore delivering eulogies and fasting are prohibited by a tradition of the prophets, while feasting is required only by rabbinic decree. Nevertheless, one who can afford to eat meat on Purim (and presumably enjoys meat) is obligated to do so. R. Chaim Elazar Spira of Munkatch discusses the arguments pro and con in *Nimmukei Orach Chaim* 695:2, and while inclined toward the requirement of eating meat at the Purim meal, he does not take a position.

49. *Bava Kamma* 71b, 72a.

created in the "divine image" (Genesis 1:26). The use of animals for food constantly reminds man of his higher status and correspondingly greater responsibilities in the divine plan. However, if man takes himself to be no more than another sort of animal, he inevitably will descend to the level of predatory beasts and forfeit his higher spiritual potential. Indeed, some individuals might champion animal causes not out of genuine compassion for animals, but due to a narcissistic wish to escape the moral obligations of civilization by identifying with lower forms of life. (Of course, this does not negate the fact that many famous vegetarians also have been humanitarians, and a high percentage of vegetarians in our society are involved in numerous causes for human betterment.)

Conclusion

Because the Torah mandates that humankind dominate nature (as responsible caretakers), allows us to slaughter animals for food, and during the period of the Holy Temple required certain animal sacrifices in addition to those of a voluntary nature, it is impossible to assert an ethical vegetarian position without qualification. That is, while vegetarianism circumvents the possibility of causing or condoning *tza'ar*

---

50. Rav recommends that meat be eaten after one undergoes bloodletting, whereas Shmuel disagrees, and recommends wine (*Shabbos* 129a). The sages state that a pregnant woman who eats meat and drinks wine will bear healthy children (*Kesubos* 60b*f*). Lean meat broiled over coals, as well as diluted wine, are a cure for both wine-induced delirium and severe heat-stroke; whereas fatty meat broiled over coals, as well as undiluted wine, relieve illness brought on by a chill (*Gittin* 67b). Also, one opinion has it that the lung is called *rei'ah* because consuming an animal's lung improves a person's eyesight (*r'iyah*) (*Chullin* 49a). A fish diet is recommended for nursing mothers, as well as sufferers from eye problems (*Avodah Zarah* 29a, *Kesubos* 60b); fish are generally regarded as an all-purpose health food (*Sanhedrin* 98a, *Berachos* 40a, *Gittin* 69b); see Schochet, *Animal Life in the Jewish Tradition*, chap. 10.
51. See n. 28 above. It has been demonstrated that all the nutrients contained in animal foods may be obtained through a vegetarian diet if one eats intelligently; see "Eating Well — The Vegetarian Way," published by the American Dietary Association, 1992, which rejects the "complimentary protein" theory. The same study states that vegans, who consume no animal products whatever, can obtain all the calcium they need from plant foods alone, without risking the health hazards that accompany high fat, high protein diets. In addition, most of the meat and dairy products available today are less healthful than they were in former times, due to the ubiquitous use of growth hormones, antibiotics, genetic modification, etc.

baalei chaim, we cannot say that meat eating as countenanced by the Torah is intrinsically wrong — or God would have forbidden it altogether. As for the divine mandate for humankind to dominate nature, if human beings could not do so, our survival would be morally impossible. We neither could cut down a tree for shelter, nor defend ourselves against predators. The entire system of creation, at least during the present phase of history, inevitably operates by the use of one species by another, and one human being by another. From a Jewish perspective, what makes us civilized is the degree to which we follow the world's "instruction manual," namely, the Torah of Israel, and the moral system it prescribes for all humanity: the Seven Laws of Noah. Within certain parameters, both codes permit animal slaughter.

The general affirmation of meat eating that characterizes the Jewish tradition indicates that it must have a more positive, redeeming aspect: Kabbalistically, this is the "elevation of the holy sparks." Normative *halacha* clearly permits meat eating. However, in this writer's opinion, the specifically contemporary issues have been insufficiently considered: *kashrus* problems that may result from an increase in sicknesses among animals created by factory farm conditions, coupled with the inevitably higher margin of error in mass production *shechitah* facilities; *tza'ar baalei chaim* as a consequence of mass production methods of raising, transporting, and slaughtering animals; proven health risks to humans due to the administration of growth hormones, antibiotics, and other drugs given to animals used for food; and the negative health and ecological consequences of meat-based diets. These are halachic challenges that can only be resolved by *Gedolei Yisrael,* those pre-eminent contemporary rabbinic authorities whose rulings are followed by observant Jews.

In favor of vegetarianism, it is clear that an individual who wishes to embrace this dietary regime as a personal preference for any of the reasons enumerated above may do so.

Beyond this, we must reiterate that vegetarianism is the diet of the Messianic Age, when exploitation and cruelty on all levels of creation will cease forever. According to all authorities, we are rapidly approaching this period. Therefore, it may not be coincidental that the moral sensitivity toward animals to which Rav Kook referred a century ago is beginning to increase in the world. Accordingly, one may embrace vegetarianism as a volitional component of his or her spiritual path.

As a postscript, I would like to include an anecdote that points out the difficulty of taking an unequivocal position on vegetarianism. While researching the present volume, I had the honor of meeting Rav Shear-Yashuv Cohen, Chief Rabbi of Haifa, and a lifelong vegetarian. His father was Rabbi Dovid Cohen, the Nazir of Jerusalem, who edited Rav Avraham Yitzchak Kook's treatise, "A Vision of Vegetarianism and Peace." After exchanging greetings with the Rav, I began to describe my work-in-progress. When I mentioned the issue of "elevating the holy sparks," however, the Rav stopped me.

"Let me tell you a story," he interjected. "A number of years ago, I visited the Lubavitcher Rebbe (R. Menachem Mendel Schneerson, 1902-1994), of blessed memory, during the period when the Rebbe was giving dollars, along with his blessings, to the thousands of visitors who streamed to his door at 770 Eastern Parkway in the Crown Heights section of Brooklyn on Sunday afternoons. When I was introduced to the Rebbe, to my surprise, he immediately recognized my name. In the course of conversation, the Rebbe asked, 'Are you a vegetarian?'

"I answered that I had never eaten meat in my life, to which he responded, 'I understand why you are a vegetarian. But what I don't understand is: how could your father give up eating meat? What about the elevation of the holy sparks?'

"'Has the Rebbe seen the remarks of the *Sdei Chemed* on this?' I asked. Replying in the negative, the Rebbe instructed his Gabbai (attendant) to bring the volume in question. There, the author states that a number of eminent Kabbalists refrained from eating meat due to asceticism, as well as the spiritual risks involved. After perusing the text for a few moments, the Rebbe smiled, and with a twinkle in his eye, replied, 'Rav Cohen, you have defeated me!'"

We must note that despite this scholarly exchange with the Rav of Haifa, the Lubavitcher Rebbe did not become a vegetarian. However, their dialogue underscores the fact that whatever one's choice of diet, eating must be approached as a spiritual task, and not merely a physical indulgence.

Sources

Primacy of Vegetarian Foods

And the Lord said: Behold, I have given you every herb yielding seed that is upon the face of the Earth, and every tree in which is the fruit of a tree yielding seed — to you it shall be for food. And to every animal of the Earth, and to every bird of the sky, and to everything that creeps upon the Earth that possesses a living soul, [I have given] every green herb for food. And it was so (Genesis 1:29-30).

Commentary 1: [The Creator] made human beings equal to the animals with regard to food, and He did not permit Adam and his wife to kill a creature and eat its flesh. Only "every green herb" may they all eat alike (Rashi, ad loc.).

Commentary 2: The purpose of eating is to extricate the good possessed by an article of food and to elevate it from the impurity and spiritual dross with which it is mixed. Since animals were then on a lofty spiritual plane, permission was not given for them to be eaten. However, vegetation such as herbs and trees were allowed, for they still needed to be refined through eating (Rabbi Yitzchak Luria, as cited by Rabbi Chaim Vital, *Sha'ar HaMitzvos, Eikev,* p. 99).

∞

And God blessed Noah and his sons, and He said unto them: "Every moving thing that lives shall be food for you; as the green herb, I have given you everything. Only flesh with its living soul — its blood you shall not eat" (Genesis 9:1-4).

Commentary: "Shall be food for you." I did not permit meat to Adam, but only green herbs; but as for you — as the green herbs that I declared free to Adam, so I have given you everything (*Sanhedrin* 57a).

"Flesh with its living soul." He forbade them the limb of a living animal; that is, as long as its living soul is in it, you shall not eat its flesh (Rashi, ad loc.).

∞

For God, your Lord, brings you into a good land: a land of water-courses, springs, and pools that come forth from the valley and hill; a land of wheat, and barley, and grapevine, and fig, and pomegranate; a land of olive oil and honey [of dates]; a land where you will eat bread without scarcity, and you will not lack anything in it (Deuteronomy 8:7-9).

Commentary 1: It is a positive commandment of the Torah to bless God after one has eaten bread [made from the five types of grain], or any of the seven types of produce [listed in the verses above] to the point of satiation. Common bread is made of wheat or barley. Spelt is included in the category of wheat, whereas oats and rye are included in the category of barley. Also concerning the seven types of produce, the Torah states, "And you shall eat and be sated, and you shall bless God, your Lord, for the good land which He has given you" (Deuteronomy 8:10) (*Sefer HaChinnuch,* Mitzvah 430).

Commentary 2: The main food for humans is bread, as our sages state concerning the commandment to recite the Grace After Meals. Bread possesses universality, for it actually includes all four elements: earth, water, air, and fire. Flour corresponds to the element of earth, for all grains come from the earth. The flour is kneaded with water. Then the dough is allowed to rise; that is, it swells and expands as a result of the element of air. Finally, it is baked, which involves the element of fire. Thus, bread includes all four elements (Rabbi Nosson Sternhartz, *Likkutei Halachos, Pesach* 3:8).

Treat Bread With Respect

The rabbis taught: Four things were said with regard to bread. It is forbidden to place raw meat on bread; to pass a full cup over bread; to throw bread; or to support a platter with bread (Talmud: *Berachos* 50a).

Commentary: The respect shown to bread instructs us as to the sacredness of life and its honor. Since human beings were created for a most lofty mission, it is particularly fitting to honor them. This should be done by showing respect even toward the medium through which they primarily derive life, which is bread. An extra measure of honor should be given to bread, for it betokens the pre-eminence of humankind. What is more, it is destined to bring humankind to a greater spiritual height, for *da'as* (intellect or wisdom) is increased through bread. As our sages taught: "An infant does not know how to say 'father' or 'mother' until it has tasted grain."[52]

Due to the bestial spirit within man, he is predisposed to eat raw meat, like all predatory animals; thus, even today on the outskirts of civilization may be found savages who consume human flesh; and the predilection toward cannibalism is shown particularly through eating raw meat. Therefore, our sages spoke with disdain of those inclined to eat raw meat, e.g., when they spoke disparagingly of the Babylonians who did so.[53]

The process of making bread for food was conceived by man due to his higher intellect and his spiritual elevation above the ways of predatory animals, through his recognition of those sublime gifts with which he has been endowed. For man was created in the divine image in order to emulate his Master in doing that which is righteous and good. Therefore, he was enlightened in that he prepared his staple foods from vegetation. Moreover, when vegetation in its raw state was insufficient to sustain him, he was all the more intelligent to invent bread, of which it is written, "And bread sates the heart of man."[54] It shall transpire in the course of time, when the human heart has been healed entirely from the moral decline that the Primordial Serpent brought about, that man shall forswear meat eating completely. For the Torah did not permit [the consumption of animal flesh] except as a concession to the weakness of the body, as a result of moral weakness of the soul and her alienation from the light of the face of her Maker; in the words of scripture, "For it your soul desires to eat flesh..." (Deuteronomy 12:20).

In addition, our sages state: "An ignoramus is forbidden to eat meat."[55] It is understood that meat is permitted to a Torah scholar only

---

52. *Berachos* 40a.
53. *Menachos* 99b.
54. Psalms 104:15.
55. *Pesachim* 49b.

so that he strengthen his Torah study, which is called the "light of the world."[56] [This light emerges through difficulty and suffering.] It is fitting that animals contribute their share to bringing light to the world, just as human beings have brought numerous sacrifices through the many wars and disasters that God has visited upon us in order to straighten the crookedness of the heart. When there shall no longer be a need for this, it is understood that Torah scholars will no longer require meat. Scripture lists among the promised blessings: "And you shall eat your bread to satiety..." (Leviticus 21:5). It is significant that in the holy tongue [Hebrew] a formal meal is synonymous with bread.[57] This alludes to the higher ethical goal [of vegetarianism] that will be realized in the future.

In any case, eating raw meat exemplifies the inferior side of human nature, while the higher aspect develops through eating bread. This is why *it is forbidden to place raw meat on bread*, for bread symbolizes civilized and ethical life, as opposed to raw meat, which indicates savage behavior. However, the civilized custom to prepare food, beginning with bread, becomes a spiritual obstacle when one uses it improperly, estranging a person from his innate disposition to be satisfied with simple foods that are sufficient for him. The intelligence with which he engages in preparing food now leads him to seek delicacies, until he is no longer content with food that merely satisfies his hunger.

This harmful conduct is even more apparent in the case of drinking, as the Torah states concerning Noah.[58] Thus, *it is forbidden to pass a full cup over bread*. Usually a cup is filled to the brim with a beverage that is an extravagance; when one drinks water to quench one's thirst, one is not particular to fill the cup. [Refraining from passing a full cup over the bread] indicates that the intrinsic worthiness of bread enables one to

---

56. Exodus 2:20; *Bava Basra* 4a.
57. I Samuel 20:24.
58. Genesis 9:20-27. After the waters of the Flood subsided, Noah planted a grapevine, from the fruit of which he made wine and became intoxicated. Thus, while Adam and Eve sinned through the forbidden fruit, Noah experienced a spiritual decline through drink. A possible allusion to this may be found in one of R. Nachman of Breslov's thirteen mystical stories, *Sippurei Maasiyos*, Story 1 (The Tale of the Lost Princess), when after failing the first test to save the Lost Princess by not eating for one day, the Royal Viceroy is given a second test by which he must refrain from drinking for one day.

attain his highest potential: to eat to satisfy his soul [rather than to indulge the senses], and to rejoice in his genuine fulfillment.

Indeed, one of the categories of showing respect for life is alacrity in fulfilling whatever is needed to preserve the vitality of the body, contradicting the view of those who despise life, who deprive the body of its basic requirements. Concerning this, we are cautioned *not to throw bread.* That is, we should not repudiate that which is necessary, such as the bread "by which a man lives,"[59] as if it were scornful. Rather, we should cherish involvement with everything that brings fulfillment of legitimate human needs, within moderation.

The seal of the signet ring of human destiny is to make clearly known to man that the ultimate quest of his life is to attain the Crown of Life: the wisdom and righteousness that comprise the knowledge of God. However, from the desire of fools, bon vivants who only find time for the sensual pleasures of temporal life, it is well to keep distant. Therefore, *it is forbidden to support a platter on bread,* in order to show one's repudiation of the statement that belittles life, when the fool declares: "I shall live in order to eat!" He supports his platter full of delicacies on bread as if bread was invented to enable him to live for no higher purpose than to enjoy the delicacies heaped upon his platter. This is not the portion of the spiritually evolved person, who eats in order to live, and with bread supports his Torah study and the divine knowledge in his heart. From the Five Books of Moses, the Prophets, and the Writings, we find that "bread sates the heart"[60] — that is, the heart of man that is prepared to understand, in order to do what is good (Rabbi Avraham Yitzchak HaKohen Kook, *Ein Ayah,* Vol. II, *Berachos,* chap. 7, par. 41, pp. 223-224).

Permission to Eat Meat as a Moral Concession

When the Lord, your God, shall enlarge your border, as He has told you, and you will say, "I will eat flesh," because your soul desires to eat flesh—after all the desire of your soul you may eat flesh (Deuteronomy 12:20).

---

59. Paraphrase of Deuteronomy 8:3.
60. Paraphrase of *Bereishis Rabbah* 48:11.

Commentary 1: The Torah teaches proper conduct, for one should not wish to eat flesh except in a time of abundance and wealth (Rashi, ad loc., citing *Chullin* 84b).

Commentary 2: This teaches that a person does not give full vent to his passions except amidst great affluence. "A lion does not roar over a pile of straw, but over a pile of meat" (*Berachos* 32a). Thus, [the condition of] "when the Lord shall enlarge your border..." will lead you to remove the veil of shame from your face, until you openly declare your desire to eat meat. This is a form of casting off the yoke of the kingdom of Heaven in order to seek that which properly is associated with the sacrificial rites alone.

The cause of all this is [indicated by the verse,] "If the place that God has chosen be too far from you..." (Deuteronomy 12:21). The closer a person comes to the divine sanctuary, the greater is his awe of Heaven, as it is written: "And My sanctuary shall you fear" (Leviticus 19:30). That is to say, from the sanctuary is drawn forth your awe of the kingdom of Heaven. However, "if the place be too far from you," then "God is far from your thoughts" (Jeremiah 12:2). Therefore, all day long you are obsessed with desire and are not ashamed to demand meat to eat. Behold, [says God,] I permit you this thing. However, you must slaughter your cattle according to the rules I have imposed upon you — not at any time but only on occasion, when your desire overcomes you (Rabbi Shlomo Ephraim Lunshitz, *Kli Yakar*, Deuteronomy 12:20).

ೞೞ

"Just as you may eat the deer and the hart, thus shall you eat them" (Deuteronomy 12:22). This may be understood according to the verse that states, "And when you trap animals or birds..." (Leviticus 17:13). Concerning this, our sages remark, "The Torah teaches us proper conduct, that a human being should not eat flesh except after such preparation."[61] If one would accustom himself to a diet of those animals that are designated for his consumption, such as the ox, sheep, or goat, he would constantly indulge his desires. But if he were forbidden to eat

---

61. *Chullin* 84a.

animals unless he goes to the wilderness to trap his prey, be it animal or fowl, which is dangerous and extremely troublesome, then his desire would be stilled. Eating is not worth such great difficulty.

Not without reason did Isaac tell Esau, "Go forth to the field and trap venison for me" (Genesis 27:3), since he did not have in his house anything that had been trapped previously. Why was he so anxious to send him into danger, but that he follow the Torah's standard of proper conduct and only eat meat that has been fittingly prepared, specifically by trapping? This would prevent [Esau] from becoming accustomed to such indulgence.

Therefore, it states, "Just as you may eat the deer and the hart, thus shall you eat them." In other words, upon this condition, that you do not become habituated to it, you may eat meat. You consume the deer and the hart only infrequently, for they are wild creatures that must be trapped; because of the effort involved, a person limits his eating of them. Thus shall you eat even ordinary meat. This is a fitting explanation of the verse that expands upon Rashi's words (Rabbi Shlomo Ephraim Lunshitz, ibid.).

০৪৪০

And God said to Moses: Tell the people, "Sanctify yourselves [in preparation] for tomorrow, and you shall eat meat, for you have wept in the ears of God, saying, 'Who shall feed us meat? We had it better in Egypt.' Therefore, God will give you meat, and you shall eat. Not for one day shall you eat, or for two days, or for five days, or for ten days, or for twenty days, but for a whole month, until it comes out of your nostrils and it is loathsome to you — because you have despised God, who is among you, and you have wept before Him, saying: Why did we leave Egypt?" (Numbers 11:18-20).

Commentary 1: When God performs signs and wonders for Israel, they are expressions of His kindness, and they are all for their benefit; for "God is good to all, and His mercies are over all His works" (Psalms 145:9) (except when "there is wrath gone out"[62] against those who transgress

---

62. Numbers 17:11.

His will, when He acts toward them with anger and the attribute of judgment to utterly devastate them). Thus, miracles can only be manifestations of complete and perfect goodness, through [the attribute of] mercy, or retribution through the attribute of judgment.

However, now that God told Moses that He would grant their request, and they would eat meat "until it comes out of your nostrils and it is loathsome to you," Moses our Teacher understood that God did not wish to give them meat in a miraculous manner, as when He gave them the "bread of heaven,"[63] [but only through natural means] (Nachmanides, ad loc.).

Commentary 2: Thus it is with all worldly desires. People complain and weep that they have not fulfilled their cravings, despising spiritual matters and heaping scorn upon them. However, in the end, that which they craved "comes out of their nostrils," and they descend to the abyss (Rabbeinu Bachaya, *Commentary on the Torah,* ad loc.).

ೞ೮೮

And Moses said: "God gives you meat to eat in the evening, and in the morning bread to satiety, for God hears your complaints that you complain against Him — and what are we? Not against us do you complain, but against God" (Exodus 16:8).

Commentary: It was taught in the name of Rabbi Yehoshua ben Korcha: Because they asked for meat disrespectfully, it was given in a disrespectful manner; because they asked for bread respectfully, it was given in a respectful manner. Here the Torah teaches good manners, that one should eat meat only at night.

Rav Achah bar Yaakov said: At first, the Israelites were like birds pecking on a dung-hill, until Moses came and designated a proper time for their repast[64] (Talmud: *Yoma* 75b).

ೞ೮೮

It was taught [in a Baraisa that] Rabbi [Yehudah HaNasi] stated: One who is ignorant of Torah is forbidden to eat meat, as it is written, "This is

---

63. Psalms 78:24.

the Torah (i.e., the law) of the animal and the fowl" (Leviticus 11:46). That is to say: whoever studies Torah is permitted to eat the flesh of animals and fowl, but whoever does not study Torah is forbidden to eat the flesh of animals and fowl (Talmud: *Pesachim* 49b).

ೞೞ

Rabbi Yochanan asked: What is the meaning of the verse, "The curse of the Lord is upon the house of the wicked, but the dwellings of the righteous shall be blessed" (Proverbs 3:33)? "The house of the wicked" refers to Pekach ben Rimalyahu, who used to eat 40 *se'ah* (a large measure) of young birds as an appetizer for his feast. "The dwellings of the righteous shall be blessed" refers to Hezekiah, King of Judea, who used to content himself with a *litra* (a small measure) of vegetables for his entire meal[65] (Talmud: *Sanhedrin* 94b).

ೞೞ

Even the animals permitted by the Torah are merely a concession to human lust and desire, just as [within certain restrictions, the Torah] permitted the Israelites women taken captive in war (Deuteronomy, chap. 21).[66] On the verse, "Because your soul desires to eat flesh" (Deuteronomy 12:20), the sages of the Talmud explain that there is a moral lesson in this expression, namely, that one should not eat flesh unless he has a craving for it (*Chullin* 84b). This shows clearly that the eating of flesh was permitted only because of necessity (Rabbi Yosef Albo, *Sefer HaIkkarim*, 3:15).

---

64. The Maggid of Chernobyl explains the metaphor of "birds pecking on a dung-hill" to mean that the Israelites were unable to elevate the fallen holy sparks by eating in a spirit of holiness until "Moses came." Kabbalistically, Moses represents *da'as*. That is, in order to rectify the holy sparks, they needed to attain *da'as*: the knowledge that mundane physical tasks such as eating are not excluded from the spiritual life, but through these mundane activities we can come closer to God; *Me'or Einayim, Emor*, s.v. *V'zeh she'amar*.
65. According to R. Avraham Chaim Na'eh, the volume of 40 *se'ah* is equivalent to 100 gallons, while a *litra* is equivalent to 12 fluid oz. In Talmudic measures, a *litra* is equivalent to 1 *log*. There are 4 *lugin* in a *kav*, and six *kavin* in a *se'ah*. Thus, the quantity of meat eaten by Pekach ben Rimalyahu was 960 times greater than the quantity of vegetables eaten by King Hezekiah.
66. See Chapter 6 above, n. 2.

Permission to Eat Meat as a Practical Concession

As long as the Earth exists, seedtime and harvest, cold and heat, summer and winter, day and night, shall not cease (Genesis 8:22).

Commentary: [They will not cease] from continuing in this unnatural fashion, which I set for them after the Flood: that the sun shall revolve spherically, tilted from the equator [hence the equinox will not be constant] and this turning will cause the change of all these seasons. Before the Flood, the angle of the Earth to the sun was such that the equinox was constant; therefore, it was constantly springtime, which was a general betterment for the elements, vegetation, and the span of life of living creatures. [Now, the Torah] says that this will be "while the Earth remains," meaning until such time that God, the Blessed One, will ameliorate the damage caused by the Flood; as He says, "The new Earth which I will make" (Isaiah 66:22), for then the sun will return, once again, to the [permanent] equinox, and there will be a general improvement of the elements, vegetation, and living creatures, [including] their length of days. This is the way it was before the Flood, as it says, "He who dies at a hundred years shall be reckoned as a youth, and he who fails to reach a hundred shall be reckoned accursed" (ibid. 65:20); and this is what is meant by, "The lands of sunrise and sunset [will] shout for joy" (Psalms 65:9) (Rabbi Ovadiah Sforno [1470-1550], *Commentary on the Torah,* ad loc., trans. R. Raphael Pelcovitz [Brooklyn, NY: Artscroll / Mesorah Publication, 1987]).

০৪৫৩০

And behold, I am about to destroy them with the Earth... (Genesis 6:13).

Commentary: I will destroy them with the Earth. I will destroy [i.e., alter] the climate of the Earth and air after the Deluge.

The angle of the Earth to the sun was altered, whereas previously the equinox was constant [day and night being of equal length] — as God explained to Job in his rejoinder. As a result, immediately after the Flood the span of human life was shortened, since weather conditions and the fruits were no longer perfect, as before. It is for this reason that man was permitted to consume the meat of living creatures after the Flood (Sforno, ibid. 6:13).

გჳეი

Why was Noah permitted to eat meat, whereas Adam was not allowed to do so? This was because Adam was in the Garden of Eden, a place of trees and the finest fruits that could possibly exist. As the verse states: "And the Lord God caused to spring forth from the ground all manner of trees, pleasant in appearance and good for food... and He said to him, 'From all trees of the garden you may freely eat...'" (Genesis 2:9,16). By contrast, Noah and his children, when they left the ark, had nothing to eat but the grass of the earth, not the fruit of trees; and if they had waited to eat until they had sown fields and planted orchards, they would have died of hunger. Yet by killing animals for food, they would acquire the trait of cruelty. Therefore, [immediately after granting Noah and his descendants this concession] the Torah forbade them the limb of a living animal (ibid. 9:4), which is the ultimate cruelty[67] (Rabbi Yitzchak Abarbanel, Genesis 9:1, sec. 3).

გჳეი

When the conditions of life radically changed [after the Flood], humankind received a new kind of food. Given man's shortened lifespan, it is reasonable to assume that [the life cycle] which formerly had extended for seven to eight hundred years now became compressed into seventy or eighty years. It is possible that all of these accelerated developmental processes necessitated the use of animals for food. Differences in temperature and changes of seasons and climates also may have been among the reasons why divine consent now was given for animal food.

Humanity thereby became less dependent on the food that the Earth yields. We already have discussed the view of our sages, which is consistent with geological findings, that before the Flood the Earth's

---

67. Citing the Abarbanel, Malbim similarly offers this rationale in his commentary *HaTorah V'HaMitzvah*, ad loc. See "Benefits of Eating Meat" in Additional Source Texts for Chapter 6.

temperature was stable and vegetation more luxuriant. Thus, vegetarian food always was available in sufficient quantity, and there was no need to derive sustenance from living creatures. The Torah does not require us to become vegetarians; it does not recoil from the consumption of meat. On the contrary, it even deems it a mitzvah to do so on Yom Tov.[68] However, if we had remained in our original physical condition, the eating of meat might never have been permitted to us, whereas now it may be necessary.

In any case, as soon as animals became permissible for food, dietary laws and prohibitions were instituted. Even later, when the Torah was given to the Jewish people, we find that no food is prohibited except animal foods. At first meat was disallowed altogether, and subsequently it was permitted only with numerous restrictions. In the vegetable realm, by contrast, no sort of plant is forbidden categorically. The prohibitions of *chadash* (new wheat), *orlah* (fruit of a tree less than three years old), and *kil'ei ha-kerem* (mixed species) are rooted in entirely different considerations (Rabbi Samson Raphael Hirsch, *Commentary On The Torah*, Genesis 9:3, based on Rabbi Mordechai Breuer's Hebrew translation from the original German).

Rabbi Simcha Wasserman on Vegetarianism

The problem with eating meat, or fish for that matter, is that you are supporting your life at the expense of another creature's life. As you get older, you actually feel this issue more strongly — especially when you see the animal's body parts. Adam was not allowed to eat meat. This means that he did not need to sustain his life at the expense of any other creature. After the Flood, Noah and his descendants were permitted to eat meat. The generation of the Flood was wiped out because the people were involved in *chamas,* a term which our sages relate to theft. The problem of stealing is living at the expense of someone else. The person who steals has benefit from something that the victim worked for, which is actually a part of his life. "The money of the tzaddikim is more precious to them

---

68. This reflects the position of Maimonides; however, see above, n. 47, for dissenting views.

than their bodies" (*Sotah* 12a). A tzaddik never takes anything that does not belong to him. Either he manufactured the object, or he worked for the money with which he bought it. Either of these two processes takes time. A person who steals an object is taking someone else's lifeblood, and in a certain sense that is tantamount to killing. The generation after the Flood experienced a "measure for measure" situation where, in order to survive, they would have to eat other creatures. The primary system of creation was not to eat meat. Now they were positioned in a secondary system.

Reb Simcha Wasserman (d. 1992) said that once he was on the subway in New York when there was a power failure, and the lights went out. As he sat in the darkness, suddenly some small emergency lights came on. The train had a generator that backed up the primary system in case of emergency. As he looked at those lights, he realized that they were not as good as the primary lights. They were very weak, supplying just enough light for the passengers to get around and leave the train. Neither were they long lasting. The power supply that kept them going was much weaker, so they were less bright and less enduring. The human body is like this, too. If there is a problem with the primary system, a secondary system takes over. If the latter fails, there is another back-up system that will take over. But these have deficiencies and side effects, since the body was not designed to operate in this way.

The universe, too, has primary and secondary systems. The secondary systems are typically not as good and have side effects. That is what happened at the time of Noah. The primary system kept the world going and did not have any side effects.

There is a theory today that the human body is designed to function better when people follow a vegetarian diet. Even if eating meat on occasion is not harmful, a meat-centered diet has negative side effects. This also suggests that meat eating is a secondary system. Compared to meat and fish, most vegetables (aside from onions and garlic which are meant to flavor other foods) do not have a significant aftertaste. In the Torah, dessert is called *kinu'ach*, something that "wipes away" something else. It wipes off the palate, removing the aftertaste left from the main course, i.e., animal foods. Like an immoral act, eating such foods may "feel good" at first, but afterwards you do not feel so well ("Vegetarianism: Jewish Eating," taped lecture by Rabbi Dr. Akiva Tatz, based on the teachings of Rabbi Simcha Wasserman).

Summary

Judaism views the world and all it contains as worthy and deserving of respect by virtue of having been created by God. Creation is an intricately interwoven tapestry that garbs and expresses the Divine Essence, and everything in the universe serves God in its own way. Thus, no creature should be disparaged. Indeed, the spiritual task of humankind, and the Jewish people in particular, is to refine and elevate all levels of creation by using the things of this world to serve God thereby, neither completely renouncing the world, nor exploiting it for the sake of ego and selfish desire.

This is why all levels of creation were represented in the rites of the Holy Temple.[69] The stones with which it was built and the metals with which its vessels were made represented *domem,* the mineral realm. The offerings of the harvest, as well as those of grain, oil, and wine represented *tzomei'ach,* the vegetative realm. Animal sacrifices represented *chai,* living things. The rites of the Holy Temple were performed by the Kohanim-Priests, assisted by the Levites, on behalf of the entire Jewish people, as well as non-Jews who sought to worship the One God; together they represented the level of *medaber,* "speaking beings," or humankind. The spiritual intent of these rites was reinforced by the music played by the Levites. From the innermost precincts of the Temple, the "House of Light, " prophecy and divine wisdom shone into the world. The entire tradition of Kabbalah is based upon this paradigm. Thus, while directed toward the transcendental, Jewish mysticism is at the same time world-affirming.

The Midrash states that God has compassion for animals, just as He has compassion for people. In emulation of God's ways, we, too, must show compassion toward all living things. However, this ethic does not reflect the moral equivalence of the species; rather, it instructs us to concern ourselves with the plight of other creatures precisely because we are human beings, created in the divine image. Although humankind is primary in the divine plan, the role of man is to be a steward over nature,

---

69. R. Chaim of Volozhin, *Nefesh HaChaim, Likkutei Ma'amarim,* 33 (end), p. 385, based on various Kabbalistic sources.

not a self-serving tyrant. Even concerning the permitted uses of animals, the Torah's underlying intention is to accomplish the benefit of all beings. Cruelty to animals (*tza'ar baalei chaim*) is forbidden to both Jews and non-Jews. This is a factor that must be applied to present methods of raising and slaughtering animals, which often are objectionable. Even in cases where the prohibition of *tza'ar baalei chaim* may be overruled in order to serve a legitimate human need, we should seek ways to avoid causing animals pain.

In the opinion of many authorities, meat eating is allowed within certain limitations as a concession to human desire. However, the Kabbalists explain that this is not merely permissible exploitation, for it accomplishes the elevation of "holy sparks," the divine life-force concealed within the animal realm. When performed in a spirit of holiness, meat eating also releases human souls that may have been reincarnated as animals. According to several Jewish philosophers, using animal products for food reminds man of his higher status in creation, and the higher moral ideals toward which he must strive. Without recognizing his Godlike potential, man inevitably will debase himself to a moral level inferior to that of animals.

Nevertheless, vegetarianism is permitted as a personal preference for a number of reasons. Arguably, the vegetarian diet has many *kashrus* advantages, as well as health benefits that make it superior to the traditional Western meat-based diet. Beyond this, a societal shift toward a plant-based diet would have positive ecological consequences. Animal activists also point out that most animals are no longer raised on small family-operated farms, as they were in the past. Given the frequently inhumane treatment of animals raised on "factory farms" and slaughtered by mass production methods, vegetarianism is consistent with the Jewish ethic of showing compassion to all creatures. Moreover, vegetarianism is associated with both the Garden of Eden and the Messianic Age. Thus, its growing popularity may signal the long-awaited end of the exploitation of one nation by another and one species by another.

May we soon see the day of universal peace that the ancient prophets of Israel envisioned, when the knowledge of God will be the foremost pursuit of all humanity, "death will be swallowed up forever,"[70] and at last, the world will become what the Merciful One originally intended it to be.

---

70. Isaiah 25:8.

Part IV:
Additional Source Texts

Sources: Chapter 1

Compassion for Animals in the Talmud, Midrash, and Zohar

Rabbi Yehudah said in the name of Rav: In all creation there is nothing that lacks a divinely-appointed purpose (Talmud: *Shabbos* 77b).

ભજી

There is nothing superfluous in the universe. Even flies, gnats, and mosquitoes are part of creation and, as such, serve a divinely-appointed purpose (Midrash: *Bereshis Rabbah* 10:7).

ભજી

[Shimon ben Azzai] used to say: Do not disparage any person and do not reject anything, for there is no man who does not have his hour, and nothing that does not have its place (Mishnah: *Avos* 4:3).

Commentary: Everything has its place in the world. Even creatures that seem to be ugly, hateful, painful, and harmful, such as insects, snakes, and scorpions, were created by God and serve His will (*Tiferes Yisrael,* ad loc.).

ભજી

And the Lord saw everything that He had made, and, behold, it was very good (Genesis 1:31).

Zohar: The verse states "everything He had made," without qualification. Snakes, scorpions, and insects, even destructive creatures are included in the pronouncement, "And behold, it was very good," for they, too, serve the One Above (*Zohar* III, 107a).

ભજી

Rav Achah declared: Through all things the Holy One, blessed be He, completes His mission — even through a snake, even through a frog, even through a scorpion, even through a mosquito (*Vayikra Rabbah* 22:2).

ભજી

Rabbi Yochanan observed: If the Torah had not been given, we could have learned modesty from the cat, honest labor from the ant, marital fidelity from the dove, and good manners from the rooster (Talmud: *Eruvin* 100b).

∝≈∾

Go to the ant, you sluggard: observe her ways and become wise (Proverbs 6:6).

Midrash: For she has no watchman or task-master standing over her, yet in the summer she prepares her food, and in the harvest season she stores it.

What did King Solomon see in the ways of the ant that he wished to teach the sluggard? The rabbis stated: The ant has three chambers. She enters neither the upper chamber because of the rain, nor the lower chamber because of the mud, but only the middle one. She only lives for six months, she has neither tendons nor bones, and her food consists only of a grain and a half of wheat; yet she goes back and forth all summer collecting whatever she finds, wheat, barley, and lentils.

Rabbi Tanchuma stated: Although her entire sustenance is only a grain and a half of wheat, she gathers all this. Why does she bother? She says, "If the Holy One, blessed be He, should decree upon me long life, I will have prepared sufficient food."

Rabbi Shimon Bar Yochai stated: King Solomon once came upon a pit containing three hundred *cur* (a large measure) that an ant had filled in the course of one summer for the coming winter. Thereupon, King Solomon exclaimed. "Go to the ant, lazy one; observe her ways and become wise. You, too, should prepare for the World to Come by performing commandments and good deeds in this world."

What does the verse mean by "observe her ways (*derech*) and become wise"? The rabbis explained: Observe her integrity (*derech eretz*), in that she flees from theft.

Rabbi Shimon ben Chalafta stated: Once an ant dropped a kernel of wheat. Her comrades came and examined it, but none would pick it up (Midrash: *Devarim Rabbah* 5:2).

CRITICAL

As the dove is whole (*tamah*), so Israel is whole-hearted [in its devotion to God]. As the dove is distinguished, so Israel is distinguished through circumcision and *tzitzis* (knotted strings on their four-cornered garments). As the dove is chaste, so Israel is chaste. As the dove stretches out her neck for slaughter, so does Israel; as the verse states, "For Your sake, we are slaughtered all the day" (Psalms 44:23). As the dove atones for sin, so Israel atones for the nations of the world. As the dove is faithful to her mate from the first moment they meet, so Israel remains faithful to God. As the dove is saved by her wings, so Israel is saved by the commandments. As the dove never abandons its cote, even upon the loss of its young, so Israel continues to observe the pilgrim festivals each year, even after the destruction of the Holy Temple. As the dove produces a new brood each month, so does Israel produce new Torah insights and new good deeds each month. As the dove flies far away [in search of food] but always returns to her cote, so Israel shall return to her land (Midrash: *Shir HaShirim Rabbah* 1:63, with *Eitz Yosef,* abridged).

Whoever has compassion for other creatures is shown compassion from Heaven; whoever does not have compassion for other creatures is not shown compassion from Heaven (Talmud: *Shabbos* 151b).

The Holy One, blessed be He, sustains all creatures, from the horned *r'eimim* (gargantuan beasts) to the eggs of lice (Talmud: *Shabbos* 107b).

Rabbi Elazar HaKapar taught: It is forbidden for a person to buy an animal or bird unless he can feed it properly[1] (Jerusalem Talmud: *Kesubos* 4:8).

---

1. R. Yaakov Emden in *She'eilas Ya'avetz*, Vol. I, no. 17, distinguishes between house pets that can scavenge freely for their own needs, and domestic animals that depend entirely upon their owners. Although one may not be culpable in neglecting the former, nevertheless, it is proper to attend to their needs before one's meal. R. Emden adds his opinion that the purchase of house pets is "a waste of money and time, as well as a distraction from Torah study." Nevertheless, a strong case can be

‿ℭℬ℺

Just as the Holy One, blessed be He, has mercy upon human beings, so does He have mercy upon animals (Midrash: *Devarim Rabbah* 6:1; similarly cf. *Tanchuma* 58:6).

‿ℭℬ℺

Even unto the smallest gnat does the mercy of the Holy One, blessed be He, extend (*Zohar Chadash, Ruth,* 94b; similarly, *Zohar* II, 106b).

‿ℭℬ℺

Rabbi Yonah expounded at the entrance to the house of the Nasi (head of the Sanhedrin): What is the meaning of the verse, "A tzaddik is concerned with the plight of the impoverished" (Proverbs 29:7). This refers to the Holy One, blessed be He, Who knows that a dog's food is meager. Therefore, He decreed that a dog's food remain in his stomach for three days before it is fully digested[2] (Talmud: *Shabbos* 155b).

‿ℭℬ℺

When Scripture speaks of the people of Nineveh, it does not say, "God saw their sackcloth and their fasting," but, "God saw their good deeds, that they repented from their evil path" (Jonah 3:10). [The King of Nineveh commanded] "Let the people and the animals be covered in sackcloth" (ibid. 3:8). What did the people do? They tethered the mother animals to one side, and the young to one side, [whereupon the mature animals began to bellow, and their young began to bleat, being unable to suckle: *Pirkei D'Rabbi Eliezer,* 4]. Then they declared before Him: "Master of the Universe! If You do not have mercy upon us, we will not have mercy upon them!" (Talmud: *Ta'anis* 16a).

---

made for the various benefits their owners derive from them, including ridding their homes of vermin, warding off thieves, and providing companionship. Also cf. R. Menashe Klein, *Mishneh Halachos*, Vol. 6, no. 216, who cites *Yad Ephraim, Orach Chaim* 167, that one should be diligent to feed his animals before his meal as an act of righteousness: sometimes a person may possess no other merit than this act, as implied by the Midrashic teaching about Alexander the Great and King Katzia.

2. For a Kabbalistic explanation, see *Sefer HaPeliah*, s.v. *Mi yachin l'orev*, p. 282.

Commentary: This was as if to say: "Just as You wish us to have mercy upon them, in keeping with the verse, 'For His mercy is upon all His works' (Psalms 145:9), so You should [set an example of this by having] mercy upon us" (Rashi, ad loc.).

ca⁊ɔ

Rabbi Tanchum Bar Chiyah said: A day of rain is greater than the day on which the Torah was given. For the giving of the Torah brought joy to the Israelites, whereas a day of rain brings joy to all nations and to the entire world, including the animals and beasts (*Midrash Shocher Tov* on *Tehillim* 117).

ca⁊ɔ

Rav Yehudah said in the name of Rav: It is forbidden for a person to eat before feeding his animal. [This is derived from the verse which first] states, "And I shall provide grass in your field for your cattle" (Deuteronomy 11:15), and then concludes, "and you shall eat and be satisfied" (Talmud: *Berachos* 40a).

Commentary 1: The four levels of creation must ascend from below to above, until the ultimate state of harmony and perfection has been attained. The mineral level benefits the vegetative level, which in turn benefits the inarticulate animal level. Afterwards, the inarticulate animal level ascends to the level of man, the speaking being. This is why human beings are required to eat last of all (Rabbi Moshe Alshech, *Commentary on the Torah, Acharei Mos*).

Commentary 2: Aside from enjoining us to recognize our obligation of active concern for the welfare of all creatures, according to the lofty station of this holy directive, it is required as an act of justice, since by means of the animal, man brings forth bread from the earth, and "abundant produce from the power of the ox" (Proverbs 14:4). Given this, the one that does the work [the animal] deserves priority in benefiting from her labors. Additionally, in order to show that humans must not exploit animals, this precept not only expresses compassion, but also reflects the justice of showing gratitude; for if not for the animal, man would not gain the necessities of life. Therefore, because one is compelled to feed his animal before eating, his consciousness is raised to know that concern for animals is not only an expression of piety and altruism, but of integrity and justice.

This, too, one must recognize: from the sole standpoint of the purpose of physical eating [i.e., deriving strength to perform work], the animal's ability is superior to his; man does not need to recognize and contemplate his advantage over the animal except in the spiritual dimension: in intellectual matters, and in the perception of God and His beneficial and holy ways. Therefore, from the standpoint of physical eating, the animal should precede man; for in general the physical abilities of most animals surpass the physical abilities of humans, as explained at great length in *Iggeres Baalei Chaim*.[3]

It also must be pointed out that a human being who lacks food temporarily can quiet the distress of his soul by pursuing various forms of spiritual gratification, due to his higher soul and intellect. However, the animal that suffers pangs of hunger has nothing with which to distract her soul. Therefore, within the implications of this commandment of our sages, which is suggested by an entire scriptural verse, may be found altruistic concern and strict justice, as well as the elevation of humankind to the radiant light of wisdom and true stature (Rabbi Avraham Yitzchak HaKohen Kook, *Ein Ayah*, Vol. II, *Berachos*, chap. 6, par. 26, p. 180).

Compassion for Animals in Halacha and Mussar

Mercy is a most praiseworthy trait. It is one of the Thirteen Attributes ascribed to the Holy One, blessed be He, as it is written, "Merciful and gracious..." (Exodus 34:6). One must also show mercy and compassion toward animals, for it is forbidden to cause animals suffering. Concerning this the Torah states, "[You shall not see your brother's donkey or his ox collapsing on the road and hide yourself from them;] you shall surely help him lift them up" (Deuteronomy 22:4). Also, one

---

3. This is a moralistic collection of fabulous conversations between various animals. Originally an Arabic work, Kalonymus ben Kalonymus translated it into Hebrew and published it in Mantua in 1517. The work enjoyed many subsequent printings, including translations into the Jewish vernaculars, Yiddish and Ladino.

must feed his animal before he feeds himself (*Berachos* 40a) (*Orchos Tzaddikim, Sha'ar HaRachamim*).

ᏟᏴᎤ

One who owns animals or fowl that depend upon him for their sustenance is forbidden to eat anything until he feeds them. As the verse states, "And I will give grass in your fields for your cattle, and you shall eat and be satisfied" (Deuteronomy 11:15). The Torah teaches that the animal's food precedes that of man. But concerning drink, man takes precedence, as it is written, "Drink, and I will give your camels drink, also" (Genesis 24:46); and it is written again, "So shall you give the congregation and the cattle drink" (Numbers 20:8) (Rabbi Shlomo Ganzfried, *Kitzur Shulchan Aruch*, 42:1; also note *Sefer Chassidim*, 531; Maimonides, *Mishneh Torah, Avadim* 9:8).

ᏟᏴᎤ

It is permissible to exert oneself on the Sabbath in order to feed one's cattle, domestic animals, or birds, since they depend upon their owners for sustenance. Similarly, one may feed one's dog; even an ownerless dog may be given a modest meal. However, it is forbidden to give food or drink to bees or doves or pigeons, nor may one cast food before them, since they are not dependent upon their owners but eat in the fields. [Therefore, this would be a needless compromise of the sanctity of the Sabbath.] Some people have the custom to feed wheat to the birds on the Sabbath during which the Song of the Sea is recited in the synagogue, but this is improper[4] (Rabbi Avraham Chaim Na'eh, *Kitzos HaShulchan* IV, 130:1).

ᏟᏴᎤ

It is permissible to let one's animal graze in the field on the Sabbath, as the verse states, "That your ox and your donkey may rest..." (Exodus 23:12), for this is its manner of resting (ibid. IV, 15).

---

4. However, there is no impropriety in putting out crusts of bread for the birds prior to the onset of "Shabbos Shirah" (*Parshas Beshalach*) on Friday afternoon.

ᏣᏍᏍᎤ

"A tzaddik considers the needs of his animal, but the mercy of the wicked is cruelty" (Proverbs 12:10). If a person does not need to eat meat and knows that the meat will spoil if he slaughters the animal for no purpose, he is forbidden to do so. If he transgresses, he also violates the prohibition of *bal tash'chis*, wanton destruction (*Chullin* 7b). However, if he needs the hide, it is permissible (R. Yehudah HeChassid, *Sefer Chassidim* 667).

ᏣᏍᏍᎤ

"A righteous man knows the nature of his animal..." If one's animal is sick or about to give birth, he should not trouble it. All the more so does this apply to one's maidservant (ibid.).

ᏣᏍᏍᎤ

Everything was created for a reason; therefore, it is forbidden to kill any creature unnecessarily (*Zohar* II, *Yisro*, 93b).[5] My master [Rabbi Yitzchak Luria, known as the holy Ari] was careful never to kill any insect, even the smallest and least of them, such as fleas, lice, and flies — even if they were causing him pain (Rabbi Chaim Vital, *Sha'ar HaMitzvos*, *Noach*).

ᏣᏍᏍᎤ

---

5. However, killing a potentially harmful insect is permissible even on the Sabbath, as stated in *Shulchan Aruch, Orach Chaim* 316:10. R. Yaakov Emden in *She'eilas Ya'avetz*, Vol. I, no. 110, rules that one may kill harmless insects (although not on the Sabbath), contending that insects and all non-domestic animals are excluded from the prohibition of *tza'ar baalei chaim*. This view is disputed by R. Yehudah Leib Graubart, *Chavalim BaNe'imim*, Vol. I, no. 43; see R. J. David Bleich, *"Animal Experimentation," Contemporary Halakhic Problems*, Vol. III, pp. 216-217, n. 33. Several Kabbalistic sources state that one should rid his home of spiders, particularly prior to the Sabbath; see R. Chaim Elazar Spira of Munkatch, *Darkei Chaim V'Shalom*, par. 1080, citing *Totza'os Chaim, Emek Beracha, Shnei Luchos HaBris, Siddur HaRav Shabsai*, et al. Also note the explanation of this in *Divrei Torah*, 9:98. Gratuitous killing of insects is strictly forbidden; see R. Moshe Feinstein, *Igros Moshe, Choshen Mishpat*, Vol. 2, no. 47. I am grateful to R. Ben-Zion Strasser, Nitra Rov of Borough Park, for these sources. I have been told by R. Aharon Pam that his father, the late R. Avraham Pam, Rosh Yeshiva of Mesivta Torah Vodaath in Brooklyn, NY, was careful not to use any means of exterminating mice, flies, or insects that might cause *tza'ar baalei chaim*.

It is best not to raise chickens. When necessary, one should simply purchase them and slaughter them. However, if they are not always available, and one must keep them on his premises, one must be extremely diligent and instruct his children and household members to be sure to feed the animals on time. Their sustenance is our responsibility, and the heavenly punishment for neglecting them is severe. Particularly if they are locked in a cage, one must show compassion toward them all the more and prepare food for them in advance, in order to avoid transgressing the prohibition of *tza'ar baalei chaim* (cruelty to animals)[6] (Rabbi Eliezer Papo, *Peleh Yo'etz, Inyan Baalei Chaim*).

ভা৪৪৩

It is customary to tell a person wearing a new garment for the first time, "May you wear it out and acquire yet a new one." However, some authorities (e.g., Mahari Weill) write that this does not apply to new shoes or garments made of leather or fur, because the manufacture of such things entails the killing of animals, and it is written, "His mercy extends over all His works" (Rabbi Moshe Isserles on *Shulchan Aruch, Orach Chaim* 223:6).

ভা৪৪৩

Love of all creatures is also love of God, for whoever loves the One, loves all the works that He has made. When one loves God, it is impossible not to love His creatures. [The converse is also true.] If one

---

6. Nevertheless, there are situations in which it may be permissible to cause a minor degree of *tza'ar baalei chaim* in order to benefit the animals; see *Teshuvos Minchas Yitzchak*, Vol. 6, no. 145. *Otzar HaPoskim*, sec. 87, cites *Teshuvos Imrei Shefer* and *Binyan Zion* to the effect that one may not cause *tza'ar baalei chaim* for the sake of financial gain, a position supported by *Teshuvos Yad HaLevi*, Vol. I, no. 196. However, other authorities permit *tza'ar baalei chaim* for financial reasons, seeing this as a form of *tzorech adam* (human benefit); see Chasam Sofer on *Bava Metzia* 32b, *Noda B'Yehudah*, Vol. II, *Yoreh De'ah*, no. 10; *Pri Yitzchak*, Vol. I, no. 24; *Yad Eliyahu, Kesavim* 3:5. While cautioning that one should conduct oneself beyond the letter of the law to avoid causing *tza'ar baalei chaim*, the late R. Yitzchak Weiss of Jerusalem's Eidah HaChareidis agrees with these latter authorities in *Minchas Yitzchak*, op cit.

hates the creatures, it is impossible to love God Who created them (Maharal of Prague, *Nesivos Olam, Ahavas Re'a*, 1).

⊙₰ఴ

Rabbi Menashe of Ilya, Lithuania (1767-1832), a leading disciple of the Vilna Gaon, once wrote: "What am I in comparison to the many forms of sentient life in the world? If the Creator were to confer upon me, as well as my family members, loved ones, and relatives, absolute goodness for all eternity, but some deficiency remained in the world — if any living thing still were suffering, and all the more so, another human being — I would not want anything to do with it, much less to derive benefit from it.

"How could I be separated from all living creatures? These are the works of God's hand, and these, too, are the work of God's hand"[7] (Author's Introduction, *Ha'amek She'eilah,* cited in biography printed with *Alfei Menashe*, Vol. II).

Rav Moshe Cordovero on Compassion for Animals

There is none so patient and humble as our God in His attribute of *Kesser* (the Supernal Crown). For He is absolute compassion; before Him there is no flaw or transgression, no severe judgment or other quality that could prevent Him from watching over [creation] and bestowing bounty and goodness constantly. So, too, should a person conduct himself. Nothing in the world should prevent him from doing good to others; no transgression or misdeed should deter him from helping whoever needs a favor, always and at every moment. Although God transcends creation, He sustains all living beings, from the highest to the lowest, and does not disparage any creature — for if He were to reject any creature due to its inferiority, none could exist for even a moment. Instead, He watches over and shows mercy to all. Similarly, a person should be beneficent to everyone, and no creature should seem despicable to him. Even the

---

7. This statement is consistent with R. Menashe's ideas regarding the kinship of all creatures presented in his *Tikkun Klalli,* of which only an incomplete manuscript is extant. I am grateful to R. Yaakov Weiss of Lakewood, NJ, for locating these sources.

smallest living thing should be exceedingly worthy in his eyes; he should consider it and exert himself for its benefit. This quality, too, comes from the attribute of *Kesser* (*Tomer Devorah*, chapter 2).

ೞಜಿ

One should respect all creatures, recognizing in them the greatness of the Creator, Who formed man with wisdom. All creatures are imbued with the Creator's wisdom, which itself makes them greatly deserving of honor. The Maker of All, the Wise One who transcends everything, is associated [with all His creatures] in having created them. If one were to disparage them, God forbid, this would reflect upon the honor of their Maker.

This is the meaning of the verse, "How worthy are Your works, O God…" (Psalms 104:24). It does not say "how great (*gadlu*)" but "how worthy (*rabbu*)," as in the verse "the head (*rav*) of his house" (Esther 1:8), indicating great importance. [The verse concludes,] "You have made them all with wisdom." That is, since Your wisdom is imbued in them, Your works are great and worthy. Therefore, a person should consider the divine wisdom within them, and not their disgrace (ibid.).

ೞಜಿ

One's compassion should extend to all creatures, and he should not disparage or destroy them, for divine wisdom extends to all creation: "silent" things [such as dust and stones], plants, animals, and humans. For this reason our sages warned us not to treat food disrespectfully. Just as divine wisdom despises nothing — since everything proceeds from it, as the verse states, "You have made them all with wisdom" (Psalms 104:24) — so should a person show compassion to all of God's works.

That is why Rabbi Yehudah the Prince was punished when he did not show pity to a calf that tried to evade slaughter by hiding behind him. "Go!" he told it. "You were created for this purpose." Compassion shields against the divine attribute of strict judgment. Therefore, suffering — which derives from [the divine attribute of] strict judgment — came upon him. But when Rabbi Yehudah the Prince had mercy upon a weasel, quoting the verse, "His mercies extend to all His works" (Psalms

145:9), he was delivered from strict judgment. The light of divine wisdom spread over him, and his suffering disappeared.

Similarly, one should not disparage any creature, for all of them were created with divine wisdom. One should not uproot plants unless they are needed or kill animals unless they are needed. And one should choose a humane manner of death for them, using a carefully inspected knife, in order to be as compassionate as possible (ibid. chapter 3).

CЗ৪О

[The *Zohar* states that while crossing a stream, Rabbi Yosé stepped on some worms and exclaimed that he wished such creatures did not exist. At this, his master Rabbi Shimon Bar Yochai declared that it is forbidden to disparage or to kill any creature, for they all serve to benefit the world (*Emor*, 106b).]

One might ask: if so, how can the Torah permit us to kill a snake on the Sabbath in the land of Israel, or [to kill any dangerous or bothersome animal] under similar circumstances?

The term "disparage" could mean either in word or in deed. Rabbi Yosé was guilty of both. First, by stepping upon the worms, he violated the prohibition of wantonly killing small creatures that are not harmful to humans [such as flies, gnats, and worms]. Second, by exclaiming, "Would that they did not exist!" he spoke disrespectfully regarding the order of the universe, which reflects upon the honor of the Creator. If a dangerous creature threatens a person, or if there is a harmful snake in one's house or courtyard, one is justified in killing it to avoid being hurt. However, if a snake is in the field going its own way, one must not interfere with it; for the snake is fulfilling its mission according to the divine will. The story cited above attests to this, as do many such stories that we have discussed elsewhere.

Even when creatures are sent on a mission to do harm, "God is good to all" (Psalms 145:9); for, in truth, this too is a good mission, since the death they cause will benefit the soul of the transgressor. God's mercy extends even to creatures that do not perform their mission [i.e., immoral people] in that He sustains them nevertheless. Thus, we are obligated to follow in His ways and show compassion toward all His works, never destroying them wantonly as long as they do not harm us. Moreover, to diminish God's creation is to diminish the manifestation of His mercies. According to the diversity of creation, through each and every species, God's mercies are evident. This is implied by the divine blessing "to be fruitful and multiply" (Genesis 8:17), as well as by the subsequent verse [in the psalm quoted above], "All Your works, O God, shall praise You..." (Psalms 145:10). That is, over each species in creation, an angel is appointed who sings praises to the Creator; and the praises of the One who sustains all creatures are increased according to the multitude of angelic hosts. One who destroys a swarm of bees or flies or a colony of ants therefore destroys the praises of God, unless these creatures are in one's house and are harmful. In this case, it is permitted to remove them, albeit in the most humane manner possible. Even this is not proper according to what we see in Tractate *Bava Metzia* (85a) concerning the nest of weasels that were found in the house of Rabbi Yehudah HaNasi. He told his maidservant to leave them alone, for "His mercies are upon all His creatures."

Thus, wantonly to kill even harmful creatures such as mice and weasels would be unseemly, since unlike snakes they do not physically afflict human beings. It would be preferable for a person to keep a cat who will consume them, as this conforms to the ways of the angels who determine how one species is subjugated to another. This may be deduced from the words of the Book of Song (*Perek Shirah*): "The mouse, what does it say? 'For You are righteous in all that comes upon us, for You have performed truthfully, and we have acted wickedly' (Nehemiah 9:33). The cat, what does it say? 'I pursued my enemies and overtook them, and returned not until they were destroyed' (Psalms 18:38)." This teaches that [the preying of one species upon another] is God's will, and reflects His absolute mercy toward the needs of His creatures.

Similarly, *Perek Shirah* concludes by describing how King David was pleased with himself upon completing the Book of Psalms, when he happened upon a frog [who contended that its praises of God were superior]. This narrative does not mean to extol the croaking of the frog, but [the songs and praises of] the angel that presides over frogs. And their leaping, too, was an expression of the spiritual inspiration that came to them from their presiding angel, who sings melodies and praises to God.

This also applies to the frog's remark [in *Perek Shirah*] that it has resigned itself to its fate, to serve as food for the stork or crane, or another bird. In other words, the presiding angel itself fulfills the will of its Maker in compelling the families of frogs not to rebel, but submit to the species designated to consume them. Therefore, it is proper to raise other creatures to prey upon destructive animals, for this follows the natural order. Thus, when Rabbi Yehudah's maidservant came to destroy the weasels, he told her to let them alone; but, nevertheless, he raised cats, for this [way of ridding oneself of pests] reflects the divine mercy, as our sages taught on the verse, "A tzaddik considers the needs of his animal..."[8] (Proverbs 12:10).

One might ask: since the calf was destined for slaughter, why was Rabbi Yehudah afflicted for saying, "Go, this is the purpose for which you were created"? To this it could be said that there might have been a transmigrated soul in the calf, and it was possible to save it for all eternity from an evil fate, from slaughter.[9] Or perhaps he should have entreated the slaughterer to postpone the killing at least for that day. [This would have served as an example of compassion to everyone present] (*Ohr Yakar*, commentary to *Zohar, Emor*, pp. 137-138).

Rav Samson Raphael Hirsch on Compassion for Animals

Everything around us was created by God and serves Him. Every force of nature is the messenger of God; matter is what God has apportioned to these forces to work with, in, and through, in accordance with His mighty laws. Everything exists in God's service, at its post, in its time, to fulfill God's Word with the means and powers allocated to it, contributing its share to Him, to become part of one all-inclusive entity.

---

8. R. Cordovero probably alludes to *Vayikra Rabbah* 27:11 and *Pesikta D'Rav Kahana* on *Vayikra* 22:28, which interpret the term "righteous" as referring to the Creator, Who "understands the nature of His animal" in mandating that His human subjects show compassion toward animals.

9. That is, the calf's *tikkun* might have been accomplished by other means, without causing it distress.

Everything serves God (*The Nineteen Letters,* Letter Three, trans. Karin Partitzky, commentary by R. Joseph Elias [Jerusalem: Feldheim, 1995]).

ભૅજ

With ten utterances the world was created. What does this come to teach us? Indeed, could it not have been created with one utterance? It was to exact punishment from the wicked who destroy the world that was created with ten utterances and to bestow goodly reward upon the righteous who sustain the world that was created with ten utterances (Mishnah: *Avos* 5:1).

Commentary: It was not with just one word, one summons of creation, that the Almighty brought this world into being, the whole of it and every detail; for if it had been created in this manner, everything would be directly dependent on God's Word for its existence, life, and functioning. Instead, He called His world into existence in ten stages; He created an abundance of forces, intermingled and functioning closely together, according to His Word — and then He separated them, so that each had to sustain the other: none was henceforth able to exist and function by itself, but had to be sustained by fellow creatures and, in turn, had to help them exist and function. In this way everything contributes according to its strength, however much or little, to the existence of the whole; and if it destroys a fellow creature, it robs itself of what it needs for its own existence (*The Nineteen Letters,* ibid.).

ભૅજ

Guided by the Torah, we have discovered the position of man within creation. He is to be neither a god nor a slave of this earthly world, but a brother and fellow worker. However, because of the nature and scope of his service, he holds the rank of the firstborn; he is to be the administrator of the Earth, and it is his task to attend to everything on it and further it in accordance with God's will. It is only from God, the source of all power, that he has received the right to appropriate the world for his own use; and with this privilege comes also the duty to take only that which the Giver has permitted and to use it according to His Will (ibid. Letter Five).

⊂ॐ⊃

The Earth was not created as a gift to you — you have been given to the Earth, to treat it with respectful consideration, as God's Earth, and everything on it as God's creation, as your fellow creature, to be respected, loved, and helped to attain its purpose according to God's Will. To this end, your mind is able to form the right image of all that exists; to this end, your heartstrings vibrate sympathetically with every cry of distress sounding anywhere in creation, and with every glad sound uttered by a joyful creature; to this end, you are happy when the flower blossoms and sad when it wilts (ibid. Letter Four).

Stories of Tzaddikim

There once was a good, honest man in whose home the holy Ari (Rabbi Yitzchak Luria) stayed as a guest. The host served him with great honor. As the holy Ari was leaving to resume his journey, he asked, "How may I repay you for the great love you have shown me?" The householder answered that after bearing several children, his wife had become barren. Perhaps [the Ari] could suggest some remedy so that his wife could bear children again.

The Ari then told the man why his wife had become barren. "You know that there was a small ladder standing in your house, upon which the chicks used to go up and down in order to drink water from a bowl nearby. Thus did they drink and quench their thirst. Once your wife told her servant girl to take the ladder away. Although she did not mean to afflict the chicks but only to clean the house, from the day she removed that ladder, the chicks suffered greatly and had to endure extreme thirst. Their cries ascended before the Holy One, blessed be He, Who pities all of His creatures. That is why it was decreed that she become barren."

The householder returned the ladder to its former place, the Holy One, blessed be He, caused his wife to conceive, and she bore children again (Rabbi Zvi Hirsch Koidanover, *Kav HaYashar* 7:20).

⊂ॐ⊃

It happened in our own generation that our master, Rabbi Yitzchak Luria Ashkenazi (the holy Ari), once looked at the face of a certain Torah scholar and told the man that he had committed the sin of causing suffering to animals (*tza'ar baalei chaim*). Deeply upset, the Torah scholar looked into the matter until he discovered that his wife had neglected to feed their chickens that morning, but she had merely let them into the yard and the street to fend for themselves. He earnestly instructed her to prepare kneaded bran and water for them every morning. Then, having rectified the problem, he returned to the Rabbi. When the Rabbi looked at him, he said, "Your transgression has disappeared. What happened?" Then the man explained everything that transpired (Rabbi Elazar Azkari, *Sefer Chareidim*, chap. 4:1).

୧୫୫୨

After the passing of Rabbi Dov Ber, the Maggid of Mezeritch (1704-1772), a number of Chassidim were sitting together, discussing the ways and habits of their late *rebbe*. One of that brotherhood, Rabbi Shneur Zalman of Liadi (1745-1813), posed a question: "Is anyone here able to explain why every morning at dawn our *rebbe* was accustomed to stroll near the lakes, where the frogs croak?"

Receiving no answer, he continued: "Then let me tell you what our *rebbe*'s intention was in doing this. Do we not read in *Perek Shirah* how every particle of creation, animate and inanimate, from the loftiest to the humblest, sings its own paean of praise to its Creator? Well, the frogs too have their own song, and the *rebbe* wanted to hear how these creatures praise their Maker" (R. Shlomo Yosef Zevin, *A Treasury of Chassidic Tales*, Vol. I, *Va'eira*, trans. Uri Kaploun [Brooklyn, NY: Artscroll / Mesorah Publications, 1980]).

୧୫୫୨

Rabbi Israel Salanter, a famous nineteenth century Orthodox Rabbi, failed to appear one Yom Kippur eve to chant the sacred *Kol Nidrei* prayer. His congregation became concerned, for it was inconceivable that their saintly rabbi would be late or absent on this very holy day. They sent out a search party to look for him. After much time, their rabbi was found in the barn of a Christian neighbor. On his way to the synagogue, Rabbi Salanter had come upon one of his neighbor's calves, lost and tangled in the brush. Seeing that the animal was in distress, he freed it and led it through many fields and over many hills. This act of mercy represented the rabbi's prayers on that Yom Kippur evening (S.Y. Agnon, *Days of Awe* [New York: Schocken, 1995]).

ભ

[One of those deported to the Nazi death camps] was a poor man who had earned his livelihood by raising chickens: the accomplished Talmud scholar, Rabbi Isaac Rosensweig. He cried out beseechingly from the window of the death train to his tormentors, who had a great laugh and spat at him. How could these "merciful Christians" comprehend the request of this "cruel Jew,"[10] surrounded by his wife and little children, who plaintively begged his oppressors, "Go to my house and give the chickens food and water, for they have not touched food or water for a whole day!" Then Rabbi Isaac noticed his comrade, Rabbi Moshe Yudah Tziltz, who had not yet been summoned by the authorities, standing at a distance. With a loud cry he called out to him, "Afflicting animals is forbidden by Torah law! Give the chickens food and water!" (Rabbi Michoel Ber Weissmandl, *Min HaMeitzar*, p. 32).

ભ

Once, while traveling from his native Poland to Israel, Rabbi Ephraim of Pshedbarz (1880-1946), author of *Oneg Shabbos,* entered the barn in which he and several companions were quartered and found a rooster asleep on his bed of straw. A comrade observed that the young scholar left and returned several times during the next hour until the rooster awoke of its own accord and vacated its place. Then Rabbi

---

10. R. Weissmandl bitterly alludes to the traditional Christian critique by which Jews and Judaism often have been denigrated throughout the centuries, that Judaism is a religion of harsh justice, while Christianity is a religion of mercy. *Min HaMeitzar,* the tragic story of R. Weissmandl's attempt to bring the plight of the Jews at the hands of the Nazis to the attention of the Allied leadership in order to stop the genocide, was translated by Abraham Fuchs as *The Unheeded Cry,* Brooklyn, NY: Artscroll / Mesorah, 1984.

Ephraim went to sleep. So sensitive to the feelings of others was Rabbi Ephraim that he even placed the comfort of a rooster above his own (Breslov oral tradition).

CRSO

Despite his aura of fear of God, Rabbi Eliyahu Lopian (1876-1970) [author of the contemporary Mussar classic, *Lev Eliyahu*] always exuded gentleness and love, not only to other human beings who are "created in the divine image," but to animals as well. Once he noticed a lost kitten that had taken refuge in the yeshiva of Kfar Chassidim. Immediately he became this kitten's patron and concerned himself with all its needs. Those who knew about this and witnessed it were amazed at how gently he placed a saucer of milk before the purring kitten every morning, and with what pleasure he watched it take each sip from the milk (Rabbi Aharon Soraski, *Marbitzei Torah U'Mussar* IV, 165).

CRSO

When he was a student at the Mirrer Yeshiva, the master Talmudist Reb Refoel Dovid Auerbach was a frequent visitor at the home of Chassidic luminary Reb Shlom'ke of Z'vihl (1869-1945). He went at the urging of his father, the *gaon* Reb Chaim, who was convinced that the greatest miracle-worker of their generation was Reb Shlom'ke.

Once when Reb Refoel Dovid knocked on Reb Shlom'ke's door, he was greeted by Reb Shlom'ke's devoted follower, Reb Eliyahu Roth. The latter was the only one in the house, as Reb Shlom'ke had gone out. Reb Eliyahu took Reb Refoel Dovid on a small "tour" of Reb Shlom'ke's humble abode, where grinding poverty and destitution were apparent in every corner. Among other sorrowful sights was Reb Shlom'ke's bed, where row upon row of moths converged.

Reb Eliyahu explained that he had wanted to buy some poison to exterminate the moths, but had been stopped by Reb Shlom'ke, who insisted that spraying them would be an act of *tza'ar baalei chayim* (causing pain to living creatures). In vain, Reb Eliyahu tried to convince Reb Shlom'ke that the moths might harm him, but Reb Shlom'ke only declared, "I have an agreement with these moths. In return for my not killing them, they do not harm me!" (Memoir of Rabbi Yisrael Hazeh, Sochatchover Chassid and disciple of R. Eliyahu Lopian, adapted from HaModia English Edition, Iyar 28, 5759/May 14, 1999).

☙❦

Once on the holiday of Rosh Hashanah, Rabbi Naftali Tzvi Berlin (1817-1896), the celebrated Rosh Yeshiva of Volozhin, Lithuania, could not find the key to the chicken-coop and was unable to feed the birds. He did not eat until a non-Jew was found, who broke the lock and fed them[11] (Oral tradition cited by Rabbi Yoel Schwartz, *V'Rachamav Al Kol Ma'asav*, p. 62).

☙❦

Lithuanian master Talmudist Rabbi Avraham Yeshayah Karelitz (1878-1953), better known as the Chazon Ish, showed compassion for animals even during his youth. Once an animal of a non-kosher species fell into a deep pit and was trapped without means of escape. [The young scholar] felt the animal's anguish in his heart. Therefore, he lowered himself into the depths of the pit and set it free (Shlomo Cohen, *Pe'er HaDor*, Part I, p. 175).

☙❦

One summer, Rabbi Yitzchak Elchanan Spector (1817-1896) was vacationing outside Kovno. Every day Rabbi Yaakov Lipschutz took the ferry and brought him all the *she'eilos* (questions concerning matters of Jewish law) that had come in the mail. Reb Yitzchak Elchanan would immediately write his *teshuvos* (rulings) and give them to Rabbi Lipschutz to take them back to Kovno and mail them.

One day, Reb Yitzchak Elchanan came chasing after Rabbi Lipschutz who was already on the boat, "Reb Yaakov! Reb Yaakov!"

Concerned, Rabbi Lipschutz ran toward Reb Yitzchak Elchanan and asked what was the matter.

---

11. As an observant Jew, he was not allowed to break the lock himself due to the sanctity of the day.

"I forgot to tell you that there is a cat that has been coming around outside the house, and I have been giving it a bowl of milk every day. Now that I am on vacation, no one is taking care of it. Please be my substitute until I return, and give it the milk" (based on a memoir of R. Yaakov Lipschutz, *Toldos Yitzchak: Toldos HaRav Yitzchak Elchanan Spector*).

გამ

On the path that led to the Ponevezh Yeshiva in Bnei Brak, Israel, sat a cat that a certain God-fearing Torah sage failed to observe as he approached, engaged in a scholarly discussion with one of his students. When the tzaddik noticed the cat, he stopped in the middle of his dissertation and remarked, "*Tza'ar baalei chaim* is a scriptural prohibition! Let's not bother the cat by passing by so closely." The master and student immediately turned around and took a different path to the yeshiva (Rabbi Yitzchak Nachman Eshkoli, *Tzaar Baalei Chaim*, chap. 13, p. 402).

გამ

At one time it happened that in a certain region there was an outbreak of fatal cattle disease. One old farmer who used to fatten cattle for the market saw that several of his oxen showed dangerous symptoms, and decided to set out to spend Shabbos in Ziditchov [in the court of the tzaddik, Rabbi Yitzchak Eizik, 1804-1872]. On Friday night, when the time came for the tzaddik to deliver his regular *derashah* (Torah discourse), all the Chassidim present pressed forward, tense and eager, the better to hear his every word. And this old man, though preoccupied with the troubles that brought him there and not really interested in the learned words of the tzaddik, nevertheless pushed his way in as vigorously as the best of them — for was this not a time-honored custom? Reb Yitzchak Eizik now began to expound the verse, "You, God, will save both man and animal" (Psalms 36:7).

As soon as he heard these words, the old farmer said to himself: "The Rebbe no doubt went to the trouble of explaining this verse only for my sake. For sure, God will save both man and animal!"

Returning to his farm, he found that of all his cattle not one had died: the epidemic had ceased (Rabbi Shlomo Yosef Zevin, *A Treasury of Chassidic Tales on the Torah,* Vol. I, *Bo,* trans. Uri Kaploun, Brooklyn, NY: Artscroll / Mesorah Publications, 1980).

CREAD

In the courtyard of Chassidic master Rabbi Nosson Dovid of Shidlovitz (d. 1865) hundreds of doves nested. Whenever the Rebbe leaned his head out of an open window, they would all flock to him in a great tumult of activity — and he would do with them whatever he would do.

It once happened on Rosh Hashanah (the Jewish New Year), as the Rebbe ascended the raised platform prior to the sounding of the Shofar (ram's horn), that a dove flew into the synagogue through an opened window, and perched on the reader's table. The Rebbe gazed intently at the bird, and then asked that a bowl of water be placed in front of it. However, due to the incline of the reader's table, it was impossible do so. Therefore, the Rebbe removed his *shtreimel* (fur-trimmed hat), and placed the bowl upon it at the proper angle, so that the dove could drink.

At last, the time came for the Rebbe of Shidlovitz to leave this world. However, as soon as his holy soul ascended from the body, an amazing thing happened: all the doves immediately flew away from the courtyard, and disappeared forever. Who can fathom the secrets of the tzaddikim?[12] (*Alim L'Terufah-Chassidei Belz,* 5 Marcheshvan 5757/1996, citing *Tiferes Avos-Biala*).

CREAD

---

12. R. Moshe of Ujhely, *Yismach Moshe, Noach,* s.v. *V'hinei HaGaon Baal Tevu'os Shor,* pp. 142b-143a, discusses the teaching of the Ari that the souls of *tzaddikim* sometimes reincarnate as doves or other birds of a kosher species, whereas the souls of the wicked sometimes reincarnate as birds of a non-kosher species. The Talmud states in *Chullin* 59a that the latter are typically predators. *Galya Raza,* p. 95, cites a somewhat different tradition that reincarnation as a dove or pigeon is designated for those who did not transgress the cardinal sins of idolatry, murder, or forbidden relations. *Sefer HaKanah* states: "One who sins with speech and action reincarnates with the wild animals of the field. One who sins with action but not with speech reincarnates with the birds of the sky. As for pigeons and doves, however, the souls of *tzaddikim* rest upon them, and [during the Temple period] they were called 'a gratifying fragrance'"; see *Sod HaShechitah Chayos U'Behamos,* p. 282.

Once our holy master, the Stropkover Rebbe (R. Avraham Shalom Halberstam, 1857-1940) visited the city of Ujhely, Hungary, staying in the home of Rabbi Lemel Schvartz. In the morning, after a long night of Torah study, the Rebbe asked R. Lemel's son, R. Mordechai, for some grain to feed the chickens and geese. The Rebbe explained: "One should emulate the Creator, Whose 'mercy is upon all His works.' It is an especially great mitzvah to show compassion toward the creatures of the Holy One, blessed be He. By doing so, one also elicits God's kindness, causing it to shine upon Israel.

"Another benefit of feeding animals is that it strengthens one's compassion. By doing so first thing in the morning, it becomes easier to show compassion throughout the day."

Thus did our master conduct himself, feeding the birds a number of times during his stay (Rabbi Menachem Mendel Halberstam of Stropkov, *Divrei Menachem.* Jerusalem, 1957, p. 144, col. 2).

⊂჻ఖ

In Elul of 5699/1939, during the worst of the battles on Polish soil, Belz was an island of quiet. The Poles had retreated, the Germans were busy elsewhere, and for a whole month the townspeople were left alone with their anxieties. To fill the governmental vacuum, a local militia was formed, manned by more Jews than Poles, in proportion to their numbers in the town. This group kept order and assisted the thousands of refugees who began arriving as soon as word spread of the relative peace in that region.

The Rebbe (Rabbi Aharon of Belz, 1880-1957) made only one concession to the political circumstances: he acquired a horse and carriage, and ordered that it be kept ready for him to flee at a moment's notice, whenever he would give the word. Otherwise, he kept his schedule exactly as before — learning, praying, receiving Chassidim, and directing public affairs.

Even in such tense times, the Rebbe's concern was for the finest details of halacha. Every evening, when his *gabbai* (attendant) would bring him his coffee for "breakfast" (his first meal of the day), the Rebbe would ask, "Did you remember to feed the horses?" Now that he owned horses, he had to fulfill the halacha to feed one's animals before oneself, and he would not drink his coffee until he was sure that the horses had been fed (Moshe Prager, *Hatzalas HaRabbi MiBelz* [Jerusalem 5760/2000], p. 10, translated by Aharon Perlow, HaModia English Edition, Av 17, 5762/July 25, 2002).

ೞ৪ಲ

One night the [yeshiva] boys were gathered on the grass listening to Reb Shraga Feivel [Mendlowitz], who was sitting on the stairs leading up to the main building. As he was speaking, mosquitoes descended on the boys, and soon everyone was scratching himself furiously. In the dark, Reb Shraga Feivel could not see what had happened, but he sensed the disturbance. When one of the students explained what had happened, he was perplexed: "If there was a swarm of biting insects here, I, too, would have felt it." For their part the boys were equally amazed that he had not been bitten at all. The next day, however, as they were learning *Yalkut Shimoni* on *Mishlei* (Proverbs) with Reb Shraga Feivel, they had their explanation. On the verse, "When a man's ways are pleasing to [God], even his enemies make peace with him" (*Mishlei* 16:7), *Yalkut Shimoni* interprets the word "enemies" as referring to mosquitoes.

Reb Shraga Feivel himself once offered another explanation for the fact that insects never bothered him. He could not recall ever having killed a fly (Yonoson Rosenblum, *Reb Shraga Feivel: The Life and Times of Rabbi Shraga Feivel Mendlowitz, the Architect of Torah in America* [Brooklyn, NY: Artscroll / Mesorah, 2001], p. 296).

ೞ৪ಲ

Rabbi Avraham Pam was a leading Torah sage and educator who inspired thousands of souls to continue the journey to the world where all of God's creatures would feel at home. He served as the Rosh Yeshiva (Dean) of Yeshiva Torah Vodaath in Brooklyn, and he was a member of the Moetzes Gedolei HaTorah of America — the council of the great Torah sages of North America. In the spirit of a Torah sage, he was an outstanding model of ethical behavior, and he was a warm and loving teacher who was known for his great sensitivity to the feelings of others.

Throughout the generations, the prophets and sages of Israel have emphasized the sacredness and importance of *kavod habriyos*, a term which literally means "honoring the creatures." The term *kavod habriyos* is used when we refer to the honor and dignity due to human beings, who are creatures created in the Divine Image. In the following story, Rabbi Pam indicates that the term can also be used to refer to the dignity due to all of God's creatures:

A number of years ago the Moetzes Gedolei HaTorah of America was concerned about new attempts within the State of Israel to divest the State of any Jewish identity. There were some secularists who argued that Israel should not be a "Jewish" state, but a "state of its citizens," and the United States was seen as a model. They wanted to abolish all laws that enacted public respect for Shabbos, the Festivals, Kashrus, and other "symbols" of our spiritual heritage. One of the new laws that they wanted to enact would have the government encourage the importation of pig meat. This law was opposed by Orthodox and traditional Jews, including most of the Sephardic population. It was also opposed by some secular-oriented Jews who felt that Israel should publicly honor basic Jewish traditions in order that Israeli culture not become a "carbon copy" of American culture.

The Moetzes Gedolei HaTorah decided to issue a public statement expressing its concern about these developments. A text was drafted and circulated among the members for their consideration and comment. As is usually the case when the Moetzes Gedolei HaTorah issues a public statement, each member of the body of Torah sages reviewed the proposed text with a fine-tooth comb, one suggesting the deletion of a sentence here, another suggesting the addition of a paragraph there, yet another suggesting a different way to structure the statement.

Then Rabbi Pam got on the phone: "It's very good, except for one problem. The sentence about the importation of pigs is written in a way that could be seen as demeaning to the pigs. *Vos iz er chazir shuldig az er iz a chazir? Der Eibishter hut em azoi bashafen!* (Why should the pig be faulted for being a pig? The Almighty created him that way!)"

Rabbi Pam added: "A statement from the Moetzes Gedolei HaTorah must be extremely careful not to undermine *kavod habriyos* — the inherent dignity of all God's creatures. Let's reword it this way..." (Rabbi Chaim Dovid Zweibel, Hamodia English Edition, Ellul 5, 5661 /August 24, 2001).

A Chassidic Ecology Lesson

In everything, even in the minutest circumstance which we created beings reckon as nothing and do not take at all into account, there is a divine intention, a divine will; and divine providence arranges the circumstances that will enable this intention to be realized in a certain way.

One day in the summer of 5656 (1896 c.e.) I was strolling with my father (Rabbi Sholom Dov Ber, the fifth Lubavitcher Rebbe, 1860-1920) in a field in the country resort of Bolivke, near Lubavitch. The crops were almost ripe, and the grain and the grass were nodding in a gentle breeze.

"Behold Godliness!" said my father. "Each movement of every single sheaf of grain and blade of grass was included in the Primal Thought of the *partzuf* of *Adam Kadmon* (Primordial Reality) — in Him Who watches and gazes until the end of all the generations; and divine providence brings this thought to realization for the sake of a certain divine intention."

As we walked on, we found ourselves in a forest. Deep in contemplation of what I had just been told concerning divine providence, and overwhelmed by the tenderness and the earnestness of my father's explanation, I plucked a leaf from a tree as I passed by and held it in my hand. As people often do and without taking particular notice, I tore off little pieces from the leaf every so often as I walked on, ensconced in thought, and tossed them to the ground.

My father now said, "The Ari says that not only is every leaf of a tree a creature with divine vitality, which the Almighty created with a certain end as part of the ultimate purpose of creation; but, moreover, every leaf contains the spark of a soul that descends to this world for the sake of a *tikkun* — in order to attain restitution.

"Just see how 'man is always liable for damages, whether awake or asleep' (*Bava Kamma* 26a). The difference between being awake or asleep is to be found in the inward faculties of *seichel* and *middos*, in the person's intellect and in his emotional attributes. The external faculties are to be found in a sleeping person, too; only his inward faculties are confused —

which explains the presence of the paradoxes to be found in dreams. And where does the difference between one who is awake and one who is asleep become apparent? In the faculty of vision. One who is asleep does not see; one who is awake can see.

"When a person is awake, he sees Godliness; when he is asleep, he does not. But 'man is liable for damages whether he is awake or asleep.' Just now we discussed the subject of divine providence — and quite without thinking, you plucked a leaf, held it in your hand, played around with it, turned it around, squashed it, tore it up in little pieces and scattered it in different places. How can a person be so light-minded in relation to a creature of the Almighty? This leaf is something created by the Almighty for a particular reason. It has a God-given vitality; it has a body, and it has life. In what way is the leaf's 'I' smaller than your 'I'?

"True, the difference is a big one. The leaf is *tzomei'ach* (vegetation) and you are *medaber* (a human being), and there is a great difference between the two categories. Nevertheless, one must always remember the mission and the divine intention of every created thing — what is the task that the *tzomei'ach* has to fulfill in this world, and what is the task that the *medaber* has to fulfill in this world"[13] (Rabbi Yosef Yitzchak Schneersohn of Lubavitch, *Likkutei Dibburim* I, 4a: 4 [Brooklyn, NY: Kehot, 1987], trans. Rabbi Uri Kaploun).

---

13. R. Aryeh Levin of Jerusalem (1885-1969) recounts a similar experience. As a young Talmud scholar, R. Aryeh left his native Lithuania in 1905 and came to the city of Jaffa in the land of Israel. He sought out his future mentor, R. Avraham Yitzchak Kook, who received him with great warmth. Once, while they were walking together in the fields engaged in Torah discussion, R. Levin picked a flower. At this R. Kook remarked, "All my days I have been careful never to pluck a blade of grass or a flower needlessly, when it had the ability to grow or blossom. You know the teaching of our sages that not a single blade of grass grows here on earth that does not have an angel above it, commanding it to grow. Every sprout and leaf of grass says something meaningful, every stone whispers some hidden message in the silence, every creation utters its song!"

R. Levin concludes, "These words of our great master, spoken from a pure and holy heart, engraved themselves deeply in my heart. From that time on, I began to feel a strong sense of compassion for all things" (based on Simcha Raz, *A Tzaddik In Our Time* [Jerusalem: Feldheim, 1976] pp. 108-109).

Sources: Chapter 2

Stories

Once the donkey of Rabbi Chaninah ben Dosah was stolen. The robbers tied it up in a yard and put before it straw, barley, and water, but it would not eat or drink. They said, "Why should we let it die and befoul our yard?" So they got up and opened the gate and let it out. The donkey walked along braying until it reached [the house of] Rabbi Chaninah ben Dosa. When it arrived, the rabbi's son heard its voice and said to his father, "That sounds like our animal." The rabbi said, "Open the door, my son, for it has nearly died of hunger." Immediately, the lad opened the door and placed before it straw, barley, and water. Then it ate and drank. Thus, it was said, "Just as the tzaddikim of old were saintly, so were their beasts"[14] (*Avos D'Rabbi Nosson* 8:8).

ൠഽ൮

[Rabbi Yossi] owned a donkey that he allowed people to rent. When the day was over, those who hired it would place their payment on its back, and the donkey would make its way home to its master. However, if the amount were too little or too much, it would not go. One day a pair of sandals was placed on its back. The donkey would not budge until they were removed [and the fee had been substituted]. Only then did it proceed (Talmud: *Ta'anis* 24a).

ൠഽ൮

Once there was an Israelite who owned a cow with which he plowed his field. He fell on bad times, and was forced to sell it to a certain non-Jew. The new owner plowed with it for six days. On the Sabbath, he

---

14. R. Moshe of Ujhely finds a biblical prototype for this principle in Jacob's separation of his flocks from those of Laban. Although this was primarily a demonstration of ownership, *Yismach Moshe* infers that Jacob also wished to prevent them from grazing in foreign pastures (Gen. 30:40). He also cites the example of Elijah the Prophet, who had to persuade the ox designated to be slaughtered as an idolatrous offering to acquiesce to his fate, since this would lead to a greater sanctification of the Divine Name; cf. *Yismach Moshe, Vayishlach,* s.v. *Vayikach min habah b'yado,* p. 356a; ibid., *Vayeishev,* s.v. *Haya ro'eh es echav batzon,* pp. 373b-374a.

also took it out to plough, but it lay down beneath its yoke. He began to beat it, but the animal would not budge from its place. Seeing that his efforts were in vain, he went to the Israelite who sold it to him and said, "Come take your cow, for she grieves after her former master. No matter how much I beat her, she refuses to budge from her place."

The Israelite realized that the cow refused to work because it had been taught to rest on the Sabbath. "I will get her to stand up," he said. When he came, he whispered into her ear: "Heifer, heifer, you know that when you were mine, you plowed all week and rested on the Sabbath. But now, because of my sins, you have been sold to a non-Jew. Therefore, I beseech you, stand up and plough." She immediately arose and began to plough.

The non-Jew said, "I beg you, take back your cow. But before I leave, tell me what did you whisper into her ear? I wore myself out with her, and even beat her, but she would not get up."

The Israelite began to mollify him and said, "It was not witchcraft or sorcery I performed. I merely whispered in her ear that she was no longer mine, and she stood up and plowed."

Immediately, the non-Jew began to tremble and exclaimed, "If a cow that has neither speech nor intellect recognizes her Creator, how can I, a human being whom my Maker formed in His own image and to whom He gave intellect, fail to recognize Him?" Straightaway, he went and converted to Judaism. Eventually he became an accomplished Torah scholar who was known as Yochanan ben Torsa ("Yochanan Son Of A Cow"). To this day, our rabbis cite his rulings. And if you wonder that through a cow a man was brought under the wings of the *Shechinah* (Divine Presence), recall that it is through a cow the Red Heifer that the purification of all Israel is accomplished (Midrash: *Pesikta Rabbasi* 14).

୯୫୨୦

[Rabbi Pinchas ben Ya'ir] came to a certain inn. They placed barley before his donkey, but it would not eat. [The barley] was sifted, but it would not eat. [The barley] was carefully picked, but it would not eat. [Rabbi Pinchas ben Ya'ir] said to them: "Perhaps it has not been tithed?" They removed a tithe, and it ate. He thereupon exclaimed: "This poor creature goes forth to do the will of its Master, and you would feed it untithed produce?" (Talmud: *Chullin* 7b).

Commentary: Concerning the donkey of Rabbi Pinchas ben Ya'ir and the amazing knowledge that our sages ascribe to it, some have sought to interpret these things figuratively. However, they do not know how to interpret correctly. In truth, the words [of our sages] should be understood in their literal sense. The meaning of the matter is that this donkey was spiritually refined and perfected in every way, according to its essence and nature. It did not attain this level of spiritual refinement in the manner of other animals, whose spiritual elevation is attained through being consumed by man. Rather, it accomplished its perfection in the course of time through its own efforts and through Rabbi Pinchas ben Ya'ir, its master. It reached a level of true refinement, comparable to that of the animals during the six days of creation.

Know: the animals as they existed during the six days of creation were spiritually loftier than mankind today, after the sin of Adam. Therefore, one should not be amazed that Rabbi Pinchas ben Ya'ir's donkey discerned what the sages of that period did not discern. This is what the Talmud alludes to in the name of Rabbi Zeira: "We are like donkeys — but not like the donkey of Rabbi Pinchas ben Ya'ir" (*Shabbos* 112b).

From this one may get a sense of the greatness of man after he will have been spiritually refined and perfected according to his requirements, and how lofty the level for which he is destined, beyond all measure. Also, from this one may understand the greatness of Adam before the sin, when he existed in his pristine state (Rabbi Chaim Vital citing his mentor, Rabbi Yitzchak Luria, *Sha'ar HaMitzvos, Eikev*, p. 99).

೧೩౪⊗

Rabbi Chaim ibn Attar (1696-1743), author of *Ohr HaChaim*, earned his livelihood as a silversmith. However, he always made Torah study his primary occupation, and his craft secondary. He would sit engrossed in Torah study until his last coin was spent, and only then did he engage in worldly matters. Once two ministers from the court of the King of Morocco came to him with a certain amount of gold. "The King has heard that you are the foremost expert in your craft," they said. "Therefore, he sent us to commission you to fashion a piece of the finest jewelry in honor of his daughter's wedding. You will be paid a princely sum. However, you must complete the work in ten days."

At that time, our master, Rabbi Chaim, still had enough money to cover his daily expenses. Therefore, he put away the gold, and returned to his holy books. However, upon his return home, he forgot all about his commission, due to his preoccupation with his studies.

On the appointed day, the two royal ministers returned and asked for the finished piece of jewelry. Then Rabbi Chaim remembered the matter, and confessed that he had not yet begun his work. Since the emissaries were both rabid Jew-haters, they were overjoyed to hear that they would have an opportunity to denounce Rabbi Chaim. They returned to the palace and told the King that the Jewish silversmith had rebelled willfully, and thus had dishonored the crown. At this, the King commanded that Rabbi Chaim be cast into a pit of lions, this being the punishment for treason.

When the police came to arrest Rabbi Chaim, he asked for permission to bring along a volume of Psalms, a few holy books, and his *tallis* and *tefillin*. They laughed at him and exclaimed, "Do you think you are going to a hotel? You are on your way to be killed in a lions' den!" However, the Jewish sage paid no heed to their words, and packed his bag. Unsuspecting, his wife asked him, "Where are you going?" He answered simply, "I shall return soon."

They took their prisoner straight to the lions' den and threw him in. The lion keeper opened an overhead window to see what would happen. However, he was amazed by what his eyes beheld. There sat our master, Rabbi Chaim, wearing his *tallis* and *tefillin*, praying and studying in a loud voice, while in front of him crouched the lions in a semi-circle, like students before their teacher, listening attentively to his words. Overcome with trembling, the lion keeper ran to inform the King. After hearing his report, the King and his royal entourage proceeded to the lions' den to see with his own eyes this awesome sight. Then he proclaimed before everyone, "Now I know that there is a God of Israel!"

The King commanded that Rabbi Chaim and his belongings be retrieved from the pit, whereupon he asked him for an explanation of the miracle.

Rabbi Chaim answered, "I refrained from my work because of my immersion in the holy Torah, therefore the Torah protected and saved me!"

The King asked his forgiveness, and sent him home in peace and with great honor (*Toldos Ohr HaChaim*, p. 11, n. 4, citing *Sefer Ma'aseh HaGedolim al HaTorah*).

಄಄

Rabbi Yisrael of Rizhin (1797-1850) related how the Baal Shem Tov and his disciples once prayed the Afternoon Service before the Sabbath in the open fields. The flocks grazing nearby gathered together and began to bleat loudly while the Chassidim prayed.

The Rebbe of Rizhin explained that all levels of creation are incorporated within humankind. Thus, when a human being accomplishes a spiritual ascent, all of creation ascends, as well. Before Adam sinned, all sentient beings occupied such a lofty spiritual level that they all perceived Godliness. During his prayer, the Baal Shem Tov elevated and perfected his portion of creation and his aspect of Adam to such an degree that even the cattle and sheep acquired greater awareness of their Maker, and they all cried out to God along with him.

According to Rabbi Elimelech of Grodzisk (1824-1892), when the Baal Shem Tov uttered the words, "[He restored the destitute from poverty,] and established families like a flock" (Psalms 107:41), the sheep immediately surrounded him. According to Rabbi Aharon of Karlin (1806-1872), all the animals stood on their hind legs like human beings, and raised their front legs toward heaven in supplication (*Midrash Pinchas* I, 22, n. 35, and *Sefer Baal Shem Tov, Yisro*, 29, citing *Beis Aharon, Bo*; also ibid. 30, citing *Divrei Elimelech, Bechukosai* and *Rimzei Shevi'i Shel Pesach*; ibid. 31, citing *Toldos Adam, Noach*).

Sources: Chapter 3

God Rewards Animals for Their Pains

The Creator decreed that all living things must die. He gave every human being a certain life-span, and He made the life-span of an animal [designated for human consumption] until its time of slaughter, substituting slaughter for natural death. However, if slaughter entails pain beyond that which is experienced in natural death, God takes cognizance of this and rewards the animal according to the extent of its suffering[15] (Rav Saadia Gaon, *Emunos V'De'os, Ma'amar* III, p. 145).

Do Not Consume the Flesh of a Living Animal

Every moving thing that lives shall be food for you; as the green herb, I have given you everything. However, flesh with its life-force, which is its blood, you shall not eat. And surely the blood of your own lives I will seek; at the hand of every living animal I will seek it, and at the hand of man, even at the hand of every man's brother, I will seek the life of man (Genesis 9:3-5).

Commentary 1: "Flesh with its life-force." [God] forbade [Noah and his sons] the limb of a living animal. That is to say, "As long as [the animal] is alive, you shall not eat its flesh" (Rashi, ad loc.).

Commentary 2: The Torah juxtaposes the prohibition of taking the limb of a living animal to the prohibition of murder because they are

---

15. Cf. *Teshuvos HaGeonim*, Vol. I, no. 375, p. 191. Maimonides seems to disagree in his *Moreh Nevuchim* 3:17, according to Ibn Tibbon's classic Hebrew translation. However, some contemporary scholars take issue with Ibn Tibbon and contend that Maimonides concurs with the Geonim on this; see Schochet, *Animal Life in Jewish Tradition*, chap. 11, n. 37. Despite the hypothesis that the view presented above reflects the influence of the Islamic Mutazilites, there is no compelling reason to assume that the Geonim based their opinion on anything other than the well-known Talmudic principle that "the Holy One, blessed be He, does not withhold recompense from any creature" (*Pesachim* 118a), cited by Rav Sherira Gaon (see Chapter 3, R. Yehudah HaNasi and the Calf, Commentary 2). Since Rav Saadia Gaon did not accept the doctrine of reincarnation, how else, from his point of view, would God reward slaughtered animals if not in the Afterlife? Presumably this applies to Rav Sherira, as well.

actually equivalent to one another. Even the Children of Noah (non-Jews) are cautioned about taking the limb of a living animal. Since the precepts given to the Children of Noah primarily concern the preservation of civilization, [this prohibition applies to them]. Although the Children of Noah were not sanctified with the precepts of Israel, the Torah gave them seven commandments for the sake of safe-guarding the world.[16] Therefore, they are forbidden to take the limb of a living animal, for this is actual murder. This prohibition is one of the fundamentals of civilization (Rabbi Nosson Sternhartz, *Likkutei Halachos, Ever Min HaChai* 1:1, abridged).

Do Not Consume the Life-Blood

Only be sure not to eat the blood, for the blood is the life, and you must not eat the life with the flesh (Deuteronomy 12:23).

Commentary 1: One of the roots of this precept is that we should not instill in ourselves the trait of cruelty, which is a most reprehensible trait. In truth, there is no greater cruelty in the world than to cut off a limb or flesh from a creature while it is still alive and eat it. I have often written about the great benefit we receive through acquiring good traits of character and distancing ourselves from evil ones. For the good will cleave to the good, and the Benevolent One wishes to do good. He therefore commands His people to choose the good (*Sefer HaChinnuch,* Mitzvah 452).

Commentary 2: It is forbidden to eat the limb or flesh of a living animal. [The Kabbalists explain that] as long as the forces of severity [that are bound up with the blood] have not been "sweetened" in their source through the *tikkun* of ritual slaughter, it is impossible to remove the spirit of evil and foolishness possessed by the animal. Therefore, eating the flesh of a living animal causes a person great spiritual harm. Moreover, it is an act of extreme cruelty, akin to that of non-kosher, predatory creatures, which eat other animals alive. These creatures represent the antithesis of holiness. The traits of holiness are mercy, kindness, and the

---

16. For source references on the Seven Laws of Noah, see Chapter 3, n. 1.

negation of all anger and cruelty (Rabbi Nachman Goldstein of Tcherin, *Nachas HaShulchan, Shechitah* 62, abridged).

Do Not Ignore the Feelings of Animals

Do not muzzle an ox while it is treading grain (Deuteronomy 25:4).

Commentary 1: This verse clearly states [that it is forbidden to cause suffering to animals.] However, some contend that this prohibition is rabbinic, citing a Talmudic opinion in tractate *Shabbos* 154b. Nevertheless, based on the Talmudic discussion before us, the foremost authorities rule that cruelty to animals is prohibited by Torah law (Rif on *Bava Metzia* 32b, et al.).

This ruling is confirmed by another Talmudic source: "If an animal falls into a pool of water on the Sabbath, one should bring cushions and blankets and set them under her, that she may get up of her own accord... One might object: by doing so, does one not rob a vessel [i.e., the object used to rescue the animal] of its readiness for further use, [an act which is forbidden on the Sabbath]? However, the prohibition of nullifying the readiness of a vessel is of rabbinic origin, whereas preventing the suffering of animals is mandated by the Torah. A Torah law supersedes a rabbinic law" (*Shabbos* 128b) (Rabbi Menachem Meiri, *Beis HaBechirah*, ad loc.).

Commentary 2: One of the roots of this precept is to instill in us a sensitive spirit, choosing what is right and cleaving to it, and pursuing kindness and compassion. By becoming trained in these habits, even toward animals that were especially created to serve us — i.e., to have compassion for them and grant them a share of that for which they have labored — the spirit of a person will become accustomed to seeking the welfare of other human beings. One will prevent them from being wronged in any way, reward them for whatever good they do, and gratify them with the fruit of their labors (*Sefer HaChinnuch*, Mitzvah 596).

ෆ෨

Upon the completion of the days of purification [after the birth of] a son or a daughter, she shall bring a sheep within its first year for an *olah* (burnt offering), and a young dove or a turtledove for the purification offering, unto the entrance to the Tent of Meeting, to the Kohen (priest) (Leviticus 12:6).

Commentary: In every instance [where the Torah mentions these two species] it mentions turtledoves (*torim*) before young doves (*bnei yonah*), except here. This is because in this instance, the [Temple official who purchases the bird on behalf of the mother] brings only one bird. If a young dove is available, he should not take a turtledove, for its mate will mourn over it and not mate with another (Rabbi Yaakov ben Asher, *Baal HaTurim*, ad loc.).

⋙⋘

You shall pay [a hired laborer] his wages on the day it is due, and not let the sun set upon it. Since he is poor, he sets his heart on it; do not let him cry out against you unto the Lord, your God, causing you to have a sin (Deuteronomy 24:15).

Midrash: This may be compared to a man who walks along with his donkey behind him. He buys a sheaf of grain and puts it in his sack. The donkey keeps following him for the sake of the sheaf that he wishes to eat. What does his master do [upon his return home]? He ties the sheaf above the animal's reach. You must say to that man, "Wicked one! All the way he ran along after it, and now you refuse to place it before him?" Thus is the plight of the day-laborer who toils all day long, anticipating his wages, but goes away with nothing. Of him it is written, "He sets his heart on it; do not let him cry out against you unto the Lord, your God," for I am gracious, and I will hear (*Shemos Rabbah* 31:7, with *Eitz Yosef*).

"The Righteous Man Considers His Animal"

A spiritually sensitive person will not cause pain to any creature, including animals; rather, he will show mercy and compassion towards them. Thus, it states: "A tzaddik considers the needs of his animal..." (Proverbs 12:10). Some authorities maintain that causing animals pain is a scriptural prohibition. At the very least, it is a rabbinic prohibition. The basic principle is that compassion and kindness must be permanently fixed in the heart of a spiritually sensitive person. His constant aim must be to give happiness to his fellow creatures and not to cause them any sort of pain (Rabbi Moshe Chaim Luzzatto, *Mesillas Yesharim*, chap. 19).

⋈

The tzaddik considers the needs of his animal and does not overfeed it. Also, he does not force it to work beyond its abilities, for he knows the "soul of his animal." However, [the verse concludes,] "The compassion of the wicked is cruelty," for afterward, [the latter] works his animal beyond its strength and capacity.

[On a deeper level,] the tzaddik knows his own "animal," i.e., his physical desires. He does not pity himself by indulging his desires, but eats only "to sustain his soul" (ibid. 30:32). However, the wicked, who feel sorry for themselves and do not break their desires, are "cruel" — for "the more flesh, the more worms" (*Avos* 2:7). Because of this, they must descend to Gehenna (Purgatory) (Rabbi Eliyahu of Vilna, *Be'ur haGra Mishlei*, ad loc.).

⋈

There are probably no creatures that require the protective divine word against the presumption of man more than animals, which like man have sensations and instincts, but whose body and powers are nevertheless subservient to man. In relation to them, man so easily forgets that injured animal muscle twitches just like human muscle, that the maltreated nerves of an animal sicken like human nerves, that the animal is just as sensitive to cuts, blows, and beatings as man. Thus man becomes the torturer of the animal soul, which has been subjected to him only for the fulfillment of humane and wise purposes, sometimes out of self-interest, at other times in order to satisfy a whim, sometimes out of thoughtlessness — yes, even for the satisfaction of crude, satanic desire (Rav Samson Raphael Hirsch, *Horeb* 2:292, trans. Dayan I. Grunfeld [London: Soncino, 1962]).

Do Not Cook an Animal in its Mother's Milk

You shall not cook a kid in its mother's milk (Exodus 23:19).

Commentary 1: Because goats often give birth to twins, it was common practice to slaughter one of them. Since goats produce an abundance of milk — as it is written, "And goat's milk shall suffice for your food" (Proverbs 27:27) — they would then boil the kid in its mother's milk. This was an act of depravity, for it is wanton gluttony to eat the mother's milk together with the flesh of her young. This law and that of sending away the mother bird before taking her young come to teach us the ways of civilization. Since the [Israelites] would sacrifice many animals during the festivals, the Torah cautions us neither to boil nor eat a kid in its mother's milk.[17] This law applies to all mixtures of meat and milk, as our Rabbis explain regarding ordinary animal slaughter (Rashbam, ad loc.).

Commentary 2: The mother animal does not live so that a person, simply by his right of ownership, may exploit her for his own purposes; rather, her milk is intended for her own young, whom she loves. The kid, too, is naturally entitled to the pleasure of its mother's loving breast. However, the cruelty of the human heart, produced by our coarse materialism and moral weakness, distorts and perverts these principles. Thus, the tender kid, according to the assessment of man's inferior ethical sensitivity, has no right to nestle against its loving mother, nor to enjoy the light of life, but deserves only to be slaughtered in order to provide food for the belly of the gluttonous human being, whose debased soul insists, "I will eat meat" (Deuteronomy 12:20).

According to this, what should be the purpose of the milk, if not to cook in it the slaughtered kid? Is this not a natural combination of these two essential foods, the milk and the tender kid that derives nurture from it?

Humanity: let your ears hear the sound behind you — the voice of God that loudly cries out, "You shall not cook a kid in its mother's milk."

---

17. Rashbam wishes to explain the meaning of this law in its scriptural context, which is the passage that mandates the three pilgrim festivals and their accompanying rites in the Holy Temple.

No, the purpose of the kid is not merely to be food for your sharp teeth, sharpened and polished by your lowliness and gluttony in eating meat; and certainly the milk is not intended to be a condiment for the satisfaction of your base desire (Rabbi Avraham Yitzchak Kook, *Chazon HaTzimchonut V'HaShalom*, 20, abridged).

Do Not Kill an Animal Together With Its Young

Whether an ox or a sheep, you shall not slaughter a mother animal and her young on the same day (Leviticus 22:28).

Midrash 1: Rabbi Yudan ben Pazi taught: Just as the Holy One, blessed be He, has compassion for human beings, so does He have compassion for animals (*Devarim Rabbah* 6:1, end).

Midrash 2: Rabbi Berechiah taught in the name of Rabbi Levi: It is written, "A tzaddik considers the needs of his animal" (Proverbs 12:10). This refers to the Holy One, blessed be He, in whose Torah it is written. "Whether it be an ox or a sheep, you shall not slaughter a mother animal and her young on the same day (*Vayikra Rabbah* 27:11; *Peskikta D'Rav Kahana*, ad loc.).

Midrash 3: Children of Israel, my people: just as our Father in Heaven is compassionate, so shall you be compassionate on Earth. Do not slaughter a cow or a sheep and her young on the same day (*Targum Yonasan ben Uziel*, ad loc.).

Commentary 1: The *Zohar* explains this as an act of cruelty, which arouses the corresponding attribute of cruelty Above.[18] This would be contrary to the essential purpose of animal slaughter, which is to transform and perfect the animal spirit. One must overcome the spirit of folly, which includes the traits of cruelty and anger; as the verse states, "Anger lies in the breast of fools" (Ecclesiastes 7:9). Therefore, ritual slaughter itself must be an expression of kindness, compassion, and enlightenment. "And you shall slaughter" (Leviticus

---

18. *Zohar* III, *Emor*, 92b. This follows the rabbinic principle that according to the trait a person expresses in this world, so is he or she treated from Above; cf. *Sanhedrin* 90a; *Sotah* 1:7; *Avos* 2:6; *Tanna D'vei Eliyahu Rabbah* 16:1, 17:19; *Tzava'as HaRivash* 142; *Nefesh HaChaim* 1:4; et al.

1:5) means that you may do so only by the most humane method. The drawing of the blade must be in keeping with the verse, "Draw forth Your kindness upon those who know You" (Psalms 36:11). It is forbidden to apply the knife with pressure (*derasah*), which is murderous and cruel (Rabbi Nachman Goldstein of Tcherin, *Nachas HaShulchan, Shechitah* 16).

Commentary 2: Egotism, love and concern for self, is the powerful drive that motivates all animal life. The sacrifice of self for the existence of another creature and devoted care for its welfare, as manifested in the animal's mother-love when the animal bears and nurtures its young, is the first move of the animal's character toward that selflessness which, in human love, represents the godliest trait in human character. This trace of humanity in the animal's character must not be blurred; indeed, it must be emphasized with particular care in our treatment of those animals that, as our offerings, are intended to symbolize a moral idea toward which man should strive.

It is this inherent trace of humanity that qualifies the animal to fill this symbolic function. The fact that the Law gives it such explicit consideration makes it clear that animal offerings in Judaism are intended solely for the promotion of human morality, in sharp contrast with the pagan concept which views the sacrificial rituals as killings performed to please the gods (Rabbi Samson Raphael Hirsch, *The Pentateuch*, ad loc., trans. Gertrude Hirschler [Brooklyn, NY: Judaica Press, 1990]).

The Mitzvah of Sending Away the Mother Bird[19]

If you chance upon a bird's nest along the way, in a tree or on the ground, whether it contains young birds or eggs, and the mother is sitting upon the young birds or upon the eggs — you shall not take the mother bird together with the children. You shall surely send away the mother, and only then may you take the young for yourself; that it

---

19. Also see Compassion For Animals in the Bible and Its Commentaries above, citing additional passages from Nachmanides and *Sefer HaChinnuch,* as well as R. Kook in the section: The Pain of Animal Slaughter Must be Minimal.

may be good for you, and you may prolong your days[20] (Deuteronomy 22:6-7).

Midrash 1: Rabbi Yudan ben Pazi taught: Just as the Holy One, blessed be He, has compassion for animals, so does He have compassion for fowl (*Devarim Rabbah* 6:1, end).

Midrash 2: "You shall surely send away (*shalei'ach t'shalach*) the mother bird." The Rabbis declared: Why does the verse use a double expression? Because one who fulfills the "sending forth" of this precept will be granted the privilege of "sending forth" a slave to freedom. As it is written, "And when you send him forth free..." (Deuteronomy 16:13).

Fulfilling the precept of sending forth the mother bird hastens the advent of the Messiah, which is associated with the expression "to send forth." As it is written, "[Happy are you that sow beside all waters,] freely sending forth the feet of the ox and the donkey" (Isaiah 32:20).

Rabbi Tanchuma said: Fulfilling this precept hastens the arrival of Elijah the Prophet [the harbinger of the Messiah], whose coming is associated with the expression "to send forth." As it states, "Behold, I shall send forth to you Elijah the Prophet..." (Malachi 3:23), and he shall come and console you. "He will return the heart of the fathers to their children..." (ibid.) (*Devarim Rabbah* 6:3).

Commentary 1: The Rabbis have stated [that if a communal prayer leader says, "Even to a bird's nest do Your mercies extend," the

---

20. For the halachic parameters of this mitzvah, see *Shulchan Aruch, Yoreh De'ah*, 292. According to the view of Rashi in *Chullin* 139b, one may chase away the mother bird without actually handling her. However, Maimonides in his *Mishneh Torah, Shechitah* 12:5, indicates that one fulfills the mitzvah only by picking up the mother bird directly, an opinion with which the Ari evidently concurs; see *Sefer Chareidim* 16:42. In a responsum concerning whether one may perform this mitzvah on the Sabbath, R. Moshe Sofer concludes: "In my opinion, one must remove the mother bird from the nest directly by hand... Thus, if one drives away the mother bird [only indirectly], according to Maimonides one would not have fulfilled the mitzvah. Therefore, one would have acted cruelly without justification [by causing the mother bird distress]. Yet if one wishes to be pious and attempts to follow the view of Maimonides, the spirit of the wise does not rest upon him [for he might harm the bird, and in this manner violate the prohibition of *tza'ar baalei chaim*]"; *Teshuvos Chasam Sofer, Orach Chaim*, No. 100. Although it is not the prevailing halachic view, the Chasam Sofer's ruling is instructive in that he accords such importance to the factor of *tza'ar baalei chaim* that it may outweigh the performance of a scriptural commandment, albeit one that is in his opinion volitional.

congregation silences him. The reason given is] "because he treats God's laws as expressions of mercy, whereas they are decrees" (*Berachos* 33b).[21] This means to say that it was not a matter of God's pity for the bird's nest, nor of His compassion extending to the mother bird and her young, since His mercy toward animals did not prevent our using these creatures for our own needs. If this had been the case, He would have forbidden slaughter altogether. Rather, the reason for this prohibition is to teach us the trait of compassion, that we should not become cruel. For cruelty pervades the soul of man. It is known that butchers who slaughter large oxen and asses are "men of blood" (Psalms 55:24). "Those who slaughter men" (Hoshea 13:2) are extremely cruel. Concerning this cruelty, our Rabbis have said: "The noblest of butchers is a partner of Amalek"[22] (*Kiddushin* 82a). Thus, these commandments with respect to cattle and fowl are not an expression of divine compassion toward them, but decrees upon us, meant to guide us and teach us good character traits (Nachmanides, *Commentary on the Torah*, ad loc.).

Commentary 2: [This precept] comes to instill in us the trait of mercy and to remove the evil trait of cruelty. Therefore, although God permitted us certain kinds of animals for our sustenance, He commanded that we not kill the mother bird and its young at one time, in order to set permanently in our souls the trait of mercy (*Sefer HaChinnuch*, Mitzvah 294).

---

21. The Gemara cites a dispute between two Amoraim (Talmudic authorities), R. Yosé bar Zevida and R. Yosé bar Avin. One opines that the prayer leader is silenced because singling out this example of God's compassion might lead to jealousy among God's creatures; the other contends that God's laws are decrees beyond mortal understanding. The Maharsha explains the latter view to mean that only when the Torah mentions God's mercy or kindness in connection with a particular law may we infer something of its meaning; otherwise, we must treat the divine commandments as decrees. They are given as such in order to increase the reward of those who fulfill them unquestioningly. The first Amora apparently shares the assumption that the law of sending away the mother bird is a legitimate example of divine mercy, but deems it inappropriate for the prayer leader to mention aloud, because his words might be understood to mean that God favors one species over another. This idea would lead to jealousy and strife (*Chiddushei Aggados*, ad loc.).

22. The nation of Amalek attacked the weary and enfeebled Israelites on their journey through the wilderness, sexually dismembering their captives; note Rashi citing *Midrash Tanchuma* on Deuteronomy 25:17-19. Amalek is a symbol of human cruelty throughout rabbinic literature, much like the Nazis in the contemporary experience.

Commentary 3: "That it may be good for you, and you may prolong your days." This phrase also is found in connection with the mitzvah of honoring one's parents in the repetition of the Ten Commandments (Deuteronomy 5:16). "That it may be good for you..." indicates that it is only natural that you should benefit from these acts. As for honoring your parents, it is readily apparent that if you do so, your children will observe this and emulate your actions when they grow up. Similarly, when your children see you perform the mitzvah of sending away the mother bird they will infer: "If this is the honor one must show the parents of animals, how much so must one honor human parents." Thus, the reward of both commandments is long life — for both commandments strengthen faith in the divine origin of creation. Just as each cause in the chain of causation proceeds from the First Cause, which is God, may He be blessed, so does each parent in the chain of life hearken back to the Parent of All. To Him we must show honor — and He shares His honor with all parents that come forth from Him, in turn (Rabbi Shlomo Ephraim Lunshitz, *Kli Yakar, Ki Seitzei*, p. 552).

The Mitzvah of Covering the Blood

If any of the Children of Israel, or a convert who joins them, traps an animal or bird that may be eaten and sheds its blood, he must cover [the blood] with earth (Leviticus 17:13).

Commentary 1: Since the vital soul cleaves to the blood, it befits us to cover the life-blood and conceal it from sight before consuming an animal's flesh. To eat flesh while the animal's blood lies before us might cause a trace of cruelty to cling to our souls. However, concerning animals that are usually domesticated we are not so commanded, since [during the Temple period] their consumption was primarily as a form of sacrifice, and their blood was impossible to cover. The Torah did not wish to distinguish between ordinary slaughter and sacrificial slaughter (*Sefer HaChinnuch*, Mitzvah 185).

Commentary 2: The precept of covering the blood with dust of the Earth is related to the trait of humility. When the Patriarch Abraham said,

"And I am but dust and ashes" (Genesis 18:27), this was an expression of humility. The rabbis state that in the merit of this declaration, the Jewish people were given the precept of covering the blood with earth. For the main rectification (*tikkun*) of the soul is through humility (Rabbi Nosson Sternhartz, *Likkutei Halachos, Shechitah* 3:4).

Commentary 3: If one should stalk and trap a wild animal — [as the Torah states: "If any of the Children of Israel...] traps an animal or bird that may be eaten..."[23] — which does not rely upon man's table, and whose food is not man's responsibility,[24] one should be ashamed of his moral inferiority, in that he is of such lowly character that it befits him to manifest his cruelty in action, no less than for any innate depravity he may possess... Therefore, the impression made by slaughtering wild animals and fowl, which are generally trapped, cannot be the same as that of slaughtering the domestic animal, which is generally to be found at her trough, fed by her master at the labor of his hand, and which becomes a burden to him in her old age when she is no longer able to work. Consequently, the law of covering the blood does not apply to a domestic animal (Rabbi Avraham Yitzchak Kook, *Chazon HaTzimchonut V'HaShalom*, 16, abridged).

Commentary 4: The obligation to cover the blood teaches us to see the shedding of an animal's blood as an act akin to murder; thus we should be ashamed to shed an animal's blood, as well. It was not deemed necessary to cover the blood of a domestic animal because it is slaughtered in an area where people are commonly found. Thus, it is preferable to leave the blood of the animal in plain sight, that it may remind others that slaughtering an animal is like murder. This is not the case with animals and birds that [typically] are trapped and slaughtered far from human habitation, whose blood is not seen. Here, by contrast, the obligation of covering the blood teaches that this is a shameful act (Rabbi Avraham Yitzchak Kook, ibid. 17, abridged).

Commentary 5: This act shows a certain cruelty, since one may choose to subsist from the Earth's produce. One did not raise [the

---

23. Leviticus 17:13.
24. *Shabbos* 155b; *Shulchan Aruch, Orach Chaim* 324:11. The same insight occurred to R. Shlomo of Z'vihl; see below.

non-domesticated animal], or exert oneself in order to provide her with food. There is no divine decree that mandates spilling her blood, killing her for no other reason than to gratify the lust for meat. Thus, the Torah states that when you shed [a non-domesticated animal's] blood, you must cover the blood with earth and not allow it to remain openly visible, as if one had no responsibility for it; for you did not labor on its behalf.

Although the Torah permitted [animal slaughter] in the days of Noah, this was because [Noah] exerted himself greatly to bring [all the animals] into the ark, and provided food for them, in order to prevent their destruction at the time of the Flood. However, since this animal did not benefit from you, and nevertheless, you shed her blood, you are required to cover the blood — unlike one who slaughters a cow or another animal that was raised through the effort of its owner, who exerted himself for her. The letter of the law concedes that he is permitted to slaughter her, and the animal willingly submits to the one who has concerned himself with her food and attended to her needs. Afterwards, the owner may benefit from the animal by taking her life; however, this [act of slaughter] must not cause her pain[25] (Rabbi Shlomo of Z'vihl, *Kuntres Yesod Tzaddik, Acharei,* s.v. *Kisui HaDam,* p. 176).

Do Not Plow With Two Kinds of Animals

Do not plow with an ox and a donkey together (Deuteronomy 22:10).

Commentary 1: [This reflects the principle that] "God has mercy upon all of His works," for the donkey is not as strong as the ox (Rabbi Avraham ibn Ezra, ad loc.).

Commentary 2: Among the reasons for this precept is the matter of causing pain to animals, which is forbidden by scriptural law. It is known that the various species of animals and fowl experience great anxiety in dwelling with those not of their own kind, and all the more so if we perform work with them. As we can see with our own eyes [by observing]

---

25. I am grateful to R. Bezalel Naor for directing my attention to this source.

those not under our control: every bird dwells with its own kind, and all beasts and other species also forever cleave to their own kind.

[Therefore,] let everyone whose heart derives wisdom from this take heed never to appoint two men for any common task who are far apart in their nature and different in their way of doing things, such as a righteous person and a wicked one, or a despised person and a distinguished one. For if the Torah made a point of the anguish this causes animals, who do not possess intellect, all the more so does this apply to human beings, who possess a rational soul by which to know their Maker (*Sefer HaChinnuch,* Mitzvah 550).

Commentary 3: Do not plow with an ox and a donkey together, for the ox chews its cud and the donkey does not. When the latter sees the ox chewing its cud, it will think that its partner is eating, and suffer in consequence (Rabbi Yaakov ben Asher, *Baal HaTurim,* Deuteronomy 22:10).

Our Animals Must Rest on the Sabbath

Six days shall you do your work, but on the seventh day you shall rest; that your ox and your donkey may have rest, and that the son of your handmaid and the stranger may be refreshed (Exodus 23:12).

Commentary 1: "Your ox and your donkey." Give it rest by permitting it to graze and eat grass from the ground. Perhaps this is not [the correct interpretation], but one should confine it in its stall? Common sense tells us that this is not rest but suffering (Rashi citing *Mechilta,* ad loc.).

Commentary 2: [How can Maimonides rule that causing suffering to animals is a rabbinic prohibition, whereas in *Shabbos* 128a] the Talmud states that it is forbidden by Torah law? [This informs us that according to Maimonides, the prohibition of *tza'ar baalei chaim* as it applies to the Sabbath] is an exception to the rule. Regarding the Sabbath, we see that the Merciful One singles out only animals that possess a "living soul" and have emotions. Since the Torah insists that they be allowed to rest on the Sabbath, our sages did not wish to make this a rabbinic prohibition, but permitted one to render a vessel unfit in order to relieve an animal's distress. This is supported by the Jerusalem Talmud: "The [Torah] mandates the rest of one's animal. Therefore, one intervenes [when an animal falls into a pit on the Sabbath] because of the suffering of animals..."[26] The Torah wishes animals, too, to experience the pleasures of the holy Sabbath[27] (Rabbi Meir Simcha HaKohen of Dvinsk, *Ohr Samei'ach, Hilchos Shabbos* 25:26, abridged).

Selected Laws of Tza'ar Baalei Chaim

It is forbidden according to Torah law to inflict pain upon any living creature. On the contrary, it is our duty to relieve the pain of any living creature, even if it is ownerless or belongs to a non-Jew. However, if an animal harms people, or if it is needed for medical purposes or for any other human necessity, it is permissible to slaughter it. Although slaughter causes the animal pain, the Torah permits it. Therefore, [according to the letter of the law] one may pluck feathers from a living goose if one has no other quill with which to write. Nevertheless, people refrain from doing so because of cruelty (Rama on *Shulchan Aruch, Even HaEzer* 5:14; cf. Rabbi Shneur Zalman of Liadi, *Shulchan Aruch HaRav, Ovrei D'rachim V'Tza'ar Baalei Chaim* 4).

૦ૐ૨

When horses drawing a cart come to a rough road or a steep hill and are unable to proceed without help, it is our duty to assist, whether they belong to a Jew or a non-Jew. The driver might strike them harshly to make them draw beyond their strength, and it is a mitzvah to prevent cruelty to animals (Rabbi Shlomo Ganzfried, *Kitzur Shulchan Aruch* 191:2).

૦ૐ૨

---

26. *Yerushalmi Shabbos, Perek "M'shilin."*
27. The *Ohr Samei'ach* defends Maimonides' classification of this prohibition as rabbinic, understanding the Talmud's seemingly contradictory statement as a way of underscoring the special nature of the Sabbath. The peace and repose of the Sabbath as defined by the Torah expressly includes animals.

It is forbidden to tie the legs of an animal or bird in a manner that will cause them pain. It also is forbidden to set a bird on eggs not of her own species, for this constitutes cruelty to animals (ibid. 191:3-4).

೦ಶ೪೦

It is forbidden to castrate either man, animal, or bird, whether of a kosher or non-kosher species, in the land of Israel or in any other land; nor may one cause sterility to any male creature, even by medicine. A Jew may not instruct a non-Jew to castrate his animal. Some authorities maintain that we are even forbidden to sell an animal to a non-Jew or give it to him on condition to share the profits if we know that he will castrate it, since [in their view] a non-Jew is similarly forbidden to castrate.[28] By [transferring the animal to the non-Jew under such circumstances], the Jew transgresses the precept, "And you shall not put a stumbling block before the blind"[29] (ibid. 191:5-6).

೦ಶ೪೦

Some authorities permit feeding live worms and insects to birds and fish, or even mice to cats.[30] However, according to the majority view, it is forbidden to use living creatures that are not considered harmful as food for other animals.[31]

---

28. According to other authorities, this prohibition does not apply to non-Jews with regard to their animals. In general, the Torah instructs humankind to refrain from interfering with the perpetuation of the species. Nevertheless, if non-Jews wish to neuter or spay their animals, there may be halachic leniencies that permit them to do so; e.g. see R. Avraham of Butchatch, *Mili D'Chassidusa*, p. 205, s.v. *V'chein nosnin l'nochri l'sares*. Concerning the Seven Noahide Laws that apply to non-Jews, see Chapter 3, n. 1.

29. Castration of both humans and animals is forbidden to Jews, as stated in *Shulchan Aruch, Even HaEzer*, 5:11-14; however, note Ritva on *Yevamos* 65b that castration is permitted in the case of a life-threatening medical condition. There is a dispute between the Tannaim as to whether castration is forbidden to non-Jews. Most Rishonim, including the *Beis Yosef*, rule that it is not; however, the *Sheiltos, SeMaG*, and *Ohr Zaru'a* disagree. For an overview, see *Aruch HaShulchan*, ad loc., 21-29.

30. R. Yaakov Emden, *She'eilas Ya'avetz*, no. 17, rules that since worms and insects are commonly eaten by birds, this reflects the way of nature and is permissible. Other authorities classify feeding the birds in one's possession as a form of human need, which therefore overrides the prohibition of *tza'ar baalei chaim*. Thus, *Teshuvos Sha'ar Asher*, Vol. II, 272:18, permits one to place live worms or insects before those birds for which he is responsible, even on the Sabbath.

CR&O

According to my limited understanding, if one sees a cat pursuing chickens in order to harm them and it is otherwise impossible to save the prey, it is a mitzvah to kill the cat. The latter should be treated no better than a murderous person who pursues his fellow, whom it is a mitzvah to kill if it is impossible to stop the aggressor by injuring him. Although it is the animal's nature to behave this way, his predatory instinct should not arouse our pity. Rather, one should pity the chickens and come to their rescue. Even if they are not one's property, it is a mitzvah to save them, in keeping with the law of returning lost possessions; if they are ownerless, one must save them due to the prohibition of *tza'ar baalei chaim* (Rabbi Shimon Sofer, *Teshuvos Hisorerus Teshuvah*, Vol. II, no. 157:2).

CR&O

[Although a Jew is forbidden to milk his cow on the Sabbath,] he may ask a non-Jew to express the milk to relieve the animal's discomfort. The milk is forbidden to the Jew for the remainder of the Sabbath. Some authorities say that the owner should buy back the milk from the non-Jew after the Sabbath for a small amount, so that it should not appear that the non-Jew milked the cow for [the Jewish owner's] benefit (Rabbi Yosef Karo, *Shulchan Aruch, Orach Chaim* 305:20).

CR&O

Since the Talmud states that we are obliged to feed the hungry [of all nations] in order to promote peace,[32] it is implicit that to some degree we are responsible for their sustenance.[33] How much more so [does this responsibility for all creatures extend] to a starving dog. In my opinion, it is a mitzvah to feed any living creature that I know to be hungry, even on the Sabbath; as it is written, "His mercy is upon all His creatures..." (Rabbi Yechiel Michel Epstein, *Aruch HaShulchan, Orach Chaim* 324:2).

---

31. See R. Nachman Yitzchak Eshkoli, *Tza'ar Baalei Chaim*, chap. 12, p. 395-399, citing Maharbitz, Vol. I, no. 244, *Kitzur Shulchan Aruch*, 191:1, et al.
32. *Gittin* 61a; also see R. Naftali Zvi Berlin, *Ha'amek Davar*, Introduction to Genesis.
33. R. Epstein cites *Tosefos* on *Shabbos* 19a.

Measure for Measure

When one harms an animal, one also brings harm upon himself (Rabbi Nachman of Breslov, *Sefer HaMidos, Rachmanus* II, 4).

∝≈∾

It is customary for a sick person to feed the birds on the rooftops in order to show compassion for other creatures. Thus he will merit receiving Heaven's mercy, as our sages state[34] (Rabbi Chaim Palagi, *Ruach Chaim*, 605:2).

Animal Fights Are Acts of Murder

It is forbidden to attend animal fights, for such events are included in the category of a "gathering of scoffers" (Talmud: *Avodah Zarah* 18b).

Codes: It is forbidden to watch a bullfight. Moreover, one who goes as a spectator and pays an entrance fee is deemed an accomplice to murder[35] (Rabbi Yaakov of Lisa, *Chavas Da'as* III, 66).

∝≈∾

Rabbi Yudan said in the name of Rabbi Shimon: All of the animals and the Leviathan will provide a circus for the tzaddikim in the World to Come. Whoever has never witnessed a circus [i.e., animal fight] in this world will be privileged to witness that circus in the World to Come[36] (Midrash: *Vayikra Rabbah* 13:3).

∝≈∾

Those who waste their time in idle jest and pit dogs against swine, or engage in other forms of *tza'ar baalei chaim*, certainly will have to give an accounting of their deeds in the next world. It would seem to be a religious obligation for anyone who sees bulls goring one another or roosters injuring one another to endeavor to separate them [if one may do

---

34. See Chapter 3, n. 85.
35. In many parts of the world, animal fights continue to be common forms of entertainment. Even today in the U.S. animal fights are legally sanctioned in Oklahoma, Louisiana, and New Mexico, although they have been outlawed in most states.

36. The Maharal of Prague explains that inasmuch as the host of this feast is God, and its participants are the *tzaddikim* in the Garden of Eden, the entire description should not be understood in a physical sense. Rather, the sea-dwelling Leviathan and the land-dwelling Behemoth are symbols of the animating principle of all existence: need and its gratification. This dualism applies even to the life of the soul. However, the Garden of Eden is the paradigm of stillness and peace. Hence the "circus" that takes place in the Garden of Eden represents the dissolution of the hunger-gratification dualism into the essential Divine Oneness. The *tzaddikim* will perceive how this dualism emanates from Oneness, remains within Oneness, and returns to Oneness. This is followed by a "feast," meaning that the resolution of this paradox will be internalized by the souls of the *tzaddikim*, and this will be their delight. As the verse states, "This Leviathan You formed to delight with it" (Psalms 104:26). See *Chiddushei Aggados* on *Bava Basra* 74b, pp. 108-109.

Maimonides in his *Mishneh Torah, Teshuvah* 8:4, lists the feast of the Leviathan as one of a number of physical allegories for non-physical realities or events. Other symbolic interpretations include: *Zohar, Terumah (Sifra D'Tzniusa)*, 176b, which, according to the commentary *Yedid Nefesh*, associates the Leviathan with the source of *klippah*; Targum Yonasan ben Uziel, Mahari Kara, and Rashi on Isaiah 27:1, which explain these symbols in a historico-political context; *Shitah Mekubetzes* on *Bava Basra* 74b, which cites R. David son of R. Yehudah HeChassid that the Leviathan represents the interface between the physical and spiritual; *Chiddushei HaGeonim* on *Ein Yaakov, Bava Basra* 74a-75a, cites *Darash Moshe* and *Akeidas Yitzchak* to the effect that the Leviathan which God "salted and put away for the *tzaddikim* in the World to Come" corresponds to the "Light Hidden Away for the Tzaddikim." These authorities also discuss the feast of the Leviathan as a spiritual event.

R. Moshe Cordovero distinguishes several meanings of the term "Leviathan": in some contexts it is a symbol of the *sefirah* of *Tiferes* (harmony, or beauty) on the side of holiness (which corresponds to the Tree of Life); elsewhere, it is identified with the unholy primordial serpent that takes the form of a circle (Isaiah 27:1: *nachash akalason*, which may be the origin of the Greek myth of the *uroboros*). R. Cordovero states that the latter exists on the spiritual plane as the source of evil, and on the physical plane as the source of all manifestations of destruction and harm; see *Ohr Yakar al HaZohar*, cited in R. Nosson Zvi Kenig's *Toras Nosson, Erchei Ramak*, Vol. IV, *levyasan* 121. Similarly, R. Cordovero's eminent disciple, R. Eliyahu de Vidas, in *Reishis Chochmah, Sha'ar Yirah* 13:65, states that one who curses himself in a fit of anger arouses "the primordial serpent, which is the Leviathan..."

Although he does not discuss the animal fight or feast, R. Nachman of Breslov in *Likkutei Moharan* II, 7:13 (end) mentions the Leviathan in a positive sense as a symbol of *Malchus* (rulership), which "enters the sea of *chochmah* (divine wisdom)" to receive sustenance for all humanity, an interpretation supported by *Tikkunei Zohar*'s pronouncement: "The Leviathan of the sea — this is the tzaddik" (*Tikkun 21*, 43b). R. Nachman indirectly alludes to the Leviathan in a negative sense as the primordial serpent in *Likkutei Moharan* II, 8:3, citing Job 41:14, et al.

Alternatively, the author of *Sefer HaPeliah*, s.v. *Ha'hey nikrah Gevurah*, pp. 98-99, asserts that there is a physical Leviathan in the ocean, and a corresponding spiritual Leviathan that presides over it in the angelic realm. He, too, identifies the Leviathan as the primordial serpent. Maharsha on *Bava Basra* 75a takes the feast of the Leviathan to be a physical event, although its significance is essentially spiritual. Nachmanides in his commentary on Genesis 1:21 mentions the Leviathan in context of the sea serpents God brought into being on the fifth day of creation. R. David Luria (a disciple of the Vilna Gaon) on *Pirkei Rabbi Eliezer* 23a, n. 35, discusses the Leviathan as an so safely], so that they will cease harming one another. All this is included in the law of assisting an animal collapsing under its burden (Rabbi Yaakov Ze'ev Kahana, *Teshuvos Toldos Yaakov*, *Yoreh De'ah*, no. 33, 74a).

Trapping Non-Kosher Animals

Any man of the Children of Israel and of the convert who dwells among them who traps an animal or a bird that may be eaten, he shall pour out its blood and cover it with earth (Leviticus 17:13).

Commentary: It would seem that the phrase "who traps" comes to prohibit the willful trapping of non-kosher animals, although the Torah permits us to derive benefit from their use. [In general, all wild animals are non-kosher, with the exception of deer and the non-domesticated species of cattle, oxen, and goats. The giraffe is another exception, although we lack any halachic tradition concerning its method of *shechitah*.] As stated in my work, *Pri To'ar*, section 117, according to the view of Maimonides one may not trap them unless he intends to trap kosher animals and inadvertently captures some of a non-kosher species (cf. *Mishneh Torah, Ma'achalos Asuros*, 8:17) (Rabbi Chaim ibn Attar, *Ohr HaChaim*, ad loc.).

---

actual sea creature in the context of a Midrashic version of the story of Jonah. Other commentators who interpret the Leviathan on both levels include Ibn Ezra, Radak, and *Metzudos* on Isaiah 27:1. This position is shared by Chassidic master R. Shneur Zalman of Liadi, *Likkutei Torah, Tzav*, s.v. *Va'achaltem*, 7a-8d, who, like R. Moshe Cordovero and others, distinguishes between two Leviathans, a holy creature and an unholy creature. R. Shneur Zalman also relates this dichotomy to that of Moses versus Pharaoh, which symbolizes the self-nullification associated with divine wisdom versus the self-aggrandizement of ego.

R. Yosef Chaim of Baghdad, *Ben Yehoyada*, Vol. IV, *Bava Basra* 75a, s.v. *Elimalei machnis rosho*, relates the feast of the Leviathan to eating the fruit of the Tree of Life in the Garden of Eden that Adam was not privileged to eat. This interpretation is similar to the approach of *Chiddushei HaGeonim* above and R. Moshe Cordovero, as is that of Lithuanian Kabbalist R. Shlomo Elyashiv in *Leshem Shevo V'Achlamah, Sefer HaDe'ah* II, *Drushei Olam HaTohu* 4:10:3 (50a-d). A translation of an excerpt from the latter may be found on www.orot.com/leshem.html.

In *Likkutei Sichos*, Vol. XV, *Asarah B'Teves*, sec. 15, p. 420, R. Menachem M. Schneerson of Lubavitch interprets the feast of the Leviathan as the revelation of the hidden meaning of the Torah and commandments that will occur during the Messianic Age. By contrast, the period after the Resurrection of the Dead, in which there will be no eating and drinking, will be characterized by a revelation of the very Essence of Godliness. This Essence, which transcends all rational categories, will be awarded in the merit of the suprarational self-sacrifice of the Jewish people throughout their bitter exile.

Sources: Chapter 4

A Kabbalistic View of History

The main purpose for which this world was created was to elevate the holy sparks and to remove the *klippah* ("husk" or covering) from that which is holy. This task particularly applies after the sin of Adam, which caused many holy sparks to fall into the realm of the external forces. This worsened during the idolatrous generation of Enosh, the generation of the Flood, and that of the Dispersion [after the incident of the Tower of Babel]. Then the Patriarch Abraham came to the world and began to elevate the holy sparks and to rectify the sin of Adam. Abraham's son, Isaac, also elevated many holy sparks. When Jacob came into the world, [he continued to engage in this task, as did his children,] the twelve tribes of Israel.

The sages of the Kabbalah explain that all Jacob's dealings with Laban, i.e., the work he performed for his two daughters and his flocks, were for the purpose of elevating the holy sparks that Laban possessed. That is why Heaven caused Laban to pursue Jacob [when he began his homeward journey to the land of Israel], for he still possessed holy sparks that needed rectification. They were elevated when Jacob and Laban feasted together beside the stone [that they had set up to affirm the pact of peace between them], and this freed all the holy sparks trapped within Laban.

This was also the purpose of our ancestors' descent to Egypt. All the lost sparks of the generation of the Flood and the generation of the Dispersion were reincarnated there. Therefore God promised the Patriarch Abraham that [his descendants] would leave with "great spoil." This promise was fulfilled [during the Exodus], as the verse testifies, "And they despoiled Egypt" (Exodus 12:36). Concerning this, our sages state, "They made it like a bird hunter's trap devoid of grain."[37] This alludes to the fact that they elevated whatever holy sparks they found in Egypt.

---

37. *Tosefos, Pesachim* 119a.

Subsequently God caused us to inherit "a desirable, good, and ample land" (Grace After Meals). Sparks of even greater holiness were reincarnated in the land of Israel because of its spiritual primacy [in relation to other lands]. If these holy sparks had been redeemed, all the holy sparks in the world would have ascended with them, and the refinement of all creation would have been complete.

Sometimes a person eats an article of food that contains a holy spark that has been greatly corrupted, although it comes from a lofty source. If he does not eat the food in a state of holiness and purity, but is drawn after his physical desires, [he places himself in jeopardy]. Not only will he fail to elevate anything, but he may be adversely affected — for he, too, had a share in the transgression that resulted in the reincarnation of that holy spark. Thus I heard from the holy Rebbe of Neshchiz that this is why penitents (*baalei teshuvah*) often return to their former ways. They are not careful to eat in a state of holiness. Therefore, the holy sparks reincarnated in the foods they eat have a harmful effect upon them. This is what happened to our ancestors as well. When they came to a bountiful land and succumbed to their physical desires, they reverted to idolatry. In truth, they were harmed by the [unredeemed] sparks (Rabbi Kalonymus Kalman Epstein, *Ma'or VaShemesh, Ki Savo*; s.v. *Amnam nirmaz bazeh inyan pnimi*, p. 192a, b; also cf. R. Chaim Vital, *Sha'ar HaPesukim, Shemos*, et al.).

The Ladder of Creation

At every rung of the ladder extending from the depths of life on Earth to the most sublime regions of the spirit, all the elements reach upwards and strive to come ever closer to the holy, divine source of life and blessing. Indeed, in nature there exists a hierarchical order that extends right down to inorganic elements, differentiated by the measure of vitality that they receive from the supreme source of the divine light. This sequential connection of the spheres of creation encompasses the mineral, vegetable, animal, and human realms. The continual rise of each constituent occurs step by step. Thus, rain falls on the Earth, it waters the Earth, it helps the seed to germinate. The seed assimilates and transforms elements in the Earth to grow into a plant. The plant is eaten by animals, and the vegetable element, thanks to this transmigration, reaches a level of existence where the soul begins to shine forth on the purely physical world. Ultimately, man consumes the flesh of the animal, which becomes part of man himself. The animal comes ever closer to the source of light contained in the spiritual soul. In this way, the different elements of nature ascend to the threshold of the metaphysical world, where the unfettered human soul will rejoin the heavenly sphere of absolute holiness (Rabbi Moshe Cordovero, *Pardes Rimonim, Sha'ar* 24:10, as cited by Rabbi Elie Munk, *The Call of the Torah, Bereishis* 9:3, trans. E.S. Maser [Brooklyn, NY: Artscroll / Mesorah Publications Ltd., 1994]).

ೞೞ

"You formed me back (*achor*) and front (*kedem*)" (Psalms 139:1). Rav Ami said: "Back" [or "last"] alludes to the act of creation, and "front" [or "first"] alludes to punishment... (Talmud: *Berachos* 61a).

Commentary: According to the design that appears before our eyes in the hierarchy of creation, we see that the higher the rung upon which a creature stands, the more its life force is concentrated in one center. Therefore, it is easier [for a higher creature] to be destroyed than one that occupies a lower level. [This principle] manifests itself in primitive creatures: even when they are cut into pieces, their life force remains.[38]

It is self-understood that in one who stands at the very height of the hierarchy of nature, namely man, this quality of concentration of the life force occupies an extremely precise position. The unique human potential to elevate all creation to the center point of concentration is indicated by the order of [the divine creative acts] described in the Torah: everything created later among living creatures is more worthy and possesses greater life force. Since man was created last of all creatures, the collective life force is concentrated within him to a greater extent than all of them. For the fundamental point of this concentration is that it should incorporate those individual powers [on all levels of creation] that

---

38. An example would be earthworms that can be torn to pieces, and each "piece" will continue to function as a complete organism.

precede it. Thus, by virtue of being last in the order of creation, man is first to receive punishment [i.e. the most prone to destruction].

This also instructs us concerning the spiritual nature of man: his destiny is such that all the powers of his soul must be focused on one sublime purpose. The concentration he bears within himself is the foundation of his being and continued existence; and his loss of this spiritual concentration is caused by "the thoughts of man's evil heart" (Genesis 6:5), that he no longer turns to his true purpose to perceive and to benefit but goes wherever the spirit of temporal desire leads him. Although for all other living creatures it is possible to exist in such a state, humankind forfeits its right to life when its soul is divorced from its concentration. Since he was last in the sequence of creation, man was formed for this unique mission: that all creatures shall be spiritually elevated in the Messianic future, joining in one common purpose; and all this will come about only when one walks the straight path that accomplishes this unification (Rabbi Avraham Yitzchak HaKohen Kook, *Ein Ayah*, Vol. II, *Berachos*, chap. 9, par. 194 [p. 332]).

Bitter Medicine

Why are most medicines bitter? This is because the physical world contains minerals (*domem*), vegetation (*tzomei'ach*), animals (*chai*), and humans who possess the faculty of speech (*medaber*). Each one elevates that which is on a lower level than itself. Animals are supposed to raise up the holy sparks by consuming bitter plants. However, if they refrain from doing so because the plants are too bitter, Heaven decrees that people must become ill. Then, due to their illness, they must eat or drink bitter remedies made from plants in order to elevate [the holy sparks they contain] to their source (Rabbi Yisrael Baal Shem Tov, *Sharsheros Zahav* 27).

Outer Form, Inner Essence

Man does not live by bread alone, but by all that proceeds from the mouth of God does man live (Deuteronomy 8:3).

Commentary: Just as a fruit is surrounded by a *klippah* (rind or husk), so does everything in creation have an inner and outer aspect. The most basic food of human beings is wheat. Surrounding the wheat kernel is a *klippah* — the straw and chaff. But the wheat kernel itself has an inner and outer aspect. Its physicality is its outer aspect, which eventually becomes waste matter and is expelled; its inner aspect is the vital force it receives from God. It is this vital force that truly strengthens and enlivens a person (Rabbi Nachman Goldstein of Tcherin, *Parpara'os L'Chochmah* 17:6, abridged).

ભ⊁⊙

The paradigm of the *klippah* and the fruit within applies to virtually every level of existence; for that which on one level is the inner aspect (*pnimius*), on the level above, comprises the outer aspect (*chitzonius*). Consider, for example, plants and vegetation. Their life-force is mainly derived from the Earth, which is part of the "silent" or mineral realm. Nevertheless, the level of vegetation is higher than that of earth. Similarly, animals are on a higher level than vegetation, despite the fact that their life force is largely derived from the latter. Indeed, this indicates their superiority. The primary purpose of vegetation is to sustain higher forms of life, and the purpose of everything is to serve humanity — albeit that human beings are dependent upon [the lower levels in the hierarchy of creation].

The dualism of the *klippah* and the fruit corresponds to that of darkness and light, as well as that of folly and wisdom. For darkness and folly possess no value but that they cause light and wisdom to be recognized. "As light is superior to darkness, so is wisdom superior to folly" (Ecclesiastes 2:13). Thus, they are analogous to the *klippah* and the fruit. In the present state of things, God wishes to preserve [darkness and folly] for the sake of free will. Their existence also contributes to the gratification God derives from Israel [when they heed the Torah and its commandments], for the revelation of God's Kingship depends upon free will.

Since the vital force is garbed in the physicality of a food article, which corresponds to the aspect of *klippah* and folly, the human trait of folly is inevitably strengthened by the act of eating. However, when a person eats in holiness, in order to have strength to serve God and thus to gratify His Will, the trait of folly is not strengthened; it receives only enough sustenance to continue to exist. Thus, the spirit of folly is subdued, and the intellect prevails. This [holy intent] shows that the crux of the matter is the inner aspect, the wisdom that is the source of life; as the verse states, "Wisdom gives life [to those who possess it]" (Ecclesiastes 7:12).

The *Zohar* explains that this is the innermost aspect of the food, as well. The divine will caused the holy life force to descend from level to level until it became garbed in the physical form of this food, which is the aspect of folly, only in order to convert the Other Side [to holiness] and darkness to light. For folly, as well, is destined to become a "throne" and a "chariot" for holiness. However, this is not the case when one eats and drinks like a glutton. Then one fails to show that everything was created for the sake of God, Who derives gratification from [our divine service]. One is trapped in the physical desire for the food, which is the aspect of folly. Thus one's folly becomes even stronger and overwhelms the intellect, until one becomes mentally disturbed, God forbid. That is, the spirit of folly increases until it impinges upon the inner aspect, the life force and the point of intellect and wisdom, forcing it to become an aspect of the verse: "They are wise men for evil, and do not know how to do good" (Jeremiah 4:22). One can no longer use his intellect constructively, but only for harm.

Through this folly it is impossible to perceive the light of the tzaddik who strives to reveal the gratification that God derives from Israel, particularly through their eating in holiness. As stated above, through eating in holiness one subdues and destroys the *klippos* and the spirit of folly. Although a devout person also experiences a slight amount of mental confusion after eating, this is only temporary. Afterwards, the holy sparks contained within the food are extricated and spiritually elevated. In their supernal source, these are sparks of wisdom, as the verse states, "They all have been made with wisdom" (Psalms 104:24); they become incorporated into one's life force, which is his wisdom and intellect. However, the physical aspect of the food, corresponding to the spirit of folly, becomes expelled as waste matter. Thus, folly is subdued, and the intellect prevails (ibid. 17:7, abridged).

Breaking the Klippos

Before the soul became enclothed in the body it was nullified absolutely within the Infinite Light; nothing obscured or obstructed the revelation of Godliness. Therefore, the soul was completely nullified within its Source. When it descended below and became garbed within a physical body, the body obstructed its perception, until "the world and all that fills it" (Psalms 24:1) seemed to possess autonomous existence. [The soul] no longer perceived the essential nothingness of all the worlds before the Infinite Light, which brings everything into existence continually.

This situation is analogous to the Shattering of the Vessels, when the sparks of *Tohu* fell and became garbed within the *klippos* of [the three lower Worlds of] *Beriah*/Creation, *Yetzirah*/Formation, and *Asiyah*/Action. The *klippos* surrounded the holy sparks from every side, until the Infinite Light could not be sensed, and they appeared to be autonomous existences. As Pharaoh declared, "The river is mine, and I made it..." (Ezekiel 29:9); he referred to [the Infinite One] only as the "God of gods."

That is, prior to the Shattering of the Vessels, the holy sparks were nullified and subsumed within the Infinite Light, which illuminated them with an encompassing revelation. However, after the Shattering of the Vessels, the holy sparks fell and became enclothed by the *klippos,* which obstructed the revelation of Godliness, just as the body obstructs the soul. Therefore, [the sparks] could not remain in the same state of self-nullification.

This is why [the forces of concealment] are called *klippos.* They are comparable to husks that surround and encompass the fruit within them, hiding it like the shell of a nut. In order to extract the fruit, there is no recourse other than to break the shell. Similarly, in order to bring forth the holy sparks from the *klippos* that conceal them, one must break the *klippos*. This was the purpose of the miracles and wonders that were performed in Egypt (Rabbi Shneur Zalman of Liadi, *Torah Ohr, Va'eira*, s.v. *Vayomer Hashem... Kach es mat'chah*, 56b-57a).

Sacrifices Are Restricted to the Sanctuary

Any man of the House of Israel who slays an ox or lamb or goat in the camp, or who slaughters outside the camp, [instead of] bringing it to the entrance of the Tent of Meeting, to render an offering to God before the Tabernacle of God — bloodshed shall be imputed to that man; he has shed blood; that man shall be cut off from among his people (Leviticus 17:3-4).

Commentary: At the root of this precept is the reason for which God designated a fixed place for Israel to bring their sacrifices and to direct their hearts to Him there. Due to the permanence of the place and its greatness, and the awe that it would inspire in people's hearts, their spirit would be influenced there for the good. The heart would be softened and humbled to accept completely the kingship of Heaven. Therefore, God restricted us from offering sacrifices anywhere but at this place, in order that there should be a complete atonement for us.[39]

The crux of the matter is that all He commanded was for our benefit, as we have written, because God in His great goodness desires the benefit of His creatures; and He said that whoever offers a sacrifice outside of that designated place, bloodshed will be accounted to him. The reason is that God permitted the flesh of living creatures to people for no purpose other than atonement or the service of human needs, such as food or healing or other necessities. However, to kill them without any useful purpose at all — this is destructiveness, and it is called bloodshed. Even though it is not the same as spilling human blood, given the superiority of humans above animals, nevertheless it is called bloodshed, since Scripture did not permit spilling it without a legitimate purpose. There is no benefit in spilling blood at a location where one was not commanded to slaughter. Rather, this is an act of wanton destructiveness, since one has transgressed the commandment of his Creator. Hence Scripture gave his punishment as being "cut off" [from the Jewish people by the hand of God, measure for measure] (*Sefer HaChinnuch,* Mitzvah 186).

A Kabbalistic View of the Sacrifices

The letters of the Divine Name *Yud-Hey-Vav-Hey* correspond to [the five levels of in the hierarchy of creation]: the soul realm is derived from the "thorn," or crownlet of the *yud,* the speaking [i.e., human] realm is derived from the *yud,* the animal realm is derived from the first *hey,* the vegetative realm is derived from the *vav,* and the mineral realm from the second *hey.* Certain spiritual rectifications must ascend from each of these four levels, and all of them are accomplished through the *korban* (sacrifice in the Holy Temple).

The salt is taken from the silent realm, which it partially rectifies; wine and oil [and grain] are derived from the vegetative realm, which

---

39. Maimonides contends in *Moreh Nevuchim* 3:32 that the sacrificial system was instituted as a concession to the need of the Israelites to express their religious feelings in the manner most common to the ancient world, substituting worship of God for pagan sacrifice. "By this divine plan the traces of idolatry were blotted out," he explains, "and the truly great principle of our faith, the existence and unity of God, was established. This result was obtained without confusing the people by the abolition of a method of worship to which they were accustomed, and which was familiar to them." This position is shared by biblical commentator R. David Kimchi (1160-1235) in his glosses on Jeremiah 7:22-23, who adds that most of the sacrifices were of a voluntary nature, a point supported by Rashi on Isaiah 43:32. R. Yitzchak Abarbanel (1437-1509) affirms and elaborates upon the Maimonidean rationale in his commentary on *Vayikra* 1:1, s.v. *HaPerek HaDalet,* pp. 10b-13a.

   However, the Kabbalists emphatically reject this approach. Nachmanides observes in his *Commentary on the Torah* (Leviticus 1:9) that Noah offered an animal sacrifice which the Torah describes as "pleasing unto God," although there was not yet a trace of idol-worship in the world. R. Nachman of Breslov is extremely pointed in his critique of the *Moreh Nevuchim* and the entire genre of rationalist philosophy it represents. In *Chayei Moharan* 411, R. Nachman exclaims: "How could anyone imagine giving vacuous reasons like these for the sacrifices and incense offering? How many awesome spiritual rectifications are accomplished in the supernal worlds, worlds without end, by the mere recitation of the Torah passages that describe these rites!" Also cf. *Sichos HaRan* 5, 40, 102, 224, 225; *Chayei Moharan* 407-425, et passim. For other authorities who oppose the study of philosophy, see Chapter 3, n. 21, Chapter 5, n. 8. Nevertheless, at least one great Chassidic master attempted to find Kabbalistic support for Maimonides' seemingly rationalistic explanations of the commandments, R. Gershon Chanoch Leiner of Radzyn (1839-1891), in his *HaHakdamah V'haPesichah* (Introduction) to his father Rabbi Yaakov of Izhbitz's *Beis Yaakov, Bereishis.*

they partially rectify; then there is the animal itself. The confession recited by the person who brings the offering corresponds to the "speaking" [human] realm. The meditation of the Kohen (priest) at the time of performing the sacrifice corresponds to the soul that dwells within. Thus, these five [aspects of the sacrifice] rectify the four levels of creation and bring into harmony [the letters of the Divine Name] from which they derive. These [five aspects of the sacrifice] also correspond to [the five levels of the soul]: *Nefesh, Ru'ach, Neshamah, Chaya, Yechidah.* [Thus, the soul of the person who brings the sacrifice is brought into harmony as well.]

[An acceptable sacrificial offering is called] "an offering made by fire, a gratifying fragrance unto God" (Leviticus 1:9, et al.). [This phrase itself describes the unification of the four letters of the Divine Name.] "An offering made by fire" (*isheh*) corresponds to the lower *hey*, which is called *ishah* ("woman"). [In Hebrew "woman" is spelled the same way as the construct of "fire." This refers to the divine life force that animates the World of Action.] "Fragrance" (*rei'ach*) corresponds to the spirit (*ru'ach*) of the World of Formation. "Gratifying" corresponds to the soul of the World of Creation. "Unto God" corresponds to the "soul of souls" [of the World of Emanation] through which the Divine Name *Yud-Hey-Vav-Hey* is completed. This is the mystery of the sacrificial offering (*korban*) that brings together (*karav*) the four powers of the Divine Name (Rabbi Chaim Vital, *Ta'amei HaMitzvos, Mitzvas Korbanos,* abridged).

CRUETO

The spiritual source of the three "lower" levels of creation is actually "higher" than the spiritual source of human beings.[40] Their source is in the World of Chaos (*Tohu*), [whereas the source of human souls is in the World of Spiritual Rectification (*Tikkun*)]. However, through the Shattering of the Vessels [at the beginning of creation, described in the *Sefer Eitz Chaim* of Rabbi Yitzchak Luria] these aspects of the divine life

---

40. The Kabbalists teach that everything in the hierarchy of the physical world has its source in the spiritual world; in philosophical terms, every phenomenon has a corresponding noumenon.

force descended lower and lower, until they became manifest as inorganic matter, vegetation, and animals. Through the sacrificial rites in the Holy Temple, they would ascend to their spiritual source and become reincorporated therein (Rabbi Shneur Zalman of Liadi, *Likkutei Torah, Tzav,* s.v. *Sheshes Yamim, Ma'amar* 2).

03 80

All sacrifices distill and elevate the vital spirit from the animal level to the human level. For animals possess the vital spirit; however, it is a bestial spirit. As such, it is kindred to the spirit of folly and the animal desires which lead man to transgress. Therefore, when a person sins [which is a consequence of the spirit of folly] he must bring an animal sacrifice in order to distill and elevate the vital spirit from the animal level to the human level.

Sacrifices engage all four elements — minerals (*domem*), vegetation (*tzomei'ach*), animals (*chai*), and man, the speaking being (*medaber*) — as is discussed in the Kabbalah. This separates the good from the bad qualities of all four elements, and brings about the subjugation of the wicked and the Other Side. Thus, the Holy Temple is called the "House of Our Life," for it is the focal point of the vital spirit of all creation.

This also sheds light on why the holiest sector of the Holy Temple is the north side; as [the Mishnah] states, "The sacrifices of the holiest degree were performed on the north side of the altar..."[41] There, all deficiencies are fulfilled. For our sages declare: "The north (*tzafon*) is lacking."[42] To this place must be drawn forth the vital spirit that is hidden (*tzafun*) in the heart,[43] thus to fulfill all deficiencies. This corresponds to "the north wind (*ru'ach tz'fonis*) that blew across the strings of King David's harp."[44] [This word-play suggests that the "hidden

---

41. *Zevachim* 5:1-5.
42. *Bava Basra* 25b. In the original Talmudic context, this refers to the appearance of the sun moving across the sky, as it varies according to the seasons. Each of the four directions is illuminated, except the north. However, in the present discourse the author invokes this statement to suggest that north is the paradigm of deficiency and spiritual darkness.
43. *Tikkunei Zohar, Tikkun* 69.
44. *Berachos* 3b.

vital spirit" that is elevated through the sacrifices is comparable to music, which separates the "good wind" from the "evil wind."] Therefore, the Levites played music in the Holy Temple; for the main way the vital spirit is elicited is through melody and song to God. This is symbolized by the north wind that blew across the strings of King David's harp, causing it to play music of its own accord (Rabbi Nosson Sternhartz, *Likkutei Halachos, HaOseh Shali'ach Lig'vos Chov* 3:24).

⋈

Through breaking the desire for wealth by giving charity, all harsh judgments are nullified. God's kindness is made manifest, and enlightenment is drawn into the world; all souls ascend, and Torah wisdom is revealed. Thus, all beings attain the knowledge that everything takes place through divine providence alone (cf. *Likkutei Moharan* 1:13).

This is reflected by the order of the Morning Prayer service. In the beginning, we recite the scriptural passages that describe the daily sacrifices and the incense offering. The sacrifices allude to the spiritual task of breaking the desire for wealth by giving charity; for offering a sacrifice was an act of charity, a "gift of the heart" (Exodus 35:5).

The verse states, "That which proceeds from your lips you shall observe and do, just as you have vowed a voluntary offering, whatever you have spoken with your mouth" (Deuteronomy 23:24). Our sages explain that this refers to charity.[45] Thus, [through our reciting the scriptural passages that take the place of the daily sacrifices] the idolatry of craving wealth is destroyed, nullifying all harsh judgments and bringing the world to spiritual perfection. Then one can begin to recite the next part of the prayer service, the *Pesukei D'Zimra* (Verses of Song), of which the *Zohar* states: "Then a spirit descends, and from it the heart receives the joy of the melody of the Levites..." These are the verses of *Pesukei D'Zimra*: the songs, melodies, and praises of God that the Levites sang and played in the Holy Temple (Rabbi Nosson Sternhartz, *Likkutei Halachos, Aveidah U'Metzia*, 3:3, abridged).

---

45. *Rosh Hashanah* 6b.

Not for Everyone

The Torah does not permit even the kosher species of animals and birds to everyone indiscriminately, God forbid, but only to one who has attained the spiritual level of *malchus* (rulership). If one is "comparable to a beast" (Psalms 49:13), they are forbidden to him. It is written, "Fear and dread of you shall be upon all the wild animals of the earth, and upon all the birds of the sky; and all the fish of the sea are given into your hand" (Genesis 9:2). The term "upon" indicates rulership...

Who is this tzaddik [whom the Torah deems fit to rule]? One whose shadow is pure, and all stand in awe of him, like Daniel in the lion's den. He and those comparable to him can slaughter and eat meat. However, others are forbidden to consume animals...

Know that when a tzaddik eats meat, he spiritually elevates the life force within the animal and brings it under the wings of the *Shechinah* (Divine Presence) (*Sefer HaKanah, Sod Mi Mutar BaAchilas Basar*, pp. 277-279, abridged).

∞

[During the Temple period, every farmer] was required to give *terumah* (the "raised offering" separated from the harvest) to the Kohanim-Priests. One reason for this tithe was to provide sustenance for the "servants of God." However, there was a second reason. Not everyone can participate in the divine mysteries and perform *tikkunim* (spiritual rectifications) through the Kabbalistic meditations on eating. Since the Kohanim alone were designated to serve God [in the Holy Temple], with the Levites assisting them, God commanded that the *terumah* be set aside for them. In His kindness, He brought it about that the holy sparks would be elevated in this way. This also helps us understand why a common person (*zar*) was strictly forbidden to partake of the *terumah* designated exclusively for the Kohen (Rabbi Moshe Teitelbaum of Ujhely, *Yismach Moshe, Shemos* 287b, abridged).

A Kabbalistic View of Eating

The Patriarch Abraham told the angels [who appeared to him in human form]: "Recline under the tree..." (Genesis 18:4), meaning under the Tree of Life in the Garden of Eden. How? "And I will bring you a loaf of bread..." (ibid.). That is, through eating.

This is the meaning of what is written: "And God said: Behold, the man... And now, lest he send forth his hand and take also from the Tree of Life and eat, and live forever." (ibid. 3:22).

God in his great mercy desires man's *teshuvah* (return), and that he should remedy whatever he has spiritually damaged. Thus, God said, "And now..." meaning: now that Adam has sinned, how can he remedy his mistake — unless he has a possible means of rectification by sending forth his hand and grasping the Tree of Life, by way of eating. He may extricate the holy sparks [that have fallen through his sin] by eating in holiness.

Thus, the verse states: "And he shall eat and live forever," meaning: through eating he will grasp eternal life. This is why Adam was banished from the Garden of Eden in order to work the land — for "in the World to Come there is no eating or drinking..."[46] Only in this world can one rectify and extricate the holy sparks (Rabbi Elimelech of Lizhensk, *Noam Elimelech, Chayei Sarah*, 10b).

෨෨෩

A kosher animal derives its life force from *klippas nogah*, the spiritual "husk" that is a mixture of good and evil. When it eats vegetation, the souls it contains are no longer trapped and bound to such a great extent, and they remember their original status. Consequently, they are not able to find rest and be silent within a kosher animal, but yearn to ascend to the human level. They constantly rise from the belly to the throat and mouth of the animal, which are kindred to the human organs of speech. This suggests why kosher animals chew their cud.

By contrast, the non-kosher species derive their life-force from the three impure *klippos* that are completely evil;[47] therefore, they do not

---

46. *Berachos* 17a.
47. Cf. *Zohar* III, 41b.

chew their cud.[48] As soon as these non-kosher animals ingest the souls contained in plants, the latter become trapped and cannot move from their place; as the verse states, "God has given me into the hands of those against whom I am unable to stand" (Lamentations 1:14). When such souls enter the body of an Israelite, however, they find rest and repose, having been restored to their former status: the level of a human being endowed with the faculty of holy speech. With the strength he derives from his food, a human being may praise God. This is alluded to by the verse, "And you shall eat... and you shall praise the name of God..." (Joel 2:26). Then all the souls attain their ultimate perfection. However, when a person is melancholy and disturbed, lacking the wisdom that befits a human being, the food that he eats finds no rest within him; he, too, "chews his cud" and experiences digestive problems, even to the extent of regurgitating the contents of his stomach.

The second sign of ritual purity in animals is that they possess split hooves, for the main thing that stands a person on his feet is wisdom. Similarly, the main characteristic of human speech is the wisdom it contains. The traits that distinguish a human being from an animal are the abilities to speak, walk on two feet, and stand erect. This is why a drunkard, whose mind is confused, cannot speak or walk properly. This, too, is why ritually pure animals possess a degree of wisdom, which is the main good. Although they walk on four legs, the vitality of the souls concealed within them extends to their feet; thus they have split hooves. However, the souls that are trapped in non-kosher animals are bound to such an extent that they cannot have any illuminating effect at all. Thus, the hooves of non-kosher animals are closed (Rabbi Nosson Sternhartz, *Likkutei Halachos, Simonei Behemah V'Chaya Tehorah*, 1, abridged).

൫൝

---

48. In Leviticus 11:4-7, the Torah identifies four animals that possess one kosher sign, but not both: the camel, the hyrax, and the hare all chew their cud, but lack cloven hooves, while the pig lacks the former, but possesses the latter. This prohibition of consuming the flesh of these animals is repeated in Deuteronomy 14:7-8. The fact that in more than 3,000 years, no other animal has been discovered that possesses only one kosher sign often is cited in support of the argument that the Torah is of divine origin. See Malbim, ad locum.

Although Adam named the various beasts and animals, we do not see that he named the vegetative or mineral realms.[49] This is because Adam refined and elevated all species of animals; by the very act of naming them, he brought about their *tikkun*. However, he did not rectify vegetation and minerals at all. That is why he was not allowed to eat meat, but consumed only vegetation and herbs.[50]

The purpose of eating is to extricate all of the holy sparks possessed by food, whether derived from the animal, vegetative, or mineral realms. Since Adam had already refined the various animals by naming them, he was not permitted to consume them. When he ate from the Tree of Knowledge, however, all of the animals sinned with him; they, too, ate of the fruit and spiritually damaged themselves. By virtue of the sacrifice Adam offered,[51] they might have attained a complete *tikkun*, but after Adam sinned, they descended to the realm of the *klippos*.

Subsequently, during the generation of the Flood, the animals and birds further damaged themselves by consorting with members of different species.[52] From then on, permission was given to Noah and his descendants to consume animals in order to rectify them. Now humans would have the task of refining the animals by consuming them, thus elevating the holy sparks to their rightful place. During the period of the Holy Temple [this task was nearly completed.] Everything was rectified through the sacrifices offered on the Altar: the person rectified his transgression by reciting the confession over the offering; the animal itself was rectified through the mystery of sacrifice; the vegetative realm was rectified through the wood used to burn the sacrifices; and the mineral realm was rectified through the salt [in which all sacrifices were dipped before burning.] As the verse states, "On your every offering, you shall offer salt" (Leviticus 2:13).

---

49. See R. Chaim Vital, *Sefer Eitz Chaim, Heichal Nukvah, Sha'ar Mayim Nukvin U'Maim Duchrin, D'rush* 3; ibid. *Heichal A-B-Y-A, Sha'ar Klippas Nogah, D'rush* 3; *Sha'ar HaMitzvos, Eikev*, et al.
50. *Sanhedrin* 59b.
51. *Shabbos* 28b. Adam offered a sacrifice from a one-horned animal as a gesture of penitence after he sinned by eating from the Tree of Knowledge.
52. Rashi on Genesis 1:12.

However, today we lack the power to refine them completely. Although [when consumed by a human being] the animal is transformed and becomes part of the human body, nevertheless, the animals of the Six Days of Creation were far superior to the human beings of today. Such was the wondrous donkey of Rabbi Pinchas ben Ya'ir. Thus, even the Amora'im (Talmudic sages) said: "[Compared to our teachers] we are like donkeys, but not like the donkey of Rabbi Pinchas ben Ya'ir."[53] This animal received its *tikkun* not through being eaten, but only in the course of time and through [the saintliness of] Rabbi Pinchas ben Ya'ir, until it finally attained its lofty level (Rabbi Avraham Azulai, *Chesed L'Avraham, Mayan* 4, *Nahar* 27, abridged).

෫෩

Everything that a sacrifice accomplishes, one's table accomplishes...[54] Thus, when a tzaddik eats with mindfulness and holy fervor he nullifies the guilt of all humanity (Rabbi Moshe Chaim Ephraim of Sudylkov, *Degel Machaneh Ephraim, Shemini*, p. 152, s.v. *Zos hachaya*).

෫෩

Whatever we eat potentially has a share in bringing about *tikkun* of the damage caused by Adam, who sinned by eating from the Tree of Knowledge. The recitation of blessings and special preparations the Jewish people make before eating — with meat, the slaughtering and salting, and with other foods, carrying out the various commandments that apply to them — is in order to rectify the spiritual damage caused by Adam. Because it was through eating that Adam sinned, we must eat in a manner that brings about a *tikkun*. This is implied by the verse, "And you shall eat, eating... (Joel 2:26). In other words, the fact that "you shall eat" is a result of the eating of Adam. Therefore, "you shall eat" in order to rectify Adam's sin, through "eating," i.e., through the commandments that pertain to eating (Rabbi Levi Yitzchak of Berditchev, *Kedushas Levi, Noach*, s.v. *O yomar, kach lecha*, abridged).

---

53. *Shabbos* 112b.
54. See *Berachos* 55a.

ය෩ෂ

You constantly must strengthen yourself in God and never despair in any way, but continually remind yourself that "the whole world is full of His glory,"[55] and God is always with you. By doing so, you will be able to strengthen yourself when you prepare to eat, and attain an "awakening of *ratzon*" — the deepest will and desire of the soul for God. These feelings arise particularly at the time of eating.

This is the antithesis of the despair that afflicts most of the world, for the feelings of depression we experience are, for the most part, consequences of how we eat. Because we do not eat in a spirit of *kedushah* (holiness), we fall into spiritual decline.

In truth, every Jew must strive to sanctify his manner of eating. Nevertheless, it is forbidden to despair for any reason.[56] On the contrary, you must strengthen yourself at all times. Particularly when you prepare to eat, you must not let yourself be weak and listless; rather, you must be like a mighty warrior.

Not only is it forbidden to slip into spiritual decline through eating, but also you must know and believe that the eating of a Jew is extremely precious in God's eyes — just by virtue of eating according to the Torah's dietary laws, and by reciting the appropriate blessings before and after. By doing so, even the simplest Jew can extricate many holy sparks through eating. Therefore, you should eat in good spirits, strengthen yourself in God, and contemplate that "the whole world is full of His glory," and God is with you. Eventually you will come to feel the "illumination of *ratzon*" while eating, and experience the most intense yearning and desire for God. This is the essence of holy eating. In this way, every Jew can elevate the holy sparks in his food and restore them completely to their supernal source (Rabbi Nosson Sternhartz, *Likkutei Halachos*, *Challah* 4:3).

ය෩ෂ

---

55. Isaiah 6:3.
56. *Likkutei Moharan* II, 78.

[The celebrated Kabbalist and close disciple of Rabbi Nachman of Breslov] Rabbi Yidel once described how after his wedding, while living in the home of his father-in-law, he ceased to experience the taste of food. Prior to his marriage he had been accustomed to dine in luxury, for he came from a distinguished family. After marrying the daughter of the tzaddik, Rabbi Leib of Strestinetz, he ate at his father-in-law's table. Due to his poverty, Rabbi Leib used plain wooden bowls that exuded an unpleasant smell from the remnants of food they had absorbed. This disturbed Rabbi Yidel to the point that he could not eat. Noticing this, Rabbi Leib asked his son-in-law to sit beside him and share the food in his plate. As soon as he did so, Rabbi Yidel tasted the most wondrous flavor! However, when he returned to his place and tried to eat the food in his wooden bowl, he was unable to do so. Again his father-in-law called him to his side, and again he tasted the most wondrous flavor. This happened several times. Finally Rabbi Leib pointed out: "It is unimportant what you eat, or how the food is served. Everything depends upon the one who eats the food!" (Rabbi Levi Yitzchak Bender, *Siach Sarfei Kodesh*, Vol. V, 141).

⳨

The spiritual elevation of vegetarian foods is accomplished simply by having faith in God and by reciting a blessing before eating, through which we acknowledge that "the Earth belongs to God, and all that fills it" (Psalms 24:1). Thus, our sages observe, "Faith is the Order of *Zera'im* ['Seeds,' the section of the Mishnah that addresses agricultural matters],"[57] and established at its beginning the tractate that deals with the laws of blessings. This alludes to the spiritual order by which all growing things are elevated to God: through our fulfillment of the commandments that pertain to them, and by our first reciting the appropriate blessing. Thus we express our faith that everything belongs to God, the simple faith that is fixed in the heart of every Jewish person, as our sages state: "They are believers, children of believers."[58]

---

57. *Shabbos* 31a.
58. Ibid. 97a.

Therefore, vegetarian foods are permitted even to those ignorant of Torah. However, our sages state that eating meat is permitted only to a Torah scholar.[59] Hence, tractate *Chullin* [which deals with the kosher laws relating to animals] is included in the Order of *Kadashim* [the order of the Mishnah that deals with the sacrificial services and matters related to the Holy Temple]. For non-consecrated animals slaughtered outside of the Holy Temple are permitted only to one who eats in a spirit of holiness and purity, whose "table is comparable to the altar."[60] The meat he consumes is like that of a sacrifice, and is sanctified. This is accomplished only by words of Torah, as it is written: "Since the Holy Temple was destroyed, the Holy One, blessed be He, has no dwelling place but the four *amos* (cubits) of the Law."[61]

When one makes his table into the "four *amos* of the Law," he recreates the paradigm of the Holy Temple and the altar. When he eats, he participates in the paradigm of the Kohanim (Priests); for just as they were privileged with an "elevated table," so is he. The fat and blood of the sacrifices corresponds to the life force within the food, and to one's desire for it. All this ascends unto God by virtue of the words of Torah, for the "fire of Torah" is analogous to the fire of the woodpile upon the altar. Through the Torah one recognizes that it is God Who imbues the food with life and imparts appetite and desire to one who partakes of it (Rabbi Tzadok HaKohen of Lublin, *Pri Tzaddik*, Vol. I, *Kuntres al HaAchilah* 7).

Nothing Left

Through the fulfillment of one's physical needs — through doing business, eating and drinking, and sexual relations — it is possible to accomplish spiritual unifications at the level of action. [Rabbi Bachya ibn Paquda,] author of *Chovos HaLevavos* (Duties of the Heart) eloquently describes this in "The Gate of the Unification of Action," and "The Gate of Divine Service," in connection with the verse, "Only for God alone..." (Exodus 22:19). Eating, drinking, and sleeping strengthen the body to

---

59. *Pesachim* 49b.
60. *Chagigah* 27a.
61. *Berachos* 8a.

serve the Creator; similarly, engaging in business enables one to provide food for himself and his family. To be sure, one who carries out these mundane activities with such intent does so with a good heart, all of his deeds being for the sake of Heaven; nevertheless, my brother, according to the tradition we have received, this is not a complete way of service (*avodah tamah*).

Thus did we hear in the name of our master, the righteous Maggid [of Mezeritch]: "What is a complete way of service? One that leaves nothing else to be accomplished. If one contemplates while eating that the strength he derives from the food is only for the sake of studying Torah and serving God, how can this be called a 'complete service'? When one is eating, he cannot pray or study the Torah. This [way of serving God through eating] is primarily for the sake of the divine service that one subsequently will perform." These were the Maggid's words. However, if while eating one engages in the mystical meditations of the Ari, in order to extricate and raise up the holy sparks from the food, liberating the good from subservience to the Primordial Kings[62] — particularly if God has graced him with the ability to visualize the permutations of Divine Names [detailed in the prayer book of the Ari] — he can perform spiritual unifications while eating, just as if he were praying. [This is a "complete service," because it is intrinsically connected to the Divine Oneness.] Fortunate is he, fortunate is his lot (Rabbi Zvi Hirsch of Ziditchov, *Sur Me'Ra V'Asei Tov, Hakdamah V'derech L'Eitz HaChaim: Kasav Yosher Divrei Emes*, s.v. *V'gam b'avodas tzorchei haguf*, pp. 112-113).

Better Than Manna

Since the Manna was spiritually beneficial to Israel, why was it given only for a limited time? Could not the All-Sufficient One just as easily have provided the "bread from Heaven" for all eternity? However, our master the Baal Shem Tov taught that we must depend upon physical sustenance in order to spiritually elevate the Earth by virtue of its

---

62. In the *Zohar* and writings of the Ari, the Primordial Kings represent the *sefiros* of *Tohu*/Chaos. They give rise to the illusion of separateness, the sense that everything we perceive somehow possesses autonomous existence apart from God.

produce. In this manner, we rectify the holy sparks that fell because of Adam's sin.

There are two *kavannos* (intentions one should bear in mind) for eating: to benefit the person, and to benefit the food — i.e., to rectify the Earth through its produce. The Manna enabled the Children of Israel to receive the Torah in its entirety. After doing so, however, it was necessary to consume the produce of the Earth again, in order to rectify the Earth. Thus, the verse states, "And they ate the grain of the land (*mei'avur ha'aretz*)[63] from the day after Passover..." (Joshua 5:11). [The author renders *mei'avur ha'aretz*," as if it were *ba'avur ha'aretz*, "for the sake of the Earth," a homiletic word-play.] That is, the Children of Israel began to eat physical food again, for the sake of the Earth, whereas previously they had done so for their own spiritual benefit, by eating the Manna (Rabbi Moshe Teitelbaum of Ujhely, *Yismach Moshe, Shemos*, p. 186a, abridged).

The Power of Kavanah

By eating just one meal during the week or on the Sabbath — indeed, by eating even one food with proper *kavanah* (intention), for the sake of Heaven, and in order to elevate one's physical nature — all of one's meals and all the foods one formerly has eaten ascend, as well. As the sages of the Kabbalah instruct us concerning prayer: one prayer recited with proper *kavanah* can elevate all the flawed prayers of an entire year.[64] Just as prayer takes the place of the sacrifices, so does eating in a spirit of holiness. Similarly, a single act performed with spiritual intent can elevate all of one's previous mundane doings, not to mention the commandments one may have performed by rote, without enthusiasm and mindfulness. However, this applies especially to eating, of which the Gemara explicitly states: "One act of eating affects the next, that it

---

63. According to Rabbenu Tam, the term *avur* indicates the old crop of grain, in contrast to *tevu'ah*, denoting the new crop that may not be eaten until the Omer offering has been brought; see *Tosefos* on *Kiddushin* 37b, s.v. *Mi'macharas haPesach achol.*

64. *Sefer HaTanya, Kuntres Acharon*, chap. 3 (154b), s.v. *Elah mip'nei she'kavanaso laShamayim*, citing *Mikdash Melech, Pekudei.*

should be similar to itself" (*Shabbos* 71a) (Rabbi Tzadok HaKohen, *Pri Tzaddik*, as cited in *Sefer Kedushas HaAchilah*, 73).

Apologizing to the Holy Sparks

The holy Rav Yaivi (an acronym for Chassidic master Rabbi Yaakov Yosef ben Yehudah of Ostrog, 1738-1791) was accustomed to eat large portions of food as a means of divine service. If he was incapable of eating more, but food still remained in the serving trays and crocks, the Rav would incline himself submissively and entreat the holy sparks in the leftover foods, that they should not bear any grievance against him for not accomplishing their *tikkun*. After reciting the Grace After Meals, the Rav would stay awake all night long, studying Torah intensely and enthusiastically with the strength he gained from the food he had eaten. In the morning, too, he would pray with great fervor (*Imrei Kodesh*, cited in *Sefer Kedushas HaAchilah*, 139).

The Sabbath and the Holy Sparks

"Thus said God, Who made a way through the sea, and through the mighty waters a path..." (Isaiah 43:16). This world, in all its vicissitudes, is like the sea; and when one encounters the Divine Presence "Whose radiance fills the entire world"[65] in all of one's physical circumstances, one accomplishes a mystical unification. [This is called a "way."] As it is written: "And protect me on this way that I go..." (Genesis 28:20), which our sages interpret to mean: "From forbidden relations."[66] The same applies to a "path."

During the six ordinary days of the week, it is difficult to attain this spiritual level, which applies only to men of God, masters of wisdom and masters of the soul. However, on the Sabbath it is easy for everyone to reach this level. Thus, God commanded us to eat, drink, and delight on

---

65. Isaiah 6:3.
66. *Bereishis Rabbah* 70:4. Sexual relations, in turn, allude to unifications on the spiritual plane, both sharing the same terminology in Hebrew (e.g., *yichudim, zivvugim*). In the scriptural narrative the *Degel Machaneh Ephraim* cites here, Jacob prays that God protect him from transgression as he leaves the Land of Israel on his way to the house of Laban in Haran.

the Sabbath day — for on the Sabbath, everything becomes one (Rabbi Moshe Chaim Ephraim of Sudylkov, *Degel Machaneh Ephraim, Likkutim,* s.v. *Ko amar Hashem*, p. 250).

❧

On the Sabbath everything rests and is refreshed, freed from the Thirty-Nine Types of Labor,[67] and becomes incorporated into the realm of holiness. The Other Side is overcome, and the knowledge of God is complete.

Thus, concerning the Sabbath, the Torah states: "[On the seventh day you shall desist,] so that your ox and your donkey may rest" (Exodus 23:12). The ox represents the physicality that derives from the side of holiness; the donkey (*chamor*) represents the physicality (*chomer*) of the Other Side. Both aspects "rest" and attain spiritual perfection on the Sabbath, when everything becomes subsumed within the holy. The Other Side, too, is subjugated and becomes a vehicle for holiness.

Therefore, when Jacob went forth from the house of Laban, he said, "And I have acquired the ox and the donkey..." (Genesis 32:6), for Jacob brought everything into the realm of holiness. [The Ari explains that] while dwelling in Laban's house, Jacob refined the holy sparks. [This corresponds to the divine service of the Jewish people during the six days of the week.] Then he went forth, and immediately entered into the holiness of the Sabbath. As the verse states [of Jacob's arrival at the walls of Shechem], "And he encamped before the city" (Genesis 33:18), which our sages interpret to mean, "He [arrived on the eve of the Sabbath and] fixed the Sabbath boundaries..."[68]

This also explains why Jacob praised himself with the words, "And I have acquired an ox and a donkey..." For he had succeeded in subjugating everything to the holy, as implied by the phrase " your ox and your donkey shall rest," which alludes to the Sabbath (Rabbi Nosson Sternhartz, *Likkutei Halachos, Kilei Beheimah* 2:3, abridged).

---

67. The Talmud enumerates 39 categories of creative work related to the construction of the Tabernacle in the desert. These categories serve as the paradigm for all mundane activities forbidden on the Sabbath (*Shabbos* 49b).
68. *Bereishis Rabbah*, 79:7.

Give Rest to Your Animal

We must draw forth the holiness of the Sabbath into the weekdays by remembering our spiritual goal. Then we can separate the human sustenance (*shefa*) that has fallen to the animal kingdom and restore it to humankind. This confusion [by which the *shefa* of humans and animals has been exchanged, is a consequence of the sin involving the Tree of Knowledge and the subsequent exile from the Garden of Eden.] It is responsible for all the difficulties of doing business and all the hard labor of the six days of the week.

The verse states: "Remember the Sabbath day, to make it holy; six days you shall work..." (Exodus 20:9). [This intimates that by remembering our spiritual goal, which is bound up with the Sabbath, we can undo this confusion.] We receive the strength to accomplish our task of extricating the human sustenance from the animal kingdom, and restoring it to humankind. [Then the animals will receive the sustenance that is their due.] Thus, we are commanded to let our animals rest on the Sabbath. As our sages instruct us: "Give rest to [your animal], that it may graze and eat,"[69] for her eating is a form of rest: The animal may eat from that which is divinely appointed for her, without exerting herself. This is possible because all sustenance has been restored to its proper place.

This, too, is why we are commanded to eat heartily on the Sabbath. Then we derive nourishment from human sustenance alone, from the effluence of divine wisdom that is holy, pure, and luminous. Through this, we attain our ultimate goal: to know and perceive Godliness (Rabbi Nosson Sternhartz, *Likkutei Halachos, Mekach U'Memkar*, 4:16, as cited in *Lechem HaPanim* 11:61).

The Sabbath Foods

"God blessed the seventh day, and He sanctified it" (Genesis 2:3). [Interpreting this verse,] Rabbi Ishmael declared: "He blessed the Manna in the wilderness, and He sanctified the Manna in the wilderness"

---

69. Rashi on Exodus 23:12, citing *Mechilta*.

(*Bereishis Rabba*, 11:2). This suggests that God blessed the Sabbath foods, imbuing them with the taste of Manna. It is known that the Manna was called "Food of the Mighty" (Psalms 78:25). Similarly the sacrifices in the Holy Temple were called "Food of the Mighty." Thus, partaking of the Sabbath meals is like partaking of the sacrifices in the Holy Temple (*Imrei Noam,* cited in *Sefer Kedushas HaAchilah* 299).

രജ്ഞ

The holiness of the Sabbath foods is comparable to that of the sacrifices in the Holy Temple. Indeed, some say that the holiness of the Sabbath foods is even greater: for a profane thing that became sanctified through a person's divine service attains a higher spiritual level than that which was holy of itself (*Yismach Yisrael, Likkutim,* cited in *Kedushas HaAchilah* 304).

രജ്ഞ

The "Feast of the Leviathan"[70] [designated for the tzaddikim in the Garden of Eden] will be made up of the foods consumed by the Jewish people at their Sabbath and Festival tables, as well as when they showed hospitality to guests or celebrated a religious event (*se'udas mitzvah*). These are the foods they are destined to eat in the Future World. Thus it is written, "And you shall eat, eating (*achol*) and being satisfied" (Joel 2:26); that is, they shall partake of that which they previously had eaten [*achol,* a play on words] (Rabbi Levi Yitzchak of Berditchev, *Kedushas Levi, Likkutim,* 7, as cited in *Sefer Kedushas HaAchilah,* 328).

രജ്ഞ

Our sages state that one ignorant of Torah is forbidden to eat meat, for this distances him from his human aspect and reinforces his animal

---

70. *Bava Basra* 74a-75a; also note *Avodah Zarah* 3b; *Chullin* 67b; *Targum Yonasan ben Uziel,* Rashi, Mahari Kara, Ibn Ezra, Radak, *Metzudas* on Isaiah 27:1; *Bereishis Rabbah* 7:5; *Vayikra Rabbah* 13:3, 22:7 (end); *Bamidbar Rabbah* 21:17 (end); *Tanchuma, Chayei Sarah* 3; *Pesikta D'Rav Kahana* 29; *Pirkei Rabbi Eliezer* 9 (23b), 10 (26a); *Aggadas Bereishis* 75; and *Yalkut Yonah* 550. All authorities explain the Feast of the Leviathan, the Wine Preserved from the Six Days of Creation, and the Wild Ox allegorically, however, some maintain that the Leviathan and Wild Ox have a physical aspect, as well; see above, Additional Source Texts, n. 36.

aspect. However, on the Sabbath such an individual may partake of meat, as well, since the holiness of the Sabbath enables all things to ascend[71] (Rabbi Shneur Zalman of Liadi, *Siddur HaRav Baal HaTanya, Sha'ar Rosh Chodesh,* 214b).

જ્રેજી

[Rabbi Aharon of Karlin once remarked]: "Sometimes thoughts of *teshuvah* — remorse about one's past, and yearning to return to God — occur to a person during the Sabbath meals; for then one comes closer to the point of truth. These thoughts of *teshuvah* may be even loftier than those that arise during prayer." He later added: "The *zemiros* (table songs) are the wings by which the holiness of the Sabbath meal ascends... " (*Beis Aharon*, as cited in *Kedushas HaAchilah,* 312).

જ્રેજી

One should be extremely joyous on the holy Sabbath, and not show even the least trace of sadness or worry. Simply "take delight in God" (Isaiah 58:14), and enjoy all the pleasures of the Sabbath, in food and drink, as well as in fine clothing according to one's means. For the eating of the Sabbath is entirely spiritual, entirely holy, and it ascends to a completely different place than the eating of the ordinary days of the week (Rabbi Nachman of Breslov, *Likkutei Moharan* II, 17).

---

71. Also cf. ibid. *Sha'ar HaMilah,* 144b. Both sources are cited in R. Bezalel Naor's *Ben Shanah Shaul,* p. 293.

Sources: Chapter 5

The Tikkun of Reincarnation

A person's transgressions may damage the soul to such an extent that it cannot be purified except by difficult means. It must enter from above [i.e., it must descend from the source of all souls beneath the Throne of Glory described in the Merkavah vision of Ezekiel] by way of the Face of the Ox [which is the spiritual source of all clean animals]. Then it must be transferred by the angel appointed over all clean animals and become garbed in one of them. Just as it was garbed in the vital soul of a human being, it is now garbed in the vital soul of an animal. Thus, it must graze like a cow, and eat straw, and perform labor, etc. and be afflicted according to its sins. In this manner, it is purified from its evil. It also shares the pangs of death when the animal dies, and then it is uprooted from this state of existence.

If the soul has attained purification, it will die by the ritual slaughterer's knife, which is on the side of holiness. If not, it will die by a blemished blade, which is on the left side [in the array of the *sefiros*, the source of severe judgment], and it will be a *neveilah* (carcass unfit for kosher consumption). As such, it remains trapped among the *klippos*. If it merits to be slaughtered in a proper manner but is cast to the dogs, it is carrion. If it is pure, an Israelite will eat it. During the era of the Holy Temple, [the animal bearing such a reincarnated soul] would sometimes merit to be offered on the altar, and it would then cleave to the side of holiness.

One who guards his soul should avoid eating meat, as it is possible that by doing so, the soul of a wicked person may cleave to him. Sometimes [such a soul] will harry a person unto death. [Yet this does not happen by chance.] "Guilt is borne by the guilty, [and merit by the meritorious]"[72] — sometimes for harm, sometimes for one's benefit. However, "God watches over fools."[73]

---

72. Rashi on Deuteronomy 22:8, citing *Sifré*.
73. Psalms 116:6.

Just as all this applies to the [ritually clean] animals whose source is the Face of the Ox, so does it apply to the [predatory] animals whose source is the Face of the Lion, and the birds whose source is the Face of the Eagle. Everything depends upon the nature of the transgression[74] (Rabbi Moshe Cordovero, *Shiur Komah, Inyan Gilgul*).

ᘓᔥᔥ

The Kohanim would eat, and the owners of the sacrifices would gain atonement (Talmud: *Pesachim* 59b).

Commentary: This alludes to the reincarnated souls that "own" or "possess" the sacrificial animals. The reincarnated soul is not concerned with its present physical life. On the contrary, it yearns for the day when it will receive its *tikkun* (Rabbi Moshe Teitelbaum of Ujhely, *Yismach Moshe, Noach*, 143b, s.v. *V'al pi zeh yisba'er*, citing *Asarah Ma'amaros*).

The Travail of the Soul

Certain evil-doers are reincarnated in minerals, others in vegetation. If the produce is consumed by a worthy person who recites a blessing over it, the reincarnated soul will receive its *tikkun*. Other souls are reincarnated as living creatures, such as kosher species of animals or birds. During the days of the Holy Temple, if a reincarnated [soul] was deserving, the Holy One, blessed be He, would cause it to be chosen as a sacrificial animal, and thus it would receive its *tikkun*. After the Temple's destruction, this *tikkun* can still be accomplished if the animal or bird is properly slaughtered with a carefully inspected blade, and then consumed by a worthy person. However, if the soul is undeserving of *tikkun*, it will be rendered carrion through slaughter by means of an invalid blade, physical injury, or another halachic disqualification. This is brought about by [the angels] who preside over the reincarnated soul.

There are souls that must be reincarnated in non-kosher species of animals, beasts, or birds. Some are reincarnated as black dogs, in which form the reincarnated soul cannot attain its *tikkun*.

---

74. In a similar vein, see Rabbi Avraham Azulai, *Chesed L'Avraham, Nahar 27, Inyan Chamor Shel R' Pinchas ben Ya'ir*.

Jewish souls may reincarnate again as Jewish children if they had begun to correct their deeds, and continue to return to this world again and again until they receive their *tikkun*. This is the mystical reason for the suffering and death of young children. However, if they do not begin to attain their *tikkun*, they are granted but three incarnations as Jews and no more.

After all this, they must descend to Gehenna to be afflicted until they have suffered [all that has been decreed upon them]. This applies to the wicked. However, concerning the righteous, the Holy One, blessed be He, prefers reincarnation to Gehenna, since they will rectify their former deeds. Even if they spent many "years" in the Garden of Eden, if God wishes to elevate them from level to level, they are judged again to a hair's breadth, and compelled to return to this world through reincarnation[75] (Rabbi Yechiel Michel Epstein, *Kitzur Shnei Luchos HaBris, Inyan S'char Va'Onesh*, abridged).

The Reincarnated Soul Knows Its Condition

A soul that has been reincarnated in an animal suffers because it is aware of its grievous condition. It may appear in a dream to one of its relatives, asking for help in order to attain a measure of relief, to whatever extent is possible — that is, if the soul merits to recall its former place or its relatives. Sometimes it is utterly deprived of relief and experiences great anguish. Such an animal may be endowed with extraordinary intelligence because of the reincarnated soul it bears. There are many true stories about such things, as many masters of the Kabbalah have written (Rabbi Moshe Cordovero, *Shiur Komah, Inyan Gilgul*).

c₃౸

"However, the flesh with its life-blood you shall not eat" (Genesis 9:4). According to the mystical doctrine of reincarnation as animals, this is comparable to consuming the flesh of one's peers. The Kabbalists state

---

75. This reflects the prevailing view of the Ari and his school. *Galya Raza*, p. 95, cites a variant Kabbalistic tradition that punishment in Gehenna precedes the purification process of reincarnation.

that if one intentionally transgresses the commandment [of consuming the flesh with its life-blood] and fails to repent, he must reincarnate as an animal that will be killed and consumed [by another wild creature]. An allusion to this is the verse, "A tzaddik considers the needs of his animal" (Proverbs 12:10); for [the reincarnated soul] will know [the reason for its fate] at the time of its punishment (*Yalkut Reuvaini, Noach,* pp. 139-140, citing Recanati).

ෆ෯ර

It is forbidden to slaughter an animal and its young on the same day because a human soul might have been reincarnated in that form, and this would cause it anguish. [That is, the animal possessed of a reincarnated soul would love its young with the same love a human parent feels toward a child.] Indeed, this would also violate the biblical precept to love one's neighbor as oneself (Rabbi David ibn Zimra, *Ta'amei HaMitzvos, Mitzvah* 302).

ෆ෯ර

The Kabbalists state that when a person is reincarnated as another human being, he does not remember his former life; however, when a person is reincarnated as an animal, beast, or bird, he does remember his former life. Therefore, the soul grieves and agonizes over how it has fallen from the heights of heaven, from the human form to an animal form (Rabbi Eliezer Azkari, *Sefer Chareidim,* chap. 33).

ෆ෯ර

Although a soul reincarnated in human form does not recall its former life, one reincarnated as an animal does remember. He knows who he is, and for which deeds he is being punished. According to my limited understanding, I would like to offer an explanation for this, comprised of one reason according to the order of nature, and a second that addresses the divine plan and purpose [of such punishments].

The first reason is that the soul reincarnated as an animal is not bound to the animal's body to such a great extent. The latter does not complement the soul, for it is not its "intended mate." Unlike the human body, it does not possess all the powers corresponding to the human soul; rather, it is like a disparate entity, within which the soul remains an isolated consciousness. The soul is imprisoned there only because of the punishment imposed upon it. Thus, during the days of its destitution and decline, it remembers all the pleasantness it had known during its former life — [as well as the evil] it had done, and what [as a consequence] was decreed upon it.

This is not the case when the soul reincarnates in human form. As such, it experiences a complete bond with the body and its sensory faculties and abilities, for the Creator determined the confluence between the human body and soul from the beginning of creation in order that the two should become one. [The human body] is its "intended mate." Therefore, it readily attains harmony and synthesis with the body's powers, and does not feel estranged. It cannot "peek through the cracks" (Song of Songs 2:9) to understand its true status. This is the reason according to the laws of nature.

The second reason is that all this reflects the divine plan and purpose, for only a human being is endowed with free will. Thus, the purpose of reincarnation in the form of a mute animal is not so that the soul may express itself through the exercise of its creative and moral abilities and improve itself thereby, for it lacks the means to do so. Rather, its will remains subordinate to the inclinations of the animal within which it dwells, since the main purpose of this form of reincarnation is that the soul may receive its due punishment. And it is a grievous punishment indeed for the human soul to dwell in squalor, within the coarse physicality of the animal. [Under these circumstances] of what use is its human cognition and memory? Indeed, by recognizing its own true nature, and by remembering the glory of the Omnipresent One that it had formerly known, the soul suffers bitterly and greatly.

When the end of its appointed time in the animal's body has come, if the soul is deemed worthy, it will be delivered into the hand of one who can accomplish its *tikkun*. However, when the soul is reincarnated in a human body, it can accomplish its own *tikkun* through free will. This form of reincarnation is not simply a punishment, for [the soul retains the faculties of] a human being. Therefore, if one remembered everything that transpired during his previous lifetime, he perforce would choose the good, and no longer possess free will.

The soul [must forget the past], just as it forgot everything when it entered this world for the first time. As our sages taught: "When a child is about to be born, an angel comes and strikes it on the mouth, causing it to forget all the Torah it had learned [while in the womb]."[76] This is meant in a figurative sense. The soul is a "portion of God Above."[77] As such, it would be unbefitting to forget in an instant all the wisdom it had possessed in the supernal world, as if it never had been there. Rather, this [forgetting] is brought about by divine providence — and possibly it may be accomplished through the agency of an angel, according to the simple meaning of our sages' words (op cit.). This also insures that the soul does not forfeit its free will. Similarly, [the necessity of forgetting one's past life] applies to reincarnation in human form (Rabbi Moshe Teitelbaum of Ujhely, *Yismach Moshe, Noach,* s.v. *V'nakdim ohd,* p. 142a, b).

Nebuchadnezzar's Madness

The Kabbalists state that [as a rule] a soul reincarnated in human form does not recall its previous lifetime; however, when reincarnated as an animal, beast, or bird, it does remember. As a result, it suffers and grieves that it has fallen from the heavens, from the human form to that of an animal.

The Holy One, blessed be He, wished to show all humanity an example of reincarnation from the human form to that of an animal through a great emperor who ruled the world: the evil Nebuchadnezzar [of Babylon]. While he was still alive, he descended from his throne and was banished to the fields, where he crawled on all fours like a beast, even appearing to all other animals as one of their own. [He suffered this fate] because he had spoken brazenly against the Exalted One. When the time allotted for his punishment had been fulfilled, he returned to his human

---

76. *Niddah* 30b.
77. *Shefa Tal, Hakdamah.*

status and proclaimed that God is the Supreme Power. As it is written: "At the end of the years [of punishment], I, Nebuchadnezzar, raised my eyes to heaven, and my intelligence returned to me. I blessed the Supreme Being, and I praised and glorified the One Who Lives Forever, Whose rule is eternal, and Whose kingship extends throughout the generations..." (Daniel 4:31). He even sent forth proclamations to all nations, describing the miracles that God wrought with him, saying: "The signs and wonders that the Supreme God has performed with me, it befits me to relate: how great His signs, and how mighty His wonders..." (ibid. 3:32-33).

Our sages taught: "If an angel had not come and slapped him on the mouth, he would have recited more than the psalms of King David."[78] This is as if Nebuchadnezzar had said, "Now that I have been punished and know that because of my evil speech all of this suffering befell me, I will only use my tongue to praise and exalt God, to recount His Glory among the nations" (Rabbi Eliezer Azkari, *Sefer Chareidim*, 33).

Tzaddikim and Reincarnated Souls

Sometimes when a person comes to extricate sparks of holiness that are related to his soul he encounters a certain spark that is deeply mired in impurity, and he is unable to extricate it and raise it up by himself. Therefore, the Holy One, blessed be He, causes the soul of a tzaddik to cleave to him through *ibbur* [i.e., the soul of a deceased person joins the soul of a living person]. This tzaddik will remain with him in order to help him perform a certain precept or contemplate a certain matter in his Torah studies, thereby enabling him to extricate the holy spark he could not redeem by himself. The tzaddik protects him from the *klippos* that come to wage war against him and prevent him from accomplishing his task (Rabbi Yosef Chaim of Baghdad, *Otzros Chaim* I, *Tikkun Ha'm'gulgolim B'Domem-Tzomei'ach-Chai-Medaber*).

---

78. *Sanhedrin* 92b. According to the fiery Chassidic master, R. Menachem Mendel of Kotzk (1789-1859), the angel slapped Nebuchadnezzar on the mouth and said, "Now let's hear how you sing!" Nebuchadnezzar praised God only after his deliverance; King David, by contrast, praised God in the very midst of his suffering and distress. I am grateful to R. Yitzchak Wolpin for this explanation.

Tzaddikim Reincarnate as Fish

Sometimes even tzaddikim who dwell in the Garden of Eden must be reincarnated for some small matter that they did not fulfill. However, they are reborn as fish that need not endure the pain of *shechitah*. Thus, the Torah refers to the death of fish as "gathering" (Numbers 11:22), as the Ari explains.[79]

One must consider this question: if the tzaddik neglected to fulfill his obligation according to Torah law, why should his case be judged any differently [than that of an ordinary person]? Why should he be reincarnated for a few moments as a fish, that will be consumed on the Sabbath or a religious feast, and immediately attain a *tikkun*, while everyone else who did not fulfill the Torah's requirements must endure various painful incarnations? If the act in question was not obligatory, why must the tzaddik endure reincarnation at all?

The answer is as follows. The Torah describes the commandments according to the straightforward sense of how they must be performed. Yet there are hidden depths of each precept that transcend the mortal mind, meanings that are understood only by the enlightened ones of each generation. For example, the *Zohar* (*Yisro*, 78a) states that a Torah scholar whose sexual conduct does not conform to the highest moral standards is judged in Heaven as if he had committed a capital offense. [If not for the *Zohar*'s words] would one have realized the severity of the Torah scholar's misdemeanor? Rather, the Torah's meaning must be understood in the plain sense. Only the enlightened sages of the generation can infer its hidden implications from the scriptural verse. However, for even such inexplicit infractions the tzaddik must be purified (Rabbi Zvi Elimelech Spira of Dinov, *Bnei Yissaschar*, *Chodesh Sivan*, *Ma'amar* 5:18, abridged).

---

79. *Sha'ar HaGilgulim, Hakdamah* 5. An earlier Kabbalistic view to the contrary is espoused by *Sefer HaKanah, Dinei Sod Chagavim V'Dagim Tehorim U'Temei'im*, pp. 272-273. The author asserts: "Although there are certain permissible species of grasshoppers, know, my son, that whenever gathering [and not *shechitah*] is sufficient [for creatures to be used as food], no human souls are present..." This rule also would apply to the kosher species of fish. However, the vast majority of Kabbalists reject this, taking the view of the Ari to be authoritative.

ເຮຣວ

"And [Abraham] fetched cream and milk and one of the herd that he had prepared, and placed these before them" (Genesis 18:8). My master, the saintly Rabbi Yaakov Yitzchak Horowitz (1745-1815), the Seer of Lublin, once asked: "Why does the Torah not mention fish as part of the meal [that Abraham served] the angels? Similarly, it states, 'Jacob slaughtered [from his flocks] for a feast on the mountain' (ibid. 31:54). However, when our sages speak [of a festive meal], they include both meat and fish."

I answered: "The main purpose of a meal is to elevate the holy sparks and to spiritually rectify reincarnated souls. The Ari states that tzaddikim usually are reincarnated as fish. This surely applies to tzaddikim of lesser status, but the great tzaddikim do not need any *tikkun* at all. During Abraham's day, the only tzaddikim were the great individuals mentioned in the Torah. [Therefore, he did not serve fish to his angelic guests]."

My master praised this interpretation, and added: "This, too, is why fish are not mentioned as part of King Solomon's feast. For then 'the moon was full' [i.e., the Jewish people had reached their spiritual zenith], and 'every man sat beneath his own vine' (I Kings 5:5). There were only new souls in the world. [Therefore, fish, which contain the souls of tzaddikim, did not need to be included at the royal banquet] (Rabbi Moshe Teitelbaum of Ujhely, *Yismach Moshe, Vayeira*, as cited in *Sefer Kedushas HaAchilah*, 164).

ເຮຣວ

Fish exemplify the mystical paradigm of the "open eye" that alludes to the World to Come and the state of enlightenment (*da'as*). Thus, fish were created in the water, which symbolizes enlightenment [as in "The knowledge of God shall fill the Earth as the water covers the sea" (Isaiah 11:9)]. It is customary to eat fish during the Sabbath and festival meals because the Sabbath and festivals are a "foretaste" of the World to Come and divine wisdom (Rabbi Nosson Sternhartz, *Likkutei Halachos, Simanei Dagim*, 1, cited in *Lechem HaPanim* I:111).

Rabbi Nosson Sternhartz on Reincarnation

"For man also knows not his time; like fish that are caught in an evil net and like birds that are trapped in a snare, so are the sons of man snared in an evil time when it suddenly falls upon them" (Ecclesiastes 9:12). This alludes to afflicted souls that often are "caught" or "trapped" in the bodies of birds or game. The Torah calls these animals by the term *tzeidah* (quarry) because of the souls trapped within them (*Likkutei Halachos, Shechitah* 2:10).

⊰⊱

The main purpose of *shechitah* is to elevate souls that have been reincarnated in the form of animals or birds. These souls were reincarnated in these lower forms because of the severity of their transgressions (ibid. 3:2).

⊰⊱

The *shochet* must be extremely pious and God-fearing. He must recite the blessing prior to the act of slaughter with deep concentration, and exercise the greatest care concerning every detail of the laws involved. Thus, he will redeem the soul within the animal and elevate it to the human level (ibid. 4:3).

⊰⊱

Birds and *chayos* (wild animals such as deer) are gentler by nature, and they are quicker and livelier than *beheimos* ("beasts," i.e., cattle and sheep). This is because *chayos* and fowl have a greater spiritual affinity with man, and more commonly possess holy sparks and vitality derived from human souls. Thus, the verse states: "Do not deliver unto the *chayos* the soul of Your turtledove [i.e., Israel]... Gaze upon the covenant..." (Psalms 74:19-20). The Psalmist entreats God not to allow these holy souls to remain trapped.

Furthermore, the name *chayos* [literally, "living things"] bespeaks their nature. They are called *chayos* because of the vitality [i.e., holy sparks] that they possess in greater measure; for the life-force is primarily that which is derived from the human level. However, beasts are so called because of the bestial spirit that they possess to a greater degree than the *chayos*.

This is why the established daily sacrifices in the Holy Temple consisted of beasts. The purpose of all sacrifices was to effect atonement and to remove spiritual impurity from the world. Therefore, it was necessary to sacrifice specifically beasts. Through the rite of laying hands upon the animal (*semichah*), man transferred to the animal his impurity — i.e., the bestial spirit that had come to dwell within him due to his wrongful actions. Because this spirit is dominant in animals, it attracts the bestial spirit in man to itself; for it is the nature of all things to be drawn to their source. Through the act of sacrifice, the bestial spirit is subjugated and destroyed.

[The laws of slaughter also reflect these issues.] Unlike beasts, *chayos* and birds require their blood to be covered with earth. The reason for this additional procedure is that they contain more human souls. Even after the act of slaughter, souls remain in the creature's life-blood. Therefore, the life-blood must be covered with earth [in order for these souls to be freed][80] (ibid. 2:11).

⊗

The Talmud rules that the *shochet* must show his knife to a sage. [On a deeper level] this is because the essential *tikkun* effected by ritual slaughter is the elevation the soul within the animal. Since the root of the soul is the wisdom of the Torah, it can only be elevated through the wisdom of the Torah. Therefore, it is impossible to accomplish the *tikkun* of slaughter except through one who possesses the wisdom of the Torah. One must show the knife specifically to a Torah sage in order to receive the spiritual power necessary for the *tikkun* of slaughter. Thus, the soul within the animal may be redeemed (ibid. 4:2).

⊗

---

80. A Kabbalistic explanation of this commandment that follows similar lines of thought is given in *Galya Raza*, pp. 99-102. The author interprets covering the blood to covering the shame of the reincarnated soul's former misdeeds.

The distinction between human beings and animals is the power of speech. That is why man is classified as *medaber*, the "speaking being." When a person sins, he descends to the spiritual level of an animal. He forfeits the power of speech, and becomes like a mute beast — in certain instances through actual reincarnation as an animal that cannot speak. However, this very silence and inability to speak is his spiritual remedy. He must bear this form of suffering, because "within the fault itself lays the *tikkun*." One must be "silent before God" [by enduring reincarnation as an animal]. Then, through undergoing the pain of *shechitah*, he may return to his former human status (ibid. 1:1, abridged).

◌෯෯◌

The purpose of *shechitah* is to elevate the soul of an animal to the human level. At first, the soul was garbed within an animal that lacked higher intellect and had no conception of God. Now it may ascend to the status of a human being, to whom it may be revealed and made known that "there is a God who rules the Earth." The main ascent of the soul consists in attaining the human level, so that the soul may come to know God. [When understood in this light,] *shechitah* is an act of compassion (*Likkutei Halachos, Eiver Min HaChai* 2:1, abridged).

◌෯෯◌

The process of spiritual decline begins with a loss of faith in the sages. This causes a lack of spiritual discernment and knowledge as a result of which one may fall from the human level to the level of an animal. When such an individual fails to return to God during his physical lifetime, he must be reincarnated in an animal. Then his punishment — and his path of return — is through suffering the pangs of *shechitah*. For God desires the *tikkun* of every creature; all punishments and afflictions are at the same time *tikkunim* that greatly benefit the soul. Thus, the reincarnated soul is elevated to its former status as a human being, possessed of wisdom and guided by true spiritual advice (*Likkutei Halachos, Shechitah* 5:2, abridged).

The Rav of Tcherin on Reincarnation

It states in the Kabbalistic meditations of the Ari that through the blessing recited over the act of ritual slaughter it is possible to elevate a human soul that had transmigrated to an animal or a holy spark present in the blood of the animal to the human level.[81] The crown of creation is humanity, in particular the Jewish people. The supreme purpose for which man was created is to know God. Thus, everyone should gaze at the divine wisdom and life-force concealed within the multiplicity of creation and strive to draw close to God through everything he sees and hears. When a person accomplishes this, he fulfills the divine intention in creation. This is why man was created with wisdom and speech: through these faculties he may grasp all this and make God's power known to others. As a result, all nations will come to know God: "They will accept upon themselves the yoke of His kingship," and all creation will reach a state of harmony and perfection.

When a spiritually refined person eats something and receives nourishment and vitality from it, the holy sparks concealed therein are raised up to a much higher level, for they become subsumed within the wisdom and life force of that person. This fulfills the purpose of all creation. However, when a person is far from this holy wisdom, because he has followed the promptings of his evil inclination — especially if he has actually transgressed — then he is comparable to a beast. Sometimes the spiritual damage he has done to himself is so great that he completely falls from the level of a human, possessing speech and intellect, and his soul is reincarnated in the body of an animal. Sometimes he falls to an even lower level.

Therefore, the *shochet* (ritual slaughterer) must concentrate intensely on the blessing he recites at the time of slaughter in order to release the blood — the blood being a vehicle for the forces of severity — and purge from it the spirit of folly that cleaves to the animal soul. By examining the knife and reciting the blessing prior to the act of slaughter, the *shochet* "sweetens" the forces of severity and redeems the transmigrated soul. He delivers the soul from the Sword of Esau, the Kingdom of the Other Side,

---

81. *Sha'ar HaMitzvos, R'eh.*

and raises it to the Kingdom of Holiness, by slaughtering the animal with the Sword of Holiness. Then the reincarnated soul is able to rise up and cleave to the soul of the spiritually refined person who eats the animal's flesh, until it attains its ultimate destiny. In such a case, ritual slaughter is a great religious task. Not only does it render the meat permissible for consumption, it also greatly benefits the reincarnated soul (Rabbi Nachman Goldstein of Tcherin, *Nachas HaShulchan, Shechitah* 19).

ᘓᘍᘓᘏ

Whenever Rabbi Yochanan finished the Book of Job, he would say, "The fate of man is death, and the fate of a beast is slaughter..."[82] At first glance this seems cruel. How can one take another living thing and slaughter and eat it? We are forced to conclude that, on the contrary, this is the ultimate act of kindness to the animal, for it enables it to ascend and become one with the life force of man. However, since man himself is destined to die, how does this help the animal to attain spiritual rectification?

We see empirically that everything in this world is subject to death; even in its fleeting existence, it is like nothing. For if a thing is fated to be burned, it is considered to be ashes already, as our sages state.[83] How is it possible that from a perfect Creator an imperfect creation may come forth — that everything is doomed to death, destruction, and loss, God forbid? How could this be, when everything was created with such wondrous wisdom, as it states, "You have made them all with wisdom" (Psalms 104:24), and divine wisdom is the source of life? Therefore, we must conclude that every appearance of death and destruction in the world is only [an illusion,] due to our lack of wisdom. As our sages interpret the verse, "'He shall die and not with wisdom' — without the wisdom of Torah."[84] The main goal is to acquire holy wisdom by overcoming corporeality and the spirit of folly that comes from the Other Side and the evil inclination. This is acquired only through the Torah.

A person must devote himself to Torah all his days with all his physical strength. Thus, he will overcome the evil inclination, the spirit

---

82. *Berachos* 17a.
83. *Menachos* 102b.
84. *Yalkut Shimoni* 898, citing Job 4:21.

of folly within him, and fully accept the yoke of the Kingdom of Heaven upon himself. He will perceive within all things the light of divine wisdom and draw close to God through the multiplicity of the world. By means of this wisdom and knowledge, everything in the world will fulfill its eternal destiny and endure forever (ibid.).

ᙅᔐᙠ

"That which is close to the soul restores the soul… That which is near the vital organs restores the bodily vitality… Rabba instructed his servant: When you buy a piece of meat for me, try to find a piece from near the place where the blessing was recited [i.e. the blessing prior to the act of *shechitah*: Rashi]" (Talmud: *Berachos* 44b).

Commentary: This is because the vital soul of the animal becomes garbed in the words of the blessing of the *shochet* at the moment of *shechitah* (*Parpara'os L'Chochmah, Berachos* 44b).

Sefer HaKanah on Shechitah

My son: my eyes once beheld an elderly man who slaughtered a cow, but he suddenly died before he could inspect [the animal's lungs for lesions]. I inquired [of heaven] and found that the calf had not deserved to die at the hand of this man. After a few days a calf was born in the home [of the family of the deceased], and that night I was amazed to observe a clear proof that this newborn calf was the man himself. Therefore, I declared, "Blessed is God… in Whom there is no wrongdoing."[85]

In another place I saw a pleasant youth slaughter an ox, and then a goat. However, both animals cried out because the youth [due to his lack of skill] caused them to die painfully. He, too, did not have a chance to inspect even one of them before he died.

Therefore, my son, withhold your hand from *shechitah*, for the questions that surround it are many; and seal your lips from making halachic pronouncements concerning the permissibility of *treifos*, for a

---

85. Paraphrase of Deuteronomy 32:4.

hairsbreadth of impurity may contaminate the whole (*Sefer HaKanah, Mussar L'Morei Hora'os V'Shochtim*, p. 307).

ೞೞ

It is written: "And you shall slaughter from your cattle and your sheep... as I have commanded you..."[86] This indicated to the Talmudic sages that Moses was commanded regarding the detailed laws of *shechitah*, which are part of the oral tradition.[87] Similarly, King Saul declared, "You shall slaughter them in this manner, and you shall eat..."[88] which shows that he instructed them verbally.

Now, listen, my son: What do [improper] slaughterers do? They raise their knives with a high hand and stand over the prostrate animal, who abandons herself to a fate she is powerless to prevent. This cruel individual pays no attention to the animal's cries; rather, he pays attention to attractive women and unworthy companions.

"Look!" he boasts. "I am great and powerful, like the Angel of Death, who holds life and death in his hands!" Then he gazes upon his portions of meat and wags his tail, rejoicing in them. His wife receives them with a shining countenance, and shows them off to her neighbors: "See how superior we are, and how prestigious is the great rabbi — greater than the Angel of Death!"

How they might live, and how they might enjoy length of days, if not for their desire to make known their status, these and these alike![89] Consider the greatness of our holy master [Rabbi Yehuda HaNasi] — yet because he failed to have compassion for a calf he was afflicted with pain, and his Torah knowledge did not protect him...

All souls destined to enter the world until the end of all the cosmic cycles (*shemitos*)[90] were present at Mount Sinai. [Together with Moses,

---

86. Deuteronomy 12:21.
87. Rashi, ad loc., citing *Chullin* 28a. The Torah was given at Mount Sinai along with its complete interpretation, which is an unbroken oral tradition.
88. I Samuel 14:34.
89. Presumably the author means to equate the slaughterers and their wives, both of whom sacrifice their compassion in favor of pride.
90. The Torah commands the Jewish people in Israel to allow the land remain fallow every seventh year, which is known as the *Shemitah* or Sabbatical Year. At this time, too, all debts are annulled. Every seven *Shemitah* cycles culminate in the fiftieth year

the souls of Israel regained the spiritual level of Adam before the first sin.[91]] Thus, at that gathering, they [and the souls of all animals present] flew away [from their bodies] and ascended [to the World of Souls]. Therefore, be careful not to take the life of any creature, for it, too, heard the Ten Commandments at Mount Sinai, which contain 68 *alefs*;[92] and without a doubt, cattle and sheep were present at the Giving of the Torah and tasted the Dew of Resurrection (*Sefer HaKanah, Sod HaShechita Chayos U'Behamos*, pp. 279-280).

---

known as the *Yovel* or Jubilee year, when all indentured servants are freed, and real estate reverts to the original owners (or their proper heirs); see Leviticus 25:3-10. The Talmud states that the cosmic cycle of creation and destruction of the world reflects this paradigm, every thousand years corresponding to one year in the *shemitah* cycle (*Sanhedrin* 97a). One ancient Kabbalistic tradition extends this concept to seven cycles of 7,000 years, which total 49,000 years. At the end of every cycle of 6,000 years, God returns the world to nothingness, and then recreates it anew; see *Sefer Temunah 3, Os Zayin*, p. 106 (also included in *Yalkut Reuvaini, Behar*, p. 80); *Sefer HaPeliah*, p. 7; also Rabbenu Bachaya, Recanati, and Tziyoni on Leviticus 25:8. Ramak mentions cosmic *shemittos* in *Shiur Komah, Shis Alfei Sh'nin*, 79a-83b (pp. 157-166), and *Sefer Elimah I, Ayn Kol Ha'aretz*, chap. 13 (5b).

R. Aryeh Kaplan discusses the subject in his commentary on *Sefer Yetzirah* 4:15, pp. 185-190; *Immortality, Resurrection, and the Age of the Universe: A Kabbalistic View*, pp. 1-15; in the same volume, also see *D'rush Ohr HaChayim* by R. Yisrael Lipschitz (author of *Tiferes Yisrael*), translated by R. Yaakov Elman, pp. 110-127. The original Hebrew version of the latter is printed in some editions of the Mishnah at the end of *Seder Nezikin*. R. Kaplan found a novel definition of cosmic cycles in R. Yitzchak of Acco's *Otzar HaChaim*, 86b-87b, that extends the age of the universe to 15.3 billion years, possibly reconciling the Jewish concept of the age of the universe with that of modern science (at least for the moment). The *shemitah* cycle of creation and destruction also corresponds to some of the most recent findings of modern physics; see Paul Steinhardt of Princeton and Neil Trunk of Cambridge University, 4.13.02, *Science*, p. 189 (published online 4.25.02 at www.sciencemag.org, classified as 10.1126/science.1070462, Science Express Research Articles).

However, the theory of cosmic *shemittos* was rejected by the Ari, whose views are widely regarded as definitive; see R. Chaim Vital, *Likkutei Torah, Kedoshim*, s.v. *Es Shabbsosai tishmoru; Sha'ar Ma'amarei Rashbi* 46a,b (cited in *Toras Nosson, Erchei HaAri z"l*, Vol. IV, *Shemitah* 390). Chassidic masters who follow the opinion of the Ari on this issue include R. Nachman of Breslov, *Chayei Moharan*, 424, with *hashmatos*; R. Shneur Zalman of Liadi, *Torah Ohr, Shemos*, s.v. *Vayomer... mi sam peh*; R. Dov Ber of Lubavitch, *Toras Chaim*, s.v. *Vayomer... lo ish devarim*; R. Menachem M. Schneerson of Lubavitch, *Likkutei Sichos* Vol. 10, *Hosafos* (18 Shevat 5717/1957), p. 176.

91. *Shabbos* 146a; also cf. *Zohar, Yisro*, 82b.
92. The letter *alef* is the first letter of the Hebrew alphabet, symbolizing the common origin of all created things. The *gematria* of the word *chaim*, or "life," is 68. Thus the Ten Commandments, which are the heart of the Torah, comprise a spiritual channel through which all beings, directly or indirectly, receive eternal life.

Stories of the Kabbalists

One day the disciples were studying together when the Rav (Rabbi Yitzchak Luria) turned and saw two ravens, their feathers plucked out, sitting in a tree.[93] He said to them, "Wicked ones! In this world you sought to destroy an entire nation, and now you come to me to take your side? Go away!" He chased them off. Mystified, the disciples asked about the exchange. He replied, "Those ravens were Balak and Balaam, who were being conducted from one hell to a more severe hell. They came to ask me to pray for them and save them from further punishment. This is why I answered them as I did" (*Shiv'chei HaAri*, 3).

☙

Once we were sitting with our master (Rabbi Yitzchak Luria), when a goat came and put its front hooves on the table, whereupon our master began speaking with it in its own language. Afterwards, he instructed me to go and buy it, and have it slaughtered for the Sabbath. He instructed Rabbi Moshe Sofino to slaughter it while performing the appropriate Kabbalistic meditations, and while reciting the blessing to bear in mind the intention to elevate the transmigrated soul within the animal. I asked my master why this soul was punished by being reincarnated as a goat, and he told me that it had engaged in intercourse by candlelight (*Ta'amei HaMitzvos, R'eh*, 101b).

☙

One Rosh Chodesh Teves in the village of Ein Zeitoun, our yeshiva completed the study of the Talmudic tractate *Chagigah*. We planned to make a festive meal for two reasons: in honor of completing the tractate, and in honor of Rosh Chodesh and Chanukah. On the first night of that Rosh Chodesh, I saw Rabbi Yitzchak Amigo the Musician in a dream. He had died three years previously from liver and intestinal disease. During his sickness, his liver had begun to disintegrate. When I saw him in the

---

93. The raven is known for its cruelty; see *Eiruvin* 22a; *Kesubos* 49a; *Sefer HaPeliah*, s.v. *Mi yachin l'orev*, p. 282; *Metzudas David* on I *Melachim* 17:4; Rashi on *Tehillim* 147:9; *Likkutei Moharan* I, 15:5; ibid. II, 4:1.

dream, he was in the great synagogue, as he often was in life. Among the members of the congregation were our master HaRav Karo, the appointed prayer-leader, and Rabbi Avraham Laniado, the Gabbai (sexton). They asked me to rectify the soul of the deceased. The deceased himself told me, "I have come so that you should rectify my soul." Then I awoke. In the morning I recounted my dream to the members of the yeshiva.

Soon afterward a group of non-Jews came to town with a calf to slaughter. The animal broke away from them and fled to my House of Study, climbing up to the porch where I sat with the other scholars beside a table stacked with holy books. The calf stood up, its hind feet on the porch and its front feet on the table. It gazed at my face, its eyes filled with tears. The members of the yeshiva saw all this and were astounded. I told them, "This is the dream I recounted to you."

We went outside and bought the calf from its owners. The calf extended its neck without any coaxing at all. We slaughtered it with the Kabbalistic meditations necessary for the rectification of the soul. Then it was inspected and found to be kosher. I told my comrades to remove the liver, and they found it to be putrid, like that of the man who had suffered reincarnation. They dissected it and found its chambers filled with blood and extremely long worms, numerous beyond count. I instructed them to be careful not to discard even the least scrap. Thus, they carefully excised the worms and forbidden fats from the rest of the carcass, not losing any edible part. In addition, I disallowed anyone outside our fraternity from partaking of it, only ourselves, with the intention of accomplishing the rectification of the reincarnated soul through the religious feast.

The following night, I dreamed again and saw the soul of the deceased. He said to me, "May your soul find peace, just as you have enabled my soul to find peace"[94] (Rabbi Chaim Vital, *Sefer Chezyonos* II, 28, as cited in *Chayei Moreinu HaRav Chaim Vital*, 8:53-59).

94. The Talmud describes how one of R. Yehudah's neighbors died without leaving family or friends to mourn his passing. Therefore, R. Yehudah gathered together ten men on each of the seven days of mourning to study and pray in the home of the deceased. Subsequently, the latter appeared in a dream to R. Yehudah and said, "May your soul find peace, just as you have enabled my soul to find peace" (*Shabbos* 152b).

୧୫୨୬

Once on Rosh Hashanah, my father [Rabbi Chaim Vital] was giving a Torah discourse beside the water after the *Tashlich* ceremony, when we saw a frog come out of the river in front of him. My father's eyes were closed while he said words of Torah, as was his custom. However, when the frog began to croak, he opened his eyes. Then he told us that a certain soul had come to hear his Torah, albeit in the guise of this frog. In honor of this soul, he began to expound on the subject of frogs, and why the Hebrew word for frog (*tzefarde'a*) can be broken into the words *tzipor de'ah*. [*Tzipor* is a bird; *de'ah* means knowledge or wisdom][95] (Rabbi Shmuel Vital, *Hagahos* on *Sha'ar Ruach HaKodesh*, 6a, as abridged in *Chayei HaRav Chaim Vital* 8:56, note 82).

୧୫୨୬

It once happened in Castile that the non-Jewish townspeople were preparing a certain bull for sport, planning to goad and afflict it according to their custom. The very night before [the bull-fight], a certain Jewish man dreamed that his father appeared before him and said, "Know, my son, that due to my sins I have been reincarnated as a bull. This bull is scheduled to endure great affliction tomorrow for the entertainment of the masses. Therefore, my son, you must save me! Let money be no object. Slaughter this bull, and when it is found to be kosher, let it be fed to poor Torah scholars. Thus have I been informed from Heaven, and I have been permitted to tell it to you. With this, my soul will rise up from the level of a beast to that of a human being again, and I will be able to occupy myself in divine service, with God's grace."

Many similar things have happened to the people of Israel. "Ask your father, and your elders will tell you..." Therefore, every God-fearing person should take this to heart while he is yet alive and possesses freedom of choice, and "know his God." May he repent for his sins and

---

95. This word-play also may be found in *Tanna D'vei Eliyahu Rabba*, 7:10. There it states that frogs impart knowledge by telling birds to drink from the streams they inhabit and not to fear; also cf. *Likkutei Moharan* I, 15:5. A Kabbalistic explanation is given in *Siddur HaAri z"l*, R. Shabsai of Rashkov, ed., in the commentary on *Haggadah Shel Pesach, Eser Makkos*, p. 12.

remove God's anger from himself, so that when his soul departs it will rest and be still, and find shelter in His shadow in the Garden of Eden. For God is gracious and merciful, and wishes to do good, and [as the Talmud states], "In the place where penitents stand, even the perfectly righteous are unable to stand" (Rabbi Eliezar Azkari, *Sefer Chareidim,* chap. 33).

❧

Once the Baal Shem Tov went into a deep trance and remained in meditation for three days and three nights. He did not know where he was. Then he saw that he was in a vast desert, far from his own familiar surroundings. It seemed amazing to him that he could have strayed into such a desert; certainly, this was no trivial matter. In the midst of such thoughts, there appeared before him a frog so big that he could scarcely tell what sort of creature it was. He asked the frog, "Who are you?" It answered that it was a Torah scholar who had been reincarnated as this frog. The Baal Shem Tov said: "You are indeed a Torah scholar," and with this pronouncement, he greatly elevated his soul.

The frog told him that it had spent five hundred years in its present incarnation. Indeed, the Ari (Rabbi Yitzchak Luria) had rectified all souls. However, because of the severity of his transgression, he had been banished to a place where people are not found, so that no one would rectify his soul.

The Baal Shem Tov asked: "What was your transgression?" He replied that he had once belittled the ritual washing of the hands by not doing so properly. The Accuser had therefore denounced him. [The Heavenly Court] answered that it was not possible to indict him for one sin. But since "one sin leads to another" (*Avos* 4:2), if [the Accuser] could entice him to commit to another transgression, the first would be counted against him as well. However, if [the Torah scholar] would remember God and repent of his misdeed, he would be cleared. Thus, he was tested again with another transgression, to which he succumbed, failing the test. This happened a second and third time, until eventually he came to violate almost every precept in the Torah. It was decreed that he be sent into banishment, and that his repentance be rejected.

Despite all this, if he had insistently knocked upon the gates of repentance, they would have received him. We know that in the case of Acher,[96] a Heavenly voice cried out, "Return, O backsliding children—except Acher.'" Similarly, the punishment for [this Torah scholar's] sin was to reject him. But if he had persisted in his repentance, they would have accepted him, for "nothing can stand in the way of repentance" (*Yerushalmi Pe'ah* 1:1).

The Accuser enticed him further, and he became such a drunkard that he was incapable of collecting his thoughts and repenting. Thus, he committed all the sins in the world. Since the first sin that had caused the rest had been his disrespect for the ritual washing of the hands, when he died he was reincarnated as a frog, which lives in the water. He was consigned to a place where people are not found, because if a Jew were to pass by and recite a blessing, or even think a good thought, this could bring about his redemption.[97]

[Having heard the man's story,] the Baal Shem Tov engaged in the rectification of his soul and elevated him, until the lifeless body of the frog was all that remained (A. Rubenstein, ed., *Shiv'chei Baal Shem Tov*, 5).

രു

I heard from the Rabbi of Polonoye and from [Rabbi Gedaliah of Linitz] that Rabbi Nachman of Kosov had a relative named Rabbi Yudel of Czudnov. Rabbi Yudel was a devoutly religious man.

It was Rabbi Yudel's way not to accept favors from others. Since he wished to live by the fruit of his own labor, he was in the iron ore business.

Once he went to a mine near which he wanted to spend the Sabbath. The local resident with whom he planned to stay asked him, "What will you eat, sir? I do not have fish, and you would not eat the meat because you did not examine [the slaughterer's] knife. Therefore, I suggest you go

---

96. Elisha ben Avuyah, a prominent scholar of the Mishnaic period, became a heretic. Thereafter, his colleagues called him *Acher,* meaning "the Other One" (*Chagigah* 14b, citing Jeremiah 3:14).

97. Literally, "bring forth the precious from the vile," paraphrasing Jeremiah 15:19.

to another mine nearby where there is a wealthy man. He certainly will have fish and his own *shochet*. You, sir, should go to him."

[Rabbi Yudel] traveled on until he came to a pond. Not far from that mine, the road passes through a pond. The water is [usually] shallow. But when there is a heavy rain or when the snow melts, the water becomes deeper. Rabbi Yudel and his wagon driver did not know that this was the case and were about to pass through, when a dog ran ahead of them and went straight into the pond, where it began to drown. It went up and down in the water, howling pitifully. Its anguished cries stirred [Rabbi Yudel's] heart, and tears fell from his eyes. He saw that it was impossible to cross the water. So he returned to the mine and asked [his former host] to do whatever he could to obtain fish for the Sabbath. The host entreated the fisherman, who caught a pike and brought it back to him.

The host remarked, "I have lived in this village for years, and I have never seen such a fish." They prepared several different dishes from it.

That Sabbath evening Rabbi Yudel was seated at the festive meal singing songs, when he was [suddenly] overcome by sleep. His father appeared to him in a dream and said, "Know that I was reincarnated as that fish. The informer whom I used to persecute during my life was reincarnated as the dog that drowned. His *tikkun* was that he drowned in order to save you, my son. I was compelled to be reincarnated as that fish because I persecuted him, and the tears that you shed redeemed me. So, be careful, my son, to have holy intentions when you eat this fish."

When he came to the Baal Shem Tov, the master told him [the dream] was true. The Baal Shem Tov said that Rabbi Yudel was a reincarnation of the Prophet Samuel (A. Rubenstein, ed., *Shiv'chei Baal Shem Tov*, 74, with variant texts; also note sec. 213 for an alternate version involving an anonymous disciple of Rabbi Michel of Zlotchov).

CвосмЭD

The Baal Shem Tov once observed a man hastily pick up a glass of vodka and drink it, forgetting to recite a blessing. "You should know," said the Baal Shem Tov, "that you just swallowed your father's soul that was reincarnated in the potatoes from which this vodka was made. For many years he yearned to be brought to a Jew who would recite a proper blessing over him, and thus bring about his *tikkun*. Now you have acted foolishly by tossing this drink into your mouth in one swallow, and casting down the suffering soul to endure reincarnation again." Suddenly, the fellow remembered that this very day was his father's *yahrzeit* (the anniversary of his death). Filled with fear and dread at the Baal Shem Tov's remark, he fell down in a faint.

From this we may understand the words of our sages: "The following verse applies to one who does not recite a blessing before eating: 'He robs his father and his mother...' " (*Berachos* 35b, citing Proverbs 28:24) (*Hanhagos HaDerech*, 37, as cited in *Sefer Kedushas Ha'Achilah*, 162).

ભ≈ŵ

I heard this from my father [Rabbi Nachman Chazan of Tulchin, 1813-1884], who heard it directly from a follower of our master [Rabbi Nachman of Breslov]:

One of our brotherhood had a dream in which he was told: If someone brings you a fish tomorrow, prepare it and bring it to the Rebbe [Rabbi Nachman]."

The following morning, a non-Jew came with a fish for sale. The Chassid purchased it and brought it to [Rabbi Nachman]. As soon as the Chassid arrived, the Rebbe asked: "Where is the fish?"

He gave it to him. The Rebbe made a disparaging remark about the fish, and then said to it: "A big *she'lo lishma!*"[98]

Then he explained that the fish contained the reincarnated soul of the father of the man who had purchased it. They cooked it in honor of the holy Sabbath, and thus it received a *tikkun* (Rabbi Avraham ben Nachman Chazan, *Kochvei Ohr, Anshei Moharan*, 38 ff).

ભ≈ŵ

---

98. The Talmud states that through studying the Torah or performing a mitzvah or good deed *she'lo lishma*, i.e., not for the sake of fulfilling the divine will, one eventually will come to do so with genuine devotion (*Pesachim* 50b). However, elsewhere the sages say of one who behaves without holy intent that it would have been better if he never had been born (*Berachos* 17a). Maharsha (ad loc.) explains that in the former case, the individual seeks honor; in the latter, he wishes to display his prowess at winning arguments, heedless of the truth.

Rabbi Yitzchak Dovid was one of the prominent Chassidim of the "Tzemach Tzaddik" (R. Menachem Mendel Hager, 1830-1884) of Vizhnitz. Once the Tzemach Tzaddik pointed out a number of ravens standing on the roof of his *Beis Medrash* (Study Hall), and remarked, "These are all *shochtim* (ritual slaughterers) who caused people to eat *treifah* (non-kosher) meat."

After hearing this, Rabbi Yitzchak Dovid went home to the community of Vilchovitz, where he served as the local *shochet*, and submitted his resignation to the communal leaders. They quickly sent a delegation to the Tzemach Tzaddik, who asked that Rabbi Yitzchak Dovid return to Vizhnitz. In the course of conversation, the Rebbe asked Rabbi Yitzchak Dovid to disregard what he had heard previously and to keep his position. However, the *shochet* demurred, saying, "I do not want to end up as a raven perched on the Rebbe's rooftop!" (*Kedosh Yisrael*, chap. 19, p. 332).

Fixing Souls

Once Rabbi Mordechai of Nadvorna and his disciples were discussing some scholarly matter in the study hall, when suddenly the holy rabbi heard through the window the sound of music. Reb Mordcheleh looked out the window to see a troupe of gypsies leading a dancing bear by a leash. In those days, it was customary for gypsy entertainers to travel from town to town.

No sooner did the tzaddik spy the bear, than he rushed out, telling the Chassidim he must purchase it, no matter the cost. He then entered into negotiations with the leader of the gypsies to buy his bear. The gypsy, a shrewd bargainer, smelled a good deal. "I can't possibly sell the bear which is the source of my livelihood." The price went up. Yet the Nadvorner was insistent on buying the bear. As his own funds were limited, he now turned to the Chassidim to contribute to the purchase of the bear. The Chassidim hadn't a clue why their beloved master should need a dancing bear, but a true Chassid doesn't question the ways of the tzaddik. Finally, the fee, an exorbitant sum, was paid to the gypsy.

The Rebbe then led the bear by its chain back to his *beis midrash* (study hall). Reb Mordcheleh stood with the bear in the middle of the hall, looked the bear straight in the eyes, and spoke these words: *"Schoen, genug getanzt!"* "Danced enough already!" Immediately, the bear dropped dead on the floor of the *beis midrash*. The Chassidim stared in amazement. Reb Mordcheleh was renowned as a miracle worker, but this was too much!

Before they had time to recover from their shock, Reb Mordcheleh commanded his faithful followers to perform a *taharah*, a ritual purification, on the dead bear. The Chassidim somehow managed to drag the hulk to the ritual bath next door for immersion in the cleansing waters. When they finished the *taharah*, Reb Mordcheleh demanded the bear be given a proper funeral, culminating in burial next to the ritual bath. From beginning to end, the Chassidim had not the slightest clue what was going on in their beloved Rebbe's mind, but they knew the thoughts of the righteous are loftier than those of average men.

Sometime, maybe days, maybe weeks later, Reb Mordcheleh revealed to them what it was all about. There once lived a very pious Jew who observed all six hundred and thirteen commandments, with the exception of one: It seems he was a great scholar and deemed it beneath his dignity to dance at weddings in order to gladden the hearts of bride and groom. When he died, his soul was summoned before the heavenly court for judgment. It was decreed that since he failed to keep this supremely important commandment, his punishment would be to reincarnate as a performing bear and dance his whole life in town after town.

"I recognized him as soon as I saw him. When I pronounced those words 'Danced enough already!' that was the *tikkun* of that poor soul. Having served its sentence and expiated its sin, the soul was thence liberated from within the body of the bear" (Rabbi Bezalel Naor, *Kabbalah and the Holocaust* [Spring Valley, NY: Orot, Inc. 2001], pp. 31-33).

The Man Who Liked to Fast

Once there was a pious man who fasted all week long. However, since he did partake of the Sabbath meals, he experienced stomach cramps. Therefore, he decided that he would fast on the Sabbath, as well, if the local rabbis would allow him to do so. Before inquiring about fasting on the Sabbath, he dreamed that two men were serving him platters of food. One served fruits, while the other served vegetables. They said to him, "Arise and eat!" But he did not wish to eat; for it seemed to him that he was still fasting. The two men urged him adamantly, but he refused to eat for any reason. At last, the men became angry with him. One told the other, "Come, let us take away the platters. This fellow has no desire for the Resurrection of the Dead!"

Upon awakening, the man became panic stricken because of his dream, fearing that he would not arise with the Resurrection of the Dead. Since he did not want anyone to know about his fasts, he sent a messenger [to the Kabbalist, Rabbi Yehudah Ftayah, 1859-1942], inquiring as to the meaning of his dream.

[Rabbi Yehudah] told the questioner, "Many human souls are reincarnated in water and salt, bread and fruit, as well as meat, fish, and fowl. When a person recites a blessing over them before eating, he performs a *tikkun* for the captive soul, which now can go on to Gehenna [where the soul is purified, before ascending to the supernal Garden of Eden.] However, if he does not recite a blessing over them, and eats without a blessing, this causes great anguish to the soul, because it did not merit receiving its *tikkun*. Therefore, when this man who ate those fruits without reciting a blessing departs from the world, his soul is compelled to be reincarnated in food. The Creator causes the food that bears his soul to be consumed by someone who does not recite a blessing, so that he, too, forfeits his *tikkun*. For the Holy one, blessed be He, metes out to a person what he deserves according to his own actions, 'measure for measure.'

"This is the mystical meaning of the verse, 'Not by bread alone does a man live...' (Deuteronomy 8:3). A soul awaiting *tikkun* is reincarnated in the bread. This 'man' does not live — does not receive his *tikkun* — 'by bread alone,' if no blessing is recited before the bread is eaten. Rather, 'according to whatever proceeds from the mouth of God,' that is, through the blessing a person recites, 'shall a man live,' whose soul was reincarnated in that bread.

"The pious man who had the dream fasted throughout the week, although not in order to atone for any sins known to him. As a consequence, many holy sparks and many souls reincarnated in the food remained without a *tikkun*. Thus, from Heaven they let him know that he did not need to fast any more, but should resume eating in order to 'resurrect the dead' who have been reincarnated in food. Since he was unwilling to eat, they accused him of not wishing to have a share in the Resurrection of the Dead. However, they did not actually say that he would not arise with the Resurrection of the Dead.

"Thus, we may interpret the verse: 'He loved the curse, so it has come upon him; he desired not blessing, so it has stayed far from him' (Psalms 109:17). The verse speaks of an evil person, who eats without reciting blessings. He harms himself, as well as the souls in the food, for 'he desired not blessing.' What does the Holy One, blessed be He, do? He prepares food for him that does not contain any reincarnated souls. For the souls prayed and wept before Him that they not be designated for consumption by this man, who would damage them even more. Therefore, the verse concludes, 'He desired not blessing, so it has stayed far from him' " (Rabbi Yehudah Ftayah, *Minchas Yehudah, Mikeitz*, p. 68).

Sources: Chapter 6

Vegetarian Foods and Spiritual Transformation

This world is made up of four levels: the mineral level; the vegetative level; the animal level; and the level of human beings endowed with the power of speech. However, the main element that binds them together is the vegetative level. For on the one hand, vegetation grows from the earth, which represents the mineral level; and on the other, vegetation sustains the vital souls of the animals and humans who consume it.

All creatures primarily receive their vitality through vegetation. Indeed, the main food of human beings is bread, "by which man lives" (Deuteronomy 8:3). Other foods do not satisfy us to the same degree. That is why we do not recite the Grace After Meals on anything but bread. Thus, vegetation causes a certain bond between humans and animals, both of which eat plants. [Eating vegetarian foods] also strengthens the bond between the soul and the body, the "human" and "animal" aspects of a person. Therefore, when one eats the "bread of the earth" in a spirit of holiness, the body becomes subdued by the soul and incorporated within it; then implicitly all four levels that comprise the body become assimilated to the soul.

The souls hidden within vegetation are even more precious and lofty than those hidden within the animal realm. [This is suggested by the Torah's metaphor that] "man is a tree of the field" (Deuteronomy 20:19) [i.e., there is an intimate connection between vegetation and human beings]. Thus, vegetation can spiritually ascend and bring together a person's animal soul and human soul, because it gives life to both.

This is the mystery of the Tree of Knowledge of Good and Evil [described in the Book of Genesis. The potential for good or evil is specifically] associated with the vegetative realm. Sometimes through eating fruits and vegetables, a person's human aspect can be strengthened and gain ascendance over his animal aspect. Extremely lofty souls are hidden within vegetation [that can cleave to the soul of a living person for his or her benefit.] However, the opposite also may take place [i.e., a damaged soul can cleave to a living person to his detriment].

Therefore, transformation from one level of creation to the next is uniquely apparent in the case of vegetation. Everything that comes into existence is of a kind with its progenitors. Human beings give birth to human beings; and each animal gives birth to its own kind; whereas vegetation comes forth from [seeds planted in] the Earth, which is an entirely different level of creation, namely the mineral level. The relation between the mineral and the vegetative is like the animal relative to the human, or like the body relative to the soul. Yet vegetation sprouts forth from the Earth, and transmutes the life force concealed within the Earth to its own nature.

In this we see vividly that vegetation possesses the power to transmute the animal aspect to the human, the bodily aspect to the soul. For the body empowers the soul to "sprout forth" and accomplish the various forms of divine service [that pertain to this physical world]; and this specifically requires that the body be subdued and assimilated to the soul. Vegetation sprouts forth and grows because the power of the Earth has become incorporated in the vegetation and transformed to it. This is actually the transformation of the body into the soul [i.e., the lower, or external level in relation to the higher, or internal level].

That is why plants need rain to grow from the earth. Rain comes from the "sweetening" of divine judgment, to the extent that the *Gevuros* (forces of severity) turn to *Chassadim* (forces of kindness). This [transformation from one divine attribute to another] ultimately brings about the transformation of body to soul (Rabbi Nosson Sternhartz, *Likkutei Halachos, Yoreh De'ah, Chadash* 3:10).

All Animals are Destined to be Kosher

"God releases the bound" (Psalms 146:7). To what does this refer? According to one viewpoint: the Holy One, blessed be He, will purify in the Future World all animals that presently are not kosher. As it is written, "That which was, so it shall be" (Ecclesiastes 1:9). Just as all animals were kosher during the generation of Noah, so shall they be in the future. As the verse states, "Therefore, as the green herb, I have given you everything..." (Genesis 1:30). That is, just as I permitted every green herb [to Adam and Eve for food], so did I initially permit every animal and beast [to Noah]. Why did God subsequently forbid them [to Israel]? To see who would accept His words and who would reject them. In the Ultimate Future, He will release all that He has bound (*asar*). [The word *asar* ("bound") is the root of the word *asur* ("forbidden"). Thus, the Midrash sees this verse as alluding to a change in the status of animals presently deemed non-kosher.]

However, some say that they will not become kosher. This position is supported by the verse that states: "[Many will be slain by God...] those who eat the flesh of swine, animals that creep, and mice" (Isaiah 66:17) (*Midrash Shocher Tov, Tehillim* 146).

Physical and Spiritual Dangers of Eating Meat

Because they habitually stood [barefoot] on the stone floor [of the Temple], ate a great deal of meat, and wore but one garment while performing the sacrificial service, the Kohanim suffered from intestinal sicknesses. Therefore, a healer was appointed to attend them and treat their illnesses. He and his assistants were constantly occupied with this task (Maimonides, *Mishneh Torah, Hilchos Klei HaMikdash* 7:14).

CRLO

Mar Zutra the son of Rav Nachman said: The Torah teaches a rule of good conduct, in that a father should not accustom his son to eating meat and drinking wine (*Chullin* 84a).

CRLO

Do not be among those who guzzle wine, among those who gorge themselves on flesh (Proverbs 23:20).

Commentary: We are enjoined to "know God in all your ways." [Even our physical nature must be used in divine service.] However, one who consumes wine and meat to excess does not know the way of God (Rabbeinu Bachaya, Deuteronomy 21:18).

CRLO

In the killing of animals there is cruelty, rage, and habituation to the evil of shedding innocent blood. Moreover, the eating of certain animals produces emotional coarseness, physical ugliness, and intellectual weakness (Rabbi Yosef Albo, *Sefer HaIkkarim* 3:15).

෴

Even the tzaddikim suffer greatly from eating meat. They must contend with the powers of impurity that are present within the meat, and wish to dwell within the body of the tzaddik. Whenever the soul departs from the body, the forces of impurity rest there. In this respect, animals and humans are the same, and both require *shemirah* (guarding) from the powers of impurity. Thus the body of a deceased person requires *shemirah,* as does kosher meat[99] (*Sefer HaKanah, Sod Mi Mutar BaAchilas Basar,* p. 278).

෴

Only a Torah scholar who is God-fearing and eats with proper intent can rectify [the sparks of holiness within] the animals the Torah deems to be pure. Therefore, our sages state: "One who is ignorant of Torah is forbidden to eat meat" (*Pesachim* 49b). His soul, which possesses only a small measure of holiness, will become fused with the soul of the animal. Unable to rectify and remove the spiritual dross that it encounters, this small measure of holiness will then depart. From this one should understand how careful a person must be not to consume too much meat (Rabbi Chaim Vital citing his mentor, Rabbi Yitzchak Luria, *Sha'ar HaMitzvos, Eikev,* p.100).

෴

A person who has [reached such a lofty spiritual level that he has regained] the divine image [that Adam and Eve originally possessed] can attain greater heights of wisdom by eating animal foods. However, the

---

99. *Sefer HaKanah* gives a spiritual reason for the requirement of *shemirah* that also applies to kosher meat. However, on the practical level, the reasons are dissimilar: the dead must be guarded from rodents, whereas kosher meat must be guarded so that it will not be exchanged for non-kosher meat.

opposite is also true. [That is, one who has not attained this spiritual level may be further debased through animal foods.] (Rabbi Nachman of Breslov, *Sefer HaMidos, Achilah* II:1).

෴

The elevation of holy sparks is accomplished especially through eating meat, which comes from those species of animals that possess reincarnated souls and holy sparks. Therefore, one cannot engage in eating meat [as a spiritual task] without being attached to the tzaddikim, through whom we are empowered to bring about this elevation of holy sparks. Thus, our sages state that one who is ignorant of Torah is forbidden to eat meat (*Pesachim* 49b) — for "even one who studies Torah but does not serve a Torah sage is considered an ignoramus" (*Berachos* 47b). One who is not attached to the tzaddikim and true sages is forbidden to eat meat, because he lacks the power to elevate the souls and holy sparks contained therein (Rabbi Nosson Sternhartz, *Likkutei Halachos, Simonei Ohf Tahor*, 2).

෴

The Torah definition of a formal meal is one at which bread is eaten. Therefore, ten commandments are associated with bread in order to sanctify the act of eating. However, one must be even more careful when eating meat. Our sages comment that the Israelites [during their wanderings in the wilderness] asked for bread respectfully; therefore, it was given to them with respect (*Yoma* 75a). As the verse states, "In the morning you shall be satisfied with bread" (Exodus 16:12). The eating of bread is associated with the light of day, which symbolizes intellect and wisdom. However, their manner of asking for meat was disrespectful; therefore, it was given to them disrespectfully. As the verse states, "In the evening you shall eat flesh..." (ibid. 16:18). Thus, one must be particularly careful about eating meat, for its potential for spiritual harm is far greater than other foods[100] (Rabbi Nachman Goldstein of Tcherin, *Nachas HaShulchan, Hilchos Shechitah*, 1).

---

100. Similarly, cf. R. Pinchas of Koretz, *Midrash Pinchas* 6:62.

☙⚬❧

The form of eating with the greatest potential for spiritual harm is the consumption of meat. Therefore, kosher meat requires supervision; meat that lacks such supervision is forbidden. We are afraid the kosher meat may have been switched with non-kosher meat. [Understood in the mystical sense,] this alludes to the possibility that through the Chamber of Exchanges,[101] the Other Side may harm the person who eats meat without proper mindfulness (Rabbi Nachman Goldstein of Tcherin, ibid. 63).

☙⚬❧

"When the Lord God will expand your border... and you will say, 'I will eat meat...' because your soul desires to eat meat...￿" (Deuteronomy 12:20). This means that if one wishes to eat meat, he should pray for three things: 1) that by doing so he will accomplish a *tikkun*; 2) that his health should benefit thereby; and 3) that he should not mistakenly partake of forbidden food. Thus, the verse specifies, "And you will say..." For a person must pray beforehand about these three things (Rabbi Yitzchak of Vorka, *Beis Yitzchak*, *R'eh*, p. 92, citing *Nifla'os Chadashos*, *R'eh*, included in *Sefarim Kedoshim*, Vol. 4; also cf. *Ohel Yitzchak*, 219).

☙⚬❧

"However, according to all the desire of your soul you shall slaughter and eat flesh..." (Deuteronomy 12:15). That is, in order to eat meat one must not do so in a state of distraction — whether due to [a negative spiritual impression brought about by the thoughts of] the *shochet,* or due to one's circumstances. Rather, the desire of his entire being for God must be present (Rabbi Yitzchak of Vorka, ibid. p. 91, citing *Ohel Yitzchak*).

---

101. *Chayei Moharan* 61; *Likkutei Moharan* I: 24 (end), 245; *Likkutei Halachos, Birchas HaShachar* 3:2, et passim. Concerning the revolving sword of flame, see *Zohar* I, 221b. Concerning the staff of Moses, see *Zohar* II, 28a.

Animal Slaughter

"God is good to all, and His mercy is over all His Works" (Psalms 145:9). Since God is merciful, how could he command that animals be slaughtered for food? How does this reflect God's mercy? The key to this mystery is contained in the beginning of the verse: "God is good to all..." absolutely good. Therefore, the verse concludes, "His mercy is over all His works."

This is the explanation: In the beginning of creation, God asked each animal if it agreed to be slaughtered, and the animal replied, "It is good." What was the reason for this? The animal does not have a higher soul with which to grasp the deeds and might of God. Therefore, in the beginning of creation God assembled all the animals before Him and said to them: "Do you wish to be slaughtered and eaten by man, if by doing so you will ascend from the level of an ignorant beast to the level of a human being, who knows and recognizes God, may He be blessed?" The animals answered, "We accept — and His mercy will be upon us." For when man eats part of an animal, the animal becomes part of man. Thus, the rite of slaughter is an act of mercy, for it enables the animal to transcend its former level and to enter the human level. The subsequent death of the human is actually life for [the soul of] the animal, for now it ascends to the heights of the angels. This is the mystical meaning of the verse, "God saves man and animal" (Psalms 36:7). If so, contemplate the mystery of animal slaughter, and you will realize that it is an act of God's mercy and compassion for all His creatures (Rabbi Yosef Gikatilla, *Sha'arei Orah*, Gate 6).

ᏟᎦᏋᏁ

The reason for [the original prohibition of eating meat] was that even creatures lacking the human faculty of intellect possess a certain spiritual superiority. They have the power of choice concerning their welfare and their food, and they flee from pain and death. As the verse declares: "Who knows that the spirit of man is the one that ascends on high, while the spirit of the beast is the one that descends down into the earth?"[102]

---

102. Ecclesiastes 3:21.

When they sinned, and "all flesh had corrupted its way upon the earth,"[103] it was decreed that they die in the flood. However, God saved some of each species for Noah's sake, and He gave Noah's descendants permission to slaughter and eat them, since animals were meant to serve humankind. Nevertheless, God did not give human beings permission to consume the soul of an animal, but prohibited them from eating the limb of a living creature. In addition, He forbade [the Jewish people] to consume blood [even that of a slaughtered animal] because it is the basis of the soul; as it is written: "For the life of any creature — its blood is bound up with its life; so I have said to the Children of Israel: You shall not consume the blood of all flesh, for the life of all flesh is the blood thereof."[104] Thus He permitted eating the flesh of mute animals after death, but not the soul itself.

This, indeed, is the reason for the commandment of shechitah and for the axiom of the Talmudic sages: "The duty of relieving the suffering of animals is a biblical requirement."[105] Moreover, this is the meaning of the blessing that we recite before slaughtering animals: "Blessed are You, Eternal One, our God, King of the universe, Who has sanctified us with His commandments and commanded us concerning *shechitah*" (Nachmanides, *Commentary on the Torah*, Genesis 1:29).

ଔଞ୍ଚ

All of God's ways are just. Why did He command us to slaughter animals for our food? Would it not be better if we were to sustain ourselves from fruits and produce? Why should we shed the blood of animals and birds, causing them great suffering? Know that this is one of the mysteries of the universe. God is beneficent toward each creature and compassionate, as it is written: "God is good to all, and His mercy is upon all His works" (Psalms 145:9). This verse informs us that slaughtering animals for food is an expression of compassion and mercy toward them [in bringing about their spiritual ascent] (*Iggeres HaKodesh*, variously

---

103. Genesis 6:12.
104. Leviticus 17:14.
105. *Shabbos* 128b.

attributed to Nachmanides or his teacher, Rabbi Azriel of Gerona; cited by Rabbi Eliyahu de Vidas, *Reishis Chochmah, Sha'ar HaKedushah*, chap. 16).

ಈೂ

One should not uproot any plant unnecessarily, nor should one kill any animal without reason. [When one slaughters an animal,] one should be as merciful as possible, choosing for it a humane death with a knife that has been inspected for any defect (Rabbi Moshe Cordovero, *Tomer Devorah*, chapter 3).

ಈೂ

Every creature derives its food from the level beneath it. *Domem* (the mineral realm), the lowest existence, is self-sustaining. *Tzomei'ach* (vegetation) is nurtured by the earth. Every *baal chai* (animal) eats vegetation; and *adam* (man), the species endowed with speech, derives food from animals. When is this [morally justifiable]? When a human being is involved in Torah study, he actualizes his highest potential and earns the distinction of being called "man." Lacking this, he is comparable to an animal. As such, by what right may he consume his peer, and what spiritual improvement can he confer upon his peer by eating it? For all food is transformed to the nature of the one that derives sustenance; and man, when he eats animal foods, effects the spiritual elevation of the animal. Now it attains the level of the species endowed with speech. However, a human who is comparable to an animal, what can he give and how can he improve what he has eaten? (Rabbi Shlomo Ephraim Lunshitz, *Kli Yakar*, Genesis 9:2, s.v. *U'mora'achem v'chitchem*, p. 31).

ಈೂ

For the soul of the flesh is in the blood; and I have given it to you upon the altar to atone for your souls... (Leviticus 17:11).

Commentary: This verse also comes to warn us not to take the life of an animal. For God did not give us the life-blood of animals, other than to effect atonement for our souls. Thus, the verse states, "I have given it to you upon the altar..." to negate any reason but this. [The life of an animal] is not given to us in order to serve our every whim. That is why a Rabbinical Court of 23 judges must preside over a capital offense involving an animal, similar to a capital offense involving human beings.[106] As for *shechitah*, the Torah did not permit it except to serve legitimate human needs, "since the soul of man desires meat"; for thus did the Owner of the World concede in giving [the lives of animals] over to us (Rabbi Chaim ibn Attar, *Ohr HaChaim*, ad loc., abridged).

CRX

Rav Pinchas, Rav Levi, and Rav Yochanan said in the name of Rav Menachem of Gallia: In the Ultimate Future, all sacrifices will be abolished, with the exception of the thanksgiving offering (*korban todah*), which will never be abolished (Midrash: *Vayikra Rabbah* 27:12).

Commentary: Animals achieve *tikkun* by rising to be a sacrifice on the altar to God. Since they do not possess *da'as* (intellect), they are spiritually elevated only by the sacrifice of their blood and fat — the repository of their soul — to God. Man, on the other hand, comes closer to God through his intellect. However, in the future, the flow of intellect will spread and reach even the animals. "They will do no harm or damage in all My holy mountain: for the knowledge of God shall fill the Earth as the water covers the sea" (Isaiah 11:9). The sacrifice at that time will be the meal offering from the realm of vegetation, and it will be pleasing unto the Lord as in the days of old[107] (Rabbi Avraham Yitzchak Kook,

---

106. *Sanhedrin* 15a; *Bava Kamma* 41b-45a. Another legal parallel between animals and humans is the law that a hired animal has "rights" similar to those of a hired worker. The animal, too, is entitled to eat on time, and payment must be made to its owner in cash; see *Teshuvos HaChida*, III, no. 458:2.

107. The sin offering will be rendered obsolete, since the desire to sin will no longer exist, as stated in *Sukkah* 52a; also cf. R. Aharon of Zhelikhov citing the Baal Shem Tov, *Kesser Shem Tov* 81; R. Nachman of Breslov, *Sefer HaMiddos, Emes* I, 8. Therefore, the only private sacrifice still relevant will be the thanksgiving offering; see *Eitz Yosef* on *Vayikra Rabbah* 9:17; *Shnei Luchos HaBris, Beis David* 1, 37a. The thanksgiving offering consisted of 10 leavened breads, 10 small unleavened loaves, 10 small unleavened wafers, 10 small scalded loaves, and one sheep, goat, or cow less than three years old. R. Kook does not question the reinstitution of the sacrificial system. However, his view is unusual in rejecting the widely held assumption that during the Messianic era, as in ancient times, the thanksgiving offering will include an animal. R. Kook maintains that since animals, too, will attain a degree of enlightenment their sacrifice would be unwarranted.

Olat Rayah I, 292, s.v. *ve-arvah la-Hashem minchas Yehudah ve-Yerushalayim*).

Why We Eat Dairy Foods on Shavuos

The verse states: "When you bring a new meal-offering to God on your festival of Shavuos (Weeks)..." (Numbers 28:26). The initial letters of the Hebrew words "a meal offering to God" spell the word *chalav* (milk). This alludes to the custom of eating dairy foods on the festival of Shavuos mentioned in the *Sefer HaRoke'ach*. We see that it is beneficial to consume animal foods in order to elevate the holy sparks they possess to the human level. Yet if it would be sufficient to eat butter and milk, without having to slaughter a living creature, this would be far better. Thus did Adam conduct himself before the first sin. Afterwards, the human soul no longer possessed the requisite spiritual power to elevate the holy sparks by consuming dairy foods alone, without slaughtering the animal and spilling its blood — for this act accomplishes the release of the animal's soul. Otherwise, the holy sparks could not ascend. Although after the first sin, animal slaughter still was deemed to be wrong, it was permitted to Noah after the Flood. However, on the day of the Giving of the Torah, the Israelites regained the spiritual level of Adam before the first sin. Therefore, it was sufficient to consume dairy foods, without slaughtering animals, and the holy sparks were elevated through milk (Rabbi Moshe Sofer, *D'rashos Chasam Sofer*, Vol. II, *L'Shavuos*, 291a).

Benefits of Eating Meat

Rabbi Yannai said in the name of Rabbi [Yehudah HaNasi]: Compared to anything that possesses the quantity of an egg, an actual egg is superior [in food value].

When Rabin came [to Babylonia from the Land of Israel] he said: A lightly roasted egg is superior to six *kaysi*[108] of fine flour.

---

108. A *kaysi* is equivalent to a *log*, which contains the volume of six eggs. According to R. Avraham Chaim Na'eh, a *log* is equivalent to 12 fluid oz.

When Rav Dimi came, he said: a lightly roasted egg is superior to six [*kaysi*]; a hard-roasted egg is superior to four; and a boiled egg is superior to the same quantity of any other kind of boiled food except meat (Talmud: *Berachos* 44b, according to Rashi).

Ϡϡ

During the period in which the Holy Temple existed, there was no rejoicing without meat. However at present, when the Holy Temple does not exist, there is no rejoicing without wine, as it is written, "Wine gladdens the heart of man" (Psalms 104:15)[109] (Talmud: *Pesachim* 109a).

Ϡϡ

Rav Nachman was unable to respond to the challenge of another sage. The next day, however, he was able to do so. When asked what had happened in the interim he replied, "At first I could not solve the problem, because I had not eaten beef the previous evening" (Talmud: *Bava Kamma* 71b).

Ϡϡ

If a person is a perfect tzaddik, all animals will fear him; as the verse states: "Fear and dread of you will be upon all the animals of the earth..." (Genesis 9:2). All creatures were brought into being to serve man, who was created in the Supernal Image. Therefore, it befits him to rule over all, and he is permitted to consume the flesh of animals (*Ma'areches Elokus*, attributed to Rabbi Peretz ben Yitzchak HaKohen, Chapter 9, cited in Rabbi Bezalel Naor's *Ben Shanah Shaul*, p. 291).

---

109. Similarly, note Ritva on *Kiddushin* 3b; *Teshuvos Rashbash* 176, etc. However, Rambam does advocate the consumption of meat as an expression of rejoicing on Yom Tov even today (*Sefer HaMitzvos*, Positive Mitzvah 54; *Mishneh Torah, Yom Tov* 6:18). This is also the ruling of *Tur Shulchan Aruch, Orach Chaim* 529. This view is rejected by the *Beis Yosef, Orach Chaim* 529; *Magen Avraham, Orach Chaim* 696:15, although the latter reverses his position in *Orach Chaim* 529:3 and 249:6; *Shnei Luchos HaBris*, as cited in *Pischei Teshuvah, Yoreh De'ah* 18:9, et al. The *Bach* on *Orach Chaim* 529 takes an intermediate stance, concurring that the consumption of meat on Yom Tov is not obligatory in these times, but may be considered a mitzvah if one does so for the sake of rejoicing on the holiday; see R. Bleich, "Meat on Yom Tov," in *Contemporary Halakhic Problems*, Vol. III.

೮ƺ೩೦

When one eats fat beef or drinks spiced wine in order to expand his consciousness for the sake of God and His Torah, or in order to fulfill the precept of delighting on the Sabbath and Festivals, the vital force within the meat and wine that had been under the influence of the realm of impurity (*klippas nogah*) is spiritually refined and ascends to God like a sacrificial offering (Rabbi Shneur Zalman of Liadi, *Likkutei Amarim — Tanya*, chapter 7).

೮ƺ೩೦

At first, Chassidic master Rabbi Levi Yitzchak of Berditchev (1740-1809) abstained from eating any kind of meat, including fowl, even on the Sabbath. However, Rabbi Chaim of Krasna [a prominent disciple of the Baal Shem Tov] entered into debate with him about this, arguing, "If you are right, for whom were these foods created? Do you think that only gentiles should be permitted to eat them?" From thenceforth, the Rav of Berditchev consented to eat fowl, even on weekdays (*Toldos Yitzchak, Zichron Tov* 5:1, as cited in *Inyanei Shabbos V'Rosh Chodesh MiToras Kedushas Levi*, p. 41).

೮ƺ೩೦

Just as there is nothing wrong in an animal eating vegetation, for the latter benefits thereby in being transformed into the body of the animal, so there is nothing wrong if a human consumes the flesh of an animal, for thus [the animal] is elevated to become part of the human body (Rabbi Meir Leibush Malbim on Genesis 9:3).

೮ƺ೩೦

God permitted humans to slaughter animals for meat only after the Flood, because reincarnation as animals only began at that time. This is why the Gemara states: "An *am ha'aretz* is forbidden to eat meat" (*Pesachim* 49b). One who devotes himself entirely to earthly pursuits and not to the service of God, who eats only to satisfy his appetite, and renders himself spiritually unfit to elevate reincarnated souls — it is enough for him to consume the Earth's produce. The descendants of

Noah were given permission to eat meat only for the sake of *tikkun* (Rabbi Moshe of Ujhely, *Yismach Moshe, Noach*, s.v. *V'nachzor l'inyaneinu*, citing *Asarah Ma'amaros, Ma'amar Chikkur Din*, II, chap. 17).

Meat-Eating and Physical Desire

In the evening, fire came forth from God, and the Mixed Multitude in their midst lusted after desire, and again the Children of Israel also wept, and they said, "Who will give us flesh to eat?" (Numbers 11:4).

Commentary: A few verses later, the Torah states: "They wept by their families..." (ibid. 11:10), upon which Rashi comments, "Concerning family matters, i.e., forbidden relations" (ad loc.).

Why are these verses juxtaposed? We may answer based upon the teaching of our sages that when one is faced with an opportunity to transgress but refrains from doing so out of reverence for God, he fulfills a negative mitzvah.[110] Lacking such an opportunity, one cannot fulfill the negative mitzvah. [This was the case with the Jewish people at that moment in history.] Indeed, through eating the manna, the food of the ministering angels, they were purified to such a great extent that they no longer had physical desires. For physical desire comes from food, as the *Zohar* states: "When one eats flesh, his own flesh derives pleasure. The bodily aspect is strengthened, and because of this pleasure one commits many sins."[111]

Therefore, "they lusted after desire..." meaning that if they would experience such a desire and nevertheless restrain themselves from sexual immorality out of respect for God, they would fulfill a negative commandment. This would not be the case if they had no desires at all. They would be unable to fulfill the negative commandment.

This is the meaning of: "The nation was weeping by their families..." concerning forbidden relations. Now that they were free of all physical desires, they could no longer fulfill these negative commandments. Therefore, "they lusted after desire." How could this be accomplished?

---

110. *Makkos* 23b; note Bartinuro on the Mishnah, ibid. 3:15.
111. *Zohar* I (*Sisrei Torah*), 89b.

[Through eating.] So they asked, "Who will give us meat?" By eating meat they again would fall prey to such desires. Then they would refrain from transgression out of reverence for God, and thereby fulfill a negative mitzvah (Rabbi Yitzchak Isaac of Spinka, *Chakal Yitzchak, B'ha'alosecha*, s.v. *V'ha'asafsuf asher b'kirbo*, 132a, b, abridged).

Vegetarianism as an Ascetic Practice

"One who is ignorant of Torah is forbidden to eat meat" (*Pesachim* 49b). The first and lowest category of humanity consists of the ignorant and unenlightened. It is improper for a human being on this level to eat meat, for a person lacking divine wisdom is akin to an animal, and it is forbidden for beings on the same level in the hierarchy of creation to consume one another.

The second category of humanity consists of those who are in touch with the higher soul, but have not fully actualized their spiritual potential. They have not overcome their material aspect and remain bound to physicality. This is the category of people who were permitted to eat meat during the generation of Noah [and thereafter]. Since their physical and spiritual aspects were commingled, they occupied a level higher than animals; therefore, this was conceded to them.

However, the third category consists of "those who have attained the spiritual heights, and they are few" (*Sukkah* 45b); for they have separated the physical and spiritual aspects, enabling them to internalize the higher intellect. Concerning one on this level, it has been taught, "If he lives, he will die; but if he dies, he will live" (*Yalkut Shimoni, Bereishis* 14). [That is, these two components of mortal man are inherently contradictory.] For him, subjecting the spiritual aspect to an excess of the physical could lead to death — and the converse is also true.

These people have reached the level our sages compared to "two tables" (*Berachos* 5a). That is, they have separated the soul from the physical aspect and can sustain each in an appropriate manner. The physical aspect, now that it has been subordinated to the soul, can be sustained by a simple vegetarian diet. Vegetation is permitted because it occupies a lower level than the bodily aspect; meat should not be eaten because it occupies the same level. The intellect, having achieved self-actualization, has no need for sustenance from physical things [but hungers only for Torah wisdom].

Thus, from time immemorial, men of spiritual attainments, possessed of divine wisdom and removed from worldly desires, having separated the intellect from the physical, removed themselves from society to dwell in the deserts and forests, far from the rest of humankind, in order to attain spiritual perfection. They refrained from consuming the flesh of animals, but sustained the body with grains, fruits, and vegetables. Heeding God's benevolent instruction to all mankind at the beginning of creation to eat only vegetarian foods, they sought to extricate the intellect from the physical and free themselves from inner conflict. Thus, the wise [King Solomon] said, "Better a morsel of bread eaten in peace than a feast in a house full of strife" (Proverbs 17:1). According to this teaching, bread and all that belongs in this category — grains, fruits, and vegetables that comprise the level below the animal realm — are the foods that a spiritually refined person should eat. For him, the consumption of meat is a "feast of strife" [because meat feeds intellect and body in a way that disturbs a person in the third category, leading to "strife" between his spiritual and physical aspects. All the spiritually refined person requires is the simple sustenance that comes from the vegetative level.]

The holy sages Rabbi Shimon Bar Yochai and Rabbi Elazar, his son, heeded this benevolent instruction when for thirteen years [during the Roman persecutions] they hid in a cave and sustained themselves with spring water and carobs (*Shabbos* 33b). Similarly, [the Talmudic saint] Chanina ben Dosa subsisted on as little as a *kav* (approximately 1.5 quarts) of carobs from one Sabbath to the next (*Taanis* 24a). Many other cases attest to the truth of our words.

The "second table," from which the perfected intellect derives sustenance, consists of the thoughts upon which one meditates while eating, and worthy actions made possible by the energy derived from physical food. The righteous acts of the tzaddik serve as food for his soul.

The prophet alludes to this in the verse: "Say of the righteous, that it shall be good; for they shall eat the fruit of their accomplishments" (Isaiah 3:10). The meaning is allegorical, as in the verse: "For you shall eat the fruit of your labors" (Psalms 128:2). That is, the efforts you make while traveling the divine path will constitute the most appropriate sustenance for the intellect, by which it will endure forever in the World to Come.

When a person sustains his soul through his spiritual labor [i.e., in both thought and action] his body benefits, as well. This is implied by our sages' praise of one who earns his livelihood by the work of his hands: "You will be fortunate in this world, and it will be good for you in the World to Come" (*Berachos* 8a). One's need for food will be minimal. Therefore, he will be "fortunate in this world," in that he will not be driven by the compulsion to acquire costly foods and delicacies, nor will he be forced to rely upon others to obtain them; and it will be "good for [him] in the World to Come," since he will be sustained by the "work of his hands" [which is his spiritual labor] (Rabbi Yitzchak Arama, *Akeidas Yitzchak, Beshalach,* Gate 41, abridged).

ᑕᔓᓍ

In addition to the knowledge of the Written and the Oral Law which the students of Rabbi Nosson Adler (1742-1800) acquired from their teacher, they inherited his devotion to the Kabbalah and the philosophy of abstinence which marks followers of this way of life...[112] Seckel Loeb [later known as the Baal Shem of Michelstadt] in his eighteenth year made a vow to abstain from eating anything derived from a living thing. This decision included not only meat and fish, but also eggs, butter, and milk. This abstinence was based, without a doubt, on assumptions taken from the Kabbalah (Rabbi Naftali Herman, *The Baal Shem of Michelstadt,* trans. M. Kuttner [Jerusalem: Feldheim, 1973], chapter 3).

---

112. This asceticism influenced the school of the Chasam Sofer, who also was a disciple of the Kabbalist R. Nosson Adler. It is said that the Chasam Sofer's disciple, Maharam Schick, abstained completely from red meat (*Darkei Moshe HeChadash*, 35). During his last years, R. Yehoshua Heschel HaKohen, Rav of Kapish and Bilgoray, and a disciple of Maharam Schick, did not eat red meat but only fowl, even on the Sabbath and Festivals (*Zichron Yehoshua, Erech Se'udah*, 10). Maharam Asch restricted his consumption of red meat and wine (*Devar Yom B'Yomo*, 52).

CRRO

The only reason a person may be punished with the Purgatory of the Grave is because he rejoices at an improper time — and "there is no joy without meat and wine" (*Pesachim* 109a). All days on which one performs *nefilas apayim* (the rite of covering one's face during the prayers of supplication) are not days of joy. Therefore, it is forbidden to eat meat or to drink wine on them.

The verse states, "Your new moons and festivals My soul despises" (Isaiah 1:14). This alludes to the pleasure that one derives on occasions when it is forbidden to rejoice. [Thus the verse may be rendered,] "The festivals you have made for yourselves My soul despises." However, days on which work is proscribed (i.e., the Sabbath and Festivals) or when the rite of *nefilas apayim* is omitted are considered days of joy. Then it is permitted to rejoice and to consume meat and wine (Rabbi Avraham Azulai, *Chesed L'Avraham, Nahar 6: The Mystery of the Purgatory of the Grave*).

CRRO

Rabbi Nachman of Breslov instructed a number of disciples to abstain from eating animal products for twenty-four hours once a week (*Sichos HaRan* 185). For a certain period of time, he instructed his foremost disciple, Rabbi Nosson Sternhartz, to study eighteen chapters of the Mishnah every day, to remain awake for two days and one night every week, and to refrain from consuming all animal products from one Sabbath to the next (*Siach Sarfei Kodesh* I, 625, citing *Avaneha Barzel*).

CRRO

Rabbi Nachman of Breslov instructed his followers to fast until the late afternoon one day each week during the six to eight week period known as *Shovevim*, when the biblical account of the Egyptian exile and redemption is read in the synagogue on the Sabbath. According to the Kabbalists, this period is conducive for each man to make amends for his share in Adam's sin of separating from his wife after the exile from the Garden of Eden.[113] In more recent times, some Breslov Chassidim have taken upon themselves the custom of refraining from any food product derived from animals for a twenty-four hour period or, more commonly, from dawn until nightfall each week during the *Shovevim* period (*Siach Sarfei Kodesh* IV, 204; Breslov oral tradition).

❧❧❧

One who is capable of sanctifying himself before His Maker should eat meat only on the Sabbath and Festivals, or on days when the supplicatory prayers (*tachanunim*) are not recited (Rabbi Eliezer Papo, *Peleh Yo'etz, Inyan Basar*).

❧❧❧

While Reb Shmuel of Lubavitch (1834-1882) was on a visit to St. Petersburg for some communal matter, one of his Chassidim came to him with a complaint: "Rebbe, in this city it is hard to come by meat that is really strictly kosher."

"And who says that one has to eat meat altogether?" asked the Rebbe. "Have not the sages of the Talmud taught us that 'an ignoramus is forbidden (*asur*) to eat meat'? Now this word *asur* at its root means *bound*. That is to say, an ignoramus feels *bound* to eat meat... One can survive without such meat that one lusts to eat." (Rabbi Shlomo Yosef Zevin, *A Treasury of Chassidic Tales on the Torah*, Vol. II, *Re'eh*, trans. Uri Kaploun [New York: Artscroll / Mesorah Publications, Ltd., 1980]).

❧❧❧

The way of Torah is to content oneself with few luxuries (*Avos* 6:4), in order to refrain from compounding the tendency toward materialism. However, a common person, one who does not engage in Torah study, surely should exercise even greater restraint in eating or drinking. As our sages state, "An *am ha'aretz* is forbidden to eat meat" (*Pesachim* 49b). Meat is associated with feasting, an indulgence for

---

113. The Kabbalists explain that the soul of Adam included all human souls, and all human souls represent a "spark" of Adam's soul. Therefore, all humankind must engage in repairing the spiritual damage produced by Adam's sin. Israel in particular accomplishes this through performing the 613 commandments and through *teshuvah* (penitence). Regarding *Shovevim*, see R. Alexander Ziskind, *Yesod V'Shoresh HaAvodah*, 12:2, citing the Ari z"l. He also mentions that some individuals refrain from eating any animal products for the entire period of *Shovevim*.

which a person has no need at all. Thus, when the Torah states. ["And when in the evening God will give you] meat to eat..." (Exodus 17:8), Rashi explains, "However, not to satiety. The Torah teaches proper conduct, that one should not eat meat to the point of satiety" (ad loc.).

An *am ha'aretz* is not what the world thinks: an utter boor who knows nothing of Torah. Rather, the term refers to those who expend all their powers of intellection on worldly affairs, preferring not to engage in Torah study. Thus, our sages homiletically explain: "It is written, 'These are the sons of Seir the Horite, the inhabitants of the earth' (Genesis 36:20). Does the rest of humankind dwell in heaven? Rather, this means that they were well versed in cultivating the earth" (*Shabbos* 85a). An *am ha'aretz* [who similarly devotes all his energies to earthly matters] is forbidden to eat meat; that is, he must limit his eating of all delicacies as much as possible (Rabbi Yosef Yitzchak Schneersohn of Lubavitch, *Igros Kodesh Maharyatz,* Vol. 2, p. 545, letter dated 7 Elul 5693-1933, s.v. *K'mevu'ar l'eil,* abridged).

ᏅᎯᎣ

Among the martyrs of the Warsaw Ghetto was the saintly Lubavitcher Chassid known as *Reb Itcheh Der Masmid* (Rabbi Yitzchak HaLevi Horowitz, the "Dilligent Torah Scholar," d. 1941). Reb Itcheh was an ascetic to a degree that was unusual in recent generations. However, many of his Chassidic peers also were careful neither to eat to excess, nor to indulge in delicacies. In the jargon of such circles, one who abandoned the life of Torah study and divine service in order to pursue physical comforts was said to be *essen kotletten* — "eating fried cultlets" — even when his standard of living was quite meager.

Once Reb Itcheh was sent to America on a communal matter as a representative of Rabbi Yosef Yitzchak of Lubavitch (1880-1950). In one of his letters, Reb Itcheh reports back to his Rebbe about what he has observed. "Our brothers in America," the great ascetic exclaims in wonder, "are *essen kotletten b'poel mamash, Rachmana litzlan* — actually eating fried cutlets, may the Merciful One protect us!" (Oral Tradition, Chassidei Chabad).

Prerequisites for Studying the Kabbalah

If your soul wishes to enter the chambers of this wisdom, you must resolve to practice and fulfill whatever I am about to write; and the Creator will bear witness that no harm will befall you in body, soul, or possessions, nor will harm befall anyone else as a result of your virtuous quest. When "one comes to attain purity" (*Shabbos* 104a) and wishes to approach [the mysteries of the Kabbalah], the first requirement is to fear God — which means to fear divine retribution. For the inner essence of fear, which is awe before God's greatness, only can be experienced through the attainment of enlightenment.

The main purpose of this instruction is "to remove the thorns from the orchard" [by refining the soul]. This is why those who devote themselves to this wisdom are called "reapers of the field (*m'chatzdei chaklah*)." To be sure, the *klippos* will arouse themselves against you, to entice you, and lead you to sin. Therefore, you must guard yourself against transgressing the Torah's laws, even inadvertently, so that [the *klippos*] should have no connection to you. Be careful not to engage in any unseemly behavior, for the Holy One, blessed be He, is exacting with the tzaddikim to a hair's breadth. Therefore, you should abstain from meat and wine throughout the days of the week [except during the celebration of a *se'udas mitzvah*, a religious feast].[114] Strive to "turn from evil, and perform good" (Psalms 34:15), and seek peace by pursuing peace. Never become irritable about any matter, however great or small, even with members of your own household; and all the more so, never become angry, but distance yourself from anger to the utmost degree (Rabbi Chaim Vital, Introduction to *Sefer Eitz Chaim* of the Ari, s.v. *Ode hakdama ... Ani hakoseiv...*).

---

114. Chassidic master R. Zvi Hirsch of Ziditchov states that this does not apply to a weak person whose ability to concentrate on his Torah studies will be negatively affected by such abstinence. However, one who can fulfill R. Chaim Vital's instructions should do so (*Sur MeRah V'Asei Tov, Prishus HaAchilah*, p. 24, n. 36).

Advice From Rav Yosef Karo's Angelic Teacher[115]

Desist from eating more than a minimum of meat, even on the Sabbath, for this weakens the soul and harms her. Similarly, you do not know how much spiritual damage drinking wine indulgently brings about. Therefore, withhold your feet from these paths and deny your soul these pleasures. Exercise the greatest vigilance in such matters.

The masses take this world at face value. They neither look, nor see, but eat and drink to the satisfaction of their Evil Inclination. Woe unto them, that the world fools them — for a hand writes Above, and afterward their deeds will be investigated and punished. Thus, it is written: "What shall you do on the day of reckoning?" (Isaiah 10:3). Fortunate are you, in that you have been warned. Cause your loved ones to listen, as well, that they may awaken from their spiritual sleep (*Maggid Meisharim, Azharos V'Tikkunim U'Siyagim*, 6, 18, combined).

Sdei Chemed on Vegetarianism

On the subject of eating meat nowadays, our master [R. Chaim Benveniste] in his *Knesses HaGedolah* (*Yoreh De'ah* 28) citing the Rashal, states that we may rely upon the Ri and the Ran, and eat meat for the sake of bodily nourishment, and not afflict ourselves at all. However, the Chida [R. Chaim Yosef David Azulai] in his *Chaim Sha'al*, 43:6, states: "It all depends upon the nature of the individual. If one can afflict oneself in order to atone for one's sins—for 'there is no person free from sin'—that is well and good." As for ourselves, what can we say to this, in such an orphaned generation when the number of our sins is beyond calculation and our plight is almost unbearable, may God forgive us.

This view is shared by [R. Raphael Pinchas Yehoshua DeSegura] in *Os Hi L'Olam*, 63c. Here we find support and justification from a well-known

---

115. R. Yosef Karo (1488-1575), author of *Beis Yosef* on the *Arba'ah Turim*, as well as the *Shulchan Aruch* (Code of Jewish Law), was one of the greatest halachic authorities of all time. He was also a profound mystic who was visited by an angelic teacher known as a Maggid ("speaker"). R. Karo would go into a trance, and speaking through his mouth, the Maggid would instruct him in both halachic and Kabbalistic wisdom. These teachings subsequently were published as *Maggid Meisharim*.

sage, may the Merciful One protect and sustain him, who for many years abstained completely from eating meat. Heaven forefend that anyone disparage him; happy will be his lot. He abstained even from wine, except when performing a religious precept (e.g., *Kiddush, Havdalah,* or the Four Cups of the Passover Seder meal).

It has been said that all of a person's labor is for the sake of food; therefore, gluttony often leads to transgression. We have already cited the words of the Ari [R. Yitzchak Luria], "Happy is the person who is able to abstain from meat and wine all week long." Also note [R. Yehudah Tiktin] in *Ba'er Heitiv* on *Orach Chaim* 134:1, sec. 3: "There is an accepted practice not to eat meat or drink wine on Monday and Thursday, since the Heavenly Court is then sitting in judgment... Happy is the person who is able to refrain from meat and wine the entire week." Also see *Yakhel Shlomo* on *Orach Chaim* 529:2.

It is true that [the Talmud states] that on the Sabbath one dines on meat and wine. However, that is a person's right, not his obligation. Our sages taught, "One should eat on the Sabbath just as on a weekday [in order to avoid taking charity]" (*Shabbos* 118a). [Therefore, the consumption of meat cannot be construed as obligatory.] This is also the ruling of [Rabbi Moshe Isserles] in *Darkei Moshe* on *Yoreh De'ah* 341.

In *Reishis Chochmah* [the classic introduction to the Kabbalah by R. Eliyahu de Vidas] (129b) there is a lengthy discussion that concludes that one should not consume the flesh of any living creature. And [R. Eliyahu HaKohen of Izmir] in *Shevet Mussar*, 192a, states that meat is only permitted to a perfectly righteous person. However, all this only pertains to the devout, and a common person is not actually forbidden to eat meat. Nevertheless, we have learned that it is correct to refrain from doing so if one is able to endure privation. Such an individual is considered mighty and holy. Also note *Kerem Shlomo* on *Yoreh De'ah* (chap. 1), which explains at length that there is no actual religious duty to consume meat and wine even on the Sabbath or Festivals.

I have recently seen the Kabbalistic work *Shiur Komah* by Rabbi Moshe Cordovero, and one of my students, who shall always remain dear to me, has shown me page 84c regarding the transmigration of the soul into the vital spirit of an animal. [There it states,] "Thus a conscientious person should avoid eating meat, as it is possible that the soul of a wicked person may cleave to him — sometimes hastening his death."

The editor adds: "In the light of this, one should never eat meat unless the divine mysteries have been revealed to him, and he knows that it does not contain the reincarnated soul of a transgressor. Similarly the Ari in *Sha'ar HaMitzvos,* in the Torah portion *Eikev,* cautions us not to eat much meat for this reason. He adds that certainly one must never consume the heart of any animal, beast, or bird, as therein dwells the life force" (Rabbi Chaim Chizkiyahu Medini, *S'dei Chemed,* Vol. 5, *Inyan Achilah*).

Reb Ahreleh Roth On Meat Eating

What can one say about the matter of *shochtim* (kosher slaughterers), since today so many people lack sincere religious commitment, due to our many sins? Woe unto us, for that which our eyes see and we are powerless to protest. Our hearts are so blocked that we cannot speak. Indeed, the prediction of our sages has been fulfilled in us: "There is no reproof..." (*Sotah* 49b).[116] One who guards his soul should flee from the place of such *shochtim.* Would that we possessed the strength to abstain from the consumption of meat altogether — but what can we do in our weakness?

Even worse is the problem of our butchers. There are so many religiously lax individuals in this profession, who are suspected of causing others to consume non-kosher meat. For the smallest profit, they buy and sell whatever forbidden foods they come across, may the Merciful One protect us! This is especially true in establishments where there is no kosher supervision. Unfortunately the butchers neglect to properly perform the excision of forbidden fats and tendons, because of the widespread lack of fear of Heaven and lack of kosher supervision, especially in smaller communities. Thus, forbidden tendons frequently

---

116. Citing R. Pinchas ben Ya'ir, the Talmud (ad loc.) speaks of the grievous spiritual decline prior to the advent of the Messiah.

are left in the meat. Fortunate are those God-fearing individuals who are abstemious and limit their consumption of flesh to that of fowl, thus sparing themselves numerous halachic uncertainties.

We do not mean to cast aspersions on everyone, for "the Children of Israel are holy," and God forbid that we denounce the majority. I address my remarks only to that minority of cases where proper and God-fearing supervisors are absent. For the sake of whoever wishes to sanctify himself before the Creator I have sought the counsel of God-fearing *shochtim*, and their advice is to eat no meat but poultry. This is sound advice for anyone who wishes to guard his soul from error, particularly in our generation,[117] as those who are knowledgeable understand (Rabbi Aharon Roth, *Shulchan HaTahor, Maamar HaPrishus MiMaachalos HaAsuros*, 1, 197b).

The Lesson of the Manna

When God provided the Israelites in the desert with Manna, He gave them the opportunity to sit at "two tables":[118] the "first table," in that the Manna sustained their physical powers without producing within them any spiritual discord; the "second table," in that the Manna made it possible for them to acquire the precious Torah teachings that are the unique "food" of the higher intellect. However, meat was not served on the "King's table" except subsequently, as a temporary measure.

And it happened that in the evening the quail ascended and covered the camp; and in the morning there was a layer of dew around the camp (ibid. 16:13). They were given the quail immediately prior to the Manna because they had complained that they desired meat. However, the quail was not given to them on a permanent basis, but only as a temporary measure. It was only meant to demonstrate that God had redeemed them

---

117. Standards in the kosher meat industry during the 1930s and 1940s of which Reb Ahreleh speaks varied greatly and were in many ways inferior to those of today. However, it would be foolish to assume that serious problems in this age of mass production no longer exist. Kosher supervision is by no means infallible, and especially in the slaughter of large animals, various halachic leniencies are widely used. Thus, Reb Ahreleh's advice is still relevant.

118. See "Vegetarianism as an Ascetic Practice" above.

from Egypt, and not [Moses and Aaron of their own accord]; as Moshe attested, "For what are we…" (ibid. 16:8).

Further proof that [the quail] was a singular concession lies in the fact that it came unaccompanied by ordinances concerning the way it was to be prepared or eaten, or its method of slaughter, as our sages state (*Chullin* 27b). God did not wish to give them meat, but to set before them the "two tables" mentioned previously. This is in keeping with the teaching of the *Mechilta*: "*When in the evening God gives you meat to eat —* from here we learn that He gave the quail with a 'dark countenance.' However the Manna, which they requested in a proper manner, He gave them with a 'shining countenance': *And bread to satiety in the morning…*"[119]

Because it was given with a "dark countenance," the quail was not lasting. It did not reflect God's true plan for them, since He did not wish to give them meat. Rather, He wanted them to know that [the Manna] that He provided them was enough to sustain life. Then they would awaken to the fact that the intellect, after having been separated from the physical, requires a different, more honorable food than this. This "food" consisted of the Torah teachings associated with the Manna.

Thus, the verse states: "I afflicted you and starved you and fed you the Manna… in order to make known to you that not by bread alone does man live, but by all that proceeds from the mouth of God…" (Deuteronomy 8:3). By not giving them meat, He made known to them that man (*ha-adam*) does not live by bread alone. The main lesson here is that physical food is needed only for the body; however, the Torah teachings associated with it constitute the nourishment of the soul. Only the latter can sustain the higher intellect, which is called "man (*adam*)"; as it is written, "Let us make man in our image" (Genesis 1:26). "Bread" [meaning all physical food] only ensures survival; whereas the food uniquely designated for the self-actualized intellect is "all that proceeds from the mouth of God," namely the related commandments and insights, by which the intellect, having transcended the physical, lives.

---

119. *Mechilta*, ad loc., 3, citing Exodus 16:8.

Thus, the Manna is called *lechem abirim,* "bread of the mighty" (Psalms 78:25). According to Rabbi Akiva, this means "food of the angels"; while according to Rabbi Yishmael, this denotes a food that was completely absorbed by the limbs, leaving no waste.[120] Rabbi Akiva thought that this "bread" was so extremely pure and subtle that it could serve as food for the higher intellect, just as it was, and enhance it; even the ministering angels (*abirim*) could have consumed it without succumbing to any conflict [between the spiritual and the physical]. However, Rabbi Ishmael contended that Rabbi Akiva had erred in his analysis, for the higher intellect cannot be sustained by any physical food, however subtle. In his view, *lechem abirim* indicates a physical food that can be completely absorbed by one's limbs (*eivarim*). The higher intellect is sustained by the divine paradigms and perspectives related to [the Manna, in the case of the generation of the Exodus, and simple vegetarian foods in the case of spiritually evolved individuals of subsequent generations; these Torah teachings are] the pathways to eternal life, as the verse states: "But by all that proceeds from the mouth of God shall a man live" (op cit.). This, too, was the sublime nature of the food given to Adam in the Garden of Eden (Rabbi Yitzchak Arama, *Akeidas Yitzchak, Beshalach,* Gate 41, abridged).

The Torah Does Not Change

God never forbade the flesh of animals to Adam; He never explicitly commanded him not to eat meat, as He did concerning the fruit of the Tree of the Knowledge of Good and Evil (Genesis 1:17). Rather, He instilled in Adam's nature the disinclination to eat meat, so that it should not be a worthy food to him, but an object of repugnance, contrary to his nature, the way vermin are repugnant as food to humans today. This was all a matter of nature, and not a commandment.

The verses clearly show the truth of this premise in several ways. First, we do not find that man was forbidden meat in the same manner as he was forbidden the fruit of the Tree of the Knowledge of Good and Evil.

---

120. *Yoma* 75b.

God would have explicitly forbidden this to him if He had so wished to command him.

Second, man's food and the way it was permitted to him was combined with that of the animals; as the verse states, "And the Lord said: Behold, I have given you every herb yielding seed that is upon the face of the Earth, and every tree in which is the fruit of a tree yielding seed... and to every animal of the Earth and to every bird of the sky and to everything that creeps upon the Earth that possesses a living soul, [I have given] every green herb for food" (Genesis 1:29-30). No one would think that God gave all the animals vegetation but forbade them meat, for they are not subject to commandments. Rather, the meaning is that God instilled in their nature a disinclination to eat meat and a desire for the herb of the field alone. As the Prophet Isaiah attests, "The lion shall eat straw like the ox" (Isaiah 11:7). [That is, in the future animals will return to their original vegetarian nature.] If so, this [vegetarian predisposition] also applies to man, for both man and animal were addressed in the same word and manner.

Third, the previously cited verse concludes with the words, "and it was so" (ibid.). This expression does not indicate the establishment of a mandate but a condition of nature, similar to [the Torah's account of] each day of creation that concludes "and it was so."

Fourth, the entire matter concerns a blessing and not a commandment. [When the previous verse declares man's dominion over] the fish, this reflects the divine will in determining the natural order. Similarly, Noah was given "everything that creeps upon the ground," as an expression of blessing.

Fifth, God prepared for man "all herb yielding seed," such as wheat, barley, legumes, and all trees bearing fruit; whereas for animals it designates "all green herbs for food," not "all herb yielding seed," and not fruit of the tree. However, when man sinned and became comparable to an animal, he was told, "You may eat all the herbs of the field." Certainly, this was not a command but indicates a natural predilection that God imbued within him, like all the other curses, the result of which was to change nature from its previous state. This does not reflect any change that may be ascribed to God, may He be exalted. The natural order can be corrupted or set aright according to the deeds of humankind. Thus, it became the nature of the serpent and the woman to hate one another as a result of their transgression, as well as for the serpent to eat dirt,[121] and for the woman to suffer the pangs of childbirth. None of this existed before. Similarly, it became part of human nature to eat vegetation like animals, which previously had not been the case; for humankind had been given only "herb yielding seed" and fruit of the tree.

In Noah, the desire to eat meat became part of human nature — whether in order to cut short the years of his life or to punish the animals that had perverted their way. "After all the desire of his soul he may eat flesh" (Deuteronomy 12:20) is consistent with the principle that God never changed His command from former days to reward any person or a nation, but only added to it in order to confer a greater reward. Although meat was permitted to Noah, it had never been forbidden to Adam previously. Rather, he had always possessed the right to slaughter animals for his own benefit; he had not possessed the desire to eat of their flesh nor to gratify his natural instincts through them. This became part of human nature in the generation of Noah. From thenceforth, animals, too, became predatory and carnivorous, which had not previously been the case. Their diet had been vegetarian, as well. Therefore, as soon as the desire to eat meat had been instilled in Noah, God said, "And surely your blood I shall requite; at the hand of every animal I shall requite it..." (Genesis 8:5). That is, although from now on it shall be the nature of an animal to kill its prey, if it should eat a human being, "I shall requite it of him." One may not in any manner derive from this that God forbade something and subsequently recanted and allowed it.

This was also the implicit view of our sages, of blessed memory, for meat was never prohibited to man. The Talmud states, "Rabbi Yehudah said in the name of Rav: Adam was not permitted to eat meat" (*Sanhedrin* 57a). It does not use the term "forbidden (*asur*)" but "not permitted (*lo*

---

121. According to the Vilna Gaon, this does not mean that the serpent actually sustains itself from dirt, but that because it crawls on the ground, whatever it eats is accompanied by the taste of dirt (*Aderes Eliyahu, Bereishis*, ad loc.).

hutar)." For God did not endow him with this nature, nor did He cause such a desire to awaken within him; rather, eating meat was a source of revulsion. This is what is meant by "not permitted." If not, who established the original prohibition, that the term "not permitted (*lo hutar*)" subsequently could be imposed upon him? Rather, Adam was "not permitted" in the sense that he was not endowed with this natural inclination; for God never recants upon His word, or "changes His mind." However, He does add to His word in order to complete His purpose (Rabbi Shaul HaLevi Morteira, *Givat Shaul, Shoftim, Ma'amar* 44, pp. 270-271).

A Chassidic Discourse on Eating Meat

The superiority of man over the animal is wisdom, which the animal intellect does not possess. Wisdom is a manifestation of the Lights of Illumination. These "lights" correspond to the four levels of the mind, which are derived from the Divine Name YHVH.[122] Because the animal does not possess wisdom, its life force does not come from the Lights of Illumination. [The animal spirit] is thus an aspect of the Lights of Fire.

Since [it is a principle of creation] that "God made one thing against its opposite" (Ecclesiastes 7:14), wherever the Lights of Illumination are absent, the Lights of Fire prevail. [The former are an aspect of the realm of holiness;] the latter are an aspect of the realm of unholiness. Therefore, it is written, "In the evening you shall eat flesh" (Exodus 16:8). Evening is associated with the Lights of Fire, as the verse states, "In the evening it shall be as an appearance of fire" (Numbers 9:15). Evening is when the light diminishes; the sun sets in the west. This is an aspect of the departure of the Lights of Illumination [i.e., the concealment of wisdom]. The Torah designates evening as the time for eating animal flesh, which

---

122. In *Likkutei Moharan* II: 67, the discourse on which the above teaching is based, R. Nachman of Breslov relates the paradigm of the Holy Temple to the revelation of divine intellect, citing the verse that describes Bezalel, who crafted the original vessels of the *Mishkan*: "I have filled him with wisdom (*chochmah*), understanding (*binah*), knowledge (*da'as*), and with every craft (*melachah*)..." (Exodus 31:2). Each term denotes a different level of consciousness, derived from the four letters of the Divine Name *Yud-Hey-Vav-Hey*; also cf. *Tikkunei Zohar, Hakdamah*.

is an aspect of the Lights of Fire. Consequently, one must be careful to eat meat in a holy manner and with great mental focus. This will enable one to subjugate the Lights of Fire.

Through their craving for meat, however, the Children of Israel empowered the Lights of Fire. As the verse states, "In the evening, fire came forth from God, and the Mixed Multitude among them lusted after desire, and again the Children of Israel also wept, and they said, 'Who will give us flesh to eat?' " It is only possible to do so through the power of the tzaddik, who is a channel for the Lights of Illumination. Through the tzaddik, one may subjugate the Lights of Fire and distill the good from the bad. Then may one partake of meat.

In truth, the Lights of Fire also derive their existence from the Lights of Illumination: from the "three colors of the eye and the pupil," which are drawn forth from the four letters of God's Essential Name YHVH. The Lights of Fire have four colors, corresponding to the four letters of God's Essential Name. They, too, derive their existence from the Divine Name, for God imbues everything with life. However, they must not be given vitality beyond what they need to exist, lest they become dominant. Therefore, through the power of the tzaddik, who is the channel for the Lights of Illumination, it is possible to eat meat; through the tzaddik, we have the ability to subdue the Lights of Fire, to extricate the good in animals, and to elevate it to the realm of holiness.

Moreover, the wisdom and intellect of holiness attains perfection through animals, by elevating the good they possess, which is an aspect of the Lights of Illumination; for animals, too, ultimately derive their existence from the Lights of Illumination. Thus, one who knows how to focus his mind while eating meat, and do so in the proper spirit of holiness and purity, can actually attain a higher level of wisdom. That is, through eating meat he may elevate the Lights of Illumination hidden within the Lights of Fire embodied by animals.

However, a person ignorant of Torah cannot accomplish this. By definition, an ignoramus is one who has not drawn close to the true tzaddikim. As our sages state: "Even one who studies Torah but has not apprenticed himself to a Torah sage is called an ignoramus" (*Berachos*

47a). Therefore, he may not eat meat, since he cannot subdue the Lights of Fire. He is distant from the tzaddikim, who are a channel for the Lights of Illumination. If he were to eat meat, the Lights of Fire embodied by animals would dominate him to an even greater degree.

This is borne out by the fact that God first permitted man to eat meat during Noah's generation. Noah was the tzaddik of his generation. Solely in his merit permission was given to eat meat, since one cannot eat meat [and rectify the Luminaries of Fire within the animal] except through the power of the tzaddik, then personified by Noah. Moreover, the main reason for this divine consent was so that man could offer animal sacrifices. Thus, Noah offered sacrifices from every kosher species. At that time, he also was given permission to eat meat, as the verse states: "Even as the green herb, I have given you all things" (Genesis 9:3). Through the sacrifices, the animal soul, which corresponds to the Lights of Fire, is subjugated and transformed (Rabbi Nosson Sternhartz, *Likkutei Halachos, Yoreh De'ah, Basar B'chalav* 2:1, based on *Likkutei Moharan* II, 67).

Selections From "A Vision of Vegetarianism And Peace"

The Just Treatment of Animals

There is a fundamental branch of human advancement that according to the present state of the prevailing culture, exists today only in the pleasant dream of a few extremely idealistic souls: an innate ethical striving for just, humane feeling that is fully attentive to the fate of animals.

Certain cruel philosophies that base their ethics on human reason, especially those that deny belief in God, have advocated that man completely stifle within himself any sense of justice for animals. However, they have not succeeded, nor shall they succeed with all their self-serving cleverness, in perverting the innate sense of justice that the Creator planted within the human soul. Although sympathy for animals is like the glow of a smoldering ember buried under a great heap of ashes, nevertheless, it is impossible for them to negate this sensitivity within every feeling heart. For failing to heed the good and noble instinct not to take any form of life, whether for one's needs or physical gratification, constitutes a moral lack in the human race.

Our sages did not agree with these philosophical views. They tell us that the holy Rabbi Yehudah HaNasi was visited with afflictions because he told a calf being led to slaughter, that had sought refuge in the skirts of his garment, "Go! This is the purpose for which you were created." His healing was also brought about by a deed, when he showed mercy to some weasels (*Bava Metzia* 85a). Our sages did not conduct themselves like the philosophers, who exchange darkness for light, for the sake of pragmatism. It is impossible to imagine that the Master of all that transpires, Who has mercy upon His all creatures, would establish an eternal decree such as this in the creation that He pronounced "exceedingly good," namely, that it should be impossible for the human race to exist without violating its own moral instincts by shedding blood, be it even the blood of animals.

Man's Original Diet Was Vegetarian

No intelligent, thinking person could suppose that when the Torah instructs humankind to dominate — "And have dominion over the fish of the sea, and over the birds of the sky, and over every living thing that moves upon the Earth" (Genesis 1:28) — it means the domination of a harsh ruler, who afflicts his people and servants merely to fulfill his personal whim and desire, according to the crookedness of his heart. It is unthinkable that the Torah would impose such a decree of servitude, sealed for all eternity, upon the world of God, Who is "good to all, and His mercy is upon all His works" (Psalms 145:9), and Who declared, "The world shall be built upon kindness" (ibid. 89:3).

Moreover, the Torah attests that all humanity once possessed this lofty moral level. Citing scriptural proofs, our sages explain (*Sanhedrin* 57a) that Adam was not permitted to eat meat: "Behold, I have given you every tree... yielding seed for food" (Genesis 1:29). Meat was permitted only to the children of Noah, after the Flood: "Like the green herb, I have given you everything" (Genesis 9:3). Is it conceivable that this moral excellence, which once existed as an inherent human characteristic, should be lost forever? Concerning these and similar matters, it states, "I shall bring knowledge from afar, and unto my Maker I shall ascribe righteousness" (Job 36:3). In the future, God shall cause us to make great spiritual strides, and thus extricate us from this complex question.

Vegetarianism and Enlightenment

When humanity reaches its goal of complete happiness and spiritual liberation, when it attains that lofty peak of perfection that is the pure knowledge of God and the full manifestation of the essential holiness of life, then the age of "motivation by virtue of enlightenment" will have arrived. This is like a structure built on the foundation of "motivation by virtue of the law," which of necessity must precede [that of "motivation by virtue of enlightenment"] for all humanity.[123]

---

123. The terms *"he'aras ha-sechel / he'aras ha-Torah"* are from Rabbenu Bachya ibn Paquda, *Chovos haLevavos, Sha'ar Avodas Elokim,* chap. 3, a favorite passage of Rav Kook.

At that time human beings will recognize their companions in creation: all the animals. They will understand how it is fitting from the standpoint of the purest ethical standard not to resort to moral concessions, to compromise the divine attribute of justice with that of mercy[124] [by permitting mankind's exploitation of animals]; for they will no longer need extenuating concessions, as in those matters of which the Talmud states: "The Torah speaks only of the evil inclination" (*Kiddushin* 31b).[125] Rather they will walk the path of absolute good. As the prophet declares: "I will make a covenant for them with the animals of the field, the birds of the air, and the creeping things of the ground; I also will banish the bow and sword, and war from the land..." (Hosea 2:20) (Rabbi Avraham Yitzchak Kook, *Chazon HaTzimchonut V'HaShalom*, chapters 1, 2, 12).

---

124. *Bereishis Rabbah* 8:4.
125. See *Sefer HaIkkarim* 3:15.

English Bibliography

Judaica Works:

Alshech, Rabbi Moshe. The Book of Iyyov: A Celestial Challenge, trans. Ravi Shahar. Jerusalem: Feldheim (1996).

Bar-Lev, Rabbi Yechiel. Song of the Soul: Introduction to Kabbalah. Petach Tikveh (1994).

Ben-Amos, Dan and Jerome R. Mintz. In Praise of the Baal Shem Tov. Northvale, NJ: Jason Aronson (1993).

Berman, Joshua. The Temple: Its Symbolism and Meaning Then and Now. Northvale, NJ: Jason Aronson (1995).

Berman, Louis A. Vegetarianism and the Jewish Tradition. New York: Ktav (1982).

Bleich, Rabbi J. David. Contemporary Halakhic Problems, Vol. III ("Vegetarianism and Judaism" and "Animal Experimentation"). New York: Ktav / Yeshiva University (1989).

Buxbaum, Yitzhak. Jewish Spiritual Practices. Northvale, NJ: Jason Aronson (1990).

Carmell, Rabbi Aryeh. Masterplan: Judaism — Its Programs, Meanings, Goals. Jerusalem: Feldheim (1991).

Cohen, Rabbi Alfred. "Vegetarianism from a Jewish Perspective," Vol. I, No. 2, Journal of Halacha and Contemporary Society (Fall 1981).

Cohen, Noah J. Tsa'ar Ba'ale Hayim: The Prevention of Cruelty to Animals. Jerusalem: Feldheim (1976) (reprint, 1959 ed.).

Cordovero, Rabbi Moshe. The Palm Tree of Deborah (Tomer Devorah). trans. Moshe Miller. Jerusalem: Targum / Feldheim (1993).

Moses Cordovero's Introduction to Kabbalah: Ohr Ne'erav, trans, Ira Robinson. Hoboken, NY: Ktav / Yeshiva University (1998).

Culi, Rabbi Yaakov. Me'Am Lo'ez: The Book of Esther, trans. Aryeh Kaplan. New York: Maznaim (1978).

Fuchs, Abraham. The Unheeded Cry. Brooklyn, NY: Artscroll / Mesorah (1984).

Ganzfried, Rabbi Shlomo. Concise Code of Jewish Law (Kitzur Shulchan Aruch), trans. Hyman Goldin. New York: Hebrew Publishing Society (1961).

Gaon, Rav Saadia. The Book of Beliefs and Opinions, trans. Samuel Rosenblatt. New Haven, Conn. / London: Yale University (1976) (reprint, 1948 ed.).

Gikatilla, Rabbi Joseph. Gates of Light, trans. Avi Weinstein. San Francisco: HarperCollins (1994).

Gold, Rabbi Avie. Baal HaTurim Chumash. Brooklyn, NY: Artscroll / Mesorah (2000).

Goldwurm, Rabbi Hersh. The Rishonim. Brooklyn, NY: Artscroll / Mesorah (1982).

------ The Early Acharonim. Brooklyn, NY: Artscroll / Mesorah (1989).

HeChasid, Rabbi Yehudah. Sefer Chasidim: The Book of the Pious, trans. Avraham Yaakov Finkel. Northvale, NJ: Jason Aronson (1997).

HaLevi, Rabbi Yehudah. The Kuzari: In Defense of the Despised Faith, trans. N. Daniel Korobkin. Northvale, NJ: Jason Aronson (1999).

Herman, Rabbi Naftali ("Judaeus"). The Baal Shem of Michelstadt, trans. M. Kuttner. Jerusalem: Feldheim (1973).

Hirsch, Rabbi Samson Raphael. Horeb: A Philosophy of Jewish Laws and Observances. London: Soncino (1962).

------ Judaism Eternal, London: Soncino (1967).

------ The Pentateuch, trans. Gertrude Hirschler. Brooklyn, NY: Judaica (1990).

------ The Nineteen Letters, trans. Karin Paritzky, commentary by R. Joseph Elias. Jerusalem: Feldheim (1995).

Kalechovsky, Roberta. Vegetarian Judaism. Marblehead, Mass: Micah (1998).

------ Judaism and Animal Rights: Classical and Contemporary Responses. Marblehead, Mass: Micah (1995).

------ Rabbis and Vegetarianism: An Evolving Tradition. Marblehead, Mass: Micah (1995).

Kaplan, Rabbi Aryeh. The Bahir (Book of Illumination). Northvale, NJ / London: Jason Aronson (1995).

------ Handbook of Jewish Thought, Vol. 2 (Avraham Sutton, editor). New York / Jerusalem: Maznaim (1992).

------ Immortality, Resurrection, and the Age of the Universe. Hoboken, NJ: Ktav (1993).

------ Inner Space. Jerusalem / New York: Maznaim (1991).

------ Jerusalem: Eye of the Universe. Brooklyn, NY: NCSY / Artscroll / Mesorah (1996).

------ Meditation and Kabbalah. Northvale, NJ / London: Jason Aronson (1995).

------ Sefer Yetzirah (Book of Creation). York Beach, Maine: Samuel Weiser (1990).

Kramer, Rabbi Chaim. Anatomy of the Soul. Jerusalem: Breslov Research Institute (1998).

Levinger, Rabbi Dr. I.M. Shechitah in Light of the Year 2000. Jerusalem: Maskil L'David (1999).

Lichtenstein, Aaron. The Seven Laws of Noah. New York: Rabbi Jacob Joseph School Press (1981).

Luzzatto, Rabbi Moshe Chaim. The Path of the Just (Mesillas Yesharim), trans. Shraga Silverstein. Jerusalem / New York: Feldheim (1980).

The Way of God (Derech Hashem), trans. Aryeh Kaplan. Jerusalem, Jerusalem / New York: Feldheim (1983).

Miller, Rabbi Moshe, trans. Zohar: Bereishit, Vol. 1. Morristown, NJ: Fiftieth Gate (2000)

Munk, Rabbi Elie. The Call of the Torah, trans. E.S. Maser. Brooklyn, NY: Artscroll / Mesorah (1996).

------ The World of Prayer. Jerusalem / New York: Feldheim (1961).

------ with Rabbi Michael Munk and Dr. I.M. Levinger. Shechitah: Religious and Historical Research on the Jewish Method of Slaughter. Jerusalem: Feldheim (1976).

Nachmanides (Rabbi Moshe ben Nachman). Commentary on the Torah, trans. Charles Chavel. New York: Shilo (1975).

------ Gate of Reward (Sha'ar HaGemul), trans. C. Chavel. New York: Shilo (1983).

Naor, Rabbi Bezalel. Kabbalah and the Holocaust. Spring Valley, NY: Orot Inc. (2001).

Orchos Tzaddikim: The Ways of the Tzaddikim, trans. Shraga Silverstein. Jerusalem / New York: Feldheim (1997)

Pick, Phillip, ed. Tree of Life: An Anthology of Articles Appearing in The Jewish Vegetarian 1966-1974. London: Yoseloff (1977).

Pinson, Rabbi DovBer. Reincarnation and Judaism: The Journey of the Soul. Northvale, NJ: Jason Aronson (1999).

Rakover, Nahum. Law and the Noahides: Law As A Universal Value. Jerusalem: Library of Jewish Law (1998).

Raz, Simcha. A Tzaddik in Our Time: The Life of Rabbi Aryeh Levin. Jerusalem:Feldheim (1976).

Rosenblum, Yonoson. Reb Shraga Feivel: The Life and Times of Rabbi Shraga Feivel Mendlowitz, the Architect of Torah in America. Brooklyn, NY: Artscroll / Mesorah (2001).

Sacks, Rabbi Jonathan. Tradition in an Untraditional Age. London: Vallentine, Mitchell (1990).

Scherman, Rabbi Nosson, ed. The Stone Tanach. Brooklyn, NY: Artscroll / Mesorah (1998).

Schneersohn, Rabbi Yosef Yitzchak of Lubavitch. Likkutei Dibburim, trans. Uri Kaploun. New York: Kehot (1987).

Schneider, Susan. Eating As Tikkun. Jerusalem: A Still Small Voice (1996).

Schochet, Elijah Judah. Animal Life In Jewish Tradition: Attitudes and Relationships. New York: Ktav (1984).

Schochet, Rabbi Jacob Immanuel. Mystical Concepts in Chassidism. New York: Kehot (1971).

------ The Mystical Tradition. New York: Kehot (second ed. 1995).

Schwartz, Richard H. Judaism and Vegetarianism. New York: Lantern (2001). Judaism and Global Survival. New York: Lantern (2002).

Sears, David. The Path of the Baal Shem Tov: Early Chasidic Teachings and Customs. Northvale, NJ: Jason Aronson (1997).

------ Compassion for Humanity in the Jewish Tradition. Northvale, NJ: Jason Aronson (1998).

Sefer HaHinnuch: The Book of (Mitzvah) Education, trans. Charles Wengrov. Jerusalem: Feldheim (1984).

Shatz, David, Chaim I. Waxman, and Diament, Nathan J. Tikkun Olam: Social Responsibility in Jewish Thought and Law. Northvale, NJ: Jason Aronson (1997).

Slifkin, Rabbi Nosson. Nature's Song. Jerusalem: Targum / Feldheim (2000).

Sonnenfeld, Rabbi Shlomo Zalman. Guardian of Jerusalem: The Life and Times of Rabbi Yosef Chaim Sonnenfeld, trans./adapted Hillel Danziger. Brooklyn, NY: Artscroll / Mesorah (1993).

Starrett, Rabbi Yehoshua. The Inner Temple. Jerusalem: Breslov Research Institute (2000).

Sternhartz, Rabbi Nosson. Tzaddik: A Portrait of Rabbi Nachman, trans. Avraham Greenbaum. Jerusalem: Breslov Research Institute (1986).

Rabbi Nachman's Advice. trans. Avraham Greenbaum. Jerusalem: Breslov Research Institute (1983).

Toperoff, Rabbi Shlomo Pesach. The Animal Kingdom in Jewish Thought. Northvale, NJ: Jason Aronson (1995).

Una, Rabbi Isak. Tierschutz Im Judentum. Frankfort Am Main: J. Kaufmann Verlag (1928).

Zaitchik, Rabbi Chaim Ephraim. Sparks of Mussar, trans. E. Van Handel. Jerusalem: Pisgah Foundation / Feldheim (1985).

Zevin, Rabbi Shlomo Yosef. A Treasury of Chassidic Tales on the Torah, trans. Uri Kaploun. New York: Artscroll / Mesorah (1980).

General Works on Agriculture, Animal Rights, Animal Welfare, Ecology, Environmental Science, Diet and Health, Vegetarianism, and Reincarnation:

American Dietetic Association. Position of the ADA: Vegetarian Diets. Journal of the American Dietetic Association, Vol. 97, No. 11 (Nov. 1997).

American Veal Association. Use of Animal Health Care Products In Veal Calves. Middletown, PA: AVA (2000).

Safety Through Science. Middletown, PA: AVA (2000).

Facts About The Care And Feeding Of Calves. Middletown, PA: AVA (2000)

Campell, T. Colin, and Cox, Christine. The China Project: Keys to Better Health Discovered in Our Living Laboratory. Ithaca, NY: New Century Nutrition (1996).

Davis, Karen. Prisoned Chickens, Poisoned Eggs. Summertown, Tenn.: Book Publishing Co. (1996).

Durning, Alan B. and Brough, Holly B. Taking Stock: Animal Farming and the Environment. Worldwatch Institute (1991).

Eisinitz, Gail A. Slaughterhouse. Prometheus (1997).

Grandin, Temple. Recommended Animal Handling Guideline For Meat Packers. American Meat Institute (1991).

Supplement to Recommended Animal Handling Guideline: Good Manufacturing Practices for Animal Handling and Stunning. American Meat Institute. (1999).

Harris, William. The Scientific Basis of Vegetarianism. Honolulu: Hawaii Health Publications (1995).

Harrison, Ruth. Animal Machines. London: Vincent Stuart (1964).

Lappe, Francis Moore. Diet for a Small Planet. New York: Ballentine Books (1987).

------ and Collins, Joseph. Food First: Beyond the Myth of Scarcity. Boston: Houghton Mifflin (1977).

Lawrence, William F. and Bierregaard, Richard O. Tropical Forest Remnants: Ecology, Management, and Conservation of Fragmented Communities. Chicago: University of Chicago (1997).

Mason, Jim and Singer, Peter. Animal Factories. New York: Harmony / Crown (1980).

National Chicken Council. Animal Welfare Guidelines. (2001).

National Milk Producers Federation. Issue Brief: Animal Care. (2000).

North, Mark O. and Bell, Donald D. Commercial Chicken Production Manual, 4th edition. New York: Van Nostrand Reinhold (1990).

Ornish, Dean. Dean Ornish's Program for Reversing Heart Disease. New York: Ballentine Books (1990).

Pimentel, David, Westra, Laura, and Noss, Reed F. Ecological Integrity: Integrating Environment, Conservation, and Health. Washington, DC: Island Press (2000).

Regan, Tom and Singer, Peter. Animal Rights and Human Obligations. Englewood Cliffs, NJ: Prentice-Hall (1976).

Rifkin, Jeremy. Beyond Beef: The Rise and Fall of the Cattle Culture. New York: Dutton (1992).

Robbins, John. Diet For a New America. Walpole, NH: Stillpoint (1987).

Schell, Orville. Modern Meat: Antibiotics, Hormones, and the Pharmaceutical Farm. New York: Random House (1984).

Shroder, Tom. Old Souls: The Scientific Evidence For Past Lives. New York: Simon & Schuster (1999).

Stevenson, Ian. Twenty Cases Suggestive of Reincarnation. Charlottesville, Va.: University of Virginia (1974, revised second ed.).

------ Children Who Remember Previous Lives. Charlottesville, VA: University Press of Virginia (1987).

United Egg Producers Animal Welfare Committee. Animal Husbandry Guidelines For U.S. Egg Laying Flocks. United Egg Producers (2000).

Hebrew Bibliography

Abarbanel, Rabbi Yitzchak. Perush Al HaTorah. Jerusalem: Hotza'as Sefarim Bnei Abarbanel (1984).

Adler, Rabbi Binyamin. Kashrus U'Treifos B'Ohf. Bnei Brak: Mishor (1986).

Albo, Rabbi Yosef. Sefer HaIkkarim. Jerusalem: Choref (1995).

Arama, Rabbi Yitzchak. Akeidas Yitzchak. Jerusalem (1960).

Asher, Rabbi Yaakov ben. Arba'ah Turim. New York: Friedman (no date).

Ashkenazi, Rabbi Bezalel. Shittah Mekubetzes. Bnei Brak (1989).

Azkari, Rabbi Eliezer. Sefer Chareidim. Jerusalem (1984).

Azulai, Rabbi Avraham. Chesed L'Avraham. Jerusalem: Yerid HaSefarim (no date).

Azulai, Rabbi Chaim David Yosef. Shem HaGedolim. New York: Scharf (1983).

Baghdad, Rabbi Yosef Chaim of. Ben Yehoyada. Jerusalem (1965).

------ Halachos. Jerusalem: Merkaz HaSefer (1986).

------ Otzros Chaim. Jerusalem: Ahavat Shalom (1990).

Bar Lev, Rabbi Yechiel. Yedid Nefesh al HaZohar. Petach Tikveh (1992).

Bender, Rabbi Levi Yitzchak. Siach Sarfei Kodesh, Vols. I, II, IV, V. Jerusalem: Meshech HaNachal (1988-1994).

Berditchev, Rabbi Levi Yitzchak of. Ohr HaEmes (ed.). Brooklyn, NY (1960).

------ Kedushas Levi HaShalem. Jerusalem: Derbaremdiger (1958).

------ Inyanei Shabbos V'Rosh Chodesh. Brooklyn, NY: Ehrlich/Chasidei Boston (1999).

Berensdorfer, Rabbi Yedidyah. Sh'nos Bikkurim: Tiferes Mordechai. Midos, Vol. II. Tel Aviv: Berensdorfer (2001).

Breslov, Rabbi Nachman of. Likkutei Moharan. Jerusalem: Meshech HaNachal (1990).

------ Sefer HaMidos. Jerusalem: Breslov Research Institute (1985).

------ Sippurei Maasios. Jerusalem: Meshech HaNachal (1990).

Chazan, Rabbi Avraham ben Nachman. Kochvei Ohr. Jerusalem: Breslov (1983).

------ Biur HaLikkutim. Jerusalem: Toras HaNetzach (1998).

Cheifetz, Rabbi Moshe; see Gentili, Rabbi Moshe (Cheifetz).

Chernobyl, Rabbi Menachem Nachum of. Me'or Einayim. New Square, NY: M'Ohr HaTorah (1997).

Chernowitz, Rabbi Chaim of. Be'er Mayim Chaim. Israel (no date).

Chriqui, Rabbi Mordechai. Rechev Yisrael. Jerusalem: Machon Ramchal (1995).

Cohen, Shlomo. Pe'er HaDor. Bnei Brak (1966).

Cordovero, Rabbi Moshe. Pardes Rimonim. Jerusalem: Yerid HaSefarim (2000).

------ Shiur Komah. Jerusalem: Kol Yehudah (no date).

------ Tomer Devorah. Jerusalem: Eshkol (1985).

Danziger, Rabbi Avraham. Chayei Adam (with Nishmas Adam). Jerusalem (1990).

De Vidas, Rabbi Eliyahu. Reishis Chochmah. Jerusalem: Ohr HaMussar (1980).

Dinov, Rabbi Zvi Elimelech Spira of. Bnei Yissaschar. Jerusalem (1990).

Efrati, R. Shimon. Shvi Zion: Kuntres Tza'ar Baalei Chaim (w/ Chiddushei HaGaon Zvi on Chullin). Jerusalem (1971).

Emden, Rabbi Yaakov. Sheilas Ya'avetz. New York (1961).

Epstein, Rabbi Kalonymus Kalman. Ma'or VaShemesh. Jerusalem: Galim (1986).

Epstein, Rabbi Yechiel Michel ben Avraham. Kitzur Shnei Luchos HaBris. Ashdod: Otzar HaSefarim / Blotnick (1998).

Epstein, Rabbi Yechiel Michel HaLevi. Aruch HaShulchan. Jerusalem: Maznaim (1987).

Eshkoli, Rabbi Yitzchak Nachman. Tza'ar Baalei Chaim. Ofakim, Israel (2002).

Feinstein, Rabbi Moshe. Igros Moshe, Even HaEzer, Vol. IV. New York: Moriah (1963).

------ Yoreh De'ah, Vol. V. New York: Moriah (1973).

------ Choshen Mishpat, Vol. 7. New York: Moriah (1985).

Feldman, Rabbi David Zvi. Yalkut Kol Chai: Encyclopedia Toranit L'Baalei Chaim. Jerusalem (1997).

Frank, Rabbi Zvi Pesach. Teshuvos Har Zvi. Jerusalem: Machon HaRav Frank (1994).

Frisch, Rabbi Daniel. Otzar HaZohar. Jerusalem: D'fus Alef-Beis (1976).

Ftayah, Rabbi Yehudah. Minchas Yehudah. Jerusalem: Machon HaRav Yehudah Ftayah (1995).

Gaon, Rav Saadia ben Yosef Fayyumi. Sefer HaNiv'char B'Emunos V'De'os (R. Yosef Kapach, ed.). Jerusalem (1995).

Ganzfried, Rabbi Shlomo. Kitzur Shulchan Aruch. Jerusalem: Eshkol (no date).

Gentili, Rabbi Moshe (Cheifetz). M'leches Machsheves. Jerusalem (1964) (reprint, 1914 Warsaw edition).

Gikatilla, Rabbi Yosef. Sha'arei Orah. New York (1986) (reprint, 1883 Warsaw edition).

Givartchov, Rabbi Shimshon of. Sefer Baal Shem Tov. Jerusalem: Machon Daas Yosef (1993).

Goldstein, Rabbi Nachman of Tcherin. Nachas HaShulchan. Jerusalem: Chassidei Breslov (1976).

------ Parpara'os L'Chochmah. Jerusalem: Toras HaNetzach (1994).

Halperin, Rabbi Yechiel ben Shlomo of Minsk. Seder HaDoros. Jerusalem (1956) (reprint, Warsaw edition).

Hebenstreit, Rabbi Yitzchak. Kivros HaTa'avah: Toras HaTzimchoni. Rzeszow (Reisha), Poland: HaTzimchoni/Schiff (1929).

HeChassid, Rabbi Yehudah. Sefer Chassidim. Jerusalem: Mosad HaRav Kook (1989).

Hirsch, Rabbi Samson Raphael. Perush Al HaChumash. Jerusalem: Mosdos Breuer (1966).

Horowitz, Rabbi Pinchas Eliyahu of Vilna. Sefer HaBris (HaShalem). Jerusalem: Yerid HaSefarim (1990).

Horowitz, Rabbi Shmuel. Avanehah Barzel. Jerusalem: Breslov (1983).(printed w/ Sefer Kochvei Ohr by R. Avraham ben Nachman Chazan).

Horowitz, Rabbi Yeshaya. Shnei Luchos HaBris. Jerusalem: Sha'arei Ziv (1993).

Horowitz, Rabbi Yosef Yoizel of Novhardok. Madreigas HaAdam. Jerusalem: HaTechiya (1964).

Ibn Asher, Rabbeinu Bachaya. Perush Al HaTorah. Jerusalem: Bloom (1995).

Ibn Attar, Rabbi Chaim. Ohr HaChaim Al HaTorah. Jerusalem: Bloom (1991).

Ilya, Rabbi Menashe of. Alfei Menashe, Vol. I. Jerusalem (1979).

------ Alfei Menashe, Vol. II, with biography, original approbations. Jerusalem (1976).

------ Kiryat Arba. Jerusalem (1995).

Kagan, Rabbi Yisrael Meir. Mishnah Berurah. Jerusalem (1996).

Koidanover, Rabbi Zvi Hirsch. Kav HaYashar. (w/ comm. Me'orei Aish and Kav Naki). Jerusalem: Sheinberger (1993).

Karo, Rabbi Yosef. Shulchan Aruch HaShalem. Jerusalem: Tel-Man (1977).

Maggid Meisharim. Petach Tikveh: Bar Lev (1990).

Klein, Rabbi Menashe of Ungvar. Mishneh Halachos, Vol. 6. Israel (1974).

------ Vol. 7. Brooklyn, NY: Mosdos Mishneh Halachos (1977).

Komarno, R. Yitzchak Isaac Yehudah Yechiel Safrin of. Nesiv Mitzvosecha V'Otzar HaChaim. Jerusalem (1983).

------ Heichal HaBerachah, Vol. IV. Brooklyn, NY: Kelilath Yofi (reprint of 1869 Lemberg edition).

Kook, Rabbi Avraham Yitzchak HaKohen. Ein Ayah al Aggados Chazal: Berachos, Vol. II. Jerusalem: Machon Al Shem HaRav Tzvi Yehudah HaKohen Kook (1990).

------ Chazon HaTzimchonut V'HaShalom (R. David Cohen, ed.) in Lachai Ro'i. Jerusalem: Merkaz HaRav (1961).

------ Orot HaKodesh. Jerusalem: Mosad HaRav Kook (1990).

Koretz, Rabbi Pinchas of. Midrash Pinchas HaShalem. Ashdod: Yashlim (2001).

Kenig, Rabbi Nosson Zvi. Toras Nosson: Shorshei Neshamos. Bnei Brak: Kollel Breslov (no date).

------ Toras Nosson: Erchei HaAri z"l. Bnei Brak. Kollel Breslov (no date).

------ Toras Nosson: Erchei HaRamak. Bnei Brak: Kollel Breslov (no date).

------ Nofes Tzufim. Bnei Brak: Kollel Breslov (no date).

------ Siddur Sha'arei Ratzon. Bnei Brak: Machon Toras Nosson (no date)

Landau, Rabbi Yechezkel. Noda B'Yehudah. New York: Otzar HaSefarim (1973). (reprint, Vilna edition).

Lechem HaPanim. Jerusalem: Chassidei Breslov (1971).

Leiner, R. Gershon Chanoch of Radzyn; see Radzyn, R. Gershon Chanoch Leiner of.

Levinger, Rabbi Yisrael Meir. MaOhr L'Maseches Chullin, Vol. I. Jerusalem: Maskil L'David (1994, reprinted 1996).

Liadi, Rabbi Shneur Zalman of. Likkutei Amarim-Tanya. Brooklyn, NY: Kehot (1982).

------ Siddur Im Dach. Brooklyn, NY: Kehot (1980).

------ Likkutei Torah. Brooklyn, NY: Kehot (1997, reprint of Vilna 1904 edition).

------ Shulchan Aruch (HaRav). Brooklyn, NY: Kehot (1976).

------ Torah Ohr. Brooklyn, NY: Kehot (1996).

Lipschutz, Rabbi Yaakov. Toldos Yitzchak: Toldos HaRav Yitzchak Elchanan Spector. Warsaw (1896).

Lipschutz, Rabbi Yisrael. Mishnayos: Yachin U'Boaz. New York: Pardes (1953).

Lizhensk, Rabbi Elimelech of. Noam Elimelech. New York: Yisrael Ze'ev Wolf (1956).

Lubavitch, Rabbi Menachem Mendel Schneersohn (Tzemach Tzedek) of. Derech Mitzvosecha. Brooklyn, NY: Kehot (1991).

Lubavitch, Rabbi Menachem Mendel Schneerson of. Likkutei Sichos, Vol. XV. Brooklyn, NY: Kehot (1980).

------ Likkutei Sichos, Vol. XXXI. Brooklyn, NY: Kehot (1992).

Lubavitch, Rabbi Yosef Yitzchak Schneersohn of. Igros Kodesh Maharyatz, Vol. 2. Brooklyn, NY: Kehot (1985).

Lublin, Rabbi Tzadok HaKohen of. Tzidkas HaTzaddik. Jerusalem: Beit Yesharim / Yeshivat Beit El (1988).

------ Pri Tzaddik. Jerusalem (1972) (reprint, Lublin edition).

Lunshitz, Rabbi Shlomo Ephraim. Kli Yakar. Jerusalem: Chadashim Yekarim (1988).

Maharal of Prague (R. Yehudah Loewe ben Bezalel). Chiddushei Aggados. Jerusalem (1972).

------ Nesivos Olam. New York: Judaica Press (1966).

------ Netzach Yisrael. Bnei Brak: Yahadus (1980).

Maimonides (Rabbi Moshe ben Maimon). Mishneh Torah. Jerusalem: Wagschal (1984).

------ Perush al HaMishnah. Jerusalem (1963).

------ Sefer HaMitzvos. Jerusalem: Wagschal (1984).

Malbim, Rabbi Meir Leibush. Otzar HaPerushim al Tanach. Tel Aviv (1978).

Medini, Rabbi Chaim Chizkiyahu. S'dei Chemed. New York: Friedman (1967).

Midrash Rabbah. New York: Gross Brothers (1984).

Midrash Shocher Tov (Midrash Tehillim). Jerusalem: Maznaim (1968).

Midrash Tanchuma (w/ commentaries Eitz Yosef and Anaf Yosef). Jerusalem: Eshkol (1972).

Mikra'os Gedolos: Chumash. Union City, NJ: Gross (1983).

Mikra'os Gedolos: Nach. Brooklyn: Heimlich (no date).

Morteira, Rabbi Shaul HaLevi. Givas Shaul. Brooklyn: Reich (1991) (reprint, Warsaw 1912 edition).

Munkatch, Rabbi Chaim Elazar Spira of. Darkei Chaim V'Shalom. Jerusalem: Chassidei V'Talmidei Munkatch (1970).

------ Nemukei Orach Chaim. Brooklyn, NY: Goldstein (1959).

Munkatch, Rabbi Zvi Hirsch Spira of. Darkei Teshuvah. New York: Talpioth (1959).

------ Be'er Lachai Ro'i al Tikkunei Zohar. Jerusalem: Beis Tzaddikim (1964).

Na'eh, Rabbi Avraham Chaim. K'tzos HaShulchan. Jerusalem (1979).

Nachmanides (Rabbi Moshe ben Nachman). Perush al HaTorah. C. Chavel, ed. Jerusalem: Mosad HaRav Kook (1960).

Naor, Rabbi Bezalel. Ben Shanah Shaul. Jerusalem: Zur-Ot (1995).

Neriyah, Rabbi Moshe Zvi. Tal HaRayah. Bnei Brak: Fisher (1963).

Papo, Rabbi Eliezer. Peleh Yo'etz. Jerusalem (1987).

Perek Shirah (w/ commentary by R. Chaim Kanievsky). Bnei Brak: Ohel Yosef (1985).

Piacetzna, Rabbi Kalonymus Kalmish Shapira of. Derech HaMelech. Jerusalem (1995).

Pirkei Rabbi Eliezer (w/ Radal). Jerusalem (1970) (reprint, Warsaw 1852 edition).

Radzyn, R. Gershon Chanoch Leiner of. HaHakdama V'haPesichah im Ma'amar Zichron LaRishonim. New York: Leiner (1949).

Rashkov, Rabbi Shabsai of. Siddur HaAri z"l. Israel (no date).

Roth, Aharon Rabbi. Shulchan HaTahor. Jerusalem (1980).

Rubenstein, Avraham, ed. Shiv'chei Baal Shem Tov. Jerusalem: Mas (1991).

Safed, Rabbi Avraham of. Galya Raza. Jerusalem: Yerid HaSefarim (2000).

Schneersohn, Rabbi Menachem Mendel (Tzemach Tzedek); see Lubavitch, Rabbi Menachem Mendel Schneersohn of.

Schneersohn, Rabbi Yosef Yitzchak; see Lubavitch, Rabbi Yosef Yitzchak Schneersohn of.

Schneerson, Rabbi Menachem Mendel; see Lubavitch, Rabbi Menachem Mendel Schneerson of.

Schorr, Rabbi Alexander Sender. Simlah Chadasha (w/ Mateh Asher). Jerusalem: Zivchei Tzedek (1988).

Schwartz, Rabbi Yoel. V'Rachamav Al Kol Ma'asav. Jerusalem: Dvar Yerushalayim Publications (1980).

Shapira, Rabbi Kalonymus Kalmish; see Piacetzna, Rabbi Kalonymus Kalmish Shapira of.

Sefer HaChinnuch (Chavel, ed.). Jerusalem: Mosad HaRav Kook (1988).

Sefer HaKanah. Jerusalem: Nezer Shraga (1998).

Sefer Minhagei Nesuin L'Beis Lelov. Jerusalem: Machon L'Mishmeres Lelov (2001).

Sefer HaPeliah. Jerusalem: Nezer Shraga (1997).

Sefer HaTemunah. Jerusalem: Nezer Shraga (1998).

Sofer, Rabbi Avraham Reuvain HaKohen. Yalkut Reuvaini. Jerusalem: Maznaim (1962).

Sofer, Rabbi Moshe. Teshuvos Chasam Sofer. Jerusalem: Makor (1970) (reprint, Vienna 1895 edition).

------ Chasam Sofer al HaTorah. Jerusalem: Machon Chasam Sofer (1987).

------ Chiddushei Chasam Sofer. Jerusalem: Hotza'as Ohr (1971) (reprint, Vienna 1889 edition).

Soraski, Aharon. Marbitzei Torah U'Mussar. Bnei Brak (1977).

------ Sh'lucha D'Rachmana. Jerusalem: Feldheim (1992).

Spinka, Rabbi Yitzchak Isaac of. Chakal Yitzchak. Brooklyn, NY: Mesivta Imrei Spinka (1990).

Spira, Rabbi Chaim Elazar; see Munkatch, Rabbi Chaim Elazar Spira of.

Spira, Rabbi Zvi Elimelech; see Dinov, Rabbi Zvi Elimelech Spira of.

Spira, Rabbi Zvi Hirsch; see Munkatch, Rabbi Zvi Hirsch Spira of.

Stern, Rabbi Shmuel Yehudah. Kedushas HaAchilah. London / Bnei Brak (1994).

Sternhartz, Rabbi Nosson. Chayei Moharan. Jerusalem: Meshech HaNachal (1982).

------ Likkutei Eitzos. Jerusalem: Meshech HaNachal (1980).

------ Likkutei Halachos. Jerusalem: Meshech HaNachal (1985).

------ Sichos HaRan. Jerusalem: Toras HaNetzach (1981).

Stropkov, Rabbi Menachem Mendel Halberstam of. Divrei Menachem. Jerusalem (1957).

Sudylkov, Rabbi Moshe Chaim Ephraim of. Degel Machaneh Ephraim HaShalem. Jerusalem: Mir (1995).

Talmud Bavli. Jerusalem: Tel-Man (1990).

Talmud Yerushalmi. Jerusalem (1975).

Tanna D'vei Eliyahu. Jerusalem: Eshkol (1990).

Teich, Rabbi Shmuel. Lahavas Aish: Kabbalas HaBaal Shem Tov V'Talmidav. Brooklyn, NY: Kollel Lev HaAri (1993).

Teitelbaum, Rabbi Chananiah Yom Tov Lipa. Levushei Yom Tov. Brooklyn: Deitch (1970).

Teitelbaum, Rabbi Moshe; see Ujhely, Rabbi Moshe Teitelbaum.

Tikkunei Zohar. Jerusalem: Yerid HaSefarim (1998).

Teshuvos HaGeonim, Avraham Eliyahu Harkavy, ed. Jerusalem (1967) (reprint, Berlin 1887 edition).

Tzava'as HaRivash (Rabbi Immanuel Schochet, ed.). Brooklyn, NY: Kehot (1975).

Tzeinvirt, Rabbi Avraham Abish. Chayei HaAri z"l (with commentary Even HaShoham). Jerusalem: Machon Daas Yosef (1990).

Chayei Moreinu HaRav Chaim Vital (with commentary Even HaShoham). Jerusalem: Machon Daas Yosef (1990).

Ujhely, Rabbi Moshe Teitelbaum of. Yismach Moshe. Brooklyn, NY: HaMatik (Bereishis, 1997; Shemos, 1999).

Viener, Rabbi Meir Yechezkel. Me'oros HaAri z"l. Jerusalem: Ginzei Maharitz (1997).

Vilna, Rabbi Eliyahu of. Aderes Eliyahu. Jerusalem (1988).

------ Sefer Mishlei Im Be'ur HaGra. Petach Tikvah: Phillip (1985).

Vital, Rabbi Chaim. Shiv'chei Rabbi Chaim Vital. Jerusalem: Yashlim (1988).

------ Sefer Eitz Chaim (Kisvei Ari z"l). Jerusalem: Kol Yehudah (1986).

------ Sha'ar HaMitzvos (Kisvei Ari z"l). Jerusalem: Kol Yehudah (1986).

------ Sha'ar HaGilgulim (Kisvei Ari z"l). Jerusalem: Kol Yehudah (1986).

------ Mevo She'arim (Kisvei Ari z"l). Jerusalem: Kol Yehudah (1986).

------ Sha'arei Kedushah. Jerusalem: Eshkol (1985).

Volozhin, Rabbi Chaim of. Nefesh HaChaim (im Hosafos). Bnei Brak: Rubin (1989).

Vorka, Rabbi Yitzchak of. Beis Yitzchak. Jerusalem: HaRim Levin (1992).

Waldenberg, Rabbi Eliezer Yehudah. Tzitz Eliezer. Jerusalem (1985, second ed.).

Weiss, Rabbi Yitzchak Yaakov. Minchas Yitzchak. Jerusalem (1969).

Yalkut Shimoni (R. Shimon HaDarshan, ed.). Jerusalem: HaTechiyah (1960).

Yosef, Rav Ovadiah. Yabia Omer, Vol. 9. Jerusalem: Ma'or Yisrael (2001).

Yolles, Rabbi Yaakov Zvi. Kehillas Yaakov. Jerusalem (1971). (reprint, Lemberg 1870 edition).

Z'vihl, Rabbi Shlomo of. Kuntres Yesod Tzaddik (published w / Rabbi Yechiel Michel of Zlotchov, Mayim Rabbim). Jerusalem: Hotza'as El HeHarim (1987).

Zhelikhov, Rabbi Aharon HaKohen of. Kesser Shem Tov. Kfar Chabad: Kehot (1980).

------ Ohr HaGanuz L'Tzaddikim. Included in Sefarim Kedoshim, Vol. 36. Union City, NJ: Gross Brothers (no date) (reprint, Warsaw 1887 edition).

Ziditchov, Rabbi Zvi Hirsch of. Sur Me'Ra V'Asei Tov (im Hosafos Moreinu HaRav Zvi Elimelech Spira MiDinov). Jerusalem: Ohr Toras Munkatch (1996).

Ziskind. Rabbi Alexander. Yesod V'Shoresh HaAvodah HaShalem. Jerusalem: Rosenfeld (1987).

Zohar. Jerusalem: Mosad HaRav Kook (1984).

Zohar Chadash (w/commentary of Rabbi Yisrael of Koznitz). Brooklyn: K'lilas Yofi (1981) (reprint, Munkatch 1911 edition).

Index

With Gratitude to

Mr. and Mrs. David E. Bronfman
and Family

Toronto, Ontario

For Their Generous Support of This Project

Dedications

In Memory of Our Beloved Husband, Father,
Grandfather, and Great-Grandfather
Dr. Lewis Sears
Leib ben Yitzchak Yaakov
Norwich, Conn.

*

Adam Lieberman
Lady Lake, Florida

*

In Loving Memory of My Mother
Phyllis (Feigel) Oder
From Danila Oder

*

In Memory of Rabbi Zelig (Sigmund) Wolkenstein
From Mr. and Mrs. Yehuda Levinson
Toronto, Canada

*

In Memory of Our Beloved Mother and Grandmother
Miriam bas Yonah
From Rabbi and Mrs. Aharon Yonah Hayum and Family
Brooklyn, NY

*

In Memory of Chaim Kanner
Chaim Raphael HaLevi ben Yitzchak
Who Captured the Hidden Order of the Universe on Film
Brooklyn, NY

*

In Memory of Israel and Esther Koslen
Yisrael ben Eliyahu HaKohen
Esther bas Mordechai
Cleveland, Ohio

*

In Memory of Rafi Estrin
Rafael Yitzchak Ephraim ben Aryeh Leib Shlomo
Pittsburgh, PA

*

In Memory of Jeffrey Berman
Yaakov Moshe ben Shmuel
Providence, RI

*

In Memory of Joshua Pearlman
Yehoshua Pinchas ben Tuvia
Providence, RI

*

In Memory of Sanford ("Babe") Pepper
Yerachmiel Shabsai ben Shlomo
Jerusalem, Israel

*

In Memory of Nosson Kurland
Nachman Nosson Yonah ben Refael Chaim Reuvain
Brooklyn, NY

*

In Memory of Rabbi Avraham Yaakov Gabbai
Avraham Yaakov ben Masoud
Mosdos Nachal Novea Mekor Chochma
Tzefat, Israel

*

In Memory of Rabbi Feivel Lebel
Meshullam Feivel ben Yonah
Brooklyn, NY

*

In Memory of Rabbi Ephraim Gelbendorf
Ephraim Dovid Yehuda ben Chaim Zev
Jerusalem, Israel

*

In Memory of Shlomo Fried
Shlomo Zalman Dovid ben Yaakov
Founder of Nesia Travel
Brooklyn, NY

*

In Memory of HaRav HaGaon R' Nosson Zvi Kenig
Nosson Zvi ben Yerachmiel Moshe
Rosh HaKollel, Breslov Kollel
Bnei Brak, Israel

*

In Memory of Rabbi Naftali Dubinsky
Jerusalem, Israel

*

In Memory of HaRav HaGaon R' Shlomo Eisenblatt
Shlomo ben Yeshaya HaKohen
Mashgiach Ruchani, Yeshivas Darkei Noam
Mosdos Boston of Flatbush
Mara d'Asra, Kehillas Mishkan Yosef
Borough Park

About the Author

David Sears is the author of *The Tree That Stands Beyond Space: Rebbe Nachman of Breslov on the Mystical Experience*, *The Flame of the Heart: Prayers of a Chasidic Mystic*, *Compassion for Humanity in the Jewish Tradition*, and *The Path of the Baal Shem Tov: Early Chasidic Teachings and Customs*. A skilled artist, he also has written and illustrated a number of children's books, including *The Lost Princess* and *Tales From Reb Nachman*. In the field of Jewish music, he has co- produced and written liner notes for several recordings by clarinetist and mandolinist Andy Statman, including *Between Heaven and Earth: Music of the Jewish Mystics*, and written liner notes for Andy Statman's highly acclaimed collaboration with fellow mandolinist David Grisman, *Songs of Our Fathers*. Since 1997 Rabbi Sears has directed the Breslov Center for Spirituality and Inner Growth, an outreach organization under the guidance of HaRav Elazar Mordechai Kenig, *shlita*, leader of the Breslov community in Tzefat, Israel.